THE COMMANDER
A Life of Barclay de Tolly

THE COMMANDER
A Life of Barclay de Tolly

There is no reliable correlation between historical significance, measured by the effect of action on events, and historical fame, measured by acclaim or volume of eulogy.
Sidney Hook, The Hero in History

MICHAEL JOSSELSON
and Diana Josselson

Oxford   New York   Toronto   Melbourne
OXFORD UNIVERSITY PRESS
1980

Oxford University Press, Walton Street, Oxford OX2 6DP

OXFORD LONDON GLASGOW
NEW YORK TORONTO MELBOURNE WELLINGTON
KUALA LUMPUR SINGAPORE HONG KONG TOKYO
DELHI BOMBAY CALCUTTA MADRAS KARACHI
NAIROBI DAR ES SALAAM CAPE TOWN

© Diana Josselson 1980

All rights reserved. No part of this publication may be reproduced, stored in a retrieval system, or transmitted, in any form or by any means, electronic, mechanical, photocopying, recording, or otherwise, without the prior permission of Oxford University Press

British Library Cataloguing in Publication Data
Josselson, Michael
 The Commander
 1. Barclay de Tolly, Michael
 2. Russia. Armiia – Biography
 3. Generals – Russia – Biography
 I. Title II. Josselson, Diana
 355.3'32'0924   DK190.6.B/   79-40527
 ISBN 0-19-215854-6

for Jennifer

*Printed in Great Britain by
Lowe & Brydone Printers Limited,
Thetford, Norfolk*

CONTENTS

	List of Illustrations and Maps	vi
	Preface	vii
	Collaborator's Acknowledgements	x
	Note	xi
I	'Your Name's Outlandish Sound'	1
II	The Man	6
III	Apprenticeship in War	16
IV	Clash of Eagles	25
V	Memel and Tilsit – Shadows of the Future	40
VI	Northern Conquest	46
VII	First in Finland	62
VIII	Minister of War	73
IX	Retreat	91
X	'All Bark and No Bite'	113
XI	Crossfire	126
XII	Borodino	134
XIII	'The Offended Fatherland'	147
XIV	Appointments in Germany	166
XV	Glory	186
XVI	The Lost Battle and the Last Journey	205
	Epilogue: The Poet and the Commander	211
	Appendix A: 'The Commander' by Alexander Pushkin	218
	Appendix B: Barclay de Tolly Private Correspondence: An Inventory	220
	Notes and Sources	227
	Select Bibliography	253
	Geographical Glossary	263
	Index	265

ILLUSTRATIONS
Between pp. 148 and 149

Barclay de Tolly. Portrait by George Dawe. War Gallery of the Winter Palace (Hermitage), Leningrad.

Auguste Barclay de Tolly, *née* von Smitten. Photo: Dr Barsewisch.

'Christel', Auguste Christine Anna von Lueder. Barsewisch Collection, Munich.

Stolben. Lithograph by H. Mützel after the drawing by J. F. Krestlingk. Barsewisch Collection.

Tsar Alexander I. Barsewisch Collection.

Empress Elizabeth. Barsewisch Collection.

Barclay de Tolly in 1816. Engraving by Carl August Senff.

Field-Marshal Prince Kutuzov. Engraving after a drawing by Hopwood.

Colonel Count Zakrevskii. Portrait by George Dawe. Hermitage.

General Prince von Wittgenstein. Portrait by George Dawe. Hermitage.

Major Baron von Loewenstern. Engraving by Alexander Albeth. Leipzig.

General Platov. Portrait by George Dawe. Hermitage.

General Prince Bagration. Engraving by Vindromini. Photo: Novosti Press Agency.

Colonel Davydov. Portrait by George Dawe. Hermitage.

Lieutenant-General Ermolov. Portrait by George Dawe. Hermitage.

The War Gallery of the Winter Palace (Hermitage), Leningrad.

The Russian army at the Battle of Smolensk, 1812. Photo: Novosti Press Agency.

The Russian army at the Battle of Borodino. Painting by Denis Dighton. Photo: Anne S. K. Brown Military Collection, Providence, Rhode Island.

The Council of War at Fili, 1812. Painting by A. D. Kivschenko, 1882. Photo: Novosti Press Agency.

Cossacks after the Battle of Leipzig, 1813. Photo: Parker Gallery, London.

Bronze bas-relief on a monument in the Barclay de Tolly Mausoleum. Photo: Cabinet of History of Arts of the Tartu (Dorpat) State University.

MAPS

	page
Campaign in East Prussia and Poland 1807	29
Campaign in Finland 1808–9	48
Campaign in Russia 1812	97
Campaign in Germany 1813	171

PREFACE

In the preface to his fragmentary *Vie de Napoléon* Stendhal warned in 1837 that the story would have to be rewritten time and again in years to come as reminiscences and other material became available. Many correctives would be needed to the legends Napoleon spun so assiduously throughout his life. Of these legends the most tenacious has been that of 'General Winter', the attempt to explain away Napoleon's defeat in 1812 as due to the snows of Russia. Stendhal himself, as eyewitness, exploded this myth: the weather in Moscow had been splendid just before the Grande Armée began its retreat on 7/9 October. By other accounts we know that the severe cold, snow, and ice, which in the end turned the retreat into disaster, only set in at the beginning of November (N.S.) when Napoleon and his ill-fated army were almost back to Smolensk.

If any single person could be said to have caused this defeat, besides Napoleon himself and his blunders, it was Barclay de Tolly. Far-sighted, convinced – at a time when the afterglow of Tilsit had not yet waned – that a showdown with Napoleon was unavoidable, Barclay set out, as Minister of War during the eighteen months that preceded the invasion, to organize and prepare Russian forces for the great contest. As commander in the field he pursued the thankless strategy of avoiding decisive battles, determined to lure Napoleon deep into Russia, keeping Russian forces intact for the day when Napoleon's army would be so weakened that it could not withstand a counter-offensive. Barclay de Tolly was not a military genius but he possessed the true wisdom of which Thucydides speaks, making careful use of his advantages – in this case Russia's vast distances – in the knowledge that things would change. Although Napoleon was informed early about Barclay's strategy, he chose to disregard the warning because it did not fit into his preconceived ideas.

A third-generation Russian from Lutheran Livonia where his Scottish ancestors had settled in the early seventeenth century, Barclay de Tolly began his active military career at the age of fifteen. He was neither a pastor as Chateaubriand claimed (perhaps because Barclay was often called 'the Minister'), nor was he the son of a pastor as Clausewitz believed. Barclay's father was a junior Russian officer who retired early to take care of his small Baltic landholdings. From this very modest background, Barclay made his career – finishing as prince and field-marshal – on the strength of his character and abilities. He did not benefit from any protection at court until the day in April 1807 when, still a little-known major-general at thirty-eight, convalescing from battle wounds, he received a compassionate visit from Alexander I and thoroughly impressed him in the course of a long conversation. A year later the Tsar's favourable impressions were confirmed during the war in Finland and from then on, except for one lapse, Barclay enjoyed the trust of his unstable monarch. The letters exchanged between the Tsar and the General – of which many excerpts appear in this volume for the first time in English – clarify dramatic episodes and throw light on the characters of both correspondents.

Barclay's strategy in 1812, not new in itself, was far from popular. His fellow generals sought his removal, the nobles were outraged by the loss of so much of their land to the enemy, and ordinary Russians, mistrustful of his foreign-sounding name, suspected treason. The hue and cry resulted in Barclay's momentary eclipse after the fall of Moscow.

But what about Kutuzov, whom Tolstoy glorified and whom Stalin described as standing head and shoulders above Barclay de Tolly? The creation of Tolstoy's genius whom generations of readers have taken to their hearts is also a legend. In his brilliant essay, 'The Hedgehog and The Fox', Sir Isaiah Berlin demonstrates that Tolstoy, for all his claims of 'undeviating devotion to the sacred cause of the truth . . . treats facts cavalierly'. Sir Isaiah particularly notes how instructive it is 'to observe the steps by which he [Tolstoy] transforms him [Kutuzov] from the sly, elderly, feeble voluptuary, the corrupt and somewhat sycophantic courtier of the early drafts of *War and Peace* which were *based on authentic sources* [emphasis added], into the unforgettable symbol of the Russian people in all its simplicity and intuitive wisdom'.

As to Stalin's estimation, it is contradicted by Marx and Engels whose judgement was that 'Barclay de Tolly . . . was, beyond question, the best of Alexander's generals, unpretending, persevering, resolute, and full of common sense'. Their verdict is confirmed by a table of ratings of the fifteen best generals in Russian history published in St. Petersburg in 1912 as part of the 1812 centenary celebrations. It shows the great Suvorov of an earlier period clearly in the lead with a total of 57 points out of a possible 60 (top 12 points for strategy, tactics, initiative, personal bravery, and 9 for coolness). He is followed by his contemporary, Rumiantsev, with 52 points, then by the heroes of 1812, Barclay de Tolly (48), Kutuzov (47), and Bagration (45). In strategy Kutuzov scores 10 points to Barclay's 9, but both receive 10 for tactics and 7 for initiative. Barclay outpoints Kutuzov in coolness and bravery. Both Barclay and Bagration reach a chilly near-perfect 11 points for their calm command in the heat of battle.

'Undeviating devotion to . . . the truth' is what one misses in the works of the more chauvinist Russian historians and military writers, both Tsarist and Soviet, whose devotion to the task of safeguarding autocracy or fanning patriotism has resulted in their making the all-Russian Kutuzov into a giant and the 'foreign' Barclay into a dwarf. As in life, so in historiography, Barclay has been the victim of corrosive xenophobia. Of late, however, some unbiased Soviet writers and scholars have looked beyond the ideological wall. Some of them have found inspiration in Alexander Pushkin's hymn to Barclay de Tolly, 'The Commander' ('Polkovodets'). While studying this poem, they have perforce been led to reflect upon what it was that so fascinated Pushkin in the history and character of Barclay de Tolly.

Napoleon's secretary and one of his countless memorialists, François Fain, introduced his book with the words: 'It is precisely because such a great number of books have appeared that I decided to publish mine. In the midst of so many divergent accounts, many a reader has been left uncertain.' Only a single book, itself incomplete and only in Russian and German, has appeared on Napoleon's great opponent, yet in all the accounts of the period that have proliferated since Fain's time Barclay has been present, usually misconceived or treated peripherally. With this book the author hopes to have repaired a defect of long standing. Andrew Marvell's words on Cromwell are well suited to Barclay de Tolly:

> So shall his praise to after times encrease,
> When truth shall be allow'd, and faction cease.

The author has great pleasure in expressing his profound gratitude for the generous encouragement, aid, and advice he has received. He is particularly grateful to Professor Erik Amburger, Georg R. von Prosch, and Dr Johann Karl von Schroeder for steering him through the maze of Livonian families, and to Miss Margarita von Weymarn for her kindness in facilitating introductions; to Philip Longworth, Professor Marc Raeff, and Professor Edward Shils for their constructive criticism of the chapters they read; to Professor Walter W. Arndt for his prompt response to the request for a translation of Pushkin's 'The Commander', which first appeared, with an early version of the Epilogue, in the *Russian Literature Triquarterly* (Fall 1974); to Baroness Adline von Campenhausen and to her nephew Baron Balthasar von Campenhausen for having so graciously given him access to Barclay de Tolly's personal correspondence; to Dr Bernhard von Barsewisch for illustrations; to Dr Henri Broms, Director of Archives Markku Järvinen, and the indispensable Kari Ketola for assistance in the Helsinki libraries; to Colonel E. Daru for permission to work on the Caulaincourt archives in the *Archives Nationales* in Paris; to the authors of the specialist studies listed in the bibliography; to Dr William C. Olsen and the Rockefeller Foundation for their hospitality at the Villa Serbelloni; to the many friends who helped in many ways, especially François Bondy, Professor Richard Pipes, Boris Souvarine, and David Walters; and to the memory of those who have departed who urged him to undertake this task, historians Constantin de Grunwald, General Serge Andolenko, and his dear friend Professor Marc Slonim.

1977

COLLABORATOR'S ACKNOWLEDGEMENTS

Michael Josselson died one month after completing the manuscript of this book. The bibliography, inventory of letters, and glossary were incomplete, however, and without help his collaborator could never have put some order into these matters. She thanks Dr Marc Raeff of Columbia University for his incalculable, multilingual generosity and helpfulness, and Dr Christopher Duffy of Sandhurst for his support. She thanks Melvin J. Lasky of London for publishing the Preface and Epilogue to this book as an article in *Encounter*, thereby providing much encouragement. Her gratitude goes out to François Bondy in Zurich, polymath and old friend; to the late Dr Sergius Yakobson in Washington; to the indeed indispensable Kari Ketola in Finland; to Mme Marguerite Weil and her colleagues at the Bibliothèque Nationale in Paris; to Dr Walter Harding of The Thoreau Society in Geneseo, New York; to Veet Charitro of Bougy-Villars; and to Margaret and Gerard Noetzlin in Geneva who have helped in a great variety of ways. I must omit many others whose help has been precious, but I cannot fail to mention most gratefully the staff of the Oxford University Press.

All errors, insufficiencies, and inconsistencies, however, are entirely the responsibility of the author and his collaborator.

1979   D. J.

NOTE

Dates: Barclay de Tolly was born on 13/24 December 1761 and died on 13/25 May 1818. That is, his dates are 13 December 1761 to 13 May 1818 according to the Julian calendar – or Old Style (O.S.) – followed in Russia until the 1917 Revolution; but by the western Gregorian calendar – or New Style (N.S.) – he was born on 24 December 1761 and died on 25 May 1818. The Julian calendar ran eleven days behind the Gregorian in the eighteenth century and twelve days behind in the nineteenth century. When no confusion in the text is possible, e.g. when events are taking place in the West and western sources are being used, dates are given in one calendar only.

Transliteration, names, titles, places: Russian names, titles, and words are transliterated from the Cyrillic alphabet according to the system in use at the Widener Library of Harvard University. Names commonly found in English usage are spelled in the manner imposed by tradition, e.g. Tolstoy instead of Tolstoi. Names of monarchs and members of royal families are usually given in English versions. Current fashion has been followed in using 'Tsar' to distinguish Russian from western emperors, while continuing to refer to mothers and wives of tsars as empresses. The spelling of place names mentioned in letters has been changed to accord with usage in the text, e.g. Barclay writing in French to the Tsar says 'Witebsk'; this has been changed to Vitebsk. For his inconsistencies the author asks the reader's indulgence.

All translations are the author's unless otherwise acknowledged.

CHAPTER I

'YOUR NAME'S OUTLANDISH SOUND'

A man who was not orthodox could not be Russian.
Dostoevsky, The Possessed

Eighteen months of savage warfare had gone by since Napoleon left the ragged remnants of his Grande Armée to straggle back from the Berezina, but at last the end came. On 31 March 1814 Paris surrendered. Eleven days later, in nearby Fontainebleau, Napoleon, abandoning his plans to trap his enemies in Paris and cut off their retreat, signed his first abdication, and failed in his attempt to poison himself.

England, the following June, gave an overwhelming welcome to its allies. The visiting conquerors, Tsar Alexander I and King Frederick William III of Prussia, along with Prince Metternich representing Austria's Emperor Francis I, were accompanied by a dazzling entourage of military and diplomatic staffs. Prominent in the Tsar's retinue was the Field-Marshal Count Michael Barclay de Tolly, whom the Russians called Mikhail Bogdanovich.*

In London Barclay de Tolly is said to have called upon Colonel Sir Robert Barclay who had served in India under the Duke of Wellington. In the course of their conversation, as recounted by the family chronicler, Hubert Barclay, the Field-Marshal told the Colonel that 'he was perfectly acquainted with his descent from the Barclays of Towie in Scotland, but that was the extent of his knowledge'.[1] ('Towie' is 'Tolly' or a variant thereof in both Gaelic and Latin.)[2] The Russian Barclay excused himself by remarking 'that having entered the army very early in life, he had had little leisure since to perfect his education or to acquire that knowledge of foreign countries or his remote ancestors, which otherwise he would have had pleasure in investigating'. According to this account, he added that news had reached him that Towie Castle had been for sale. To acquire that castle was an attractive thought, he admitted, but being of Russian birth and with his destiny now inseparable from that of Russia, he had dismissed the idea.[3]

The story of these Barclays – and of Towie Castle, still standing in Aberdeenshire in the north-east corner of Turiff parish on the road to Banff – goes back to the time of the Norman Conquest.

In the extensive literature existing on the Scots Barclay family in all its lines, legend and conjecture are more plentiful than documentation for the early

---

* The patronymic Bogdanovich comes from the russianizing as Bogdan of all names starting with Gott-, or God-. The father of Michael Barclay de Tolly (BdT hereafter in Notes) was named Gotthard.

days.⁴ There is general agreement, however, on a Normandy origin, tenantship as provost or lord in 1086 in southern England in one of various manors called Berkley or Berkeley (Berchelei or Berchelai, meaning birch trees), with settlement in Scotland probably during the twelfth century. Recent research casts doubt on the widespread view that the Scottish Barclays are an offshoot of either of the Berkeley families of Gloucestershire. The name probably comes from the village of Berkley (Berchelei) near Frome in Somerset. Here in 1086 the Norman tenant-lord (under Roger Arundel) was a certain Robert, thus Robert de Berchelei. It is presumably his line which appears in Scottish records near the end of the reign of Malcolm IV (1153–65): Robert and Walter de Berkeley. In the following reign of William the Lion (1165–1214), but still in the twelfth century, a wealthy female descendant, Agatha de Berkeley, married Humphrey son of Theobold de Adevil(l)e who was probably son of Humphrey, lord of the chapelry of Adevile in Normandy.* Agatha's husband took the name of his wealthy wife and was given title by William the Lion to the Berkeley estates in Scotland. From this family, then, by female descent, came various branches of the Barclays of Scotland including the Mathers line which is said to have produced the Russian Field-Marshal (as well as famous Quakers and bankers) and the Towie line which completed Michael's name. The spelling of its components evolved through the centuries: the first mention of Tolli instead of Towie occurs in 1457 and it was at the end of the fifteenth century that some of the family began to spell the name Barclay.⁵

The Barclays built the present Towie Castle in the latter half of the sixteenth century, finishing it in the time of a Patrick Barclay who placed a prophetic inscription over the doorway in 1593:

> In tym of Valyth [wealth] al men s[eem] friendly
> An friend is not knowvin but in adversity.⁶

The Barclay arms are incorporated in the walls with the motto of the Towie line: 'Aether Doe or Die.'

The Barclays, in common with the majority of Scots, eventually became Protestants and, like many of their countrymen, especially younger sons, some Barclays turned to the Continent and Scandinavia to make a living or fight for their convictions. A David Barclay fought in the army of Gustavus Adolphus, later became a Quaker and fathered a renowned Quaker apologist. A William Barclay of Towie was banished and took refuge in Sweden, where his son became a major-general and was ennobled.⁷

In 1621 two Protestant brothers, Peter and John Barclay, merchants, were to be found in the Baltic city of Rostock in the Duchy of Mecklenburg. The brothers' exact relationship to Sir Patrick Barclay, son of the man who completed Towie Castle, has not been traced. Their kinship with the Towie Barclays is based on a letter of 'safe-conduct' issued from Banff to Peter and John on 4 April 1621, signed by Sir Patrick, local Banff officials, and a 'Minister of the Word of God':

---

* Adevile: now Addeville, commune of St. Côme-du-Mont, canton Carentin, arrondissement St. Lo, département Manche.

Peter and John are legitimate full brothers, sprung from a legitimate marriage and honest parents, the father foresooth being an honest man, named Andrew Barclay, sprung from the same family as the present Baron of Tollie . . . [8]

A letter of 'safe-conduct', equivalent to an identity card, was a commonplace of those turbulent times, when the tocsins of the Thirty Years War were sounding from every belfry. When the brothers arrived in Rostock they found the once powerful and privileged city already suffering from the decline of the Hanseatic League and the unsteadiness of trade, and threatened by the Swedish–Polish war. Peter Barclay and three of his sons stayed on, nevertheless. John Barclay decided to go on to Norway, where he founded a branch of the family which became extinct in 1907. Peter's eldest son, Johann Stephan Barclay, moved eastwards to Livonia and in 1664 settled in another old Hanseatic city, Riga. He was the founder of the Russian Barclay line – a line marked ever after by the singularity of Livonian life.[9]

Rising a short distance from where the river Dvina flows into the Baltic, Riga was fortified and developed as a diocesan see by Bishop Albert of Bremen in 1201, on the site of a simple and ancient trading outpost. With the coming of the Hanseatic League, Riga became a flourishing and cosmopolitan town, serving as the bustling ante-room to Russia; all trading routes for merchants from northern Germany to the great markets of Novgorod and Smolensk, whether by the Baltic Sea, the Dvina, or overland, passed through it.[10] Riga became the capital of Livonia, which in those days encompassed today's Latvia, part of Estonia, and part of Lithuania. When the first Barclay arrived in Riga, it was already a captivating city. Steeply gabled houses and warehouses lined its clattering streets. Great guildhalls like the impressive Schwarzhaüpterhaus testified to the standing of mercenaries, merchants, artisans, even scribes and clerks.[11] Dominating the scene were St. Mary's Cathedral and the churches of St. John, St. James, and especially St. Peter – though it was only later generations of Barclays who saw the completion of St. Peter's airy, three-tiered wooden steeple soaring higher than the towers of Chartres. Eight generations of Barclay de Tollys were to make Riga and Livonia their home.

German culture and the German language had been firmly implanted through the Teutonic members of the Livonian Order of the Knights of the Sword who ruled the region for three hundred years. Their mission was the conversion of the heathen Livs, Letts, Ests, and Kurs, a mission given equal importance with the crusades in Innocent III's papal bull. In the sixteenth century the Knights were weakened by the advent of Lutheran Protestantism and swept away by invading Russians. Significantly, the Balts never shared in the Orthodox religion of the Russian invaders; Baltic churches were stripped of their Roman trappings and consecrated to sober Lutheran worship without ever passing through the Orthodox rite. German cultural and linguistic predominance (with an indigenous Livonian flavour) was thus reinforced, especially among the landed aristocracy and middle class, and it survived successive invasions of Poles, Swedes, and Russians, and even Peter the Great's incorporation of the whole region into the Russian Empire in 1721.

Although the Livonian Knights were disbanded as an Order, they were able individually to retain their immense estates and vast powers. Their Protestant descendants, often intermarrying with the Swedish nobility, particularly during the eighty years of Swedish supremacy (1629–1710), continued to dominate the scene. Clustering around these great Baltic barons there grew up in time a patriarchal network of lesser landowners who followed the same patterns of marriage and intermarriage. Livonians of German–Swedish stock could normally find cousins almost anywhere in the Baltic area. All the non-Teutonic elements were absorbed into the prevailing Germanic–Livonian culture. After Peter the Great, however, all the gentry, high and low, were themselves absorbed into the imperial system of service. From that time on until the repressive reigns of the last two Romanovs, the political allegiance of the Livonian upper classes was unmistakably Russian.

More and more tradesmen had followed in the wake of the Livonian Knights, and Riga had become a thoroughly commercial town when Johann Stephan Barclay settled there to practise law in 1664. During the next century the ethic of gain and the sentiment of autonomy became even more deeply imprinted. Kant's favourite pupil, Johann Gottfried Herder, who left Koenigsberg to teach at Riga's venerable *Domschule* in 1764, bears witness to Livonia's prevailing twin spirits of commercialism and liberalism. In his youthful fervour the writer-philosopher (who dreamt of becoming the great reformer of Russia – if only he could get Catherine the Great's ear) inveighed against Riga's mercantile spirit: 'Here everything, including learning, is measured in figures and weights . . .'[12] On the other hand, after sojourning nearly six years in Riga, he concluded: 'Perhaps never again in my life will I be able to live, act, and teach with such freedom and without any restraint as in Livonia . . .'[13]

Long before the question of abolishing serfdom was raised in the rest of Russia, some of the Livonian nobility and landowners – partly prodded by their Lutheran consciences – were introducing half-measures in that direction. The Livonian Baron Karl Schultz von Ascheraden had already in 1764 scandalized his peers by freeing the peasants on his estate from outright bondage, changing their status to that of in-duty-bound tenants. Twelve years later the exalted Livonian pietist, Julie de Krüdener (known to history as The Lady of the Holy Alliance and as Alexander I's *directeur de conscience*), exclaimed on a visit to Germany at the age of eleven, 'Thank God, here all men are free!'[14] She forthwith determined to free all her serfs – her father, Baron Otto Herman von Vietinghoff, 'half-king of Livonia', is said to have owned fifty thousand – as soon as she was able to.*

The Livonian upper classes (like their serfs) enjoyed a degree of liberty which was not permitted to their Russian peers, but Herder scolded them for falling far short of civilized aspirations: 'Livonia, thou province of barbarism and luxury, of ignorance and presumptuous tastes, of freedom and slavery, how much there is to be done to destroy slavery, to eradicate ignorance, and to

---

* Abolition came to Russia as a whole only in 1861, but under Alexander I the German–Balt landowners granted full personal freedom to their serfs, though without giving them land, in Estland in 1816, Courland in 1817, and Livonia proper in 1819.

spread culture and freedom . . .'[15] This Livonia was still, after all, a part of Russia – but it was a Russia without the dominance of the knout and the Orthodox Church, without the black inertia. Seen from the West, Livonia was indeed the ante-room to Russia, providing foretastes of benighted backwardness. Seen from the Russian Court or from Moscow, however, Livonia was hardly distinguishable from the West. Alexander I's Swiss tutor, Laharpe, writing to the Tsar about the high cultural level and wealth of the Baltic provinces, and even daring to compare Riga with St. Petersburg, explained to his pupil that German influence accounted for the happy combination of enlightenment with prosperity.[16]

In the 1800 census Riga's population of thirty thousand consisted of 43 per cent Germans, some 25 per cent Letts, fewer than 15 per cent Russians, and the rest a mélange of nationalities. There was much coming and going through its narrow streets, and the port attracted foreign ideas as well as foreign products. During the endless winters the yellow lights seen in the snow-mantled houses were often being used for reading. Riga boasted its own distinguished publisher. There was, besides, the stimulus of frequent visitors like Johann Georg Hamann, 'Wizard of the North', a friend of Herder and, like him and Kant, also a Koenigsberg philosopher. His ideas brought intellectual ferment to Riga and his eccentricities brought Riga to the attention of intellectual Europe.

Despite the 'barbarism . . . ignorance . . . and slavery', despite the melancholy northern climate with its bitter long winters, this then – cosmopolitan, hospitable, thriving, striving, Lutheran, Germanic, and relatively liberal – was the Livonia where generations of Barclays were formed and prospered.

Johann Stephan Barclay was admitted to the bar in Riga in 1664 and, as public prosecutor, signed his name – with perhaps more enterprise than justification – Johann Barclay de Tolli, using the title 'dominus'. His wife (Anna Sophia von Darenthal, daughter of a fellow lawyer in Riga) bore him three sons. Two of these became officers in the Swedish army; the eldest, Wilhelm, succeeded his father and was appointed first as an alderman of the Great Guild, then as city alderman in 1730, and later quartermaster of all Riga. He was known as Wilhelm Barclay de Tollie and owned two estates in Livonia. The widest interpretation of the genealogical implications of the 'safe-conduct' had by now been established by family tradition. Wilhelm's coat of arms, with inscription, hangs in St. Peter's in Riga, where his descendants could eye it covertly during the long sermons. Succeeding generations of Livonian Barclays were chiefly prominent in two professions: the army and the magistracy. They distinguished themselves in both, serving with competence, devotion, and loyalty. To the proud municipality they furnished aldermen, a city treasurer, and two burgomasters – high, honourable callings in a city which had through centuries enjoyed an autonomous status and a generous and broad-minded administration. In the army they furnished many senior officers and eventually one field-marshal, Michael Andreas Barclay de Tolly.[17]

CHAPTER II

THE MAN

> The man who obeys dutifully is worthy of being some day a commander.
>
> *Cicero, De Legibus*

In the 1760s, a traveller journeying some seventy versts (about fifty miles) due south from Riga would have crossed into the Polish-held northern part of Courland (the old Samogitia, now Lithuania) and would have reached the locality of Zheime. Situated in this locality was a small estate: Pamushis. It was here, on 13/24 December 1761, that Michael Barclay de Tolly was born. The entry in the baptismal records at Zheime reads: 'Michael Andreas, son of Barclay de Tolley of Pamushis was baptized here in 1761 *Dom. p. Nat.*', i.e. on the Sunday after the Nativity.[1]

Michael was a fourth-generation Livonian Barclay. His great-grandfather was 'dominus' Johann Stephan Barclay who founded the line; his grandfather was Wilhelm, whose coat of arms hangs in St. Peter's in Riga. His father, Gotthard, born in Riga in 1726, served in the imperial Russian army, leaving it at the age of twenty-four with the gentlemanly rank of lieutenant. Three years later he took steps to establish himself and a brother, also a lieutenant, in the Livonian Body of Knights, basing their right to a baronial title, somewhat tenuously it would seem, on the 1621 'safe conduct' issued from Banff by Sir Patrick Barclay, Baron of Tollie, to Peter and John Barclay in Rostock.[2]

Gotthard, who had bought the estate of Luhde-Grosshof (in the central Livonian district of Walk), was twenty-nine when he married Margarethe Elisabeth von Smitten, who came from a long line of Swedish army officers originally named Smitt. Margarethe was 'heiress' of the manor of Beckhof, an hour's gallop from Luhde-Grosshof, and she and Michael's father were married there, but she did not live long enough to realize her inheritance. Beckhof came eventually to Michael not through his mother but through his wife, also a von Smitten – a cousin – who purchased it from her brother.[3]

Michael's parents produced five sons and one daughter. Two sons died at birth or within months. One elder brother, Erich, survived. Older than Michael by three years, he became a major-general attached to the Tsar's suite, also married a von Smitten first cousin, and outlived Michael by one year. Michael and Erich and their families were close in later life, and Erich's son Andreas was adjutant to his uncle during the Napoleonic war. Four years after Michael's birth a younger brother was born – Heinrich – who became an artillery major in the Russian army and died at thirty-nine. Finally, Michael's junior by nine years, came his sister Christine.[4]

But Michael never lived at home with his whole family. One year before he was born his father fell into debt and was obliged to sell Luhde-Grosshof at auction. He very probably only leased the small Pamushis estate where Michael was born, soon giving that up to lease the estate of Laiksaar in the north-western Livonian district of Pernau, where the two youngest children were born. He eventually died in Laiksaar (when Michael was twenty) without ever establishing himself as a landowner. Michael is reported to have said that his father possessed a substantial fortune, but lost it through mishaps and adversities as a result of his kind-heartedness and boundless generosity. He is usually described as a 'non-wealthy nobleman', i.e. poor.[5] In any case he was ill able to afford the upbringing of his second son, and when Michael was only three, before the younger children were born, the child was sent off to St. Petersburg to be cared for by his maternal aunt and her husband, the Vermeulens, who became his foster-parents. When Michael's mother died in Laiksaar in 1771, shortly after giving birth to Christine, this little sister was also sent to the Vermeulens to become a foster-daughter. Christine was two at the time, and Michael was eleven. While growing up, Michael had had close contact with his parents and elder brother for only his first three years, and how well he knew his younger brother is not certain. Since the Barclays, von Smittens, and Vermeulens were all closely allied by marriage, however, family feeling was not broken off by this severance and warm relationships were developed despite distance. Michael was able to maintain a glowing sentiment of kinship with all branches of the Barclays; even in the crucial year of 1812 he worked in 'a few minutes with the dear, good Barclay family' on a short inspection trip to Riga, where his cousin was mayor.[6] But the immediate family to whom Michael was attached was his avuncular foster-family in St. Petersburg.

The institution of fosterage was far from uncommon among the nobility and landed gentry of the time. It supplied parents for orphans, children for childless families, educational and marital opportunities inaccessible at home. It helped level out family size and the costs of rearing each new generation, and it greatly strengthened the bonds of Livonian interrelatedness. Vermeulen, Michael's foster-father (and uncle by marriage), had himself been brought up by a foster-father (and uncle by marriage). He had been taken to the court of Frederick the Great by his foster-father, a well-known mathematician, had become a lieutenant in the Prussian army, had run away and returned to Russia, and become a brigadier in the Russian army. Michael was brought up on the campaign tales of Brigadier Georg Wilhelm Vermeulen. Vermeulen and his wife, Auguste Wilhelmine von Smitten, a sister to Michael's mother, had no children of their own and were very well pleased to take charge of their three-year-old nephew and later of his little sister Christine.[7]

Michael's leaving of the parental home at such an early and impressionable age, however, may have explained some of his later character traits, notably his reserve and taciturnity. The fierce drill Vermeulen received in Frederick the Great's army no doubt left a heavy Prussian imprint on Michael's upbringing as well. The primacy of discipline, with all the systematic punctiliousness, exactitude, and precision, with all the selfless submission to command and perfect loyalty implied in the Frederician notion of *Korpsgeist*, permeated the boy's early training.

The home atmosphere of the strict and devoutly Lutheran Vermeulens in St. Petersburg was God-fearing, dutiful, earnest, simple, and, at the same time, formal. The household, though seigniorial, was of modest substance, with servants closely supervised by Aunt Auguste who capably maintained standards of distinction and dignity in a framework of simplicity. There was a spirit of piety but not of bigotry: Livonian tolerance prevailed. While there is nothing to indicate a warm and open family life, summers in the country at Enge – a small Estonian property the Vermeulens took on when Michael was thirteen and Christine four – must have been comparatively free and easy, with the children playing in the long grass, exploring the birch copses, and regaling themselves with cranberry *kissel* and milk. Whether in town or country, obedience was the cardinal virtue, and thrift and industry were inculcated by precept and example.

Michael and Christine were always reverently devoted to their foster-parents. Michael's adult letters to his 'Most gracious Aunt' were filled with repetitious assurances of 'lifelong filial devotion' and 'forever keen feelings of gratitude', along with expressions of his wife's deference, 'who with due reverence kisses your hands'; and they seem to be something more than mere ceremonial tributes. His references to his aunt's motherly care, motherly sympathy, and continued affection convey in effect 'the sincere feelings of a man who will always venerate his mother in your person'.[8] (She died only three years before Michael; the foster-father died when Michael was twenty-eight.)

It is clear that Livonian family relationships were of a completely different order from those obtaining in most Russian households of the time, where children were normally treated with indifference and brutality. This disparity in upbringing, inevitably affecting personality development, attitudes, and beliefs, was fundamental in setting Michael apart, in later life, from his Russian compatriots.

Vermeulen, who was nearing forty when Michael came to him, had been severely wounded in the Seven Years War and was retired and pensioned soon afterwards. Although their means were limited, there were many books, there were intellectuals in the family background, and the Vermeulens were unusually well educated for their milieu. Michael began to appreciate reading, in the manner of many a lonely child, and he is said to have read assiduously, marking the passages which touched him. His fare must have included the standard works on the exploits of Alexander, Hannibal, and Caesar, of the Marshals Saxe and Münnich, Prince Eugene of Savoy, and the Duke of Marlborough – as well as obligatory works of piety. By the time Christine joined the household he was already a self-contained, self-controlled boy, enrolled for a military career, and giving satisfaction on all counts; he was considered to be an able, talented boy. Having a vivacious little sister to cherish and protect gave him a welcome outlet for his affections, especially as her arrival followed soon after the death of his real mother, an event which may have stirred up early, unavowable feelings of abandonment. The children became highly attached to each other and this attachment lasted throughout their lives, being most clearly expressed by

Michael's eventually becoming a loving foster-father to Christine's own daughter.

When Michael was only six, he was inscribed as a lance-corporal in the Novotroitskii Cuirassier Regiment and, at eight, he was advanced to sergeant. Until the age of fifteen he lived at home with the Vermeulens, however, and his foster-father was responsible for his education, purportedly an 'excellent' one. At fifteen, the standard age, he went on active duty and was transferred to the Pskovskii Rifle Regiment, where he was promoted to the rank of cornet two years later, in 1778.

This apparently precocious military career was normal for the time. As Madame de Staël observed in St. Petersburg, 'all education is finished at fifteen; every one rushes into a military career as soon as possible, and all the rest is neglected.'[9] Ever since Peter the Great had instituted compulsory gentry-service (full time from the age of fifteen until disability), the nobility had been forced to provide army or civil service and the bourgeoisie had used the army to enter the gentry class: 'the ambition of every bourgeois is to make his sons officers, so that they will be in the privileged class', Madame de Staël noted. In theory young men could enter the army only as privates, after establishing their educational qualifications, for which the parents were responsible. If commissioned, they became automatically gentlemen, if not already so by birth. On attaining the rank of major, they became 'hereditary gentlemen'. In practice, the equal-opportunity system of starting as a private was circumvented by the early enrolment of privileged children, with promotions occurring before they entered on active duty at fifteen or sixteen. Compulsory gentry-service was abolished by Peter III on his accession one year after Michael's birth, in 1762. But the tradition of service to the Tsar was so well established that army enrolment remained routine for sons of the nobility and upward-striving bourgeois. In the case of sons of petty and impoverished nobility, there was no practical alternative career. The system provided an enormous class of ill-educated 'gentlemen' army officers.

Michael's 'educational qualifications' at the time of his promotion to cornet read as follows: 'He can read and write Russian and German, and is knowledgeable in fortifications.'[10] Dissatisfied with these lean attainments, Michael devoted all his spare time off duty to assiduous study in an earnest programme to improve his education. He never succeeded in losing his Baltic–German accent in speaking Russian – a fact which did him no good in the great crisis of his later life. He became, however, proficient in French, the upper-class language of Russia – all his official correspondence including that with the Tsar was to be in French – and he was adept at finance, later showing mastery in all matters of accounting. Unlike his father, Michael had a good head for figures.*

During the next eight years Michael served without occasioning any special notice from his superiors, who saw in him 'only a front-line officer who would

---

* BdT's letters show him constantly handling money matters, land transactions, and inheritances for all his relatives; he was the businessman of the family, and as a government administrator he shouldered enormous financial responsibilities.

execute all commands to the point of pedantry'.¹¹ The Prussian–Lutheran shell of his early training showed no signs of breaking.

In 1786, at the age of twenty-five, he was commissioned lieutenant.

There are no portraits extant of Michael as boy or youth, but from the various portraits of him in adult life we can form a clear idea of his appearance. He was tall and well built, with a bearing at once elegant and military, erect and commanding. His carriage and manner are said to have 'denoted distinction and unusual composure; from the first glance he instilled confidence and esteem'.¹² During battles it was noticed that he seemed to grow even taller. A slight limp and a stiffness in his right arm and hand were caused by wounds. He had a high-domed head, a feature later accentuated by his baldness, and a long, rather pale face. His dark-brown eyes, under well-formed eyebrows, were large, and he had a strong, straight nose, well-modelled lips, cheeks bordered by comely, curling side-whiskers, with all features powerful and well proportioned, marked by an expression of intelligence. A virile, aristocratic head, an imposing man.

He was a man to admire or to hate, not one for casual conviviality. Social rapport between equals was something his childhood never taught him. But he was happy enough when it was appropriate for him to be mainly either giver or taker. The model for his attitude towards superiors and benefactors was clearly derived from his relationship with his foster-parents. He overflowed with deep feelings of gratitude and loyalty towards those who helped and guided him forward. With subordinates, on the other hand, there is a hint of his fondly protective relationship with his much younger sister. His manner with troops was curtly affectionate and he cared for their needs as no other commander then thought to do. It was considered remarkable that even under stress he eschewed insults and abuse. Since Russian soldiers normally knew no other treatment than loud cursing, howling injustice, and violent displays of temperament, interspersed from time to time by uproarious camaraderie or bouts of sentimentality, Michael's moderation, impartiality, and imperturbability, far from endearing him, often made him seem remote and indifferent.

Nevertheless, he was basically successful in these sonlike or fatherlike roles. Camaraderie with his peers was more elusive. 'In dealing with his equals he was always courteous and obliging, but never became close friends with any one.'¹³ A core of solitude remained from his companionless formative years. The high-living world of the officer class where most of his life was spent could in any case provide few candidates for congeniality. When power and position finally gave Michael the opportunity to succumb to the temptations of St. Petersburg society and enjoy the normal excesses of a Russian officer's life, he found that frivolity and excess had no appeal for him. He preferred always to live within his means, whereas it was not unusual for high-ranking officers to pilfer army funds to cover gambling debts or to squander on extraordinary luxuries. Conscience-driven himself, he did not set himself to judge his lax, worldly, Orthodox fellow soldiers, but neither did he feel like joining in: he never allowed himself 'anything superfluous, shunning all large parties, disliking card games'.¹⁴ Since parties and card games – that is, heavy drinking and gambling – were the standard off-duty occupations, not to participate required exceptional strength of character, but also marked a man as an outsider. In family gatherings and with less profligate friends, however, Michael was at ease, and he developed a reputation as a hospitable host at more sober entertainments: 'He enjoyed gathering his army colleagues and subordinates around him and hearing the opinions of the young during meals; he seldom took part himself in these talks, but listened attentively and from time to time showed his agreement by an approving smile . . .'[15] He liked plain living at home and relished it in the field. Even when he was a general he often bivouacked with the common soldiers, sleeping in the open. Once the Tsar had to seek him out in a 'wretched barn', and again, after the battle of Borodino, a fellow general was shocked to discover Barclay fast asleep on a cottage floor alongside his exhausted aides-de-camp and orderlies. His staff had some cause to envy their fellows at other headquarters. After one of Michael's adjutants transferred to Field-Marshal Kutuzov's staff, he spoke feelingly of the excellent food prepared there 'by some of the Tsar's cooks': 'It was completely unlike the modest suckling pig with horseradish handed to Barclay de Tolly every day, served on English pewter, not on imperial solid silver dishes as at Kutuzov's . . .'[16]

Michael was also set apart by his attitude towards books, his serious study of military treatises, and his avidity for new ideas. Russian officers in general were an ignorant lot, many even illiterate, and what libraries the rare readers among them had, normally consisted entirely of light reading in French, 'but not one book on war'.[17] When, foreseeing financial straits in 1812, Michael wrote to his wife suggesting she sell various household properties, he asked particularly that his books, maps, and correspondence be spared.[18]

He possessed a keen, quick, probing mind, though his lack of education meant that his scope was limited. A critical subordinate clearly did not intend a tribute when he wrote: 'Also peculiar was his uncommon independence of mind; virtually nobody could have any profound or durable influence on him . . . his opinions and decisions, good or bad, were always his own . . .'[19] Those well disposed towards him emphasized his rare common sense and 'truly extraordinary' administrative and organizational abilities.[20] Simple, earnest, kindly, unpretentious, modest – these are words applied to Barclay almost to the point of shadowing the superlatives invariably attached to two of his most fundamental and uncontested traits. One of these was his utterly unblemished honesty. The most hostile of contemporaries recognized his perfect probity (a virtue remarkably uncharacteristic of milieux close to the throne), while friends saw his honesty as a part of the whole: 'A supremely noble, independent character, heroically courageous, equable, and in the highest degree honest and disinterested . . .'[21] In view of the prevailing corruption and self-enrichment even in the highest ranks of Russian society, Michael's integrity evoked strong feelings, whether of admiration or detestation.

His amazing cool-headed courage was the other characteristic universally recognized. His manner under fire placed him at the heart of the heroic tradition: 'In battle and in difficult moments, he displayed an imperturbable composure, and nothing could bring him out of countenance. This perfect laconic calmness lent an extraordinary quality to his magnificent personal courage . . .'[22]

Michael himself, however, wished most of all to be identified with two qualities which he selected for his motto in 1815, after the central crisis of his life had been resolved. They were his own comment on his character: loyalty and patience.

Finally, underlying all the characteristics of the man gleamed a quality which has been best described as 'his extraordinary spiritual loftiness'.[23] At the crucial turning points of his life, there can be no doubt that his character, as well as historical circumstance, determined his fate.

In 1791, at the age of thirty, Michael Barclay de Tolly, following in the safe footsteps of his elder brother Erich, married a maternal cousin, Helene Auguste Eleonore von Smitten, known as Auguste. She was born at the von Smitten family estate of Beckhof in 1770.[24]

We must hope Auguste was a charming bride, though in the portrait we have of her in her days of glory, she appears less than attractive. A heavy-set matron bedecked in jewels and court decorations, with a beribboned lace bonnet topping her auburn hair, she gives the impression of being authoritarian, self-important, and demanding. Her features are heavy and fleshy; the smallish brown eyes seem shrewd and critical.

Appearances may deceive, however. Auguste and Michael were a devoted couple. It is perhaps significant that the nine-year gap in their ages was the same as that between Michael and his young sister and that Auguste was called by the same name as Michael's foster-mother. The satisfying roles of paternalistic elder brother and obedient son could be combined in this marriage, especially since Auguste responded with just the necessary proportions of dependence and domination. Auguste's fundamentally welcome mothering even followed Michael into the field, where she made his adjutants spoon-feed him home-made decoctions. Loewenstern, Barclay's adjutant in 1812 and 1814, was under solemn oath to Auguste: 'It was terribly funny to see me struggle spoon in hand with the Commander in Chief and watch his grimaces as he swallowed. But he was meek as a lamb in everything involving his wife . . .'[25]

The couple actually lived together very little, either at Beckhof or in St. Petersburg where they sometimes had apartments, since Michael was often absent on campaigns or inspections. But his letters to her – those extant are all written after twenty years of marriage – are always affectionately tender, full of concern for her health, and deal mostly with such matters as his securing a promotion or a long overdue pension payment for a relative – usually hers. There were gossipy tales of how Auguste exploited Michael's predisposition to be accommodating to the demands of family connections. At least some of these criticisms originated with biased, malicious, and envious courtiers in St. Petersburg who were disarmed by Michael's uprightness and therefore took their revenge on Auguste. Said Langeron, one of the French generals in the Russian service, echoing this gossip: 'General Barclay was a man of utter probity; but unfortunately he was married, and too often dominated by his wife;

who was not so scrupulous . . .'[26]

The quality of feeling between Michael and his wife is somewhat obscured by the old-fashioned formality of their letter style. Michael invariably signs himself 'your faithful Barclay'. In the one extant letter of Auguste to her husband, she addresses him as 'My dear beloved Angel!' and repeatedly refers to him throughout as 'dear angel . . . dear good man . . . dear beloved husband'. She prays that she be soon allowed to hurry into his arms, thanks him with a kiss for his love, and ends, 'I embrace you with ardent love, Your forever faithful wife, A. Barclay.'[27] Michael's letters to his 'liebes Weib' do not meet this level of ardour despite a 'dear angel' of his own here and there. Still, a birthday letter to Auguste after two decades of marriage testifies to an enduring affection. He tells her that next to Providence, 'I am indebted to you, my wonderful wife, for all the joys of my life.'[28]

There are pleasant conjugal touches in Michael's letters, as when he sends her twelve ells each of two fashionable shades of 'good-quality velvet' from Bohemia, or when he complains that 'We suffer here from lack of wine, please be so kind as to send some.'[29] And some of Michael's accounts of memorable episodes impart the texture of relationships as he would not have revealed them to anybody else. Thus on 17/29 June 1811 he writes to Auguste from St. Petersburg of returning with the Tsar from a tour of inspection:

> As we drove from the soldiers' school to the arsenal we met the Emperor's mother. He made us stop and stood erect in the calèche in order to greet his mother with all due reverence. I stood next to him and supported myself with my crippled hand on the edge of the calèche. His Majesty noticed this, and thrust his right hand under my arm, telling me, I shall hold you, don't strain your arm. All this is certainly proof of the particular favour which he bestows on me at every opportunity. For me it was therefore nothing unusual; the public, however, noticed it and the news of it spread like fire throughout the town . . .[30]

The only child of Michael and Auguste to survive infancy was a son named Magnus, often called Max. He is in fact the only recorded offspring of the couple, although there were other pregnancies.[31] After much disappointment, Magnus was born a long seven years after their marriage. Like most army children, he did not see a great deal of his father. After Magnus's birth, however, practically every letter from Michael to Auguste ends with 'a kiss for Magnus'.

Both before and after Magnus's birth, Michael and Auguste often had various Livonian boys and girls under some degree of tutelage in their home. One, a Vermeulen connection named Friedrich, was a special protégé, sent to the Barclays in 1796 to perfect his Russian and receive Michael's sponsorship in the army. Other young men also lived with the Barclays in St. Petersburg, 'learning to speak, write, and read Russian'.[32] When it became clear that Magnus was to be an only child, the couple turned to fosterage to fill their home. A bevy of Livonian girls lived under their protection at various times – Lina, Catherine, Jenny, and Christel. Of these the last three were cousins to one another and to Magnus. Lina's father was an Estonian landowner; Catherine's father a Russian noble married to a first cousin of both Michael and Auguste; Jenny was

Auguste's niece: her father a dignitary in Riga, her mother Auguste's sister Johanna; and Christel, the last to join the family, was Michael's niece, child of his beloved sister Christine, who had married a delightful but impoverished landowner. Lina von Helffreich, Catherine Murav'ev-Apostol, Jenny von Tornauw, Christel von Lueder – four young girls to be fostered and cherished, with every advantage that living under the Barclay wing conferred. These advantages became even more desirable after Auguste was admitted to the imperial Order of St. Catherine in 1809 and thus enjoyed the enviable privilege of being able to nominate a young lady of noble birth to the exclusive schools supported by the Order. Of the four girls, all but Jenny were appointed maids of honour at court. Lina and Christel were maids of honour to both empresses, Alexander I's wife and his mother, and Catherine was maid of honour to Alexander's sister, the Grand Duchess Catherine. After a visit to his sister the Tsar wrote that the sixteen-year-old Catherine was 'a heavenly creature'.[33] The presence of heavenly creatures in his household certainly gladdened Michael's heart and the hearts, no doubt, of his staff officers as well. The influence of the Barclay milieu is in any case fairly clearly reflected in the marriages of their protégées to distinguished army officers, none less than a general by the end of his career.[34]

It seems there was an especially close relationship between Michael and his niece Christel (diminutive of Christine), and that she was a true 'foster-daughter', considered by both Michael and Auguste as their own child. She was formally adopted as their foster-daughter in 1810 when she was seven, though the matter had probably been arranged much earlier.[35] She remembered that occasion in 1810, describing in her memoirs the three-hundred-verst week-long winter voyage (in a new covered sledge with two lovely horses) to reach the Barclays' impressive house ablaze in the glow of St. Petersburg street lamps. Here a lasting emotional attachment developed between Michael and his niece, and a lasting tension between her and Auguste. Here, before Christel's critical eye, Aunt Auguste preened herself for court appearances, adjusting the pink bow of her newly acquired St. Catherine insignia – the highest order in the land for women, but no reason in seven-year-old eyes for any self-satisfaction. Despite the fosterage arrangement and evident worldly advantages, Christel's parents had qualms about letting the child loose in her uncle's fashionable city establishment: 'As he lived on a great footing as Minister of War in Petersburg, my parents could not bring themselves to send their child there, and my dear uncle agreed to that. So I was educated at home, very simply, such as the modest means of my parents permitted and as it sufficed for the custom of the time . . .'[36] Christel was finally 'handed over' at fourteen to her foster-parents. According to her account: 'In the arms of my good uncle I felt the love of a father, but he only showed it, for good reasons, when we were alone. Indeed, when he heard steps approaching he immediately let me out of his arms . . .'[37] It is also Christel who records that Barclay's dying thought was for her. Auguste, according to Christel's memoirs, embraced her, sobbing: 'You were his last word. I shall love you as his child.'[38]

Unfortunately there is a dearth of documents on Barclay's private life. The somewhat melodramatic memoirs of his nymphet niece seem to be just slightly out of tune with his personality as it emerges from other sources. Just as there seems to be a dissonance between the 'wonderful wife' of Michael's letters and the malicious description of Auguste by the daughter of one of Livonia's oldest families:

> The superbly elegant life of the princess was in strong contrast with our simple country lifestyle which was much more harmonious. Just imagine, when the princess gave a large party, twelve servants in livery were kept busy; and even when there were fewer guests, a servant always stood behind each chair, often snatching away the plates before the guests had time to swallow their last bite. The princess was a fast eater . . . and after all she is served first . . .[39]

It is not easy to imagine Michael, the dutiful, God-fearing soldier, feeling truly at home in the ostentatious household Auguste kept during her last years. But he was a kindly man, and a dutiful, God-fearing husband, and he seems to have accepted his Auguste as a 'gift of kind Providence', recognizing the good-heartedness and ignoring the social climbing.[40] It is, however, somehow appropriate that it was Christel's son who eventually, when Michael's direct line ended, inherited his title and became the future Prince Barclay de Tolly-Weymarn.

CHAPTER III

APPRENTICESHIP IN WAR

> Where a battle has been fought, you will find nothing but the bones of men and beasts; where a battle is being fought, there are hearts beating.
>
> *Thoreau, A Week on the Concord and Merrimac Rivers*

In 1787 Barclay de Tolly was twenty-six and a lieutenant in a Jaeger corps – something new in the Russian army. Jaeger regiments were light infantry troops of crack riflemen, and their officers were usually chosen from among the best.[1] Barclay was considered to be in this superior category, although after a whole decade of active duty and training he still had not tested himself in battle. But when Turkey, provoked by Catherine the Great and encouraged by Britain, France, and Prussia, declared war on Russia in August 1787, action beckoned, all the more attractive because it was located in an exotic, faraway setting.

A chain of well-placed fortresses manned by large garrisons of Turks and their Tatar vassals guarded the northern border of the Ottoman Empire and adjoining areas. The frontier, starting deep inside what had been old Russian territory, turned westwards through the Moldavian steppes to enclose most of the Balkan peninsula. The Ottoman land forces were aided by a numerically powerful Turkish fleet patrolling the north coast of the Black Sea.

The Russian land forces were divided into two separate armies without unified command – an arrangement habitual throughout Tsarist military history, invariably creating plagues of rivalry and animosity among the Russian generals. One army of about forty thousand men, known as the Ukrainian Army, was commanded by the able, experienced, independent, though ailing Field-Marshal Count Pyotr Rumiantsev, one of the richest, most powerful, and most ostentatious of Russia's warlords. Even on the field he conducted himself in flamboyant fashion, travelling with a huge, orientally luxurious train of personal possessions. He had severely damaged the Turks in the last Russo–Turkish war; now his main mission was to cover Potemkin and link up with the relatively insignificant force supplied by Russia's ally, Austria.

The other Russian army of only about ten thousand men, known as the Ekaterinoslav Army, was about three hundred miles to the south-east, moving slowly westwards along the north shore of the Black Sea towards Ochakov. In command was Gregory Potemkin, Prince of Taurida (the Crimea), now popularly remembered as creator of those 'Potemkin villages' which marked the route of Catherine's provocative journey to the Black Sea, the journey which itself helped bring the war about.[2] Potemkin was the most famous and influential of the Empress's lovers, and proved himself eventually to be a remarkable statesman and colonizer. The lifelong favour he retained with Catherine, a woman more than generous, and the unlimited opportunities he enjoyed for pocketing fabulous sums of state moneys enabled him also to live, even when on campaign, in the style of an eastern potentate.

Barclay, now with the rank of captain, was assigned to Potemkin's Ekaterinoslav Army and was named adjutant to Lieutenant-General Prince Victor-Amadeus Anhalt-Bernburg. From the beginning of Barclay's career, he was fortunate in his field commanders. The first was Major-General von Patkul, who recognized Barclay's promise and, upon retirement, highly recommended him to Count Friedrich Anhalt. This Anhalt – for curiously and confusingly Barclay's second and third field commanders both came from the small German state of Anhalt, made up of several petty principalities just south of Brandenburg – was a remarkable man. After retiring at fifty-one from a brilliant military career under Frederick the Great, he accepted an invitation from Catherine in 1783, entering her service as lieutenant-general and supervisor of all Jaeger regiments. He had many interests – later he was president of the Free Economic Society – and he was a great teacher. Barclay's competence grew and his mind was kindled and broadened under this second field commander.

The commander to whom Barclay was assigned in Potemkin's army, Prince Anhalt-Bernburg, was also an exceptional person and he had a determining influence on Barclay's development, reinforcing his basic qualities and giving the young adjutant not only an example but above all the encouragement he needed to consolidate his self-confidence. Barclay's respectful, filial attachment to the Prince gradually turned into the easiest and most rewarding masculine relationship in his experience. Anhalt-Bernburg's personal qualities, as described by the Prince de Ligne, were remarkably similar to those later attributed to Barclay:

... of a modest and sublime simplicity which would make him appear to be the slightest of officers in his army; he is everything, and wishes to appear as nothing; ... is in love with gunshot and duty; exposing himself to danger more than he ought to; bringing out the virtues in everybody else; attributing to them what is due to himself; full of delicacy of soul and spirit; ... likeable; ... observant; ... unbending in his principles. ...[3]

Here was a pattern for Barclay, and an affinity soon developed between the two, based on their similar characters and their common nurture in Germanic culture and the Frederician spirit.[4]

The first Turkish bulwark confronting Potemkin's Ekaterinoslav Army was the great fortress and naval base of Ochakov on the north shore of the Black Sea at the entrance to the Dneprovskii Liman (*liman*: Turkish for lagoon). Ochakov had already changed hands more than once in Russo–Turkish history and was thus invested with strong emotions on both sides. Four miles across the Liman lay the Russian fortress of Kinburn, which the Turks in turn were vainly trying to overcome, and as long as these two opposing fortresses were in opponents' hands, no shipping in the Liman could be safe. At first Potemkin dismissed Ochakov as 'a contemptible place which would not last out a week's siege';[5] but the garrison of Ochakov counted 18,000 men compared to the 10,000 in the Ekaterinoslav Army, so he was not tempted to try to take the fortress by storm and even held back during a crucial Turkish sortie (27 July/7 August 1788) which his General Suvorov had brilliantly turned to Russian advantage. But Suvorov's initiative had been unauthorized and Potemkin sulked and would not attack.

Potemkin's passive siege which stretched on month after month probably cost the Russians many more lives than they would have lost through an assault exploiting Suvorov's tactics. Over the Liman floated the stench of sailors' corpses, and the pounding crossfire of fortress cannonballs filled all the returning supply carts with buzzing piles of dead and wounded. There was a steady toll from disease, aggravated by a shortage of medicines and ignorance of hygiene; from stifling heat and later from freezing cold; as well as from enemy action in daily skirmishes.[6]

For many of the men it was a relief to engage in battle, at least at the outset. The Prince de Ligne has left a vivid description of one of the skirmishes in which Barclay took part:

On 29 August [1788], forty Turks at the most, skirting the sea and climbing the slopes, advanced to fire their rifles at the battery where Prince Anhalt had just relieved General Kutuzov. It was the same Kutuzov who in the last [Turkish] war had received a bullet through his head, behind his eyes, and incredibly had not lost his sight. Yesterday the same general received a similar head wound just under the eyes and he will die, I believe, today or tomorrow . . .

The Chasseurs [Jaeger] . . . did not wait for orders from Anhalt who had just reached the scene; they ran about in confusion, trying to chase off these forty men, who were soon reinforced by more than three hundred of Hasan Pasha's soldiers. To save the first battalion Prince Anhalt had to attack with the second battalion. A bullet grazed him and went on to wound the shoulder of the Comte de Damas, a French volunteer. Prince Anhalt lost almost all of his officers but defended the battery which the Turks were already attacking. He continued to fire stubbornly at them and threw them back.

Hardly had they disappeared in their entrenchments when more than two thousand more Turks came out with flags flying. Prince Anhalt barely managed to rally his Chasseurs and attacked the Turks. There were hundreds of them firing away without stopping, hiding in the slope's crevasses, and they could not be dislodged.[7]

This sortie took place just over a year after the beginning of the war. Barclay was one of the few officers to survive unscathed, and Kutuzov, even more remarkably, survived despite his wounds.

Further long months went by without a Russian attack on the citadel. Large siege guns had arrived from Kherson, and the Sevastopol fleet, after having twice defeated the Turkish armada, was cruising offshore. Even the Turkish citizens of Ochakov wondered why no attack was forthcoming, while the Empress in St. Petersburg was reluctantly shedding her illusions about Potemkin's military worth. Finally Catherine's increasingly impatient prodding stirred Potemkin, on 1/12 December 1788, to order preparations for the assault.

Heavy storms and blizzards caused another delay, but on 6/17 December at eight in the morning Potemkin finally gave the signal to attack. Prince

Anhalt-Bernburg was in charge of two assault columns, riding at the head of the second one himself. The two columns first assailed Hasan Pasha's hilltop castle, attacking from both sides. After a short, savage battle during which Barclay fought sword against scimitar in a particularly exposed position, they took the castle and swept on to the citadel's Istanbul Gate. The besieged Turks used their every defence, concentrating an intense fire – all they could summon – on the attacking Russians. The deep moat filled with fallen Russians of the first column, but over their corpses the second column, Barclay's, pressed on. In an hour and a quarter the Russian forces fought their way to the ramparts and were able to take possession of the bastions, the Prince using Barclay 'in all the most perilous places'.[8] The Turkish defenders fled for refuge into the houses of the civilian inhabitants – and all were slaughtered together. The Russians spared no one. Consumed with a passion for vengeance and booty, they continued the butchery for three full days. Potemkin had promised unlimited plunder and he tolerated indiscipline to such a degree that officers were afraid to intervene, even when confronted by the utmost savagery. The ferocious discipline normally imposed on the Russian soldier had been suddenly withdrawn by the Commander-in-Chief, as Potemkin bid for personal popularity with his troops, and Barclay was never to forget the resulting spectacles of unleashed cruelty.

Finally there was no loot left to take. The stripped bodies of the Turks were piled up on the frozen Liman where they were said to be greatly admired by the ladies of Potemkin's seraglio, who amused themselves until the thaw by taking sledge-rides around the 'ghastly pyramids' of frozen flesh.[9] Ochakov was unmistakably in Russian hands once more, Potemkin was again in Catherine's favour, and rewards were distributed to the survivors. For his courageous role in the assault Barclay was awarded his first decoration, the gold-rimmed red enamel cross of St. Vladimir Fourth Class, as well as the gold Ochakov medal. He was also promoted to major.[10] His new assignment was with the Iziumskii Light Cavalry Regiment and he remained with Prince Anhalt-Bernburg as a senior duty officer.

All through 1789 Major Barclay was with the Prince in a number of engagements and assaults, becoming even more attached to his superior after receiving the news of his foster-father Vermeulen's death. As leader of a cavalry regiment Barclay was always in the vanguard of the action, his towering silhouette already a symbol of the coolest courage as he faced smoking Turkish cannon and clashing broadsword with manifest calm. He took part notably in the successful battle of Karshany, north-west of Ochakov; two weeks later in the victorious assault on the fortress of Akkerman on the estuary of the Dnestr; and north again in the bloody occupation of Bender, upstream on the Dnestr.

After Barclay was called away from the Turkish front, to join the army in Finland, the Russian forces – both Rumiantsev's army in Moldavia in the north and Suvorov with the Ekaterinoslav Army – continued winning. At great cost in men and money Russia was victorious on all fronts in this southern war, and on 29 December 1791/9 January 1792, a peace treaty was signed at Jassy. The Ottoman Empire surrendered Ochakov with all the Black Sea territory between the Dnestr and the Southern Bug (including the site where Odessa later developed), and the Sultan signed an *ex post facto* final agreement accepting Russia's annexation of the Crimea.

While Russia was thus occupied on her southern border, her northern neighbour, Sweden, seized the opportunity to try to regain territory in Finland. Catherine and her court, fretting at Potemkin's idling before Ochakov, were, despite ample warning, taken by surprise when Gustavus III opened a second front in the summer of 1788, leading an army exaggeratedly reported to be of thirty thousand men through Swedish Finland towards Russian Finland, boasting to the ladies of Stockholm that he would soon be celebrating his victory in St. Petersburg with a Te Deum at the Cathedral of St. Peter and St. Paul and a grand ball at Peterhof.

There was little to bar his way to St. Petersburg. Russia had assumed that any trouble from Sweden would come by sea, not land. On Potemkin's bidding Catherine had sent almost the entire Russian army to the southern front (though keeping back enough forces to stand ready in turbulent Poland). Now, as Gustavus advanced, Catherine took what immediate steps she could to meet the emergency. At best, at the beginning of hostilities, the Russian commanders in Finland, Count Ivan Musin-Pushkin and General Mikhelson, disposed of only about six thousand men. But special detachments were hastily improvised. The Comte de Ségur in his *Mémoires* described the St. Petersburg scene:

Everywhere coachmen, domestics, and workmen young and old were being hastily assembled, equipped, and drilled. I still have a delightful caricature . . . showing these grotesque, colossal recruits being dragged into formation and drilled by children pulled out of military school, standing tiptoe on chairs and benches in order to straighten these gigantic, bearded rustics' necks, heads, and chests, and place rifles on their shoulders . . .[11]

The Empress also ordered five hundred horses to be held in readiness at each of the relay stations between Moscow and St. Petersburg, to rush new recruits from Moscow, though some of the foreign diplomats were convinced the preparations were for hustling Empress and court to the safety of Moscow. Catherine shivered at the closeness of the Finnish border – 'To tell the truth, Peter put his capital too close!'[12] – and seemed reconciled to the loss of St. Petersburg. She was determined, however, to give battle to Gustavus at Novgorod or Moscow, or if need be even at Kazan' or Astrakhan – thus anticipating by twenty-four years the policy pursued by Barclay and her grandson Alexander in 1812.

As it happened, no withdrawal in depth proved to be necessary, nor the sacrifice of St. Petersburg. The performance of Gustavus lagged far behind his threats and promises, at least at the beginning of hostilities. He was hampered by ignorance of the business of war, by worn-out, inadequate equipment, famine in Swedish Finland, and a politically inspired officers' mutiny at home. He was also unsuccessful in ridding himself of opposition leaders: when he dispatched to Holland Baron Göran Magnus Sprengporten, a Finnish colonel who was one of the chiefs of a pro-Russian separatist secret order, Sprengporten 'routed' his trip through Russia and, once there, stayed, while the Russians, recognizing an important defection, treated him lavishly. 'Colonel Sprengporten . . . was made a colonel in the Russian army on Monday, a chamberlain on Tuesday, and promoted to major-general on Wednesday.'[13] Some twenty years later Sprengporten became the unpopular first Russian Governor-General of Finland, to be replaced a few months later by Barclay de Tolly.

Gustavus thus failed to achieve victory in the first skirmishes and engagements of the war, and even in the major naval battle of Hogland in July 1788.[14] Total defeat threatened when the Danes entered the war, invading Sweden in response to their treaty obligations to Russia, but it was precisely this invasion which turned events to Swedish advantage. The Swedes resolutely threw out the intruders, and this victory for Gustavus on home territory enabled him to rally his countrymen, convene the diet, quell the mutiny, and inflict several defeats on the Russians during the rest of 1789 and in 1790.

Meanwhile some of the Russian forces were transferred to Finland from the Turkish front. Among those transferred were Prince Anhalt-Bernburg, Barclay, and their troops. They arrived in Finland in April 1790, after an important interlude in St. Petersburg where the forty-six-year-old Prince was offered the highest command post in Finland, to replace Count Musin-Pushkin. The Empress was flatly dissatisfied with Musin-Pushkin's performance and she was impressed and attracted by the formidable reputation Anhalt-Bernburg had acquired in the Turkish campaign. His stubborn insistence, however, on being given full powers with the title of Commander-in-Chief threw Catherine into a rage. She had not observed at first hand, as he just had, the disastrous effects of divided commands; she saw only the impertinence of conditional acceptance of her imperial offer. For days she refused to speak to him and in his stead appointed Count Nicolas Saltykov.* The Prince, giving no outward sign of disappointment, went to Finland as one general among many.

On 20 April/1 May 1790, soon after arrival in Finland, Anhalt-Bernburg led an attack to recover the important twin positions of Kernakoski and Pardakoski. The Russians were repulsed with heavy losses, and the Prince was mortally wounded. Feeling his death approaching, he called Barclay and, in a dramatic scene, bequeathed him his sword, exhorting him always to use it for the glory of Russia. Barclay gravely accepted this bequest, and the sword and a miniature portrait of the Prince were with him from that day onwards, on every campaign. This four-year attachment, severed when he was twenty-eight, was the deepest experience in friendship of Barclay's life.

The war in Finland continued until the middle of August. Barclay was assigned to serve under General Igelström, who replaced Anhalt-Bernburg. In July the Swedes demolished the Russian fleet at Svenskund, costing the Russians fifty-three ships and nearly ten thousand men, about as many as the Turks lost in the fall of Ochakov. On land the fighting was also bitter, though less catastrophic to either side. Barclay was promoted from the lower to the higher grade of major. General Igelström reported: 'Barclay was dispatched to

---

* Not to be confused with Catherine's early lover, Serge Saltykov.

all the most dangerous spots and, in the midst of savage and incessant fire coming from all sides, he carried out all missions with firmness and an untiring spirit. . . .'[15] He showed uncommon courage and *sang-froid*.'[16]

Diminishing foreign support for Gustavus, and Catherine's desire to be free of Swedish complications in order to end the Turkish war and deal with her Polish problems led both sides to seek peace. On 3/14 August 1790 a treaty was signed at Verelä without territorial gain for either side. No one was really satisfied with the outcome, however, and there was no reason to believe that trouble would not eventually recur. Eighteen years later Barclay was again to fight in Finland, for the final expulsion of the Swedes and the annexation of Finland.

Following the end of the war with Sweden, Barclay was posted to St. Petersburg and, during this short lull, took leave to get married on 22 August/2 September 1791. He had just proved himself again in war, this time without the supporting presence of Anhalt-Bernburg. Barclay's position was promising, his reputation excellent, his means enough, with help from Aunt Auguste, to establish a household. His brother Erich had shown the way, and the von Smittens were already part of the family. The bells of the Lutheran church of Tarwast, near Beckhof, rang with a certain inevitability as well as customary joyfulness for the marriage of Auguste von Smitten and Michael Barclay de Tolly.

Their married life began auspiciously with the naming of Barclay as battalion commander in the St. Petersburg Grenadier Regiment.[17] With this regiment he took part in the Polish campaign of 1792, only a few months after the wedding, and thereafter in the Polish war of 1794, the last of Catherine's wars and the last of the eighteenth-century partitions during which Poland was squeezed, plundered, and dismembered by Russia, Austria, and Prussia. In the first partition in 1772, Russia had gained the lion's share. Soon after the signing at Jassy of the treaty of peace with Turkey, Russia again invaded Poland, and the second partition in 1793 divided the spoils between Prussia and Russia. During this campaign, an important one for Barclay's military development, he gained useful information on partisan tactics from his regimental commander, Prince P. D. Tsisianov, 'the Caucasian specialist' in guerrilla warfare.[18]

The third partition followed the outbreak of a Polish revolt in 1794 led by Thaddeus Kosciuszko, the famous patriot and military leader who had served the Americans in their War of Independence. Kosciuszko rallied popular support, promised freedom and land to the peasants and, despite a poorly equipped and largely improvised army, managed to throw the Prussians out of the country and fought the Russians on equal terms. The Poles succeeded in taking Warsaw and Grodno, slaughtering the Russian garrisons of both cities. Catherine summoned her generals to deal with the crisis and the Russians struck back, taking fortified Vilna by storm, overcoming fierce Polish resistance. Barclay fought with verve, again distinguishing himself in this operation, and also in the battle near Grodno where he led his battalion to help destroy a Polish army. Finally Suvorov took the fortified Warsaw suburb of Praga, and

Kosciuszko was captured. Polish resistance collapsed. In this third partition of Poland, in January 1795, most of her land was annexed by Russia.

At the end of this war Suvorov, aged sixty-five, was made a field-marshal. He was enchanted, but his fellow generals were bitterly jealous and some of them resentfully asked for their discharge from the service, setting a precedent for like conduct when a similar situation confronted Barclay in later years. But at this stage Barclay was only promoted to lieutenant-colonel, and transferred to the Estonian Jaeger Corps as commander of the first battalion. For his decisive action at Vilna he was awarded the very prestigious white cross of the Order of St. George Fourth Class. He wrote to his foster-mother that he had at last achieved a position which provided him with income sufficient for his needs.[19]

The Empress Catherine died in November 1796 and her son, Paul I, became Tsar. Lieutenant-Colonel Barclay was put in command first of the Fourth Jaeger Battalion, subsequently renamed the Fourth Jaeger Regiment, and later took command of the Third Jaeger Regiment. In name he remained its commander for the next fourteen years. Under Tsar Paul, Barclay was promoted to full colonel for his exemplary command of this regiment, and on 13/25 March 1799, some nine months after becoming a father, he was appointed major-general (with Auguste now proudly entitled to be addressed as a general's wife: *General'sha*). His career was progressing, his virtues recognized, and the ageing and arrogant Prince Repnin, one of Catherine's field-marshals, after inspecting General Barclay's regiment on the Prussian border, stated categorically: 'He will go far.'[20]

In his advancement from cornet in 1778 to major-general in 1799 at the age of thirty-seven, Barclay had been rifleman, cavalryman, staff officer. He had travelled from the Black Sea to the north shore of the Gulf of Finland and as far west as Warsaw, and had met great varieties of men; and with his Orthodox compatriots had fought Muslims, Protestants, and Roman Catholics. He had become a master of siege, assault, guerrilla, and battle tactics on all kinds of terrain, and had learned the taste both of victory and of defeat. From a trained but untried young officer he had turned into a seasoned warrior, earning, over and over, the respect of his superiors, and even the respect of his subordinates. He had gained a true friend and lost him, without ever losing the inheritance left from this friendship, of which Anhalt's sword was sign and symbol. By his own efforts he had attained financial independence, and had become a solicitous husband and father.

During these years he had also been given opportunities for witnessing scenes of the greatest barbarity and splendour – cruelties, massacres, savagery, and the flaunted opulence and sumptuous field-style of some of the Russian generals. He had observed the dehumanizing results of indiscipline; the cost to the country of moodiness, jealousy, preferment- and popularity-seeking among the leaders; and the consequences of faulty planning and organization. All these things that he observed ran counter to what was most deeply ingrained in his own character. Indeed, it was as well that he had the friendship and guidance of a man like Anhalt-Bernburg during his first exposures to such experiences, while his own character was forming. The years of apprenticeship built solidly on the foundation formed by his background and early training. In pursuing his profession and his destiny he thus rejected the goals, methods, and manners of the most eminent military models of his day. His loyalty to Russia and the Tsar was composed of other stuff, starting with loyalty to his own principles and to the ideals which had by now become part of himself.

CHAPTER IV

CLASH OF EAGLES

> Besides creating the modern state the French Revolution became the mother of modern war . . . it brought conscription, the nation in arms, the mobilisation of all the resources of the state for unrelenting conflict.
>
> *Butterfield, Napoleon*

What might be called the 'Prussianization' of the army from top to bottom dominated Paul's short and despotic reign, and many officers, lacking Major-General Barclay's early immersion in Prussian traditions, resented the end of easy-going army life and suffered, sometimes mortally, from the inhuman discipline. With the tacit support of a number of embittered guards regiments, a handful of conspirators put an end to Paul's reign in 1801. Paul's eldest son, Alexander I, aged twenty-four, acceded to the throne of Russia. Alexander had been privy to the plot to depose his father, without expecting his father's assassination (which may well have been accidental), and the resulting tremors of unacknowledged guilt affected him long afterwards in important ways.

Napoleon was then still First Consul and had not yet released his immeasurable ambition for conquests. It was not unrealistic for France's enemies to think in terms of a dependable agreement with Napoleon during that one year – March 1802 to April 1803 – when France was at peace with all Europe. The Tsar's devoted friend and adviser, Prince Adam Czartoryski, saw in Alexander the potential 'arbiter of peace for the civilized world, the protector of the feeble and oppressed', and the inaugurator of a 'new era in European politics'.[1] Nor did this notion then appear to be a visionary's idle fancy. The Tsar's enlightened upbringing, his sensibility, his liberal impulses seemed to predispose him for just such a role. But the optimism reflected in Alexander's letters to Napoleon in 1801 and 1802 was short-lived. The impossibility of coming to adequate terms with the French predator soon became apparent. The last illusions about his character and ambitions were shattered when Napoleon in rapacious and rapid succession had the Duc d'Enghien kidnapped on German soil and promptly shot; proclaimed himself Emperor of France – the first to assume the title since Charlemagne; seized the crown of Italy, annexing the Genoese Republic; and began assembling a mighty army to invade England, boasting, quite correctly, that he was keeping Europe in suspense in the expectation of the great event he was preparing.[2] Alexander's judgement of Napoleon by this time was that he was an insatiable 'scourge of the world: he wants war; well he shall have it, and the sooner the better.'[3]

The Russian and Austrian armies prepared then for war, hoisting their battle flags in accordance with the design of the Third Coalition, which grew out of the Anglo–Russian alliance of 11 April (N.S.) 1805. When news reached Napoleon that the double eagles were again aloft, he abandoned his projected expedition across the Channel, and on 27 August (N.S.) 1805 ordered his 160,000-strong 'Army of England' to leave their Channel camps and start, within forty-eight hours, on a march to the Rhine. Enlarged and reorganized, the Grande Armée was ordered to proceed by 'the fastest and most direct routes to the Danube'.[4] Napoleon planned to have his seven army corps, with Murat's cavalry and the Imperial Guard, converge on the upper Danube in time to cripple the Austrians before the Russians could intervene.

Napoleon's calculations proved correct. He trapped Austria's General Mack at Ulm, forcing him to surrender on 19 October (N.S.) with his garrison of 40,000 men (of whom only a quarter managed to escape), while a Russian army of 40,000, under General Kutuzov, was still some 270 kilometres away.[5] With the enormous French army now closing in on him, Kutuzov made a skilful withdrawal across the Danube in the direction of Znaim in Moravia, trying to link up with another Russian army of 35,000 under General Buxhoevden and with some 25,000 remaining Austrians. Time and again Kutuzov, who proved himself the equal of the French in cunning and ruse, managed to avoid a major battle.

A third Russian army of 30,000 under General Bennigsen, with Barclay de Tolly commanding the advance guard, was meanwhile waiting unhappily on the border between Russian Lithuania and Prussian Poland. Alexander's friend the King of Prussia had refused to allow the Russian troops to pass over Prussian territory. Only after Marshal Bernadotte's corps, heeding Napoleon's instructions on 'the fastest and most direct routes', took an unauthorized short cut through the Prussian territory of Ansbach, did the King of Prussia finally accede to the Tsar's request; and even then, only on condition that Bennigsen take a detour which, he claimed, meant a further loss of two weeks and prevented his army – including Barclay's vanguard – from reaching the combined Russo–Austrian forces under Kutuzov in time for the battle of Austerlitz.[6]

Kutuzov was commander-in-chief in name only. Alexander, against Czartoryski's advice, had put himself at the head of the Russian army, something no Russian sovereign had done since Peter the Great. Outrage at Napoleon's conduct blinded the Tsar to his opponent's military genius and diplomatic virtuosity. Nor did Alexander understand the deficiencies in his own armed forces and in those of his allies. He had no conception of the problems created by the great distances the Russian armies had to travel to join the Austrians, nor of the inadequacy for the task of Russian supply services. His presence at the front, and his habit of surrounding himself with a flattering group of incompetent military advisers, provoked feuds and intrigues. But being at the front, with plumes, pomp, and power, was irresistible to young Alexander. Life in Gatchina, where Catherine had sometimes allowed her grandsons to visit their parents, had been lived to the beat of a drum corps, and strictly regulated by Paul's orders for peasant, soldier, and courtier alike. Instead of being surrounded by demanding tutors (one of them preaching the Rights of Man), the boys were constantly gratified by the salutes of high-ranking officers manifesting respect bordering on worship. The ceremony of power was the essence of military life in Alexander's experience, from which he had developed an outright 'paradomania', while remaining ignorant of the realities and responsibilities of warfare.

Alexander's unfounded respect for Austrian battle advice persisted despite continuing and egregious blunders by the Austrian generals in this campaign and despite the memory of their 'grotesque display of timidity and disloyalty' when last Russia and Austria had fought as allies, in 1799.[7] In vain did Kutuzov warn against giving battle to the French straight away, and least of all on the terrain near Austerlitz chosen by the Austrian commander Weyrother. Temporizing did not suit the Tsar's heroic image of himself, and the habits of a courtier restrained Kutuzov from the traditionally unthinkable act of speaking up firmly in opposition to the sovereign's decision. Nor would Kutuzov press his point with the Austrians, whom he despised, nor with the group of young, inexperienced generals in the Tsar's suite – of whom it has been said that they 'lost the battle of Austerlitz to spite Kutuzov'.[8]

On 20 November/2 December 1805 the sun of Austerlitz, an image of victory in Napoleonic annals, set disastrously for the allies, costing them some 26,000 men and all their artillery. The French victory was as complete as could be; and the whole campaign had lasted less than six weeks. Austria sued for peace. The Russian armies, accepting one of Napoleon's conditions, withdrew beyond the borders of Russian Poland, and the Third Coalition, which Prussia, to its own eventual undoing, had refused to join, fell apart. Unjustly, the blame fell on Kutuzov, and Alexander, weeping bitter tears and accusing him of cowardice and 'a passion for retreat', never forgave him.[9] Prince Czartoryski, who was at the Tsar's side throughout the catastrophic day, had a different opinion: he blamed the Tsar's presence, which undermined Kutuzov's ability to exercise true battlefield command.[10] Kutuzov was removed as commander-in-chief and appointed governor-general of the city of Kiev.

This first year of warfare in Alexander's reign was all in all an unhappy year for Russia. For General Barclay the career officer, it was a year of disappointment at not being in the thick of the fighting; he had had all the slogging and waiting of war without any of its chances for glory: it was a year to practise patience in. But also he grieved for Russia's defeats and for the Tsar, finding it intolerable that defeat should touch this young, godlike emperor. Family grief mingled in these reactions and Barclay chafed to avenge both his Tsar and his younger brother, Major Heinrich Barclay de Tolly, to whom the war had brought death (at Wenden, in Livonia) at the age of thirty-nine.

Between the sorry ending of Austerlitz and that still to come at Friedland, the Russian army showed itself in a different light, and Barclay de Tolly was to distinguish himself as a gifted leader in battle. The scene was the battlegrounds of Prussia during the very severe winter of 1806–7, when horses survived only by eating thatch stripped from the cottages and soldiers prowled endlessly all winter long digging for food buried by the peasantry.

Although Prussia had not joined the Third Coalition, the agreement between Alexander and the forever wavering Frederick William III (which had been designed to entice Prussia into the coalition) remained in force. A series of reversals of Prussian policy now resulted after all in war with Napoleon. Alexander, true to an earlier pledge to come to the aid of Prussia at the call of the Prussian royal couple, and eager to avenge Austerlitz, ordered his forces to redeploy along Prussia's borders, ready to move in support of the Prussian army. This army still enjoyed the reputation it had acquired under Frederick the Great, but it was led by tired old men, and in performance the Prussians proved no match at all for Napoleon's modern Grande Armée.[11]

At Jena and Auerstadt on 2/14 October 1806 the Prussian army was virtually annihilated and their surrender of Magdeburg and Lübeck completed the catastrophe. Of Prussia's once invincible power, there remained only a unit of 15,000 troops under the able and excellent General Lestocq, plus the garrisons of Danzig and Graudenz. The crucial mistake made by the Austrians the year before in failing to await the arrival of the approaching Russians had been fatally repeated by the Prussians. The consequence was that the Russian armies, which were intended each time as a strong supporting force to the more numerous Austrians or Prussians, found themselves facing Napoleon's Grande Armée almost on their own.

Only on 22 October/2 November 1806 did a first Russian army cross the Prussian border. It consisted of four divisions totalling about 67,000 troops and 276 cannon. Their commander was Barclay's superior, the veteran General Bennigsen, originally from Hanover – tall, tough, rash, over sixty and still scrambling for recognition – who only a year before had been delayed by the Prussians at the border. The campaign which now began stretched over a roughly equilateral triangle with its points at Warsaw in the south, the fortress of Thorn in the west, and royal Koenigsberg in the north, where the King of Prussia and his court had taken temporary refuge when they saw Berlin was about to fall to the French. Framed by the broad Vistula in the west and the Narew in the south-east, the whole region glittered with rivers, streams, lakes, and swamps, and was interspersed with wooded areas: an ideal terrain for defensive tactics. At the beginning of the campaign, however, a precocious thaw accompanied by torrential rains turned the roads into mires, impassable by heavy cannon, many of which had to be abandoned. The private wagons of the officers cluttered up the routes and impeded progress. The foot soldiers struggled knee-deep, and often waist-deep, in mud. Both sides were at an equal disadvantage, but it was left to Napoleon to claim that only the intemperate weather and the short winter days prevented him from annihilating his opponents.[12]

Despite the dragging mud, Bennigsen and his staff managed to speed ahead to Pultusk, about fifty kilometres north of Warsaw, and began deploying troops. Barclay, heading the vanguard, rushed to Plock on the Vistula, south of

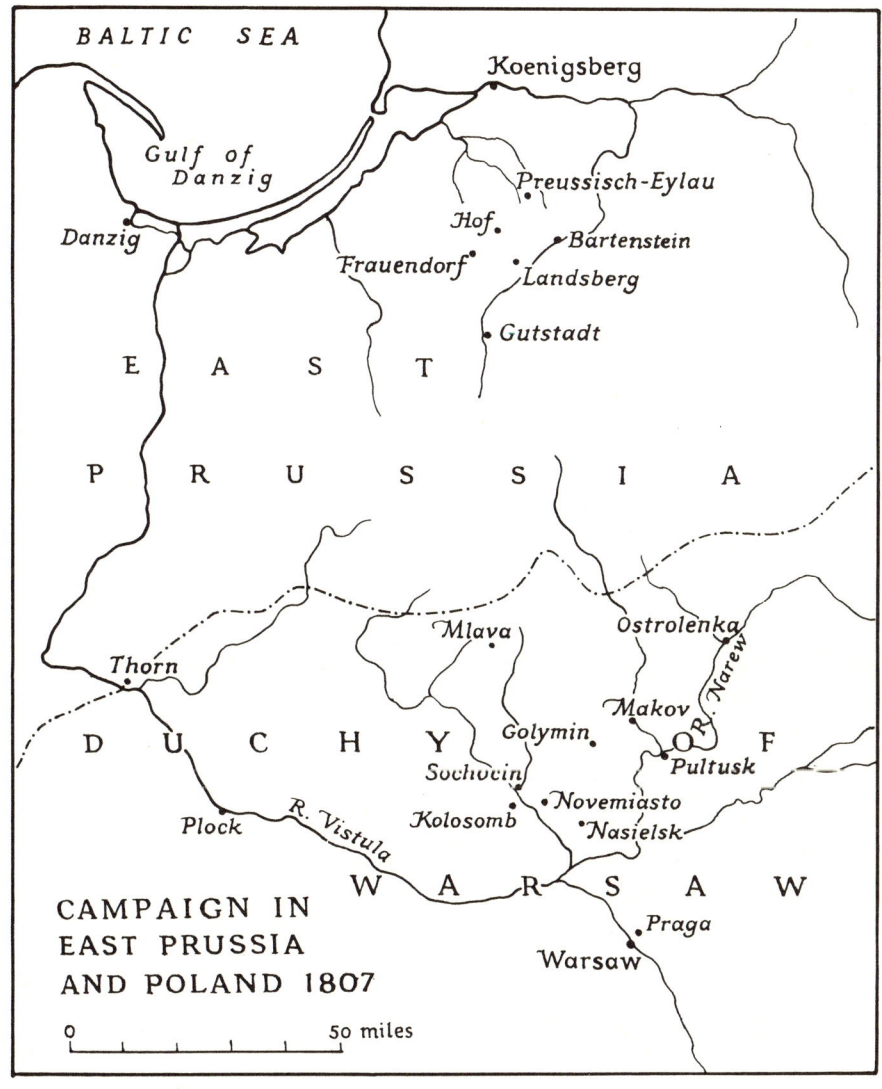

CAMPAIGN IN EAST PRUSSIA AND POLAND 1807

Thorn.* Thorn was headquarters for the Prussian General Lestocq, who had spread out along the lower Vistula what bedraggled troops remained to him after the previous year's defeats. Bennigsen's 6th Division, under General Sedmoratskii, occupied Praga, the north-eastern suburb of Warsaw.

Everything seemed to be going smoothly for the Russians except for a shortage of bread. As long as the Russian armies were advancing rapidly, their system of living primarily on food seized from the inhabitants was fairly successful, however devastating to the populace. When the forces were concentrated in one area over a period of time, however, as was the case during this campaign, true famine resulted for both army and civilians, with 'prodigious' mortality and horrors.[13] Although the campaign had only just begun, Barclay's advance guard felt the pinch acutely, since the hostile Polish inhabitants of Plock desperately hid both bread and grain. Barclay and his officers used up army funds and then emptied their own pockets to buy rare supplies of bread, meat, and wine for the troops, but the cash to feed five thousand ravenous men very soon ran out. The soldiers, having to fend for themselves, tried to seize the needed supplies by force, whereupon the population fled with its remaining crumbs. The situation, grim for soldiers and peasants alike, drew Barclay and his men closer together, and talk of Barclay's exceptional concern for the soldiers' welfare spread among the troops.

On 4/16 December 1806, a full six weeks after Bennigsen's army had penetrated Prussian territory, a second Russian army, under General Buxhoevden, finally arrived north of Pultusk. It also consisted of four divisions headed by proven commanders, but it was in poor shape, having been through Austerlitz, and lacked its full complement of men, horses, weapons, and ammunition. Reinforcements under General Essen I were coming up, however, and, all told, the Russian troops, including infantry, cavalry, artillerymen, and engineers, now numbered 159,900 men and 624 pieces of artillery.[14]

With three of his armies thus on the march – or at least trudging through the mud – Alexander was hard pressed to appoint an overall commander. His dilemma was great, since Kutuzov was in disgrace and junior generals could not properly be considered. 'It is difficult to describe the embarrassment in which I find myself', wrote the Tsar to Count Pyotr Tolstoy, his *homme de confiance* in the field. 'Who is the man among us who enjoys universal confidence and who combines military talents with the severity indispensable for the post of commander? I myself know of no such man!'[15] Finally the Tsar's choice fell on the sixty-nine-year-old Field-Marshal Count Kamenskii who had fought with distinction in Catherine's Turkish wars. Kamenskii's age was in itself not a matter for concern, for had not Tsar Paul put Suvorov, also aged sixty-nine, at the head of the Russo–Austrian armies fighting Napoleon in 1799? But Kamenskii was no longer in possession of all his faculties. To no avail he protested to the Tsar that he thought he was too old for the army, could not stay

---

* Barclay's detachment was of elastic composition, changing from battle to battle. At Plock it consisted of one infantry regiment, one Jaeger regiment, five squadrons of light cavalry, two regiments of Cossacks, and one battery of horse artillery: altogether about 5,000 men. – Bennigsen, 'Zapiski . . .' (Jan. 1897), 85.

in the saddle, was half blind, and could no longer read a map or see what he was signing.[16]

Arriving in the field and no doubt feeling that some action was expected of him, Kamenskii briskly ordered an immediate general advance against the French, although two of the three Russian armies were not yet on the scene. He himself went to join Bennigsen at Pultusk. When he heard that the Russians were taking up positions between the Vistula and the Narew, Napoleon moved headquarters to Posen, mid-way between Berlin and Warsaw. His first objective was to dislodge the Russians from Praga and the Prussians from Thorn. His army would then be able to cross the Vistula at these two pivotal points, to outflank the enemy on the right or left, or trap him altogether. He advanced his right flank (Murat and Davout) towards Warsaw, his left flank (Ney, Bessières, Bernadotte) towards Thorn, and his centre (Augereau and Soult) was to press across the Vistula at Plock, where Barclay's ill-nourished advance-guard detachment was posted. 'Always keeping all . . . corps within mutual supporting distance', in accordance with Napoleon's time-proved principle, the Grande Armée, far superior to anything the Russians could concentrate at any single point of the disputed area, now moved forward with perfect co-ordination.[17] When Warsaw fell to Murat's cavalry without a fight it was a signal success for Napoleon's strategy, a severe setback for the Russians, and was mistakenly hailed by the Poles as a hopeful step towards the recovery of their independence.

Lestocq, with the small Prussian force at his disposal, could not hold out at Thorn against Ney's onslaught, and withdrew to the east. The news of the fall of Thorn, coupled with Sedmoratskii's precipitous flight from Praga, caused Bennigsen on 20 November/2 December 1806 to order a general withdrawal of all the forces under his command. The natural barrier of the Vistula was abandoned to the enemy, and Bennigsen pulled out of Pultusk and moved northwards towards Ostrolenka, hoping to be joined there at last by the slowly approaching divisions of Buxhoevden's army.

Barclay's detachment was thus no longer the advance guard but had become the rearguard, covering Bennigsen's retreating divisions. At this point Barclay took the initiative of detailing Cossacks to swim through the ice floes on the Vistula to observe the enemy's movements. The frozen, frightened prisoners brought back by these Cossacks informed Barclay that the French corps of the centre were not stirring; there were no preparations for pursuing Bennigsen. Barclay's report persuaded Bennigsen to turn around with the main body of his army and go back to Pultusk, whence he continued westwards towards the river Wkra. Barclay's detachment once again therefore became the vanguard, with the mission of protecting the crossings of the Wkra at the neighbouring villages of Kolosomb and Sochocin. Here Marshal Augereau's VIIth Corps assaulted him on a wide front and Barclay's close-knit, embattled detachment was in great danger of being outflanked. In vain Barclay looked for promised reinforcements but they had been bogged down in the sodden ground and were unable to reach him in time. Using every varied resource at his command – infantry, Jaeger, light cavalry, Cossacks, and horse artillery – Barclay fought fiercely until nightfall, holding back for hours the whole enemy corps, but was finally forced to withdraw in the direction of Novemiasto on the road to Pultusk.[18] His faultless performance contributed to his growing reputation for courage and skill.[19]

These short though sharp encounters between enemy advance guards and various troop movements and manœuvres in the area eventually led to a major battle, the battle of Pultusk. Napoleon was determined to be first at Pultusk and there to prevent the crossing of the Narew. He therefore sent Lannes ahead at full speed. Covering forty-five kilometres in a single day, Lannes almost won the race, but when his advance guard reached Pultusk, they found it already occupied by a Russian detachment commanded by General Baggavut. For once the Russians had been faster than the French and were able to fight them off. In the meantime Kamenskii, rising to the occasion, had recalled Bennigsen from the unsuccessful expedition to the Wkra. The bulk of Bennigsen's army, though not all, arrived at Pultusk on 13/25 December 1806. 'Tomorrow we hope to have the enemy as our guests,' Kamenskii advised Buxhoevden at Makov, ten kilometres to the north.[20] Kamenskii had no expectations of victory, however, and he instructed all divisional commanders that in case of failure at Pultusk all Russian troops should seek refuge on their native soil in *sauve-qui-peut* fashion. After this surprising pronouncement, the old Field-Marshal, who had been only seven days in the field, laid down his command and took his leave.[21]

When the Russians first sighted the approaching Lannes at ten o'clock on the cold, wet morning of 14/26 December, their troops were positioned between the outskirts of Pultusk on their left and a copse on their right. Half hidden in the dripping woods, Barclay's detachment formed the right flank.* To his left he had Sacken's 3rd Division and farther on, forming the left flank, was the 2nd Division of Lieutenant-General Count Ostermann-Tolstoy. In front of Pultusk, Baggavut's detachment was meant to defend the town.

Lannes, having lined up his two infantry divisions and his cavalry, moved forward through the mire and heavily bombarded the Russian centre. Almost immediately he also attacked Barclay's and Baggavut's positions. The latter lost ground, which was regained by Ostermann-Tolstoy's infantry. Lannes's troops were driven out and the lost, muddy terrain was retrieved. The attack on Barclay's position was equally furious. 'Despite his bravery and fearlessness,' Bennigsen reported, 'Barclay had to yield to the impetuous attack.'[22] The French momentarily invaded Barclay's copse and seized a battery, only to lose it again. Just as Ostermann-Tolstoy had come to the rescue of Baggavut, Sacken came to Barclay's rescue. Lannes called off his attack on the Russian right flank and waited for the arrival of a new division from Davout's corps for a fresh assault. Running into heavy Russian grapeshot fire, this new French division nevertheless pressed forward. At this point Bennigsen ordered Barclay to mount a bayonet charge. The charge was carried out brilliantly – a 'remarkable action' – and Bennigsen, appraising the situation, decided to pass to the attack on the

---

* Barclay's detachment at this point was composed of the 77th (Tenginskii) infantry regiment, three Jaeger regiments, and five squadrons of Uhlans. Some of his Cossacks were stationed one kilometre ahead, along with most of the cavalry.

entire front. Four French generals were wounded and Lannes himself was grazed by a bullet. Lannes soon realized that he had failed in his mission and, as darkness set in, began withdrawing. The victory was Russian. To some, like the Duc de Fezensac, Pultusk marked the turning point in Napoleon's chain of victories: 'his star began to pale' and it was the beginning of 'half-successes' and 'incomplete triumphs'.[23]

At the end of this strenuous day Barclay, like his fellow soldiers, longed for 'a glass of hot tea and a few hours' rest on wet straw', but he was anxious concerning the whereabouts of one of his batteries. Wearily therefore he set out in the company of his adjutant, three junior officers, and a Cossack to search for the missing six cannon. Losing their way in thicket and brush, they found themselves riding alongside an infantry regiment which they mistook for one of their own, when the 'Qui vive?' of a French sentinel stopped them in their tracks. A salvo of rifle fire followed immediately. Barclay and his five companions threw themselves headlong into the sodden undergrowth and held their breath while the pursuing French horsemen passed them by. This was the first time, said Friedrich von Schubert who was one of the party, that Barclay ever lost his already legendary sang-froid.[24] The thought of this close shave in a situation brought on by his own foolish error was in fact one to keep Barclay tossing the night through on his bed of wet straw.

All in all at Pultusk about 3,500 Russians lost their lives, while the French, who usually minimized their losses, spoke of 2,200 casualties on their side. Bennigsen was rewarded with money and a medal, while four of his generals and one colonel received the Order of St. George Third Class. They included Ostermann-Tolstoy, Baggavut, and Barclay. About Barclay, Bennigsen wrote: 'I must pay due tribute to General Barclay, whose remarkable action in this battle further heightened the reputation he already enjoyed in the army.'[25] Indeed his and Ostermann-Tolstoy's exploits were those most talked about within the army and contributed to raising army morale.

In reporting to the Tsar, Bennigsen was particularly lavish in praise of himself, however, and clearly overstated the extent of his victory when he claimed to have defeated Napoleon. Napoleon was not on the battlefield at Pultusk; he was twenty kilometres away at Nasielsk. He had dispatched most of his corps towards Golymin where he believed the bulk of Russian forces to be concentrated, and when he realized his error it was too late to redirect large numbers of troops to Pultusk, so impassable were the intervening roads for even the short distances involved. Marshals Augereau, Davout, and Soult, therefore, were in Golymin, where they found awaiting them only Prince Golitsyn's 4th Division, reinforced by Dokhturov's 7th Division from Buxhoevden's army. The Russians, though greatly outnumbered, put up stiff resistance during the ensuing battle which was fought simultaneously with that of Pultusk on 14/26 December. The next morning, however, the two Russian divisions had to give ground, and joined Buxhoevden at Makov. The news of this engagement reached Bennigsen at midnight. He decided his position would be stronger to the north and, abandoning hard-won Pultusk, withdrew once again to Ostrolenka.

The war at this point was at a stalemate, the armies exhausted, and the weather made it impossible to continue the fight. Officers and soldiers of both sides were happy to go into winter quarters. Harness repair shops were set up and biscuits baked in great quantity. The soldiers relished the warmth and food, and the officers, somewhat revived, manœuvred for rank instead of for victory.

Before leaving, Kamenskii had named as his successor Buxhoevden, who was senior in rank to Bennigsen. The Tsar, however, was so impressed by the ephemeral Pultusk victory that he appointed Bennigsen, refusing to be influenced either by seniority or by the fact – of the kind which usually loomed large – that Bennigsen had been the first to break into the bedchamber of Alexander's father on the night of the murder. The rivalry between Buxhoevden and Bennigsen was fierce, as was so often the case with the Russian generals. The Livonian Buxhoevden treated German-born Bennigsen as a 'foreigner', though he had been in Russian service a quarter of a century, and tried in every way to damage his reputation. Coolly ignoring Buxhoevden's challenge to a duel, Bennigsen took over as commander-in-chief on 1/13 January 1807, while Buxhoevden was posted to Riga as governor-general.

The army's respite was to be brief, hardly more than a fortnight's quiet after settling into winter quarters. The King of Prussia argued convincingly that the French were unaccustomed to the climate and unprepared for a winter war and that this was therefore the moment to take the offensive. Neither the Tsar nor his generals in the field needed urging. Still preening themselves after Pultusk, they were eager for more successes. And now the terrain was tempting: a hard freeze had set in, the earth and lakes were frozen solid, and only a few days' march separated the belligerents. A quick attack could take the French by surprise, and possibly end the war. So, on 4/16 January 1807, only seventeen days after Napoleon had ceased operations, the Russian forces, an endless grey mass of men and horses brusquely dislodged from the snugness of their shelters, marched to the west, in a driving snowstorm. Leading the way into the whiteness were three advance guards, commanded by Barclay, Baggavut, and Markov. The main army consisted of the left flank under Ostermann-Tolstoy, the centre under Dokhturov, and the right flank under Tuchkov IV, one of five brothers who all became generals. Backing them were considerable reserves.

Bennigsen's plan could have worked had not Marshal Ney, acting against Napoleon's orders, taken the initiative and moved out of his assigned winter quarters even before Bennigsen began his advance. Russian scouts soon discovered that Ney had already covered a considerable distance. His advance guard was at Gutstadt, half-way from Mlava to Koenigsberg. Ney, on his side, when he detected some Russian vanguard detachments, quickly fell back. Instead of the great surprise attack on Ney's supposedly sleeping forces, small skirmishes took place between some of Bennigsen's and Bernadotte's detachments.

As soon as Napoleon learned what was going on he alerted his other marshals to abandon winter quarters. In a solid front they moved massively northward to confront the Russians. Bit by bit the formidable pressure exerted by the combined force of the Grande Armée squeezed the Russians back in the direction of Koenigsberg. The actual engagements were fought mostly by the three Russian vanguards now once more transformed into rearguards and placed under Prince Bagration's overall command.

Barclay's task was to cover the left flank of the main army, and in the circumstances it was a bloody task. During a harrowing series of clashes at Frauendorf and again at Hof, Barclay's detachment withstood French onslaughts even while being forced to lose ground all the time. Reporting on Frauendorf, Barclay wrote:

> I continued the withdrawal without haste and in good order, under the constant bombardment of the numerous French artillery . . . I cannot sufficiently praise the courage, endurance, and coolness in action of the men of my detachment. Every order was executed perfectly and without confusion, and this in the face of the numerically far superior enemy force, who disposed of the necessary means to destroy us. I am convinced that it was due to the exemplary behaviour of our troops that the attempts to annihilate us were thwarted.[26]

Time after time the French tried to cut off his rearguard, but Barclay showed great ingenuity in manœuvring: wherever they turned, the French found some of his artillery or infantry or cavalry barring their way. It was clear to Barclay that he was being steadily forced back to Hof, but he knew he was making progress for the French as slow and difficult as possible. Now, underlining this role, Bennigsen sent him instructions to hold out as long as possible, to give the main army time to take up position for a major battle.

Suddenly the French forces surged forward while the news spread that Napoleon had arrived on the scene to take matters in hand. 'This news did in no way bother Barclay,' according to Mikhailovskii-Danilevskii (who celebrates Barclay's sang-froid to a hyperbolic degree),[27] but still he knew what a bad situation he was in. As he himself said:

> In any other circumstances, I would have withdrawn in time so as not to have my entire detachment wiped out to no purpose by an enormous enemy force. But some of my officers brought back the news from headquarters that our army was still on the march and had not taken up final positions. Therefore I considered it my duty to sacrifice myself with my entire detachment to a superior enemy, since by withdrawing I would have attracted the enemy after me and hence exposed our whole army to great danger.[28]

This battle at Hof on 25 January/6 February 1807 was by far the most important rearguard battle of the campaign. No reliable figures of Russian losses are available, but they were immense.[29] Speaking of one of his regiments, the 19th Kostromskii Infantry – which three times heroically repulsed the French cavalry, each time turning about to advance again, firing to the beat of their drummers – Barclay described his pain at seeing the 'almost total annihilation of this incomparable regiment. The French made off with [the regiment's] guns and all its flags except for one, torn from the hands of [a French cuirassier] by cadet Tomilovski of the Iziumskii Hussars' (Barclay's old regiment after Ochakov).[30] The Petersburg Dragoons, crushed by the weight of French numbers and unable to stand their ground, trampled in their panic flight over two supporting battalions.[31] Concluding his report to Bennigsen on the action at Hof, Barclay did not make light of the costs: 'My brave comrades and I can find comfort only in the thought that, by having stuck to our position, we saved the army from a sudden attack of the entire enemy force. That was our mission and that our aim, and if this was accomplished, then all sacrifices were justified.'[32]

This mission was accomplished – despite all débâcles Barclay 'conducted himself so well that his lines were never pierced'[33] – and the sacrifices did gain enough time to permit Bennigsen to take up a more suitable position farther north at Preussisch-Eylau rather than at Landsberg as originally planned. Considering what happened seventy-two hours later in this little, frozen town of Preussisch-Eylau, however, the ultimate value of the sacrifices is open to discussion. As usual, the question of retreat versus battle had been decided under the pressure of immediate events and feelings. Bennigsen recognized the prudence of awaiting possible Austrian and British aid (after the Baltic opened) rather than committing the empire 'under very inauspicious circumstances . . . to the fortune of a single action'.[34] The general feeling of the army, however, worn down by night marches and constant scrounging for pitifully inadequate food, was violently against further retreat, 'for indeed a Russian force was never by character of composition or system calculated to retreat . . .'[35]

Even among reliable sources, estimates of the numbers lined up by each side at Preussisch-Eylau vary considerably. For the French, the figures given are between 67,000 and 80,000; for the Allies – the Russians plus Lestocq's corps of Prussians – they are between 63,000 and 82,500. Let us say roughly 70,000 men on each side, with a slight numerical superiority in favour of the Allies. Bennigsen's main forces were drawn up facing the town, along a ridge behind Preussisch-Eylau. The position stretched from the village of Schmoditten in the north to the village of Serpallen in the south. No bread had been sent to the battlefield and the troops had no food for the next two days. Barclay's depleted detachment, battered, tired, cold and wet, unfed, and mourning all the comrades fallen in the last two bloody days of battle at Frauendorf and Hof, was given the task of defending the town of Preussisch-Eylau during the day of the 7th (26 January/7 February), in order to prevent French troops from being able to shelter there during the night. The situation became critical at about four o'clock in the afternoon when Soult's Corps tried to invest the town. Barclay and his men resisted in house-to-house fighting until they were driven back to gardens – brittle, ice-sheathed, and now bloodied – at the eastern edge of the town. Here Barclay collected the remnants of his troops and obstinately led them fighting their smoke- and snow-blinded way back to the town's main square. At this point a fresh Russian detachment finally arrived on the scene and bayoneted its way to the centre of the town. Together they drove out the French, killing and wounding a great many and taking five hundred prisoners. According to what may be an apocryphal story, this was the 'historic' moment when Napoleon, rarely given to flattery of the enemy, wanted to know the name of the general 'who barred his route to Preussisch-Eylau with such courage and consummate skill'.[36]

What is known with certainty is the fact that in the approaching dusk, as

Barclay was leading a final cavalry charge trying to rout the last of the French from the church and the cemetery, he was hit in the arm by bone-smashing grape and unhorsed by the impact. Unconscious and about to be trampled to death, he was snatched up from under horses' hoofs by a sergeant of the Iziumskii Hussars. The sergeant slung him across the saddle and swept him off to the nearest dressing-station. Immediately the news was rushed to Bennigsen. Distressed by this 'misfortune to them all', he referred feelingly to Barclay as 'this valiant and splendid general', and spoke of 'the entire army's greatest sorrow' that Barclay had to leave the field.[37] Night fell on the gutted town of Preussisch-Eylau which, thanks primarily to Barclay, remained in Russian hands. But in itself the town was of no use to the Russians, and at ten in the evening Bennigsen gave orders to vacate it in silence without arousing the enemy.

Barclay's night was one of groans and fevers in frost so intense that scalpels and saws dropped from the freezing fingers of medical orderlies. At daybreak on the 8th (27 January/8 February 1807), while jolting by sledge towards a hospital in Koenigsberg, he was deafened by the cannonade with which the Russian army opened hostilities. The French batteries replied in kind and from then on throughout the day the opposing artillery thundered over the howling wind. The battle proper of Preussisch-Eylau was under way on empty stomachs and in a temperature of −26 °C. With roughly equal forces the contestants battered each other nearly to a standstill. Napoleon, reproaching himself for not having summoned Bernadotte's Corps to this major battle, looked in vain for Ney to arrive from the north: he arrived only at ten o'clock that evening. The Russians seemed finally to have the best of it and nobody saw this more clearly than Napoleon: 'The Russians have received reinforcements; but we have almost used up our artillery shells. Ney is not appearing, and Bernadotte is far away; it would seem that it would be better for us to go to meet him.'[38]

But Bennigsen did not know what Napoleon was thinking. What loomed in Bennigsen's mind was the news – which reached him well before it reached Napoleon – that Ney's vanguard had arrived on the north of the Russian right flank. Bennigsen's constant dread of being outflanked and eventually surrounded was kindled by this news. Ulm, Austerlitz, Jena, and Auerstadt all testified to Napoleon's genius for this strategy, and Bennigsen was determined to avoid encirclement. At eleven o'clock he summoned his generals who, still mounted, formed a circle about him. Despite their urging to continue the action, Bennigsen announced and maintained his decision to withdraw from Preussisch-Eylau to Koenigsberg. (It was only at midnight that he and his staff shared a bowl of potatoes, their first food of the day; his soldiers, however, got along on frozen snow.) Bennigsen later defended his position thus:

Let every experienced military man judge whether it was not more advantageous for me to withdraw to Koenigsberg. There I could let the army pull itself together, obtain care for the wounded, get the guns back into condition, pick up new supplies of shells, strengthen Koenigsberg's defences, and leave to Napoleon the snowy fields, the deserted Preussisch-Eylau, and the empty villages round about where he would find neither provisions nor care for the wounded nor reconditioning for his artillery.[39]

By leaving the field at Preussisch-Eylau, however, Bennigsen gave Napoleon the chance to boast of a victory precisely because 'the enemy was in retreat'.[40] But the real upshot was indecisive, even in the light of Frederick the Great's definition of victory: 'to compel your opponent to yield you his position'.[41]

Although Napoleon had no intention of remaining long in the snowy fields and deserted town, he did revisit the scene of the slaughter the next morning and for several days thereafter. All witnesses agreed that it was 'the most horrible scene of carnage ever observed in a war . . . there were some ten thousand human corpses and three to four thousand horse cadavers, and about six thousand Russians in the process of succumbing to their wounds'.[42] Napoleon himself described the scene as a 'horrible spectacle, which duty had rendered necessary', and he had himself painted on horseback (in the famous picture by Gros) looking down with compassion on the wounded soldiers bleeding against the white, snowy ground.[43] Marshal Ney's comment, after silently inspecting the field of battle, was simply: 'What a massacre, and all for nothing!'[44]

From 15,000 to 26,000 Russians were killed or wounded, and from 18,000 to 25,000 French, according to different sources. A total of from 33,000 to 51,000 in all. Nine Russian generals were wounded and six or seven French generals, as well as Marshal Augereau, while one French general was killed. For the surviving leaders there were the usual advancements and decorations. Barclay's remarkable performances were rewarded by promotion to lieutenant-general, the order of St. Vladimir Second Class, and, from the King of Prussia, the order of the Red Eagle. More important, he had earned the notice and gratitude of the Tsar.

Barclay was lucky to have been among the wounded who were rescued from the field and who survived the sledge journey to Koenigsberg. Shortage of medical officers meant in general that only promising cases were taken. Even men who might have been saved but who would most likely have been unfit for future service were economically left behind, 'for the finances of the empire did not admit of this burthen'.[45] Arrived in Koenigsberg, Barclay found himself in the confusion and horror of a town where the wounded were being dumped by the thousand and many were dying from want of medical attention. 'The town was overflowing with wounded; it was impossible to find shelter for everybody, nor to dress the wounds immediately,' wrote Madame de Krüdener in her Koenigsberg diary; 'the entire population was busy making bandages.'[46] Barclay's case, however, like many others, called for more than bandages. He was moved as soon as possible to the austere but less crowded city of Memel, farther from the front, where the Prussian royal couple also took refuge. Auguste rushed there to provide home nursing, bringing with her Caroline von Helffreich (known as 'Lina'), the first of the Barclay de Tollys' foster-daughters. Over forty bone fragments had to be extracted from the wound. There was of course neither antisepsis nor anaesthesia, no notion of sanitation nor of trained nursing; and access to medical treatment depended a good deal on rank, chance, and favour, if one can believe the account left by Lina's daughter:

One Sunday afternoon, as Barclay was drowsing in his bed, his wife, exhausted from the long hours spent at his bedside, had lain down in her room, locking her door. The servants were out strolling in the strange town; only Lina, aged thirteen, stayed home. Suddenly she heard some one at the front door and timidly went to open it. It was the Tsar's personal physician sent by his master. Lina announced the physician's arrival to Barclay and was about to withdraw quickly, when the doctor asked her to help him and fetch a bowl of tepid water. 'Please hold the bowl here,' said he, and taking out his surgeon's knife, began to remove bone splinters. Blood flowed profusely, but the general remained composed, and the trembling Lina tried to support him as best she could.[47]

Despite all this, a year and three months after Preussisch-Eylau the wound was healed, leaving only a certain impairment of mobility in his right arm and hand. A very noticeable change took place in his handwriting (it became larger, sloppier, more illegible), but it is clear that with patience and perseverance Barclay had succeeded in re-educating his right hand. Because of these fifteen months of invalidity, Barclay was spared active participation in the dénouement which followed his exploits at Pultusk, Frauendorf, Hof, and Preussisch-Eylau. Meanwhile both sides again burrowed into winter quarters and spent the next four months licking their wounds and replenishing their ranks and supplies.

CHAPTER V

MEMEL AND TILSIT – SHADOWS OF THE FUTURE

> I am of the opinion that an alliance with Russia would be very advantageous, if it weren't such a whimsical thing.
> *Napoleon to Talleyrand   14 March 1807*
>
> An alliance of France with Russia has always been the object of my desires.
> *Alexander to Napoleon   12/24 June 1807*

About six weeks after the battle of Preussisch-Eylau, the Tsar, in expectation of a hard campaign, sought to consolidate the alliance between Russia and Prussia. A meeting between the two monarchs and their chief advisers was set up at Bartenstein, a village close to Preussisch-Eylau but unscathed by battle. At nearby Memel, a two-day visit (25–26 March/6–7 April 1807) to raise the downcast spirits of King Frederick William III and Queen Louisa preceded the official meeting at Bartenstein.

Upon learning that Barclay was also in Memel, having his wounds mended, the Tsar called upon the General at his lodgings. This was the first time the two had met face to face. Although details of their lengthy conversation are not recorded, the meeting was a consequential one in the sense that it established an immediate and lasting rapport. Despite the absence of documentation, it is unlikely that the meeting had been intended as a simple courtesy call. The Tsar had already heard much of Barclay's personal courage and overall competence and, since Alexander was ever seeking ability and unquestionable loyalty, he would have been very eager to meet Barclay, to sound him out and assess him. What were the General's views of the recent campaign? What of the state of the Russian army, of its equipment? What were the prospects of a decisive victory over Napoleon? What tactics would serve best? Barclay had had time to ponder such questions and he was given to plain speaking; his simplicity and his grasp of the problems involved was no doubt a bracing change from the ignorant flattery the Tsar was generally used to in his entourage. In a world where treachery was the norm, loyalty was always the first quality sought by Alexander – combined, if possible, with ability; and in the able Barclay he could not fail to perceive a dedicated fidelity. The informality of the scene, with the host in bed receiving a sickroom visit, was an ideal setting for bringing out Barclay's character, and even the homeliness and orderliness of the quarters, so removed from the luxury customary with most of the generals and so attractive to the compulsively neat Alexander, would have contributed to making this first impression a remarkable one.

At the beginning of the year the Tsar had faced the desperate problem of trying to find a man 'who enjoys universal confidence and who combines military talents with the severity indispensable for the post of commander', and the Kamenskii débâcle had at least demonstrated that ability was more important than parentage. The Memel meeting now laid the ground for Barclay's rapid advancement by establishing the essential element: confidence. As a first token of the Tsar's appreciation of Barclay's qualities, he sent his surgeon to the General on the following day, and the last of the bone fragments were removed in the scene little Lina so vividly recalled. During the weeks that followed, weeks of disarray and disaffection among the Russian generals, the Tsar again found the occasion to express the regard which had crystallized during his talk in Memel: before the end of April Barclay was given command of the 6th Division (replacing the deceased General Sedmoratskii), and the Tsar wrote to him: 'I am convinced that you will welcome this appointment as a further sign of my confidence in you.'[1]

From Memel the Tsar went on to Bartenstein; signed the Bartenstein Convention with King Frederick William III to reinforce their alliance (14/26 April); talked about plans for a Europe free of Napoleon; and inspected the troops who were to do the freeing. Neither Austria nor England welcomed the invitation to join the Bartenstein Convention, and in two months it became irrelevant. At the time, however, there was no shadow on the Bartenstein entente except for Prussian grumblings about Bennigsen and his failure to exploit the 'victories' at Pultusk and Preussisch-Eylau. The Prussians complained that Bennigsen's withdrawals after gaining the advantage were inexcusable, but the Tsar had already congratulated Bennigsen, complimenting him on being the first 'to vanquish the hitherto invincible'.[2] Besides, who could replace him? The Tsar went so far as to discuss possible replacements with Hardenberg, Chief Minister of Prussia - General Essen I came out first on the list - but in the end he left Bennigsen in place as commander-in-chief.

It was Bennigsen, therefore, who was on the spot when the armies soon clashed again and the French army demolished the Russians. The place was Friedland on the river Alle, the date 2/14 June 1807, and the consequences unthinkable a week, even a day, earlier.

Friedland was alarmingly close to the Russian border, and, with this major defeat, a French invasion of Russian territory suddenly became a possibility which had to be reckoned with. Immobilized in Memel, Barclay confronted the problem. Freed by his convalescence from immediate involvement and the press of day-to-day duties and decisions, he was able to consider all possibilities and achieve a long-range view. What this view was is known from the conversations he had at this time in Memel - in an 'intimate atmosphere' - with the Prussian diplomat and historian, Barthold Georg Niebuhr, who was financial councillor to Hardenberg.[3] Barclay's plan was based on the classical Fabian, delaying, strategy; as Niebuhr's account was later summarized, Barclay's proposals were essentially as follows: by way of skilful withdrawal, to lure Napoleon into Russia's heartland, farther and farther from his base of operations, wearing him out with short engagements and maximum harassments, making him use up his supplies, and only then tendering him 'a new Poltava' with all the force of Russia's well-preserved armed strength and with the aid of the climate.[4]

Barclay's thinking was clearly of a different order from Catherine's when, at the beginning of her Swedish war, she had contemplated the panicky possibility of falling back, even as far as to Astrakhan. He, on the contrary, worked out details, constructing a policy of carefully planned retreat designed as an entrapment manœuvre to yield eventual victory. According to Ranke, he was the first one to have done so.[5] As it turned out, however, Barclay's ideas would have five years to ripen slowly before they were needed. In the immediate situation, the military rout at Friedland produced an equally serious political problem – the Russian generals and nobles split into dangerously unstable 'peace' and 'war' factions which then rapidly turned into so-called 'French' or 'English' parties.

Bennigsen, in announcing the 'woeful event' ('ce funeste évènement') at Friedland, had asked the Tsar's permission to negotiate an armistice.[6] Alexander, unable to believe what had happened, responded bitterly: 'I was far from expecting such tidings as I have just received from you, General, after having entrusted you with such a splendid army. . . . If you have no way to extricate yourself . . . other than to seek a truce, you have my permission to do so, but only on condition it be done in your own name.'[7] Bennigsen thereupon sent the following message to the French: 'After the bloodletting of the last few days . . . I would like to alleviate the sufferings caused by this destructive war and therefore I propose an armistice.'[8] While the Tsar was reluctant to let Bennigsen ask even for an armistice, Napoleon wanted more: a truce, to him, now seemed a mere first step towards gaining Alexander as an ally, a notion which only a very short while before he had thought of as 'a whimsical thing'. Yet before the month was out the amazing volte-face was accomplished: Alexander and Napoleon were as brothers, the Russian defeat had turned into an alliance with the enemy, and the Prussians had lost out in every way.

One of the first steps in this rapid, but tortuous, evolution was the Tsar's realization that the Prussians had been right in their assessment of Bennigsen. After Friedland their judgements became even more severe, as Hardenberg's: 'The battle of Friedland was the most irresponsible and most unnecessary defeat, resulting from a complete lack of talent and sound thinking.'[9] Two British officers who witnessed it likewise testified that 'from the commencement of the battle it was manifest that we had a great deal to lose and probably little to gain'.[10] General Sir Robert Wilson, another British observer at Russian headquarters, warned that 'if Bennigsen retains the command the Emperor will finally lose his throne'.[11] Bennigsen himself in his memoirs admitted that it would have been better to have avoided the battle and that the decision to fight had depended on him alone.[12] Belatedly Alexander confessed that he could not understand how 'St. Petersburg' had formed such a high opinion of Bennigsen: 'He is not at all well thought of in the army. They find him indolent and spiritless – we owe our victories at Pultusk and Eylau not to any talent attributable to him but to the bravery of our armies.'[13]

Alexander had recovered from Austerlitz; he had every expectation of recovering from Friedland. At Bennigsen's headquarters, however, defeatism was rife. Russian officers proclaimed their disillusion with fighting for the sake of the Tsar's Prussian friends. A 'Peace Party' was formed with Grand Duke Constantine as its head. A Prussian general attached to Bennigsen's headquarters, and no doubt feeling very isolated there, described the atmosphere: 'The officers at General Bennigsen's table speak without any restraint of the need to conclude peace with utmost haste; no one seems to imagine that the Emperor might think differently, and in general these gentlemen ... feel sure of succeeding and carrying out their plan even against the Emperor's intentions.'[14] Another report from the same aggrieved Prussian source describes the abandon with which Bennigsen's camp cursed the war and declared themselves beaten: 'how little these people watch their tongue', he said, as they intrigued against the Tsar, under Constantine's lead.[15]

Widespread as was the defeatism of the Russian generals, it is nevertheless not true, as has been said, that of the generals only Barclay de Tolly was still in favour of fighting.[16] There were others, as for example Lieutenant-General Ostermann-Tolstoy, who had fought with Barclay at Pultusk, was wounded just before Friedland, and was a fellow invalid in Memel. Some prudently left their opinions in doubt or shifted with the wind. Puzzling, for instance, is the case of General Prince Bagration, a favourite of Suvorov in the old days and always a favourite with the troops. A fawning letter he wrote from his rearguard headquarters to Grand Duke Constantine could be interpreted as taking sides with the Peace Party.[17] Though not averse to intrigue, it is implausible all the same that Bagration should have plotted against the intentions of the Tsar, and indeed quite the contrary was true according to Napoleon's envoy to St. Petersburg, General Savary, who reported that Bagration was generally considered as anti-French and anti-peace.[18]

To work on his brother the Tsar, Constantine contrived to deliver personally the dispatches reporting on first contacts with the French, contacts in which the French had gone out of their way to be courteous and charming. Constantine used every kind of pressure to bring Alexander round to a completely new outlook, even going so far as to warn that failure to give in to the officers' clamour for peace might result in Alexander suffering the same fate as their father. The Tsar acquiesced to the extent of accepting the idea of a personal meeting with Napoleon, while simultaneously marking his resistance by issuing orders against fraternization with the French by any one, including his brother: only the negotiators were to cross the French line. Nevertheless the rumour quickly spread at Bennigsen's headquarters of an impending meeting between the two sovereigns, and the Peace Party felt it was gaining its point.

There followed a strange dance, two steps forward, one step back, turning in a circle, changing partners, changing places, and finally changing sides. The figures of the dance were being improvised and only Napoleon seemed to be sure of his footing. After two years of fighting Napoleon, two years of various on-and-off (though disappointing) alliances with England, Austria, Prussia, and Sweden, and only two months after the new Russo–Prussian agreements of Bartenstein, here suddenly was the Tsar's brother along with the Commander-in-Chief of Russian forces and a whole clique of generals making overtures to the enemy and almost threatening the Tsar. No wonder St. Petersburg, steeped in hatred of Napoleon as Antichrist, was talking of Bennigsen as a traitor. But Napoleon's approaches to Alexander were seductive while the Prussian protests and reminders were irritating. Ironically, while Alexander was moving in Napoleon's direction, Bennigsen danced in the opposite direction, now assuring the Tsar that Russian losses at Friedland had been greatly exaggerated (as was in fact the case) and claiming to be ready to fight the French again, this time victoriously. Bennigsen's startling turnabout may have stemmed from 'a sudden surge of self-assertiveness in a man who felt he had been weak', as Herbert Butterfield suggests, or from an equally sudden and chilling realization that while Alexander had so far chosen to overlook Bennigsen's role in Tsar Paul's assassination, he might not excuse the loose talk bordering on treason which Bennigsen tolerated in his mess. This reversal of roles, with Bennigsen 'now being the optimist, the enthusiast for war, is a problem of psychology, a study in moods. . . . Any puff of wind might have altered history.'[19] No wind blew hard enough, however, to counteract the alluring visions Napoleon was holding out to Alexander of two great world-straddling eastern and western empires, a division of glory more realistic, it then seemed, and certainly more thrilling than the Bartenstein prospects now crushed in the Friedland defeat.

Only eleven days after this battle, then, the combatants met in the famous ornate wooden pavilion erected for the occasion on a raft on the river Neman' near Tilsit. Alexander had discovered, or so he said, that he too hated England and its 'obnoxious egotism'. For over a week the two emperors talked, dined, and rode about the countryside together, occasionally with the King of Prussia trailing along as a poor Lepidus on the scene, helplessly watching as Napoleon flattered Alexander into forgetting his oaths of undying friendship for Prussia. The two emperors were very busy exchanging cravats, handkerchiefs, and pledges. Talleyrand and Prince Kurakin worked diligently to draw up the articles of alliance and on 25 June/7 July 1807 the Treaty of Tilsit was ready and was signed two days later, along with a punitive Franco–Prussian Treaty. Finally, decorations and embraces were exchanged. Among those decorated by Napoleon's hand was Bennigsen, but the Tsar, having satisfied the army by the Peace of Tilsit, lost no time in dismissing his commander-in-chief, allowing him to retire to his large estate near Vilna, in Lithuania.

Alexander now hastened to return to St. Petersburg, where he found antagonism to the Tilsit realliance to be even stronger than he had feared. In Moscow too, and in the country at large, the news from Tilsit caused unrestrained anger. Against the Tsar were his mother, the Dowager Empress Maria Fedorovna, whose court was a seat of power; his favourite sister, Grand Duchess Catherine; the nobility, with few exceptions; the merchants, who foresaw the ruin of their trade through the embargo on Britain; those of the military who had not witnessed Friedland; the clergy, who had preached a hundred Sundays against Holy Russia's idolatrous enemy; and finally, though less articulately, those who had prayed against this French Antichrist or had lost members of the family fighting him. All these, summarily named 'le Parti anglais' by the French, considered that Alexander's Tilsit arrangements deeply offended Russian honour. In their eyes the defeats of Austerlitz and Friedland were lamentable setbacks, while the Peace of Tilsit was a true disgrace. Commenting on the constantly growing disaffection in St. Petersburg, the Swedish Ambassador, Count von Stedingk, reported to his King that 'gruesome things are being said'.[20] All things French were hated. Napoleon's envoys, first General Savary and later General de Caulaincourt, were ostracized (at first) by most of St. Petersburg society.[21] The nobility preferred instead to fill the theatre where Vladimir Ozerov's *Dimitri of the Don* was playing – a new epic drama of Russia's great victory over the Tartars in 1380, crammed with patriotic harangues and calls for revenge.

From the beginning Tilsit was a source of conflict and ambivalence. 'God has saved us,' Alexander wrote to his sister from Tilsit: '. . . instead of being sacrificed, we have come out of the struggle with a sort of lustre.'[22] But we also have the word of the French Count Montgelas, Bavaria's Minister of State, that at the moment of signing, Alexander muttered that he had thereby at least gained time.[23] The French historian Vandal wrote that 'In 1807 Alexander did not yet want a new war, but had moments of foreseeing 1812.'[24] Denis Davydov, poet as well as adjutant to Bagration, declared: 'The year 1812 already stood amongst us Russians with its bayonct up to its sockct in blood.'[25] The departing Minister of Foreign Affairs, Budberg, who was likewise convinced that the Tilsit friendship treaties contained all the ingredients for later conflict, insisted that 'We must employ this moment of repose in preparing the means of resistance against another attack.'[26] What is likely is that the 'enigmatic' Tsar's silence, stubbornness, and 'sovereign dissimulation' hid not a uniform, calculated policy but a fluctuating mixture of feelings, attitudes, and ideas.

As for the various articles signed at Tilsit, including those 'secret and reserved', they outlined a series of steps leading Russia into conflict with Britain; extended Napoleon's Continental System, closing ports, including Russian ports, to British trade; slashed Prussian territory by half and left the rest under French occupation; set up under French control the Duchy of Warsaw consisting of formerly Prussian-held Polish territories, thus giving Napoleon direct access to Russia's border; vaguely promised French help to Russia against the Turks; and promised partnership in any European war. Danzig was also made a free city.

There is no evidence of when, exactly, Barclay imparted to the Tsar his strategy for coping with invasion. Had Alexander himself put the problem to Barclay in Memel or, in the glowing aftermath of the meeting and following the shock of Friedland, did Barclay hurry to proffer comfort in the form of a saving strategy in case the worst did come to the worst? If Alexander had this strategy in mind, the evolution of his thinking is clarified. He could thus write to his sister from Tilsit in wonderment at spending his days tête-à-tête with Napoleon – 'I ask you if all this doesn't seem like a dream' – and yet very well write to her again, fifteen months later: 'Bonaparte thinks that I am nothing but a fool. *He who laughs best laughs last.*'[27]

CHAPTER VI

NORTHERN CONQUEST

> 'Mong Russian troops was oft a name
> Inscribed upon historic page,
> Come hither in the arms of fame
> Long ere the war's first stage –
> Barclay, Kamenskii, Bagration,
> Well known to every Finnish son;
> And conflicts sharp were rightly feared,
> Where'er these men appeared.
>
> *Johan Ludwig Runeberg, The Songs of Ensign Stål*
> *(translated from the Swedish by C. B. Shaw)*

During the fifteen days that Alexander and Napoleon spent in each other's company in Tilsit they conjured up a world divided between them. Napoleon was wrong, however, in believing that his chief enemy, Britain, would be intimidated by the mere threat of an alliance between France and Russia. Britain remained firm. Hence Articles 4 and 5 of this treaty of alliance had to be implemented. Article 4 directed Alexander to mediate between England and France to make concessions to Napoleon. Article 5 stipulated that, if Britain refused, Sweden, Denmark, and Portugal were to be ordered to close their ports and declare war on Britain. According to the treaty, any of these three which refused to do so would be treated as an enemy and, in the case of Sweden, Denmark would have to declare war on her.

As was foreseeable, though Russia's mediation efforts ended in her severing relations with Britain and joining Napoleon's Continental System, there was no question of Sweden declaring war on Britain since, as Napoleon well knew, Gustavus IV Adolphus had sworn to die in battle sooner than make peace with the 'Corsican usurper'. The Tilsit alliance thus led directly to war between Russia and Sweden, despite the Russian assurances sent from Tilsit itself that 'whatever turn events may take, His Swedish Majesty may always count upon the sentiments of friendship and attachment' of the Tsar.[1] Napoleon urged Alexander to wrest Finland from Sweden, 'your geographical enemy', thereby securing the safety of the capital and 'protecting the fair ladies of St. Petersburg from ever again being disturbed by Swedish cannon'.[2] Napoleon assured Alexander of his full support, even promising him Stockholm into the bargain.

The Tsar welcomed the opportunity to restore his popularity by way of a predictably victorious campaign against Sweden in Finland. A British assault on Copenhagen and the capture of the Danish fleet gave Alexander the signal for invading Finland. At dawn on 9/21 February 1808 a Russian force of approximately 24,000 men crossed the Russo–Swedish border at Frederikshamn without a declaration of war, and Alexander thus renewed the centuries-old feud over Finland, eighteen years after the peace treaty of Verelä.

This time Alexander chose impetuous Buxhoevden to be supreme commander of the Russian forces in Finland. Under his leadership the Russian army moved briskly forward in three roughly parallel columns. On the left, following the Gulf of Finland shoreline, one column (the 17th Division and part of the 14th), commanded by General Nicolas Kamenskii, younger son of the old Field-Marshal, advanced towards Helsingfors. Buxhoevden and his staff were in this group. Farther inland on a parallel route moved Prince Bagration's column (the 21st Division). The third column, led by General Nicolas Tuchkov (the 5th Division), struck out northwards towards the key road junction of Kuopio on Lake Kallavesi. To Tuchkov's rear, and inside Russian territory, Barclay de Tolly, his arm still in a sling, was preparing his new 6th Division to enter Finland as a reserve force.

All Russian divisions were under strength. The officers and other ranks had hardly recovered from the previous winter's devastating fighting in Poland and Prussia, and now they found themselves in the midst of an even harsher winter, with temperatures hovering between $-15°$ and $-25°$ C. Lakes and rivers offered no obstruction since they were frozen solid, but heavy snowfalls had transformed the roads into narrow lanes between shoulder-high snowbanks. The wheels of the gun-carriages had to be fixed on to small sledges, while foot soldiers, inspired by the contraptions they saw Nordic hunters using, fashioned themselves rudimentary skis.

Facing the Russian aggregate of about 24,000 men was a Swedish army of 19,000, its rank and file consisting mostly of hardened Finnish soldiers. About one-third of this force was safely ensconced behind the thick, granite walls of fortress Sveaborg – the 'Gibraltar of the North' – stretching over several small islands just outside Helsingfors. The main body of the Swedish army in Finland was concentrated at Tavastehus ready to give battle to the invaders. But since it was greatly outnumbered, Sweden's newly appointed supreme commander in Finland, the one-eyed Field-Marshal Klingspor, ordered a general retreat to the north as soon as he reached Tavastehus.

The Russians, leaving a force behind under Kamenskii to cope with Sveaborg, advanced speedily and unopposed in pursuit of the enemy, whose withdrawal up the coast of the Gulf of Bothnia set the pace for the Russian advance. In the unprotected south, another group of Russians occupied Åbo, at that time Finland's capital, and Buxhoevden took it over for his headquarters. A single battalion took the Åland Islands while a somewhat larger unit landed unopposed on the Isle of Gotland. In central Finland, Tuchkov's column overcame moderate resistance to seize Kuopio, essential for safeguarding supply lines. Expecting Swedish withdrawal all the way to the Finno–Swedish frontier at the head of the Gulf of Bothnia, Buxhoevden rushed over-hasty congratulations to the Tsar on the successful occupation of all Finland.[3]

Thus, less than two months after the invasion, Alexander announced to Napoleon on 5/17 April 1808 that 'all of Swedish Finland has been conquered

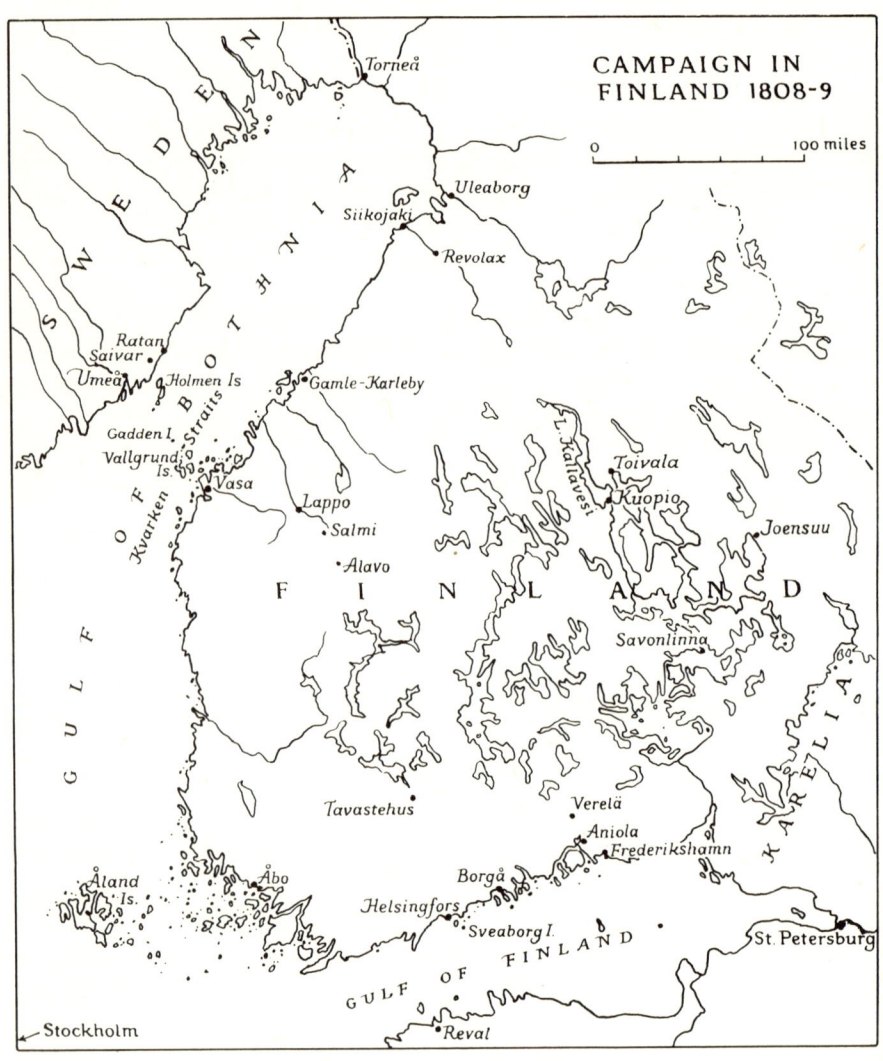

and only Sveaborg's fortress remains in Swedish hands', and there was good reason to believe that Sveaborg would soon capitulate.[4] Alexander went on to say that King Gustavus had been inciting the Turks against Russia and had locked up the Tsar's minister in Stockholm. In retaliation the Tsar had proclaimed Swedish Finland a Russian province. At the same time and for the same insubstantial reason, Russia formally declared war on Sweden.

Although the Tsar's Sveaborg prediction, made with full knowledge of behind-the-scenes bargaining, was soon to prove correct, his assertion of the complete conquest of Finland was decidedly premature. St. Petersburg, however, received the proclamation with joy and the Tsar's reputation was largely restored. Alexander, tireless in acknowledging gratitude to Napoleon for good advice, saw public opinion reverse itself in judging the French alliance. Napoleon's Ambassador Extraordinary, General de Caulaincourt, helped by abundant funds, now became a centre of attraction for the St. Petersburg society which had previously cold-shouldered him.

While St. Petersburg was celebrating, however, and even before, the fighting on the Finnish shores had been becoming less favourable to the Russians. During the chase up the coast of the Gulf of Bothnia, the pursuers were getting weaker, the pursued stronger. The Swedish army, retreating in good order, was constantly being reinforced by small groups of officers and men crossing the Gulf from Sweden to Finland. The Russian detachment at their heels, farther and farther from supplies, urgently required reinforcement. Buxhoevden, therefore, as soon as Kuopio had fallen, ordered Tuchkov and his 5th Division to turn immediately towards the coast. Tuchkov demurred, complying only partially. Lurking in the neighbourhood of Kuopio, he warned, was the renowned Savolax Brigade, 3,000-strong, who would jump at the chance to retake Kuopio and smash the Russian supply system. Buxhoevden ignored this report and repeated his order. This time Tuchkov dared not disobey. On 7/19 March he moved out of Kuopio, leaving behind a force sufficient only to protect his lines of communication. At Gamle-Karleby he joined up with units commanded by Raevskii and Kul'nev, but even so the effective strength of the contingent now under his orders did not exceed 4,600 men – and there were no reserves within 600 kilometres. By this time the Swedes had more than a two-to-one superiority in men and it was clearly only a question of time before Klingspor would give battle.

Only one day after Alexander's boast to Napoleon that all Finland was conquered, the first Russian setback occurred. On 6/18 April 1808 at Siikojoki, the northernmost point reached by the Russian advance guard, the persistent myth of Russian superiority was damaged. In this first defeat, Russian losses came to 350 (dead, wounded, and missing). The people of Sweden and Finland were exuberant and the morale of the victory-starved Swedish army was restored. Only nine days later another Russian unit of 1,500 men was surrounded at nearby Revolax, losing one-third of its component and having its wounded commander taken prisoner. This was the unit which Tuchkov had left behind, hoping to safeguard Kuopio, but Buxhoevden had ordered it, too, to move west.

With the road thus free to Kuopio, Klingspor did not hesitate. He dispatched

Colonel (later General) Sandels to take charge of the 3,000 men whose presence near Kuopio Tuchkov had reported. Sandels quickly occupied Kuopio and, meeting no resistance from the small Russian force retreating before him, dashed on, threatening the Russian border towns in old Russian Finland. All along his route his Savolax Brigade roused the local population to action and formed partisan bands. Buxhoevden, properly alarmed by this situation largely of his own making, ordered whatever reserves were nearby to move against Sandels. The nearest and first to arrive on the scene were three of Barclay de Tolly's infantry regiments.

Apart from dispatching Sandels to Kuopio, Klingspor did not take advantage of his victories at Siikojaki and Revolax. The western front remained quiet for a whole six weeks, mainly because the spring thaw was flooding the rivers, making them impassable. The action shifted to the central front where a clash was in preparation between Sandels and Barclay for the possession of Kuopio.

Meanwhile, without bloodshed, the great fortress of Sveaborg capitulated to the Russians. Kamenskii's besieging force of 6,500 men was outnumbered by the fortress's garrison of 7,503 and outgunned by its 2,000 pieces of artillery. What lead and powder could not have achieved, however, was accomplished by ruses, tricks, and bribes: 'golden bullets', they were called, or in the words of the Tsar, 'golden rain'. On 25 April/7 May the garrison surrendered and was set free after its officers promised not to take up arms again in this war, though few of them kept their word.

When Barclay's corps, numbering a formidable 7,500 men, began pressing ahead, Sandels quickly abandoned his forward positions and retired to Kuopio.[5] Barclay's progress, however, was not unimpeded. He was harried constantly by guerrilla forces. All Finland was now passionately roused to a people's patriotic war; the whole nation from the Åland Islands to Karelia seemed to rise against the Russians. Everywhere there were guerrilla bands of local peasants, armed with scythes, clubs, pikes, and knives, led by regular army officers or non-commissioned officers, among them many who had been obliged to surrender at Sveaborg. They particularly threatened Barclay's supply lines. They pounced upon small outposts and on details of foragers, but they also engaged in bolder actions. In one of their most daring raids against Barclay's division, the partisans destroyed a whole supply transport, burned pontoon equipment, and killed off most of the escort; they also killed some 400 horses by cutting the veins in their forelegs.[6]

Despite constant harassment of this kind, Barclay's men reached Kuopio on 7/19 June 1808, one week after they had set out in pursuit of Sandels who, eluding Barclay's advance guard, managed to escape with his men and guns to the north shore of Lake Kallavesi where he took up position at Toivala, with fourteen kilometres of water between himself and Barclay.[7] No sooner was Sandels chased out of Kuopio, however, than Barclay received orders to move westward, leaving behind only just enough men to defend the Kuopio supply routes. It was the Tuchkov situation all over again: the same orders in the same circumstances which several weeks earlier had had such disastrous consequences for the central front. Klingspor had resumed his coastal offensive and had forced the Russians to withdraw another 100 kilometres south, to the neighbourhood of Vasa. Meanwhile Buxhoevden, blaming the Russian setbacks at Siikojaki and Revolax on Tuchkov's dilatoriness and his 'needless stop at Kuopio', had removed Tuchkov from the command of the western front and appointed Raevskii in his place.

Buxhoevden's operational plan, which was not well thought of in the War Ministry, called for Barclay to go to the rescue of the hard-pressed Raevskii. Somewhat reluctantly, therefore, Barclay marched off from Kuopio with about two-thirds of his troops, laboriously ferrying them across the multitudinous Finnish lakes and rivers, since the guerrillas had destroyed all the bridges. Just when their destination was almost in sight, the vanguard being only 150 kilometres short of reaching Lappo, a small town held by the outposts of Raevskii's right flank, Barclay received alarming news from Kuopio. Under cover of the morning mist on the lake, Sandels had assaulted Kuopio, and although he had been beaten back, another attack was expected at any moment. The Finnish guerrillas, moreover, had received firearms and were taking over Russian outposts and disrupting supply lines all through the area, the Savolax district. Barclay knew that the troops he had left at Kuopio were not strong enough to withstand determined enemy attack, much less to carry out additional orders for a pre-emptive strike at Sandels's encampment across the lake at Toivala.

Barclay's conflict was clear: between his lifelong regard for discipline, and his profound respect for the lives of the men entrusted to him. Was he to obey, pursuing his march towards Klingspor's left flank while leaving almost 2,000 men to their doom in Kuopio; or to disobey, rescuing his Kuopio garrison, safeguarding the supply lines essential to the whole Russian army in Finland, and perhaps destroying Sandel's force? There was no time to seek Buxhoevden's approval for the second alternative, nor was it likely that approval would be forthcoming. In the end, offsetting Barclay's true horror of disobedience, there was the Tuchkov precedent, a complete object lesson in the consequences of compliance in such circumstances. Barclay could not betray his own judgement, nor the lives of men under his care, even at the risk of his career and at the price of the severe guilt feelings attaching from childhood to any defiance of authority. Dispatching only one of his infantry regiments and 100 Cossacks to augment Raevskii's force, he retraced his steps to Kuopio as fast as he and the rest of his troops could go.

They arrived just in time to thwart another attempt by Sandels to retake the town. As soon as Barclay had repelled the assailants, he threw his energies into preparations for an offensive to dislodge the Swedes from their haven across the lake at Toivala. The preparations included assembling means for carrying men, cannon, and supplies across the fourteen kilometres of water. Kuopio resounded with the hammering of rafts, and Barclay even summoned a specialist engineer from St. Petersburg to help in constructing specially large flat-bottomed vessels. Barclay's boldness had infected his troops, fierce feelings of loyalty had surged up, and their fighting spirit was aroused. All were eager to vanquish Sandels once and for all. The arrival of fifteen gunboats, which Barclay had called for to protect the convoy across the lake, brought excitement in Kuopio to a head. But in the midst of all these satisfying activities, near mid-July 1808, Barclay was taken ill. He asked for, and was granted, leave. Buxhoevden, probably not without malice, sent the recently censured, but obedient, Tuchkov to take over the Kuopio command.

Nothing is known about this illness. Sickness was common among all ranks of the Russian army and several commanding generals on the Finnish front had gone back to the capital for brief rests. Barclay's slow recovery from his recent wound may have weakened his resistance. It is possible to speculate that he felt emotional turmoil stemming from the guilt of disobedience, even disobedience prompted by the highest motives, and from the internal conflict between two of the most deeply-seated and hitherto inviolable principles of his whole being. Back in Kuopio, Barclay is likely to have lived his decision over and over again, wearing himself out in the process. He must repeatedly have turned over in his mind Buxhoevden's apparent blindness to the strategic importance of Kuopio, blindness to the fact that as long as Sandels was permitted to operate in central Finland, the areas bordering on Russia would remain unsafe. Sleepless nights would have been followed by days of over-intense activity, with Barclay straining to rush through the action which would vindicate his decision. This mental turmoil is quite likely to have taken a physical form; but most of all, his illness, whatever its nature, was probably exacerbated by Buxhoevden's angry reaction to this act of insubordination on the part of one of his generals, especially a general whom he disliked. Ever since Barclay had sided with Bennigsen two years earlier in East Prussia, Buxhoevden had borne a grudge. Feeling his reputation and career to be in jeopardy surely spurred Barclay's request for leave at this particular time.

Barclay's fellow generals were naturally divided in their opinions. Some, of course, would not even consider the possibility that an officer could ever go against orders and take responsibility into his own hands. Others blamed not only his indiscipline but his judgement, and charged him with postponing the final expulsion of Sweden from Finland. Against this it was argued that even if Barclay had followed orders, it was unlikely that his and Raevskii's combined forces could have defeated Klingspor at that time. Still others approved Barclay's choice, and among these was the ultimate arbiter, Tsar Alexander.[8] Approbation by the highest authority removed guilt, conflict, open criticism, and possibly symptoms all at once.

In any case, Barclay recovered sufficiently, within a month, to be able to attend the Tsar's Councils of War in August. Besides the Tsar, Council members included War Minister Arakcheev, General von Knorring, and General Marquis Filippo Paulucci, a Sardinian who had entered Russian service in 1807. During Barclay's stay in the capital from August through the remainder of the year 1808, he took part in frequent consultations on the Finnish war. To have his opinion sought by the Tsar and listened to in the councils of the mighty was healing solace indeed, and no doubt also the magnificent setting of imperial power and ceremony, however foreign to his Lutheran soul, could only do him good at this point.

During the early summer months the Russian situation had been worsening on both the western and southern fronts. The Åland Islands and the Isle of Gotland were retaken by the Swedes. The Swedish fleet, aided by the British, gave battle to the Russian navy and unsuccessfully attempted landings near Åbo. Raevskii, lacking after all the Barclay reinforcements, was defeated at Lappo, and again at Alavo and Salmi. His battered force retreated towards Tavastehus. Buxhoevden sent Nicolas Kamenskii to replace Raevskii in mid-July.

The Tsar was in a sombre mood. The sudden reverses of his army came just at the time when his second infant daughter died. He was also feeling abandoned by Napoleon: Alexander had counted on Napoleon mediating between Russia and Turkey and opening a second front in southern Sweden. A combined French–Danish landing under General Bernadotte had been promised as far back as April. But the French emperor was beset by a crisis of his own making in Spain. Alexander, although never officially notified that the Bernadotte expedition had been cancelled, knew well enough that only Napoleon could have called it off, and it was an angry and resentful Tsar who snapped to Caulaincourt, 'Never mind, I'll try to manage it alone!'[9] For the time being, however, all prospect of a Russian invasion of Sweden seemed out of the question, and the general feeling in the capital was wary. When Alexander consulted the members of his War Council in August 1808, Barclay's recommendation to pursue both defensive and offensive operations in Finland, since Buxhoevden by this time had over 40,000 men at his disposal there, was rejected in favour of a purely defensive policy.

By the end of the summer Buxhoevden's land forces rose to 44,000 and Klingspor realized he was greatly outnumbered. The merest possibility of an invasion of Sweden meant that sizeable portions of the Swedish army had to be kept on home territory. Klingspor was forced to withdraw again to northern Finland, suffering several defeats on the way at the hands of Kamenskii. Sandels, too, after hearing of these setbacks and knowing himself threatened both by the lake expedition from Kuopio set in motion by Barclay and now from the rear as well, at last gave up Toivala and withdrew northwards. The end of the Finnish campaign was in sight.

On 12/24 September a demoralized Klingspor proposed an armistice. Buxhoevden, who had not yet heard of Sandels's departure, agreed, and five days later signed a truce. But St. Petersburg, which had better communications and knew about Sandels, disapproved. The Tsar had set off to meet Napoleon at Erfurt and in his absence the Council of Ministers ordered Buxhoevden to break the truce. The Russians resumed their offensive and by 1/13 December all of Finland was finally in Russian hands. Meanwhile in October the Tsar returned from Erfurt full of confidence, convinced that in the following year his armies would penetrate deep into Sweden (a Russo–Danish partition of Sweden was presumably on the Erfurt agenda) and would capture Stockholm, thereby showing the world that Napoleon was not the only one who could occupy foreign capitals. Because of his premature truce Buxhoevden felt obliged to ask to be relieved of his post. His request was granted in early December and he retired to his farm in Estonia. To succeed him Alexander chose the old and cautious General von Knorring.

The first part of Russia's war against Sweden came to a close with the end of the year 1808, but the easy victory originally foreseen by Alexander, when he undertook the conquest of Finland as a simple way to regain popularity, had turned into an almost year-long seesaw of advance and retreat, flight and pursuit, while no one bothered about 'justifying' the war. And the spectacle of the Russians and the Swedes fighting each other on Finnish soil served permanently to heighten Finnish national feeling. When, during the remarkably uneven course of events, the Russians tried to destroy the guerrilla movement by making it mandatory for Finns to swear allegiance to the Tsar, some townsmen complied, but the response from the peasant population was virtually nil. In small communities the local pastors had to perform the oath-taking ceremony during Sunday services: the peasants simply stayed away. The remarkable resistance of the Finnish people and their signal triumphs in five engagements of the war became legendary, still serving in the 1840s as inspiration for the Finnish national poet, Johan Runeberg.[10]

To be the first governor-general of conquered Finland, the Tsar appointed Baron Sprengporten, the sixty-eight-year-old Finnish leader who had defected years earlier from the Swedish army to the Russians and for more than two decades had preached that Finland's true welfare lay in becoming part of the Russian empire. A new period thus began in Finnish history. For upwards of a century, until 1917, Finland remained a Russian Grand Duchy.

Back in the early, euphoric days of the Finnish campaign, when a quick Russian conquest seemed assured and the taking of Stockholm the next easy step, the Tsar had sought Barclay de Tolly's advice about an idea, initiated by Arakcheev, the Minister of War, which was then being mooted in the imperial entourage: an invasion of Sweden across the Gulf of Bothnia. Barclay was extremely sceptical, and argued against the plan. Any expeditionary force would find itself at the mercy of the more powerful Swedish fleet. 'To land in a poor country, devoid of the means of subsistence for a large invading force, with little protection from the weak Russian fleet, was to court disaster.'[11] Barclay did not make a final pronouncement, however, but diplomatically asked for time to develop his thoughts further and submit them to the Tsar in writing. A month later, after the unexpected Russian setbacks and the lowering of Russian morale, Buxhoevden warned the Tsar, on 7/19 May, that a Gulf invasion would require an army of at least 50,000 men over and above the forces already engaged in Finland, along with an escort of 200 gunboats and a fleet of line vessels.[12] The project was therefore shelved, but not forgotten. Barclay, taking advantage of his sick leave to work out a new approach, submitted his memorandum on the subject in December 1808. In it he again warned of the huge hazards of a crossing, but he agreed with Arakcheev's new suggestion that they might be lessened by crossing on ice instead of water, thus avoiding the whole problem of gunboats and battle fleets. Traversing an immense frozen surface would certainly be dangerous but, if meticulously prepared, it could be risked. An operational plan for a three-pronged attack on Sweden during the coming coldest winter months was worked out. The Russian force nearest to the Swedish shore was the one headed by Prince Bagration. It was to be reinforced to bring it to above 20,000 men. The Gulf was paved with islets like stepping-stones leading from Finland to the Åland Islands. Starting out from the Åland Islands, Bagration's force would be within relatively easy reach of Stockholm. Farther north, another and much smaller force – led, in the end, by Barclay – would leave from Vasa and cross the narrowest part of the Gulf, the part called Kvarken, roughly 100 kilometres from shore to shore. The destination would be the town of Umeå whence this second force could move either north or south as the situation might warrant. At the very head of the Gulf a third force would move overland into Sweden.

At the beginning of 1809 Barclay was given the Vasa front, taking over from Prince Golitsyn. In a further shuffle, General Count Shuvalov was put in charge of the northern front. All in all, the Russian forces in Finland now numbered some 48,000 men, including those on garrison duty. They had amongst them 127 cannon.

On his arrival in Vasa, Barclay was appalled to discover that very little had been done by way of preparation for the march across the ice. Supplies were insufficient and his force short of ammunition. The Vasa depots were empty, and it would take another three weeks, Barclay figured, to equip his units suitably. Bagration and Shuvalov faced similar problems, and all the generals had qualms about the expedition. The Tsar, angered by the delays, issued a special rescript amounting to a severe dressing-down of the Commander-in-Chief, who thereupon asked for discharge. Old Knorring had been sent early to Finland to take charge of preparations and expedite them, but his slowness was quite unsuited to the situation. Caulaincourt urged the Tsar in early March, as winter waned, to send War Minister Arakcheev, who after all had had the 'great concept' of a Gulf crossing in the first place, to hurry things along. This Arakcheev did, and very effectively, not by expediting supplies, but by bullying and cajoling, and by informing Barclay that the Tsar was about to visit Finland: 'I am sure you will want to welcome him with Swedish trophies!' As for Barclay's objection to having to proceed on inadequate instructions, Arakcheev retorted: 'A general of your quality does not need them.' The War Minister made his message even clearer by adding fulsomely, 'For once I would rather be in your place than be a minister; there are many ministers, but Providence has reserved the crossing of the Kvarken for General Barclay de Tolly.'[13] Bagration summed up the resigned reaction of the generals in the field to these proddings: 'Order us and we'll go.' 'I request you', wrote Arakcheev to Barclay, 'to proceed at once to carry out the Emperor's orders.'[14]

At least the Swedes seemed to present few problems. General Golitsyn, Barclay's predecessor at Vasa, had sent out a patrol of ten Cossacks under Lieutenant-Colonel Kiselev who had made their way half-way across the ice and back without causing any alerts. Rumours had reached the Swedes of what the Russians were attempting, but they were discounted as being absurd by the Swedish general in command of Umeå.

Barclay split up his forces, leaving one regiment behind to guard Vasa. The rest he divided into a main body, composed of one grenadier and one line infantry regiment, 200 Cossacks, and six guns, which he placed under General von Berg's command; and a smaller unit, led by Colonel Filisov, consisting of two infantry battalions, 100 Cossacks, and two guns. Altogether there were 300 Cossacks and 3,500 other troops. Barclay left orders for four additional regiments, still on their way to Vasa from Shuvalov's force, to follow him immediately on arrival.[15]

The question of numbers, however, was not of paramount concern to Barclay, who was relying mainly on the element of surprise. (His departure from St. Petersburg had been kept secret; even his wife was told only at the last minute.)[16] What did worry him was the possibility of the ice breaking, stranding him in the snowy wastes of Sweden. Not only was the frozen Kvarken famous for its cracks and fissures disguised under the snow cover, but its history was one of frequent break-ups due to sudden storms which drove the whole icy passageway out to sea. For the moment, however, all was frozen hard and, after making last-minute arrangements for guides and extra provisions, Barclay joined the main body of his troops on the island of Vallgrund outside Vasa.

Thirty-six hours before the invasion, Barclay sent ahead a ski-patrol of sharp-shooters and Cossacks under Kiselev, who already knew the way from his earlier reconnaissance. The first night this scouting party gained the island of Storgrundset off the Swedish coast and captured an astonished Swedish patrol. The following night they sighted near the shore a detachment of fifty Finnish troops of the Swedish army. The Finns put up a strong resistance, but were outnumbered two to one. All were killed except for one officer and nine men who surrendered. The rifle fire was clearly audible in Umeå, but the imperturbable Swedish commander ordered only a minimum of precautionary measures.

Meanwhile Vallgrund and a sister island twenty kilometres from Vasa were the assembly points for Barclay's forces. Cold and wind whistle through the accounts of the crossing from Vallgrund onwards: 'As far as the eye could see, an immense desert of snow; the granite island appeared to be dead nature's tombstone. No sign whatsoever of life . . . no trees, no bushes . . . no means of protecting oneself. There were 15 degrees [C.] of frost, but the troops had to camp without fire and without tents . . .'[17]

From Vallgrund, then, the real march began at five in the morning of 8/20 March. The men moved forward silently into a weird landscape:

The troops met with almost insuperable difficulties from their very first steps on the icy field. A few weeks earlier, a heavy storm had broken up the ice, piling up enormous blocks into mountainous barriers . . . these mountains of ice gave an extraordinary impression of waves frozen suddenly in the midst of convulsive movement. The marching was becoming more and more difficult. The troops had to climb the ice-blocks, sometimes to heave them out of the way; or struggle out of the hard-frozen snow. Perspiration pearled the soldiers' brows. At the same time a biting, piercing north wind was rising and threatened to turn into a hurricane which might again break up the ice under their feet. . . . The problem of moving the artillery through this icescape meanwhile delayed the forward march . . .[18]

Twelve weary hours after starting out, Barclay's forces had covered about forty kilometres and reached the Swedish islands of Storgrundset and Gadden, barren resting-places where again there was nothing with which to make fires.

The first detachment, in line with Barclay's pincer plan for taking Umeå, was to go on, after resting, towards the mainland via Holmen Island, but was not to attack until the second detachment reached the Umeå estuary. At Holmen Island, however, they were held up the following morning, at five o'clock on 9/21 March, by an engagement with the enemy and were able to reach the mainland only that evening, sixteen kilometres from Umeå.

Barclay now took personal command of the second detachment. After a short, comfortless break on Gadden, they set off again that same midnight, bone-stiff and teeth chattering, for the last lap of the crossing. Previous difficulties now seemed as nothing in comparison. It took them eighteen hours to cover the remaining sixty kilometres, bringing them finally to the misty wasteland of the Umeå estuary in the evening of 9/21 March: 'When the exhausted soldiers finally reached the estuary, they could hardly move. It would have been impossible to envisage an attack; the troops bivouacked on the ice, only one kilometre away from the enemy. . . . A few abandoned ships on the shore were cut into firewood; in the beneficent warmth of the fire, the soldiers recovered their spirits . . .'[19] A characteristically patriotic refrain sounded in Barclay's praise for his soldiers in his official report (and has echoed since through all Russian accounts): 'Only Russians', he wrote, 'could have coped with the enormous difficulties.'[20] Two hundred of his soldiers had one or more limbs frozen during the crossing.

At dawn on 10/22 March, after a reasonable night's rest, Barclay's detachment quickly overran the first line of the Swedish defence. Thereupon the Swedish commander, General Cronstedt, vastly overestimating the size of the Russian forces, dispatched one of his officers to treat with Barclay. The officer was told that if Cronstedt wished to plead for mercy he would have to do it in person. Cronstedt did not hesitate. Not only did he think himself outnumbered but he had just been shaken by rumours of serious political upheaval in Stockholm. He therefore announced his readiness to surrender Umeå and sign a cease-fire. He accepted all the stiff terms Barclay laid down. A few hours later Barclay's troops – those who were not casualties of the cold – made their triumphant entry into Umeå, finding sufficient provisions to last them a full month. In addition, they took possession of all the Swedish guns and shells, rifles and ammunition.

'I could, of course, have forced the enemy to give battle,' Barclay reported back to the Commander-in-Chief, Knorring, 'and in all likelihood would have gained the advantage. . . . Our forces were of roughly equal strength, but unlike the Swedes who were fresh, our men were exhausted . . .; also the enemy had some artillery, while ours was delayed; but all things considered, we had little to gain and would perhaps have suffered harm; it would have been very wrong of me and unworthy of my Sovereign's trust, had I chosen to sacrifice the common good for my own glory . . .'[21] On the face of it, Barclay protests too much. But one may surmise that glory-seeking of the kind he describes was standard practice and furthermore that glorious deeds of that kind were the only kind of military deeds likely to gain ready appreciation, imperial or popular.

Barclay had reckoned to remain at least a month in Umeå, using it as a base for operations in the north, and planned to combine with Shuvalov to 'force the enemy to lay down his arms in the face of his Imperial Majesty's victorious army'.[22] As soon as he had reached Umeå, in fact, Barclay dispatched Colonel Filisov with one infantry regiment and 100 Cossacks in the direction of Shuvalov's force.

Two days after Barclay's arrival in Sweden, however, Knorring sent him the startling, and at first sight disappointing and deflating, order to return forthwith to Vasa. There had indeed been political upheavals in Stockholm, providential ones from the Russian point of view: on the very day of Barclay's entry into Umeå, Gustavus IV Adolphus had been overthrown. Bagration, who had reached the Åland Islands, had already signed an armistice there. Barclay delayed three days, however, in obeying the order to return, thereby giving his men time to rest, and counteracting their natural reaction to having gone through such perils and exertions for apparently no reason; he also thus avoided giving the Swedes the impression of a constrained withdrawal. He managed, on the contrary, to make good political use of his departure, by issuing an uplifting proclamation to the inhabitants of Umeå in which he explained that the Tsar's sole intention in sending a military force into central Sweden had been to hasten the conclusion of peace, a peace which would serve the well-being of the entire Swedish population. 'Therefore,' he added, 'not only were all personal belongings of Umeå's inhabitants left untouched, but all captured arms and ammunition, provisions and supply depots are being returned intact.' The gratitude of the populace can have been equalled only by their amazement, as the departing conqueror proclaimed his altruistic reasoning: 'To serve our own self-interest by taking any spoils with us, or destroying or reducing to a state of uselessness any of the objects fallen into our hands, would negate our peaceful purpose.'[23]

Barclay reported back joyfully on the political advantage achieved through generosity and discipline (apart from the inevitable incidents caused by some always troublesome Cossacks):

During the short time the Russian troops spent on the Swedish shore, they behaved in an orderly fashion in all respects: not a single inhabitant of Umeå had grounds for the slightest complaint; the conduct and discipline of the Russian soldiers caused general astonishment. I was proud to hear the innumerable tributes to the victorious army whose arrival had been viewed by the native population as auguring endless misery . . .[24]

'With tears in his eyes', the governor of Umeå, leading a delegation of noblemen, merchants, and artisans, had voiced the Swedes' gratitude, saying that 'the entire population would forever honour the name of the beneficent Emperor Alexander'.[25]

On 15/27 March, just one week after starting out, Barclay led his troops back across the Kvarken, through the same perils, hazards, and hardships as before. For the return trip, however, since secrecy was not a problem and speed somewhat less essential – though there was still a race against a possible break-up of the ice – Barclay whenever possible employed his Cossacks and their horse power to help transport the cold and weary soldiers. Many were thus saved from frostbite and sickness. Some, including Barclay de Tolly, were marked for life by the Kvarken crossing: for the rest of his days he suffered from recurrent chills. He wrote to his foster-mother from Vasa, 'My health is not what it used to be, and I have become very sensitive to bad weather. Also, my right arm is suffering from lack of mobility.'[26] But, though he arrived back in Vasa in a state of general exhaustion, his wife was there waiting for him and her care and attention were excellent remedies. For Kvarken veterans in general the sense of heroic brotherhood was powerful, and they could imagine their progeny's boast: 'My ancestor was with Barclay de Tolly on the Kvarken!'[27] As it turned out, the Kvarken crossing had no major military significance (it helped Shuvalov obtain Swedish capitulation in the north), but it resounded with glory at the time and ever since: a feat, Viskovatov states, 'which belongs among the most memorable in [Russian] war annals'.[28]

By delaying his return over the Kvarken, Barclay missed the first moves of Alexander's elaborate enterprise to make Russian sovereignty attractive to the Finns. While Barclay's troops were just setting out on their return march, the Tsar, having convened Finland's Diet, arrived on 15/27 March 1809 in the small town of Borgå to inaugurate the parliamentary session with all the imperial trappings at his command, from triumphal arches to grand balls. Prominent in his suite were his Ministers of Foreign Affairs and of War, and the Assistant Minister of Justice, Michael Speranskii, whom everybody knew to be the *de facto* prime minister. After a magnificent procession, with salvo after salvo of guns and church bells peeling, the Tsar reined in at the mayor's house, where he was to stay, and was greeted by the 127 deputies of the four estates. (The fourth estate here was the peasantry.) His Imperial Majesty then issued an overwhelmingly popular proclamation to the Finnish people guaranteeing that Finland's fundamental laws, i.e. their right to practise their own religion and their other established civil rights and liberties, would be maintained for ever. In the Lutheran church, from a throne adorned with Finland's arms, the Tsar – now also Grand Duke of Finland – accepted oaths of allegiance and opened the Diet with an address which Governor-General Count Sprengporten translated into Swedish, the language of the upper classes in Finland. The purpose of the whole glorious show was not, to be sure, to install self-government – the Diet was not empowered to issue decrees, only opinions, and after staying in session a very short while it was not reconvened until 1863! – but to provide Alexander with a platform for proclaiming the privileged status he was conferring on Finland, thus helping to assuage the passions aroused by the Russian invasion and the breaking-off of the centuries-old link with Sweden.[29]

After Borgå the Tsar continued on the same mission at Helsingfors – at Fortress Sveaborg 900 guns thundered triumphant volleys – and at Åbo. Here, after the ceremonials, with another triumphal arch, Alexander addressed himself to military, diplomatic, and civil affairs. Furious with Knorring for having accepted an armistice when Bagration and Kul'nev had almost had Stockholm in their hands and Barclay and Shuvalov had been all set for conquest, the Tsar ordered the immediate ending of the truce and the continuation of the war until Sweden was ready to break with England. Russian arms should not be silent, he ordered, even during future negotiations with the enemy.

The Tsar was affable and charming with everyone except General Knorring whom he pointedly ignored. Knorring took the hint and asked to be relieved of his post. He was told curtly to stay on until a new commander-in-chief was chosen.

The other generals, however, had good reason to be pleased. Barclay and Prince Bagration were made full generals; Count Shuvalov was raised to lieutenant-general; and Kul'nev to major-general. There were rewards as well for other ranks. The luckiest were those, like Barclay's men, who had actually set foot in Sweden – they received two rubles; for those who had got only as far as the Åland Islands – one ruble; and for all others – a silver medal. For Arakcheev, father of the Kvarken crossing, there were high honours and tributes from the Tsar.[30] Auguste Barclay de Tolly was also not forgotten: on 26 March/7 April 1809 she received the diamond badge, lesser class, of the Order of St. Catherine, personally bestowed upon her with elaborate ceremony either by the Dowager Empress or the Empress herself, respectively Grand Mistress and Deputy Mistress of the Order. This investiture was a rare and coveted honour, the highest available to a woman, and limited to ninety-four holders. (The grand cross of the Order was restricted to members of the imperial family and twelve others, usually foreign queens or consorts.)[31]

Knorring did not have to wait long for his resignation to be accepted. Ten days after returning to St. Petersburg, the Tsar chose his new commander-in-chief for Finland. An acrimonious exchange of letters between Knorring and Sprengporten, both contending for the finest house in Åbo, served as a pretext for removing the Governor-General at the same time. During the Tsar's Finnish trip he had come to realize that Sprengporten was a difficult character and not at all popular with his fellow Finns. In place of both, combining the posts of commander-in-chief and governor-general, the Tsar appointed Barclay de Tolly, hero of the Kvarken. From the time of their first meeting in Memel, Alexander had felt Barclay shared his own fundamental 'love for order, clarity, and hierarchical discipline',[32] and now the Tsar wrote to Arakcheev that 'he liked him [Barclay] better every hour'.[33] Thus, in mid-April 1809, at the age of forty-seven, Barclay to his own surprise became Russia's most important representative in the new Grand Duchy of Finland.

Barclay was not the only person to be surprised. This appointment flouted seniority and he knew that his promotion would make him many enemies. He had the foresight to entreat the Tsar to preserve full confidence in him even if his actions should be interpreted and judged unfavourably by envious persons.[34] The Tsar's answer, loud and firm in an imperial rescript of 29 May (O.S.) 1809, went beyond what Barclay could have hoped for: 'In giving you command of my army in Finland, I have only followed the course dictated by justice and by the esteem I have acquired for your military talents and your personal character. Based on these motives, the opinion I have of you will never vary; by itself this will suffice to ward off envy if ever envy rises against you.'[35]

The Tsar was as good as his word. A swarm of generals, especially titled generals, buzzed with outrage. The civil service by this time had become effectively a reserve of the nobility, rigidly tied to seniority, and the old families intended the army to be the same. Among those who felt personally offended by Barclay's appointment and voiced their rancour at having been passed over were Generals Prince D. V. Golitsyn (who had originally been scheduled to lead the Kvarken crossing), N. A. Tuchkov, Dokhturov, Uvarov, Count P. A. Tolstoy, P. K. Essen, Sacken, Count Ostermann-Tolstoy, the Princes Gorchakov, and Count N. Kamenskii.[36] Some of these asked permission to retire from the Tsar's service. A few, to their chagrin, the Tsar dismissed outright. In other cases, notably those of Generals Tuchkov and Dokhturov, he ordered their retention. To Dokhturov he went to the trouble of explaining:

In warfare, opportunities to distinguish oneself cannot be chosen; not everybody can have the same opportunity at the same time. But when military circumstances are such that some one has the chance for distinguished action, it would be doing an injustice to the entire service to reward such action by promotion based only on respect for seniority. Therefore I have made it a rule never to abide by such considerations.[37]

Along with all the vituperation, Barclay also received expressions of support. Fellow General Count Shuvalov, for instance, who could appreciate Barclay's Kvarken exploit better than most, wrote encouragingly: 'I can assure you that you have only been justly requited for your worthy deed; everyone is full of admiration for your expedition.'[38]

By obtaining the Tsar's specific advance support against any attackers, Barclay had dealt quickly and effectively with the situation created by his rank-jumping appointment. He refused to become embroiled in army politics. With his double job in Finland, he had his hands full.

CHAPTER VII

FIRST IN FINLAND

The reward of a general is not a bigger tent, but command.
Oliver Wendell Holmes, Jr., 'Law and the Court' (1913) in Collected Legal Papers

While the family settled into the Governor's quarters – in that 'finest house' in Åbo so sharply disputed by Knorring and Sprengporten – Barclay was governing Finland with his left hand and using his right to try to conquer Sweden in accordance with the orders of the Tsar.[1]

The Russian army in Finland – serving the functions of both occupation and invasion troops – had a strength of 39,000 in mid-April 1809 when Barclay took overall command. A quarter of this force, 10,000 men, Barclay sent off under Shuvalov, re-invading Sweden by the overland route, proceeding down the coast of Västerbotten province to invest Umeå. Barclay gave three tasks to Shuvalov: to hold on to the region until peace was signed; to threaten the Swedish interior if the enemy made difficulties during peace negotiations; and to reassure the civilian population 'that Russia's sole aim is to secure peace'.[2] (Presumably the Lutheran conscience had certain conventional military loopholes.)

The problem of supplies made this assignment extremely difficult to carry out; it was indeed the key problem for both sides during the whole Swedish campaign. One factor particularly disadvantageous to the Russians was the naval situation, which prevented Barclay from sending either reinforcements or supplies over the Kvarken Straits. The Russian Ministry of Marine was incapable of providing Barclay with even the skimpiest minimum necessary to challenge Swedish supremacy in the Gulf of Bothnia. Barclay had originally planned to send provisions and his own former force of 6,000 from Vasa to Umeå as reinforcements for Shuvalov. One of his first actions as commander-in-chief had been to build a flotilla at Vasa, but he found it a nearly hopeless struggle to get the needed armaments out of the Ministry of Marine; provisioning could not be held up that long. Therefore, to supply the troops in Sweden, the roundabout land route was the remaining alternative, but six hundred kilometres – the distance from Uleaborg in Finland to the Russian positions in Sweden south of Umeå – was too long for efficient haulage: stocks would be consumed or spoiled en route. Consequently there appeared to be no choice but to forage locally – for 10,000 men. The problem of finding food in the barren eastern provinces of Sweden, however, had been a major reason Barclay had originally given in warning against a Kvarken invasion. The Swedish command, which included Sandels, Barclay's old enemy from Kuopio, faced similar problems despite shorter supply lines. Prospects of food shortages were behind the repeated Swedish quests for truces during this campaign and behind the temptation of the Russian field commanders to accept them. Although the Commander-in-Chief was obliged to accept Alexander's reiterated refusals even to consider a whole series of truce proposals offered by the Swedes to the successive Russian commanders Shuvalov, Alekseev, and Kamenskii, as early as mid-May Barclay was instructing Shuvalov and informing the Tsar that 'the most important task before new offensive actions could be envisaged was to find food supplies for the troops'.[3] Thus respites in the action were provided for, even while keeping to the letter of the Tsar's explicit orders, and in one case, on 22 June/4 July, when the Russian commanders saw their stocks of bread and flour nearly finished, the Emperor did agree to a short breathing space.[4]

While Barclay, as commander-in-chief, was struggling with the realities of blood and hunger in Sweden and the sword-rattling of his monarch in St. Petersburg, he was simultaneously coping daily with his administrative duties as governor-general. For lack of time as well as lack of inclination, he normally avoided as much as possible the heavy burden of ceremonial which could have been his lot. On 7/19 July 1809, however, Tsar Alexander returned to Finland for the closing of the Diet in Borgå, and Barclay's every minute was occupied with solemn and splendid pageantry. The burghers of the town, the mayor, the deputies, the Barclay de Tolly household, and the general population, had a wonderful time. The Tsar delivered the concluding speech, pledging to take note of the Diet's petitions and promising full understanding of the problems of the Finnish people. This done, Alexander and Barclay proceeded to a timely inspection of Fortress Sveaborg. For six hours (parades and inspections were still Alexander's favourite pastime) the Tsar examined the miles of casemates cut from solid rock, the enormous magazines, the barracks accommodating 12,000 men, and the existing garrison of 4,000. From these July visits to Borgå and Sveaborg the Tsar took back to St. Petersburg a firm impression of civil order, military strength, and granite leadership. His judgement had been right: in Barclay, hero of the Kvarken, there was an administrator of very high gifts.

The Tsar's presence at Sveaborg had the usual effect of arousing self-sacrificing patriotism and was thus well timed to stimulate resistance to the British, who were engaging in one of their half-hearted attempts to relieve pressure on their Swedish allies. British warships were roaming the Gulf of Finland. They completely controlled the sea lanes from Kronstadt to the Finnish ports, and took a toll of thirty-five Russian cargo vessels during the summer months. Russian warships, frigates, coasters, and galleys (the last oar-propelled vessels in naval history) fought stubbornly, however. Conforming to Alexander's expectations, the Russians yielded only *in extremis*; the case is cited of a forty-four-man crew of which every single one was killed or wounded.[5]

Thwarted and damaged at sea and beset continuously by supply problems, the Russians fought all summer up and down the grim north-eastern coast of Sweden, with repeated lulls both official and unofficial, and a constant shifting of advantage. What is of particular interest is that Barclay applied in dealing with his trusted field commanders the crucial lesson he had learned the year before. When sending Kamenskii to take over in Umeå on 23 July/4 August, Barclay authorized him to use his own judgement whenever a quick decision was necessary, and promised to back him up.

No sooner had Kamenskii arrived in Umeå than he faced just such a situation. Without time to get Barclay's approval, Kamenskii found it necessary to withdraw northwards to escape being surrounded. In due time a bloody battle was fought north of Umeå at Saivar where the Russians eventually gained the upper hand, and at Ratan where, because of the guns of the Swedish fleet, matters went considerably less well. Thanks to Kamenskii's initiative, however, the Russians escaped becoming fatally surrounded. Kamenskii's troops were tired, underfed, underarmed, and outnumbered. After another retreat even farther northward, followed by a southward advance, Kamenskii conditionally accepted an armistice proposal, subject to Barclay's approval. Not only did Alexander refuse to authorize this approval, but Kamenskii was judged very severely in St. Petersburg, both for the truce and the retreat. Barclay therefore faithfully dispatched a strong communication to the Tsar. After listing the reasons for retreating, Barclay complimented Kamenskii on extricating his troops from the enemy pincers. The Commander-in-Chief stated his opinion that the advantages of withdrawal exceeded the problematic gains of a hollow victory. He vouched for Kamenskii without reserve: 'I have full confidence in Kamenskii's battle experience. . . . An army which has at its head such a skilful, enterprising, and valorous commander is indeed fortunate.'[6] The Tsar's reaction was a complete turnabout, quick, glowing, and very satisfactory to Barclay, as well, of course, as to Kamenskii: 'I fully recognize the soundness of Count Kamenskii's dispositions; they deserve the highest praise, and have revealed Kamenskii as a highly competent general.'[7] In the end, in fact, Kamenskii received the Order of St. Alexander-Nevsky for the Saivar victory – with diamond insignia 'for exceptional service' – and a reward of 12,000 rubles!

The Tsar's Foreign Minister, Count Rumiantsev, was much less amenable to Barclay's reasoning about Kamenskii. To improve Russia's bargaining position in the peace negotiations, which started in late summer (26 July/7 August), Rumiantsev wanted victories and put steady pressure on Barclay to produce them. Rumiantsev was concerned not with food or fleets; he simply wanted Stockholm. But in the end Barclay's Stockholm invasion force (headed by General Steinheil) never got beyond the Åland Islands. The peace negotiations vacillated as the military balance kept changing. Rumiantsev and the former Russian ambassador to Stockholm, Count David Alopaeus, bargained for Russia; diplomat General Count von Stedingk and Colonel Skjöldebrand for the Swedes.[8] At one point the military situation was so favourable to Sweden that Stedingk wrote back to his government: 'If next summer we could land 25,000 men in Finland and if at the same time we armed the Finnish population, Finland will be ours again.'[9] Finally, however, the Swedes conceded the loss of Finland as 'a sad but unavoidable necessity', and the Russians relinquished as impracticable the idea of trying to vanquish Sweden. The Åland Islands remained the main point of contention. If the Russians took them, they threatened Stockholm; if the Swedes kept them, they threatened Finland. Comparing Finland to a valise, Caulaincourt said that leaving the Islands to Sweden was like 'taking the valise and giving away the keys'.[10] The fact that Barclay de Tolly had a force on the Islands was probably decisive. Five months after Barclay became commander-in-chief and five weeks after negotiations had begun, against a background of military manœuvres and encounters which showed neither side finally able to overwhelm the other, the Treaty of Frederikshamn was signed on 5/17 September 1809. It was just one hundred years since Peter the Great had defeated Charles XII at Poltava, dislodging Sweden from its place among the great European powers. The Frederikshamn peace again humbled Sweden; she officially ceded all of Finland and the Åland Islands to Russia.* The Russo–Finnish frontier with Sweden was fixed along the river at Torneå.

In Europe little heed was taken of this war fought at its far-off northern fringe. The headlines as usual were captured by Napoleon, spectacularly intriguing and warring in Spain. No bombastic war bulletins were sent out from Åbo or Umeå, announcing great victories. The fact that the numbers involved were relatively small, especially the numbers of casualties after Europe had become used to figures on the scale of Jena–Auerstadt and of Preussisch-Eylau, made the war in Scandinavia look like a sideshow. Even inside Russia the war caused little excitement outside official circles. Some voices, like Prince S. G. Volkonskii's, were raised against 'that unjust war against Sweden'.[11] In many public places the King of Sweden was actually toasted.[12] All those in Russia who persisted in hating Napoleon and despising the Tilsit Treaty considered the conquest of Finland as 'a crumb' thrown to Alexander by Napoleon.

It is worth recalling that the conquest of Finland had not, in fact, been the real objective when Alexander sent his armies over the border in February 1808: he set out to comply with the Tilsit arrangements and to punish the Swedish king. Only after the early successes in Finland and on Napoleon's urging did the Tsar start thinking seriously in terms of conquest. After Napoleon failed to give him support, obtaining Swedish recognition of this conquest seems again to have been secondary in the Tsar's war aims as he continued the campaign on Swedish soil, hoping to take Stockholm and show the world that he was as great a conqueror as the Corsican. For his part, Napoleon's initial idea appears to have been mostly to get a firmer hold on Alexander, his 'ally', his 'confederate' – though Alexander furiously rejected the latter term. The surprising upshot of all this, however, was that Russia's north-west boundary was moved 500 kilometres farther from St. Petersburg. Napoleon would have done better to have listened to outspoken Caulaincourt's warning: 'Who will stop this colossus once he has his finger on Torneå and an elbow on Constantinople?'[13] When at last the peace was signed and Russia's finger on Torneå became official, Kutuzov,

---

* The following December the state of war between Sweden and Denmark was terminated; and in January 1810 Sweden signed a treaty with France and adhered to the Continental System, barring British ships and British trade from its ports.

then Governor of Kiev, expressed the classical Russian view of the event: 'If only the dead could know what has happened here, both Peter and Catherine would rejoice over the fulfilment of their most cherished aspirations.'[14] True appreciation of Russia's gain, however, came only three years afterwards in 1812 when Finland undertook the defence of the Baltic shores with her own troops. As a Finnish historian has concluded: 'History is hardly likely to possess another instance of a conquest having borne such fruit.'[15]

On the day of the signing of the Peace of Frederikshamn, 5/17 September 1809, Barclay de Tolly was made a Knight of the Order of St. Alexander-Nevsky. The Order had been conceived by Peter the Great and named in honour of the Russian hero-saint who defeated the Swedish invaders in 1240. Barclay's feat was the lesser one, but none denied his meriting the award. Written in gold upon the star of the insignia was the fitting motto of the Order: For Labour and Fatherland.[16]

In the imperial rescript conferring on Barclay de Tolly the office of Governor-General of the Grand Duchy of Finland, the Tsar cited Barclay's 'striving for the good and dedication to liberal principles'. 'It is because I know this to be so,' the Tsar continued, 'that I am convinced that your nomination to this post will be beneficial to the general welfare of the country and its population.'[17]

'Striving for the good' – the phrase rings deeply true of Barclay de Tolly. There cannot indeed have been many Russian generals or administrators to whom the description would readily apply. 'Liberal principles', however, is a surprising phrase, except in the particular historical context.[18] Barclay's appointment took place just when the Tsar's liberal inclinations were at their strongest, before they were frightened away by the prospect of actually realizing reforms, which would, he discovered with dismay, encroach on his autocratic powers. Talk of liberalization had begun immediately upon Alexander's accession and, with the emergence of Speranskii, reforms moved from mere speculation into the drafting stage. Speranskii probably hoped to make Finland a model in some ways for Russia herself and he was keen to create an administrative structure which could merge directly into a future liberalized Russian administration.[19] The government of Finland was to be an instrument for facilitating both Russian reform and eventual total Finnish absorption into the empire. Local customs, language, and religion were respected; rights and privileges far greater than those allowed to the Russian nobility – though similar to those enjoyed in the Baltic provinces and the Ukraine – were preserved. The 'autonomy' of the Grand Duchy, however, only extended, in the most theoretical way, to legislative or administrative matters. The language of the rescript to Barclay reflects that lip-service, as it reflects the mood of the moment in St. Petersburg. At the same time it is difficult to imagine anyone better suited than Barclay to carry out a policy based on the particular kind of 'liberal principles' desired. His Livonian background prepared him to respect the cultural and religious autonomy of the Finns, his 'striving for the good' promised justice and fair-dealing to the new subjects of the Tsar, his personal authority enhanced his authoritarian role, and his unquestioning devotion to tsarist autocracy ensured that he would thwart any urges to real political independence in the Grand Duchy. Barclay certainly never saw himself in any other role than that of faithful servant to an all-powerful Tsar.

Barclay's first reaction, in fact, to some of Speranskii's administrative proposals was to balk at any lessening of the governor-general's absolute power. Speranskii, aided by a number of Finnish notables, had proposed a Governing Council, presided over by the governor-general, consisting of twelve Finnish members to be chosen for three-year terms by the estates in consultation with the governor-general. This less than wildly liberal suggestion was at first very strongly opposed by Barclay. In relation to police powers, for instance, he was clear and succinct: 'In this sector the governor-general has no need of any special council, which would only hamper decisions instead of acting expeditiously; it must be taken for granted that a council would lose itself in endless deliberations, forgetting that what is required is action!'[20] In relation to finances, he was again equally outspoken on a council's uselessness. He added, uncompromisingly: 'There must be no limits to the authority and power of the governor-general.'[21]

The Borgå Diet was still in session while Barclay was formulating his 'thoughts' on the matter for Speranskii and the Tsar, and the Governor-General could not have known that it would be half a century before the Diet was reconvened. He clearly saw no good in representative or even consultative government and expected only inefficiency and interference from both parliaments and councils: 'It would be preferable to do without a governor-general altogether than have one who is not invested with full power and authority to enable him to prevent, repudiate, and put a stop to the abuses which perforce are a natural consequence of a deliberative body.'[22] In a voice familiar to all ages, here spoke the military leader charged with civil administration, especially in time of war. Barclay's soldierly reaction to the Governing Council idea was no doubt reinforced by his recent experiences in St. Petersburg where he had sometimes seethed with impatience at the waste of time of similar council meetings.

These attitudes come out in a long, detailed memorandum (28 June (O.S.) 1809) on administration policy, dealing primarily with financial structure, police, and justice.[23] It is clear that Barclay had thought a great deal about these matters. It was a new field for him and he knew it; in fact he asked Speranskii to go over the memorandum carefully before submitting it to the Tsar. Many years later, in 1889, when opposition in Russia to Finland's 'internal autonomy' among the so-called 'Finn-devourers' began to flourish, K. Ordin, then a steward at the Imperial Court, used Barclay's memorandum to buttress the argument that Alexander I had never intended Finland to have a liberal administration. Ordin made much of Barclay's mind being 'fresh and foreign to . . . quasi-liberal passions'.[24]

It was perhaps just this freshness of mind that brought Barclay in the same memorandum to except judicial authority from the otherwise full powers he claimed for the governor-generalship. In the context of the memorandum, Barclay's statement was in any case refreshing: 'A governor-general must not assume the role of judge, because he must not be in a position to exercise influence on the application of laws in the courtroom.'[25]

Only one month later the actual experience of governing Finland brought about a complete reversal in Barclay's views on a Governing Council, and he began urging that the Council be established as soon as possible. As he explained to Speranskii: 'The war and the absence of probity in almost every branch of the existing administration are the cause of stagnation in the executive. On the one hand, action is being paralysed and, on the other, abuses and disorderliness have crept in, making for a situation which must absolutely be remedied.'[26] Barclay had by now realized that the Governing Council could act as a new broom and bring in a new level of responsibility. Some such instrument was necessary to clean up the corruption and introduce efficiency into the system. He could not do it alone, being also involved with the war: this letter to Speranskii was written just after Barclay dispatched Kamenskii to Umeå and just before the peace negotiations began at Frederikshamn. Military operations against Sweden were reaching a climax and calling for Barclay's attention. He also had to have workable machinery to keep the hinterland in order. Finland was not just a piece of conquered territory and Finnish affairs were therefore far more complicated than he had expected at the beginning. Speranskii, choosing his words to underline his intention that Finland be treated differently from all the simply tax- and tribute-bearing conquered territories of Russia's past expansions, recognized this situation: 'Finland is a state and not a province; one cannot govern it on the side and amidst a multitude of current business.'[27]

On 2/14 September 1809 a courier finally brought a letter from Speranskii informing Barclay that his recommendation to establish a Council had been accepted by the Tsar.[28] The final decree was now being drawn up. Speranskii also passed on a bit of diplomatic expertise to the neophyte Barclay, cautioning him to see to it that the translation from French into Swedish be done by competent hands, in fact by 'the Bishop of Åbo, who is reputed to be the only person [in Finland] writing in classic-style Swedish'.[29]

Everything was thus set for the Council's first meeting, which Barclay shrewdly made into a ceremonial occasion designed to capture Finnish enthusiasm both for the end of the war and for 'independence', channelling these emotions into loyalty to the Russian crown. The Council's inaugural meeting took place in Åbo on 20 September/2 October 1809, two weeks after the Peace Treaty of Frederikshamn officially ceded Finland to Russia. The Governing Council, as Speranskii later wrote, was 'established not on the basis of a constitutional right, but exclusively by a decision of the government', but the exuberant Finns had no thought on that day for such matters. It was a moment of euphoria and, in reporting the opening to the Tsar, Barclay's language became very elevated: 'Blessed are the people who are ruled by Your Imperial Majesty with wisdom and mercy! . . . The 20th of September 1809 will for ever be remembered as inaugurating an epoch of happiness for the entire population of the Grand Duchy of Finland.'[30] Describing how 'everyone' felt joyous about the self-government 'so graciously' bestowed, Barclay concluded his exultant report: 'I considered it my duty to confer on this happy celebration, which embraced the city's entire population and many visitors from nearby places, the dignity and splendour it justly deserved.'[31]

The city of Åbo, the most ancient in all Finland, glowed with festivity. As night fell, the thirteenth-century castle and the Lutheran cathedral were illuminated by thousands of candles and flambeaux. After the formal opening ceremonies, the Governor-General mingled with the crowd in the streets. The Governor's lady was with him, dressed to contribute her share of 'dignity and splendour', feeling all eyes upon her flashing St. Catherine's cross and the General's red sash with the red and gold badge and the red and silver star of St. Alexander-Nevsky. Barclay's son Magnus, just turned eleven, revelled in the glory and excitement. The family party was completed by Barclay's foster-daughter Caroline von Helffreich, who had enjoyed such a dramatic moment as his nurse at Memel and who lived with the Barclay de Tollys during this whole period. An impressionable adolescent, Lina keenly observed all the signs of Barclay's vast popularity among the Finns. Though flamboyance was not his style, for reasons of public policy he approached it that evening. A tall, impressive figure, limping slightly, combining the dashing aura of the Kvarken hero with the authority of military and civil chief, gorgeous in the green, white, and gold of his General's uniform, he was sought out by the many he had already come to know in almost half a year's rule, and by all those others who hoped to benefit by coming close to the source of power, or who simply wished to meet a fair-minded governor. Even those who dared not approach, eyed him eagerly as the inaugurator of 'an epoch of happiness for the entire population'.

The next day, Barclay presided over the first working session of the Governing Council. Speaking in French as usual, he emphasized that the Tsar, in ratifying the appointment of the Council, had acted in accordance with Finland's ancient constitution – a diplomatic formula which neatly avoided the question of constitutional rights. After the members of the Council had been sworn in, he no less diplomatically declared how flattered he felt to have been put at the head of the assembly representing this 'highly esteemed nation'. In his concluding remarks on the role of the Governing Council, however, there was no ambiguity of meaning: 'Your own devotion to your task gives me great pleasure and also confidence that you, Gentlemen, will assist me in my efforts aimed entirely at the general welfare of this province, in accordance with the designs of His Imperial Majesty.'[32]

Baron Tandefelt, president of Vasa's Appellate Court, expressed the Council's gratitude for the Tsar's decision and paid homage in glowing terms to Barclay's 'great merits, his amiable personality, and intelligence'. The declarations of thankfulness to the Tsar, however, contained an undertone of uneasiness about the sincerity of His Majesty's repeated promises to maintain Finland's ancient laws. Barclay, less sensitive in the circumstances to the notion that what is given can be taken away, did his best to assuage their fears. More than that, he wrote firmly to Speranskii impressing on him how important it was to give the Council a free rein in everything which did not touch on foreign affairs or military matters. In reporting to Speranskii on the first Council meeting, Barclay flattered himself, he said, that the Governing Council would do everything to strengthen the bond of confidence which already existed. 'And does this not conform with the liberality and humaneness of the Tsar?'[33]

As Council chairman, Barclay was *de jure* chairman of its two departments, legislative and economic, each with six Finnish members of high estate (including the country's Chief Accountant), who 'subserviently' informed, requested, presented, wrote, or reminded His Excellency the Governor-General about all current business and, according to the minutes of the meetings presided over by Barclay, decided matters very much as he indicated. Barclay in turn 'subserviently' proposed matters to His Imperial Majesty, such as forgoing the collection of the 1808 saltpetre tax because of war dislocations to the Finnish economy; or passed down to the Council what 'His Imperial Majesty . . . in his mercy has pleased to stipulate' regarding, for example, reimbursement of out-of-pocket parliamentary expenses.[34] The Council's deliberations were usually conducted in Swedish with only an occasional diversion into French or German – certainly a strain for Barclay, accustomed to French for all official business, but a politic concession to the spirit of independence. Despite language problems, however, he knew how to make the Council function, and he rapidly turned this group of twelve into a successful instrument of government and was able to absent himself from most of their meetings (the chair then being taken by the senior Finnish member). From the beginning Barclay led the Council into efficient, down-to-earth decision-making. Within days it had set up the various administrative offices – secretariat, military, finance, ecclesiastic, accounting, and auditing – and had determined staff allocations for each. So favourable was Barclay's experience with the two departments, in fact, that he soon became convinced that the framework of the Council's responsibilities should be extended. He worked steadily to this end and his endeavours were eventually rewarded at the beginning of the term of office of his successor, General Steinheil, who fortunately shared Barclay's views on the subject.

The political temper in Finland during this period was, of course, far from uniform; nor did the signing of the Peace Treaty mean that Sweden overnight lost all interest in Finland. Swedish propaganda was being brought into Finland and circulated by travellers and others with the aim of discrediting Russia in the eyes of her new subjects. Barclay raised the problem in the Governing Council, roundly condemning toleration of such insidious subversion in a 'well-organized and peaceful state'.[35] The public prosecutor was therefore given the limited censorship task of examining literature arriving from abroad – and St. Petersburg was given yet another example of how the Governing Council did 'everything to strengthen the bond of confidence'. Showing a proper military flair for intelligence, Barclay similarly inspired the Council to impound all documents in the possession of the homeward-bound Swedish officials of the Royal Swedish War Commission. These documents were to be 'immediately gone through and studied in case something with regard to the defence of the country, its economic well-being, or accounting . . . could serve for information . . .'[36]

The work of governing the Grand Duchy was not made easier by the

Governing Council's agenda being loaded with all sorts of trivial matters which not only took up Council time but which Barclay had patiently to sort out and pass on to Speranskii for the Tsar's information and decision or approval. On the one hand this arrangement did mean that every Finnish subject had a chance of access to the sovereign – an extraordinary fact in itself and another indication that Finland had indeed a special status quite different from that merely of a conquered country. On the other hand it meant that the Governor-General had to concern himself with sick leave for a vicar or the plea of a Swedish major's widow for help in collecting payment for land she had sold in order to emigrate to Russia; or the tangled marital affairs of a maidservant and a cobbler; and that he had to pass on to the Tsar the divorce request of a woman whose murderer-husband had been sentenced to life imprisonment.[37]

Outside the Council, Barclay had also to deal with a great variety of matters, deciding the fate of Russian deserters, repatriating families of Swedish officers, determining compensation for war damages, or making appointments to all sorts of administrative posts.[38] One of his last official acts in Finland, typical of his political action there in general, was to present to the citizens of Uleaborg a large commemorative gold medal struck in St. Petersburg by order of the Tsar. It was Russia's grateful acknowledgement of the food supplies the Uleaborg citizens had voluntarily provided for General Kamenskii's troops in an hour of great need.[39] Finnish loyalty to Russia and Russian gratitude; Finnish inclusion in the glory of the Empire as symbolized in tsarist gold; and above all the fact that such voluntary contributions would no longer be required – these were themes important to the policy Barclay pursued to promote fidelity in a vanquished people.

Among the nobility there were some pro-Russians of long standing; some irreducible elements remaining loyal to Sweden; and the great bulk of the upper classes, who had been gradually switching allegiance to Russia, especially after the opening of the Borgå Diet and even more after the Peace Treaty and Barclay's inauguration of the Governing Council. The common people showed the same divisions, but followed more slowly, remaining for a long time deeply suspicious of the invaders and holding to their newly acquired sense of national consciousness. Always in the background throughout that first year was the possibility of rebellious outbreaks. The prosperous Finnish soldier–farmer communities, for instance, which the Swedes (anticipating Arakcheev) had established in many parts of the country and which had fought the Russians with distinction in 1808, saw little gain in changing allegiance; but eventually the practical advantages of peace and order, without loss of civil rights, brought about their acceptance (and that of the Finns as a whole) of the new sovereign. Barclay's job as commander-in-chief had ended in a Peace Treaty; his work as governor-general brought a new degree of civil order to Finland while maintaining a large measure of independence. He had in fact contributed significantly to securing a tranquil and loyal acquisition for the Empire and, indeed, an 'epoch of happiness' for the Grand Duchy itself.

In addition to his military and administrative tasks, Barclay also had a number of representational duties, and Auguste certainly used the Finnish period to develop the arts of formal hospitality and official sociability which she would be called upon to practise from then on. But Finland was a country of granite, of rough shores and dark forests lightened only by the dancing birches, of little wooden houses and iconless churches, and the Finns were frugal, brooding, and correct, like Barclay's own people in Livonia. The Governor-General's family in their central pew listened meekly to the same threats of hellfire as did all the simpler citizens of Åbo. They shared the same ideals of hard work, honesty, and duty. Feeling at home with these people, Barclay could be at his best. Here he was recognized for his 'amiable personality and intelligence' as well as for those 'great merits' which won him recognition wherever he went, even where personal affinity was lacking. Ever the Russian patriot, the loyal and obedient servant to the Tsar, he could voice no objection to a transfer, but it can easily be surmised that he was sorry to leave Finland. The last period especially, after the Swedish war was ended, had been a welcome one of relative tranquillity in a hectic life, despite the volume of office work. Lina, the foster-daughter, wept when they left, crying that 'these Finns are such lovely people . . . they esteemed and appreciated their Governor-General and, when the time came to leave this lovely country, they were loath to let him go.'[40]

What had happened was that Arakcheev, envious of Speranskii and piqued at having been kept out of the Committee of Five charged with planning reforms of the central administration, had been quarrelling with his master and friend, the Tsar. Finally they patched matters up and in the process Arakcheev resigned as Minister of War to take over the chairmanship of the Department of Military Affairs in the reconstructed State Council.

Alexander chose Barclay de Tolly to be the new Minister of War. On 1/13 January 1810 he was appointed to his new post. The formal announcement was made on 20 January/1 February. Accompanied by his family, he returned to St. Petersburg.

CHAPTER VIII

MINISTER OF WAR

> A power has now drawn near the frontiers of Russia; it is France, and she will certainly not be satisfied to stay where she is – if one can judge the future by the past or by the manifest intentions of the French Emperor with his unlimited ambition to use any means to dominate Europe . . .
>
> War Minister Barclay de Tolly's first memorandum to Tsar Alexander, February 1810

The St. Petersburg where Barclay now settled had been changing and growing prodigiously. The sound of the hammer was everywhere as the expanding imperial city was being modernized from baroque to neo-classical. The new style was triumphant in the mammoth buildings still under construction for the Admiralty, next to the Winter Palace, and for the General Staff and Ministry of Foreign Affairs which were opposite the Palace. From this concentration of army, navy, and foreign service establishments clustered around the Tsar, the Nevsky Prospekt stretched down to the Fontanka river. It was here, on the river's embankment, that the Barclays lived. Gardens across the Fontanka had now given way to the fashionably pilastered Imperial Office of Privy Affairs, built to house more of the Tsar's swelling bureaucracy. Midway along the wood-paved Prospekt, after the stone Kazan' bridge built by Kutuzov's father, the colonnaded Cathedral of Our Lady of Kazan' stood practically completed, its two great alabaster archangels at each end destined to yield place in 1837 to twin statues of Barclay and Kutuzov.

Pushkin called St. Petersburg the 'martial capital', but even more was it the social capital, and it gave Barclay, now forty-nine, a moderate welcome. Although in government circles his reputation as an accomplished field commander and administrator was fairly well established, the climate he encountered was on the whole one of indifference. The French Consul-General reported home that the Russians found Barclay meticulous and good at detail – damning praise, at best – but too modest in background for his new position.[1] To the nobility, Barclay was always an upstart, and until recently a mere divisional commander. Still, it was known that the Tsar liked him, and above all he replaced the 'ogre', Arakcheev. One of Barclay's first moves was to establish his independence from his predecessor, allowing no meddling in the affairs of the Ministry of Military Ground Forces (as the War Minister's jurisdiction was then titled).[2] If Arakcheev, whose chief contribution had been the vast improvement of his own branch, the artillery, expected Barclay to act as his 'secretary'

– in his new, senior, post in charge of military affairs in the State Council – he had completely misjudged the character of his successor.³ The two men, though they succeeded in maintaining a correct relationship, were opposites. Florinsky had aptly summarized Arakcheev's reputation among his contemporaries as 'dissolute, reactionary, ambitious, rude, vindictive, and perversely cruel to a degree verging on sadism'.⁴ The only qualities Barclay had in common with him were devotion to the Tsar and an innate talent for organization and administration. But while Arakcheev, to inflate his own power and prestige, was bent on centralizing in his own hands all links to the Tsar's private chancery and to the various commands, Barclay, on the basis of his own campaign experience and with the authority of his impressive battle record, chose to give greater elasticity to all departments under his control and greater freedom of action to key commanders in the field. Not that he himself was a free agent. Like all high state officials his position in relation to Alexander was that of a servant, committed to do the Tsar's bidding.

Barclay immediately set in motion plans for reorganizing the Ministry. Aided by a handful of experienced generals, all specialists in their respective fields, and by Prince Peter Volkonskii, Chief of the Quartermaster-General's Department (which had the role of a modern general staff), he sought to increase the effectiveness of the Ministry's components.⁵ The outcome was a new structure which began functioning in January 1812 and survived until the 1860s.

Barclay's first weeks in office were largely devoted to formulating a proposal for the defence of Russia's western frontiers. It was a difficult task. The boundary, stretching for some 1,100 versts (700 miles) from the Baltic to the Ukraine, ran through perfectly flat land. Except for a few rivers and a small area of marshland, there were no natural obstacles to cause the slightest trouble to an invader, as had been amply demonstrated in earlier times during invasions by Poles, Lithuanians, and Swedes. The vulnerability of the western frontier had preoccupied the Russian military before now. In 1796 a plan had been formulated to have nine fortresses guarding the boundary at 75- to 95-mile intervals. But the project was never carried out.⁶ The whole distance between Riga and Kiev had in fact no fortified points, none of 'those mighty nails' valued by Frederick the Great. Across the river Neman' lay the Grand Duchy of Warsaw, Napoleon's creation, serving as an advance operational base for his army. Farther north was prostrate Prussia, its major fortresses in the hands of French garrisons. The absence of an adequate armed force in this, the most exposed part of Russia, further aggravated the danger: 'It is here that we are the least of all prepared to defend ourselves in a war which may decide our very existence,' lamented Barclay.⁷

Within three weeks of his formal appointment, Barclay produced for the Tsar a detailed proposal for meeting the threat from the west.⁸ The Minister of War saw his most pressing tasks to be, first, to build up fortresses and other defensive works in depth; second, to move all possible troops to the area; and third, to create the framework for a much larger field army.

Although the Tsar was still not decided whether Napoleon was ally or enemy, and still on amiable, if mistrustful, terms with him, he accepted Barclay's proposals and encouraged him to go forward with their implementation. From then on Alexander participated eagerly in the discussions on war preparations. As was his nature, he wanted to be informed on the smallest details. Remembering Austerlitz, he also set himself to improve his scanty knowledge of real warfare. As personal adviser and mentor he took on a Prussian former general-staff officer, General von Phull. This pedantic, narrow-minded war theorizer instructed the Tsar with ponderous daily lectures on the tactics of Frederick the Great. Later, Phull's counsel almost brought disaster to the Russian army.

On the matter of fortifications Barclay realistically pointed out that while only a cordon of fortifications could properly guarantee the safety of the western approaches, the enormous cost would be unbearable considering the already heavy drain, mostly military, on the Empire's coffers. The wars with Turkey, France, and Sweden had weakened the economy, and income from foreign trade had fallen off since Russia had joined Napoleon's 'Continental System'; the paper ruble had declined by four-fifths in 1810. Fortresses, besides, were only one item in the military budget, which had to cover the complete equipping of an enlarged army – armament, uniforms, transportation, forage, indeed all necessities. When Arakcheev had taken over, he told Barclay, there was not a single musket in good condition nor any reserve supplies.[9] Apart from Arakcheev's building up of Russia's artillery, nearly everything remained to be done. Furthermore, the construction of a fortress cordon, Barclay estimated, would require some twenty-five years. Therefore he recommended a minimal barrier along the irregular broken line formed by the lower Dvina and upper Dnepr. At the northern end of the line, at Riga, the Livonian Knights had left a bastion; at the southern end, at Kiev, the historic 'mother of Russian cities', was the Pechersk fortress; both needed repairs and improvements. Between these two Barclay proposed the immediate erection of two more fortresses, one at Dünaburg (Russian Dvinsk, some 130 miles south-east of Riga), where there were also ruins of a Livonian Knights' fortress, and one at Bobruisk on the Berezina, roughly 180 miles north of Kiev. Reinforcing the line at strategic points were to be several fortified camps stocked with two to three months' supplies and room for between 10,000 and 50,000 men. (The idea of a huge fortified camp to which an entire army could withdraw, as proposed by General Phull, was not contemplated until the summer of 1811.) Moscow would remain the major supply depot and also the centre for recruiting new troops. Large stores of grain and war equipment were also to be stored at Smolensk, Pskov, and Kremenchug. Barclay further proposed a more advanced operational line running via Pinsk to Vilna, to be built, time and money permitting, some 180 miles west of the Dvina–Dnepr line, leaving the latter to serve as a fall-back position. The Tsar again agreed and early in March 1810 Barclay sent out secret instructions for a survey to select the best locations.

Time ruled otherwise, however. The advance line was never realized at all, and even the Dvina–Dnepr operational line was not ready when invasion came, despite Barclay's urgent commandeering of numerous battalions to do the work. In October 1810 Major-General Oppermann, Inspector of the Engineering

Department and head of the military topographic service, confidently reported to Barclay that within a year the four major fortresses would be ready to withstand a direct assault or long siege. Offering somewhat premature congratulations he concluded: 'Never except in the time of Peter the Great have such considerable engineering works been undertaken and executed inside of a year . . .'[10] But when Napoleon actually struck, only Riga, Kiev, and Bobruisk were at all ready. By themselves they hardly constituted a 'line' of defence.

Russia's land forces at the time Barclay took over the Ministry totalled approximately 200,000 men. Most of these were deployed in three major areas far enough apart to cause considerable logistical strain, remote from the crucial western front. In the north there were the occupation forces in Finland; although the war was over, there remained the risk of Sweden, perhaps aided by England, becoming troublesome again, especially after Napoleon's former marshal, Bernadotte, was elected Crown Prince of Sweden. Far to the south, in Transcaucasia, troops were needed to ward off an attempt by Persia to recover northern Azerbaidjan. Then, in the south-west, Russia had been engaged since October 1806 in another seemingly interminable struggle with Turkey – a war which Napoleon was not keen to see come to an end – and which tied up numerous Russian units occupying Moldavia and Wallachia.

It was clearly the Turkish war which was draining off most of the military manpower and resources, and Barclay undertook a long struggle with the Foreign Minister and Chancellor N. P. Rumiantsev to bring it to an end. Speaking as 'a faithful son of the fatherland', Barclay appealed to Rumiantsev's patriotism, emphasizing that Russia's best and bravest troops were wearing themselves out with Turkey, leaving nothing but green recruits to look after the western frontier.[11] Barclay began working on the Foreign Minister in August 1810, telling him insistently, though in the most delicate of diplomatic terms, that his co-operation was needed to prepare for war with France.[12] Nevertheless, more than a year later Rumiantsev, unconvinced, was still in all sincerity calling Russia's alliance with France 'one of the most beautiful creations of the genius of Napoleon'.[13]

Still Barclay pounded at him, pointing out the other ruinous results of the Turkish war: food shortages; insufficient fortress guns, shells, and powder; depletion of the treasury. 'A quick and advantageous peace', Barclay urged, might be easily arranged by dropping some of the Russian conditions, insisting only on the annexation of Moldavia and Wallachia, and giving full powers to the commander-in-chief to negotiate an honourable settlement. To the Foreign Minister's pretence that he himself was willing enough but the Tsar would never consent to dropping any demands, Barclay replied by requesting Rumiantsev to take on the mission of presenting the facts to His Majesty in 'a manner appropriate to elicit consent'.[14]

Although the Turkish campaign limped on despite Barclay's efforts, a Napoleonic war scare at the beginning of 1811 helped him achieve a certain degree of preparedness. After various measures flouting the Continental System, on 19/31 December 1810 the Tsar issued a new commercial tariff imposing heavy duties on imports arriving overland and hitting especially hard at luxury goods from France. A sharp diplomatic and military escalation was the result. Of the nine Russian divisions aligned against Turkey, five were moved north to the upper Dnestr, within less than a day's march of southern Poland. And one of the divisions stationed in Finland was ordered to march to the upper Dvina.[15] The Russians were now poised to occupy the Grand Duchy of Warsaw and continue westwards to the river Oder, if the war scare should turn into war.

In January 1811 Barclay in fact advanced a plan for a pre-emptive strike at Poland, to eliminate the pro-French Warsaw government and link up with the Prussians to lay waste certain regions and deprive Napoleon's armies of their base of operations.[16] (At the end of 1811 Barclay submitted another 'lay-waste' proposal. These projected devastations of non-Russian territory, similar to Spanish practices at the time, were oddly premonitory of 1812 scorched-earth tactics. It seems clear that military considerations outweighed any others in Barclay's mind.)

Napoleon, however, was not yet ready for a real confrontation and the war scare faded. Barclay resumed his efforts to halt the Turkish war. Finally Kutuzov was ordered to take over the Danubian front and, since he was considered a cunning and crafty politician as well as tactician, this step was seen as a good omen for peace negotiations. The Tsar, still full of resentment against Kutuzov, left it to Barclay to inform the old general, now approaching sixty-six, of his appointment, and Barclay used the occasion to make clear his hopes and intentions, telling Kutuzov he was destined for the glory of concluding peace.[17] Kutuzov soon opened the way to peace by outsmarting the Turks, despite their three-to-one superiority in men, at the battle of Ruschuk on the Danube. But as late as April 1812 Barclay was still prodding the Tsar: 'When I look at our left flank, I am always tormented by the difficulties stemming from the continuing war with Turkey . . .'[18] Finally, when the imminence of Napoleon's invasion of Russia was inescapably clear to everyone, Alexander at last authorized Kutuzov to negotiate a peace and the Treaty of Bucharest was signed on 28 May (N.S.) 1812. In the end the Tsar gave up Russia's claim to Moldavia and Wallachia and had to content himself with annexing Bessarabia.

Russia's military manpower needs could not nearly be satisfied, however, simply by moving troops from other fronts. Three massive serf levies were ordered during Barclay's ministry, and previous standards of fitness could no longer be maintained: Sir Robert Wilson had written of the 1806 draft that no man even with bad teeth was enlisted.[19] The first ukase (16/28 September 1810) called for a levy in 1810 of three out of every five hundred souls of the population, to be followed in 1811 by four more out of every five hundred. The third levy in early 1812 (ukase of 29 March/10 April) drafted an additional two out of every five hundred. Since a levy of one out of five hundred produced roughly 32,000 recruits, then these three altogether brought over 350,000 new soldiers to the training depots. Systematic conscription was nothing new in Russian history; in fact Russia was first in this field, as Richard Pipes has noted. From Peter the Great to 1870 annual levies of peasants and dwellers in trading communities supplied Russia's huge standing army:

Although a recruit and his immediate family received automatic freedom from serfdom, the Russian peasant regarded induction as a virtual death sentence; required to shave his beard and to leave his family for the remainder of his life, the prospect he faced was either to be buried in some distant place or, at best, to return as an old, perhaps disabled man to a village where no one remembered him and where he had no claim to a share in the communal land. . . . The farewell given a recruit upon induction . . . resembled funeral rituals . . .[20]

These sad rituals were performed in every hamlet during these two pre-invasion years, raising the army's strength to approximately 490,000 men, exclusive of Cossacks and the troops engaged in garrison and administrative duties. In all, thirty-six recruits' depots were set up in the provinces closest to the western frontier. Once the new conscripts had been assigned and assimilated, the total manpower of the Russian army could be broken down roughly into 380,000 infantry, 62,000 cavalry, 43,500 artillery, and 4,500 engineers or sappers.

The 380,000 foot soldiers were distributed principally to regiments of imperial guards, grenadiers, Jaegers and, most of all, line infantry.[21] These regiments totalled 514, which included 350 service battalions. The six imperial guard regiments had three service battalions apiece, but for the others, Barclay saw to it that every unit had two front-line battalions and a third, weaker, depot battalion.[22] The 62,000 cavalrymen made up squadrons of guards, cuirassiers, dragoons, hussars, and uhlans – altogether 410 squadrons, not counting the Cossacks.[23]

At the start of the 1812 war the Russians could theoretically put 350 infantry battalions into the field to face some 487 battalions of the Grande Armée, i.e. the French had nearly a 25 per cent advantage. In cavalry strength the armies were about equal, 410 Russian squadrons (plus Cossacks) as against 418 squadrons on Napoleon's side. But Russian horses were the best cavalry horses of Europe, heavy, strong, hardy, lively, and highly trained. Only in artillery did the Russians have, at least on paper, a slight numerical advantage: 1,600 pieces against 1,393. This seeming advantage could become a drawback, however, for Russia's high proportion of artillery to infantry had already, in the previous war against Napoleon, made the army dangerously slow.

In the course of March/April 1812, as three Russian armies began deploying in the west, Barclay effected an important transformation of army structure: he introduced the corps – a large and self-contained tactical unit modelled after the French. The three armies in the west were thus subdivided into a total of twelve infantry corps and five cavalry corps (plus the *corps volant* of the Cossacks). In addition several reserve corps were being formed.[24]

Before the Napoleonic wars, the collection of military intelligence in times of peace had been regarded as a fairly unimportant activity and one which scarcely figured in the duties of the diplomatic services. In the two years preceding the war of 1812, however, Paris became keenly interested in securing every kind of information about Russia. Thus in 1810 Napoleon's first step was to send out for reliable literature about Russian history and Russian characteristics. Then French diplomats were suddenly expected to pay as much attention to the gathering of intelligence as to informing the courts of Europe of French policy 'or of what Napoleon wanted them to believe French policy was'.[25] One of the best-placed of these external agents was Edouard Bignon, the future historian, who served Napoleon by seeking out military intelligence from within Russia while acting as Minister Plenipotentiary in the Grand Duchy of Warsaw.

Russia could have no counterpart to Bignon in Warsaw since the Grand Duchy was a French *chasse-gardée*. But a Major Prendel of the Kharkov Dragoon Regiment, attached by Barclay as an ostensible aide-de-camp to the Russian Ambassador at the court of Saxony, provided the Minister of War with a flood of precise information, military and political, and not only about the Grand Duchy. Prendel had already been on a similar delicate mission to Vienna and he was known for his skill, zeal, and reliability. Barclay reminded him nevertheless to be 'discreet, alert, and extremely careful'. Prendel's exhaustive reports backed by statistical tables were forwarded by the Ambassador through diplomatic couriers to Barclay, who summarized and noted some of the most useful bits: the head of police in Lemberg could be bought for 6,000 florins plus a fur-lined coat for his wife; Napoleon was considering replacing the Bavarian crown prince; the Hungarians were discontented; and so on.[26] Barclay also put the Russian ambassadors in Berlin, Vienna, Munich, and Stockholm on their toes, outlining his intelligence requirements and sending them a basic questionnaire listing in detail all the information needed.

For Paris, the key capital, Barclay spotted a promising candidate in the person of Colonel Chernyshev, one of the Tsar's aides-de-camp attached to the Russian Embassy there and serving as special courier for Alexander's personal correspondence with the French Emperor. Chernyshev, who one day would himself become Minister of War, was on the move frequently between St. Petersburg and Paris and, young and dashing, was a welcome guest in Parisian salons. Barclay asked and received the Tsar's permission to use him for espionage. In September 1810 Barclay sent Chernyshev his instructions. He was to collect full and exact information on French military relations with her vassals and allies; the French army – numbers, locations, organization, supply depots, fortresses, morale; their best generals, with descriptions and evaluations; and French terrain, resources, and civilian population. He was also to collect maps and, 'at any price', secret projects, plans, studies, and confidential reports on troop movements and operations. He was to use supposed 'temporary missions' or any other pretext for travelling about, keep his connection with Barclay an 'absolute secret', and report only through his Ambassador, Prince Kurakin.[27] To help carry out his investigations Chernyshev established contact with an employee of the French War Administration who went by the name of Michel and had been for the last seven years an agent in Russian pay. Despite extremely tight security measures Michel, with the aid of several accomplices, contrived to see and copy, on their way to the binder, the fortnightly situation reports prepared for Napoleon. This very successful operation came to an end, however, when, owing to Chernyshev's haste and negligence, Michel was finally caught, tried, and shot – after Chernyshev himself had safely returned to St. Petersburg in the spring of 1812.[28]

Barclay's initiatives in military intelligence were not by any means limited to espionage: he was also urgently concerned with counter-espionage. His field commanders in western Russia, for instance, received secret alerts impressing on them the need to guard against 'ill-intentioned people', often disguised as travellers, monks, or beggars, hanging about fortress construction sites.[29]

An ironical footnote to Barclay's role in intelligence is that he himself was probably spied upon, though not by the French. If the gathering of intelligence abroad under diplomatic cover was something new, spying at home went back to ancient times and had been systematized by Peter the Great; his *Probrazhenskii prikaz*, or Police Bureau, was an enormous centralized apparatus he invented to deal with political 'crimes'. Informers, *agents provocateurs*, and penetration agents were employed against potentially subversive internal enemies of Russian absolutism. Thus in 1810, Barclay's first year at the War Ministry, the secret police at Alexander's behest developed an intensive surveillance of freemasonry in the capital. Briefly suppressed during Catherine's reign, freemasonry did in fact in Alexander's time become a breeding ground for the Decembrists. The Chief of the Secret Police, de Sanglen – who was Moscow-born, descended from Huguenots, and had once been a lecturer at Moscow University – himself joined the *Petra k istine* (Peter and Truth) lodge, the better to spy upon possible dissidents. On orders from the Tsar he also spied on the State Secretary, Speranskii, causing his downfall, and upon his own boss Balashov, the Minister of Police. In Vilna in 1812 this great intriguer turned up on Barclay's staff as Chief of the Military Police (called, since the days of Peter the Great, *general gewal'diger*, roughly meaning 'jailer') of the First Army, worming his way into Barclay's confidence. It is altogether unlikely that de Sanglen's presence in that spot was accidental.

All in all Barclay's intelligence efforts were productive and crucially important in enabling him to adjust the deployment of Russian troops to match his knowledge of Napoleon's war preparations. In 1811, as soon as the French Emperor made the decision to increase Marshal Davout's Ist Corps to 70,000 (or almost twice that of the next largest French formation), Barclay was able to react immediately to the information and speed up the movement of troops towards the western frontier. At the same time he formed the Russian Sixth Corps under the conscientious General Dokhturov to serve as an advance guard. Similarly, as Napoleon began assembling another large corps along the Elbe river, Barclay created a counterpart in Prince Bagration's Volhynian army (which later became the Second West Army). Up to the very beginning of hostilities the War Minister's informers gave him a sound basis for countering Napoleon's moves almost step by step, at least as far as he could with the Russian forces available. Only the estimates of enemy forces were inadequate and misleading: the intelligence Barclay received was good as far as it went, but in the circumstances, with Napoleon collecting new allies almost up to the last minute, it was impossible for it to go far enough.

Reorganizing the army structure, redeploying troops, recruiting and training large numbers of new soldiers, carrying out surveys, constructing new fortifications, repairing roads, setting up intelligence networks – these were only a few of Barclay's activities in preparing to meet the French threat, and they were all costly. Estimates on the low side put military expenditure during 1810, his first year in office, at more than 147 million silver rubles, over half of the total state budget – although this proportion appears moderate compared to military outlays in Peter the Great's time: 96 per cent of revenues in 1705![30] While no essential expense was spared, the Minister of War kept a keen eye on disbursements and cut down on waste, even when his economy measures made him exceedingly unpopular with those affected. He did not hesitate to abolish posts 'for officials who really do nothing except upset the work of their offices and are a source of considerable expense', specifically in the commissariat and rations services (where fortunes could be made) and, in many towns, in the superfluous posts of commanding officers, town-majors, and town-adjutants: 'According to their qualifications and merit, such officers could be usefully assigned to the construction work of fortresses . . .'[31] In his crackdown on useless expenditure, the services concerned with provisioning, particularly in Moldavia, drew Barclay's fire. Repeatedly he called his sovereign's attention to 'unworthy and illicit dealings there', equally detrimental to the treasury, to the soldiers, and to morale. In the end Barclay's scorn for the indolence and venality of such officers was equalled only by the hatred felt by the victims of his stringent management.

For the common soldier, Barclay showed an unprecedented concern. In all the armies and navies of the world at that time the men were considered simply as war material, an obdurate mass to be lashed into effectiveness, minimally stoked, and yet expected to perform with verve, giving up life eagerly for king, emperor, or little-father Tsar. Barclay was unusual in two ways. He thought that men should be treated as men, not as machines or beasts. And he recognized that humane treatment was productive. Upon noticing in several regimental reports a high incidence of sickness and deaths, Barclay wrote revolutionary (though diplomatic) words to the General concerned:

It is my opinion that there is no reason for the increase in sickness and even mortality other than the lack of moderation in punishment, the draining of the men's strength through exhausting drills, and the absence of abundant food. Your Excellency must know from experience the inveterate habit in our troops of basing all military science, discipline, and order on cruel and corporal punishment; it even happens that officers treat their soldiers inhumanly, as if they had neither feeling nor reason. Even though these barbarous ways have long ago been little by little transformed, we still punish small faults very severely. At present we still drill the men for very long stretches and even twice a day, which only results in calling down punishments on the lazy and on those who have difficulty in understanding. For food we give the soldiers nothing but bread, and their faces reflect neither health nor vigour; nay more, by their colour and thinness one can spot whole companies and even battalions of sick and ailing men . . .[32]

Barclay's real compassion for 'those who have difficulty in understanding' and even for the 'lazy' set him apart not only from the normal, barbaric majority in the officer class but also from its few abstract humanitarians. To these he sent out a logical appeal: 'The Russian soldier has all the highest military virtues: he is brave, zealous, obedient, devoted, and not wayward; consequently there are certainly ways, without employing cruelty, to train him and to maintain discipline . . .'[33] The Minister of War made it quite clear that he was placing responsibility squarely on the divisional commanders for 'attentive supervision of how officers treat the lower ranks' and for results obtained: 'I have given the order that I be provided monthly with an extract of the regimental reports on the number of sick cases, according to which I shall judge the aptitudes and zeal of the regimental commanders . . .'[34] He sent duplicates of these injunctions to the leading divisional commanders and the leading military governors of Russians towns.

He struggled everywhere for relatively decent rations for the troops, even when this involved dangerous conflict with the navy. The same sea-duty allowance (ten kopecks) was bureaucratically meted out by the naval authorities for supplementing the basic ration (bread), regardless of the availability or cost of foodstuffs at different ports. Barclay pointed out that, as a result, the troops serving with the fleet along the Finnish shores, where food was scarce and very expensive, were inevitably going to fall sick from undernourishment. What, he wanted to know, was the Admiral going to do about it? And to make sure of the Admiral's reactions, Barclay added that he was expressing His Majesty's will.[35]

It cannot be said that Barclay transformed the Russian army into a humane institution. He realized that rigid discipline was a necessity for turning serf recruits into disciplined soldiers. Subject to arbitrary authority since birth, and virtual slaves once in the army, they responded only to strict and systematic treatment. One cannot say how far his reforms would have gone if he had had a completely free hand and a great deal more time as Minister. In the field he was always recognized as 'a commander who, like no one else, cared for the needs of his soldiers'.[36] As a war minister he was something new in Russian history and his attitudes had some impact. The Russian soldier in any case had reason to be grateful for the dissemination of Barclay's notion that starving the troops was false economy.

Civilians, especially foreigners, were also part of Barclay's concern, and this concern, too, was unusual for a military man of that time. It could give rise to peaks of intense anger, like that he fiercely directed upon the leadership of the Danubian army which was tolerating disorder and excesses provoking streams of complaints from the helpless population. For Barclay hated indiscipline as much as he loathed brutality.

Junior officers – in cases both of brutality and indiscipline – were the immediate offenders, though Barclay knew their attitudes and behaviour depended almost entirely on their superiors. Apparently his admonishments concerning their conduct towards soldiers and civilians did have their effect, since serious offences of this kind by junior officers had declined noticeably by 1812.

By that time Barclay was heard to complain only about the inadequate number of junior officers, a source of considerable confusion in an army constantly on the move. But recruitment and formation of sufficient personnel of good quality for the lower ranks was difficult. Edouard Bignon observed that the Russians had good men in the top ranks but were the worst off of any European army for subalterns. The cause, he said, was the lack of regard shown to lieutenants and captains and the near impossibility of promotion without highly placed court intervention.[37] The junior artillery officers were the worst off of the lot, according to Sir Robert Wilson, especially since high-ranking favourites with no artillery experience were often given command of batteries for the day of a battle in order to reap the glory.[38] Even as Minister of War Barclay was in no position to do anything about overturning the institution of favouritism: only the Tsar could have done this but he, of course, thrived on it. Nor could Barclay change the whole social and educational system which produced many ignorant, uncouth, thieving officers who in turn were despised and maltreated by their military superiors. Nevertheless he did strive to awaken the Tsar to their plight and the military danger inherent in it: 'It is essential that we improve the lot of the junior officers and non-commissioned officers, who are worse off than the ordinary soldiers! . . .'[39]

As the preparations for war went forward, Barclay's reputation grew, though his popularity remained limited. He was made personally uncomfortable as well as ministerially concerned by reports that the native peoples of Livonia and Estonia now revered Napoleon as their future liberator, expecting him to expel the nobles, free the peasants, and inaugurate 'a life without law or let'.[40] Recurrent droughts in these two provinces had intensified the misery of the exploited peasant serfs, creating a mood verging on revolt. (Ironically, it was the threat of war itself that caused the postponement of the reforms envisaged just then for the Baltic provinces.) Ambassador de Caulaincourt's comments to Napoleon showed the balance of esteem, despite rampant xenophobia, to be in Barclay's favour: 'He is described as a good administrator. The Russians don't like him because they consider him a foreigner; nevertheless there are no complaints against him, which is saying a good deal and speaks in his favour. As to the Emperor, he appears to be very pleased with his services. . . . *C'est un homme très distingué* . . .'[41] The Tsar was seeing much of Barclay and indeed was liking him more than ever; this 'honest and heavy German', who preferred self-approval to self-advancement, stood out against the mass of sycophants.[42] Alexander's courteous and public solicitude for Barclay's crippled arm impressed civilians and military alike: this was the time (17/29 June 1811) when Barclay was able to write to his wife of 'the particular favour which he bestows on me at every opportunity'.[43]

Not since they were written had anyone tampered with Peter the Great's Army Regulations of 1716. Not only had the changes in warfare – huge armies over vast areas with expensive equipment – made them obsolete, but Barclay's field experience had shown him how confusing was the chain of command and how the overlapping of duties produced wasteful rivalries between units. He had assumed office with his mind set on remedying the situation. He appointed, under his own chairmanship, a commission of competent general officers (Prince Volkonskii, Generals Oppermann, Meller-Zakomel'skii, and others) to prepare the new set of rules, and a small working group under Mikhail Magnitskii, a public figure of some renown, to submit first drafts to the commission.[44]

The new regulations, which took almost two years to complete, were awkwardly titled 'Regulations for the Functioning of a Large Army in the Field' but were referred to, because of their yellow binding, as the 'Yellow Book'.[45] The book consisted of 161 pages containing 514 numbered and succinct articles. The first part devoted 61 articles to the powers and prerogatives of the supreme commander, the general staff, the commanders-in-chief, corps and divisional commanders, and their respective staffs.

The very first paragraphs dealt with the paramount question of the relationship of the supreme commander to the Tsar. The supreme commander represented the Tsar and was invested with his authority. When the monarch was present at army headquarters, however, the supreme commander was automatically relieved of that authority, which reverted to the Tsar, unless the latter specifically ordered him to remain in overall command (§18). The observance of this article became a question of first importance in 1812.

Among the responsibilities of a commander-in-chief was the maintenance of order in his army wherever it might be (§23). He was accountable for his troops' carelessness or misdemeanours, if these were brought to the Government's attention and had not been punished by the commanders concerned (§25). Barclay's experience and horror of laxity in discipline, his memories of Ochakov, were reflected in these and similar clauses. Any negligence on the part of a commander-in-chief in exercising his authority was considered an offence and, depending on its seriousness, could lead to recall, outright dismissal, or court martial (§26, §27).

The second and larger part of the Yellow Book dealt with the functions of fifteen branches of the army. The role of the Military Police, for example, was covered in ten general rules broken down into very specific detail. Among the duties of the Military Police Chief (*general gewal'diger*) were the uncovering, reporting, and punishing of such infractions as boisterous revelry, drunkenness, card games, and the presence of loitering or disreputable females (§160). The *general gewal'diger* was also responsible for requisitioning all horses and carriages belonging to individual officers in excess of the limit prescribed by the army, turning the extra horses over to the artillery park and auctioning off the unauthorized vehicles, dividing the proceeds amongst the non-commissioned officers and convoy escorts of his command (§170). Barclay's attitude towards luxury and dissipation within the army was evident in these rather perfectionist articles.

Nothing, in sum, seems to have been overlooked in this very thorough piece of work. Barclay's Regulations remained in force – with a few minor additions appended ten years later – until the 1860s and 1870s, when the army was completely reorganized by Count Miliutin, who had had twenty years as Alexander II's Minister of War and a relatively liberal era in which to do the job: the emancipation of the serfs, in particular, made for a completely new recruitment situation.

Judgements on the value of the Regulations have been consistently favourable, from Schubert's contemporary view of their 'immense benefit for Russia' and his optimistic assessment that their creation was 'in itself sufficient to have Barclay de Tolly's name for ever extolled in Russia',[46] to quasi-official present-day Soviet recognition that they constituted 'an outstanding event in the history of the Russian army',[47] and 'a very important charter'.[48]

The Tsar made comments and suggestions throughout the period of preparation, and eagerly signed the first page of the final document on the day it was put in his hands (27 January/8 February 1812). It went immediately to the printer and was distributed to all officers and other officials concerned. On the same day the Tsar also approved Barclay's new structure for the Ministry, now to consist of seven departments and a number of special services including a newly created Committee on Military Science to replace two previous branches on ballistics and topography.[49] A few days later the Tsar bestowed on Barclay for his ministerial accomplishments the Order of St. Vladimir First Class. It was now less than five months before the Grande Armée was to cross the Neman'; Barclay's essential reorganizations and reforms were completed just in time.

When Russia's old ally, Austria, signed under heavy pressure an alliance with France in April 1812, all Metternich's unconvincing attempts to describe Austria as 'neutral', although warring, did not pacify Alexander. (Metternich later secretly assured him that Austria would contribute only 30,000 men and would restrain them near the border.) The Tsar, very angry, told Barclay of a scheme for rousing the Slavs in the Balkans against Austria and helping them unite with the rebellious Hungarians. Alexander instructed Admiral Chichagov, the father of the scheme, 'to use all possible means to stir up the Slavic populations in order to lead them to our ends'.[50] Chichagov's chief collaborator was the Greek patriot who had been in Russia's service since after Tilsit, Count Capodistria, who was assigned to supply money and arms to the Serbs and direct propaganda through a consular network in the Ottoman Empire. So carried away was Chichagov by his imperial mission that when he became head of the Moldavian army, now the Army of the South (replacing Kutuzov after the Bucharest Treaty of May 1812), he proposed attacks not only in Dalmatia and Illyria but on Constantinople itself. For a moment, until he was ordered northwards out of harm's way, the foolhardy Admiral threatened to undo Barclay's endeavours for peace with Turkey.

In joining with France, Austria had only followed Prussia's example, though Prussia's reasons were far more compelling: French troops occupied all key Prussian fortresses and fortifications. Until Napoleon applied the final pressure of threatening war, however, King Frederick William III, the third man at Tilsit, still considered throwing in his lot with his old ally Alexander. In a letter to the Tsar dated 16 July (N.S.) 1811, the King stressed their 'mutual interests'.[51] The Prussian General Scharnhorst visited St. Petersburg and signed an agreement (5/17 October 1811) of military co-operation. Plans were afoot for forming a German Legion under General Gneisenau to operate behind the French lines.[52] And Barclay, heartened by these developments, immediately drew up an operational plan: if the French crossed the Oder and the Vistula, the armies of Russia, Prussia, Poland, and Sweden were to attack.[53] This was a wasted effort, however, since Napoleon forced an alliance on Prussia on 24 February (N.S.) 1812. The Tsar sent word to the King that Russia intended all the same to let Prussia gain the advantages of a Russian victory over Napoleon regardless of the Franco–Prussian alliance.[54] This seemed optimistic for French hegemony in Europe was now almost complete. The only countries not aligned with France were England, Portugal, Sardinia, and Sweden (the fear of Bernadotte's persisting loyalty to Napoleon was unfounded), all at the extremities of France's central European mass of empire and alliances. Alexander knew, however, that this mass lacked cohesion, while the problems of his own vast, map-covering empire were, by comparison, insignificant.

Among the foreigners flocking to St. Petersburg after their own countries had become dependencies of Napoleon was Baron Ludwig von Wolzogen, a native of the Duchy of Saxe-Meiningen and erstwhile aide-de-camp of the King of Württemberg. After having served four years in the Russian army Wolzogen was introduced by his protector, General von Phull, to the Tsar. Alexander liked him, took him into his confidence, and soon the thirty-eight-year-old Wolzogen shared with Barclay, Phull, and the Tsar in the secrets of planning for the forthcoming campaign. The newcomer was attached to Barclay's staff and sent by him at the Tsar's behest to survey once again the terrain between the four rivers Dvina, Neman', Dnepr, and Bug. Barclay's eight-point written instructions were based on the original defensive plans he had submitted to the Tsar and which the Tsar had approved in the spring of 1810. But, knowing that sooner or later offensive action would be required, Barclay wanted Wolzogen to prepare a dependable estimate of the terrain's suitability for both kinds of warfare.[55] From July until September 1811 Wolzogen made an exhaustive study of the region and submitted his findings to Barclay in eight detailed reports.[56]

Wolzogen's mission was complicated by his having received a different oral briefing from the Tsar and Phull. For them his job was to locate a site for the entrenched camp which was at the heart of Phull's proposed strategy; eventually he selected Drissa, 160 miles inside the border. Reduced to its bare bones, Phull's plan called for dividing Russia's main forces into two separate armies of which the larger would withdraw to a fortified camp modelled after the Bunzelwitz camp of Phull's idol, Frederick the Great, while the smaller one would operate against the enemy's flank and rear. (Phull's plan had been developed in bits and pieces in separate lectures to the Tsar; only six years after the war did Phull put it on paper in an historical essay attempting to justify his scheme.) All his ideas were based on flanking positions and movements and on the unexamined assumption of Russian numerical superiority. Despite his sober evaluation of Napoleon's military genius and war-hardened army, Phull confidently expected to see this army so weakened by its march to Drissa that it would be immobilized before the camp, neither daring to attack nor to expose its right flank by trying to bypass the camp in the direction of St. Petersburg. On the other hand, if Napoleon's destination turned out to be Kiev and the rich Ukraine, the role of the two Russian armies would be reversed: the Second

Army was to withdraw to Bobruisk fortress and farther, while it would be up to the First Army to smash Napoleon's left flank. Beyond this first phase of the conflict, Phull had nothing to offer. The Tsar, failing to see the limitations of this abstract conception, gave Phull's scheme his unofficial nod. But Barclay's plan was also kept, and all essential reconnaissance and cartographic activities throughout the period of war preparations corresponded to Barclay's design.[57]

As the threat of war increased, other strategic proposals were offered in abundance, mostly in ignorance of Barclay's having long ago worked out a basic strategy which he had been implementing since early 1810 with imperial approval. Almost all these new proposals were very general in nature and almost all struck the same note as Barclay's, counselling defensive operations until such time as the enemy was weakened through exhaustion and its supply lines lengthened beyond usefulness. Wolzogen's plan added an argument of merit, suggesting in effect that Napoleon's unusual gifts would always give him the advantage over his opponents in a pitched battle, because he could think and act faster. Therefore Wolzogen recommended avoiding major battles unless having a great superiority in numbers, adequate supplies, and a strong position – with a secure line of withdrawal in case of need. To outwit a commander of genius, said Wolzogen prophetically, one must show perseverance in adversity, operate with cold wisdom, and mix prudence with vigour.[58]

Thinking along the same general lines as Barclay's was apparent in the policies put forward by Prince Volkonskii, Admiral Mordvinov, the French expatriate Count d'Allonville, and the Dutch colonel in Russian service, Baron Tuyll van Serasken. Particularly pleased by the latter's project, which fully confirmed his own, Barclay noted that van Serasken 'has outlined the correct and only applicable principles'.[59] Others supporting a protracted defensive war included Count Lieven, Colonel Chernyshev, Sweden's Bernadotte, and Prussia's special envoy von Knesebeck, who was in a position to have known of Barclay's talks with Niebuhr in 1807.

Many of the proposals held up as an example of sound strategy Wellington's successful campaign in the Peninsular War, overlooking the difference in terrain between Torres Vedras and the endless flatlands of western Russia. There were also some proponents of a pre-emptive strike in the Duchy of Warsaw and of a scorched-earth policy there, ideas which Barclay was putting forward at this time. Finally, some, notably Generals Bennigsen and Bagration, advocated an outright offensive war. This view was shared by most of the educated public.

The suggestions and projects piled up, but no choice was made. Barclay went ahead with his preparations despite imperial vacillations, the Tsar sometimes favouring his Minister's energetic plans for anticipating Napoleon with strikes in Poland and Prussia, sometimes going back to Barclay's formulations in Memel in 1807 for leading Napoleon to his ruin, and sometimes foreseeing a quick victory by lying in wait in Phull's fortified camp. In the spring of 1811 Alexander had revealed separately to the King of Prussia and to Caulaincourt (who took notes and repeated the conversation to Napoleon in Paris on 5 June (N.S.) 1811) the primary Russian strategy for withdrawal.[60] Alexander had pointed out that Russia was huge, there was plenty of margin for ceding terrain and drawing Napoleon far from his country and resources while Russia conserved a well-organized army, and that Russia was prepared for perseverance, endurance, and suffering: 'I would rather pull back to Kamchatka than cede provinces and sign treaties in my capital. . . . Frenchmen are brave, but long privations and the bad climate will distress and discourage them . . .'[61] Barclay's current enthusiasm for beating Napoleon to the draw thus seemed after all to be out of order in this scheme of things, especially in terms of Alexander's *mot* to Caulaincourt: 'I will not be the first to draw my sword, but I shall be the last to sheath it . . .'[62]

During all this time the burden on Barclay was very great, though on the whole he thrived on the work, became concentrated and ever more forceful under stress and with the awareness of the tremendous stakes. Nevertheless constant adaptation to the Tsar's changing opinions, the fencing with advisers and ministers with discordant views, and the incessant efforts of persuasion produced frustration and strain.

For diversion there was chiefly the family circle. Keeping an eye on Magnus's education, and ushering his flock of foster-children to the Lutheran church on the Nevsky Prospekt, the same church, the meeting place for Germans, Swedes, and Balts, where he had spent his boyhood Sundays. Included in the family circle were now his elder brother Erich (at that point a colonel in the engineers on General Oppermann's staff in St. Petersburg) with his wife Margarethe (first cousin to Erich, Michael, and Auguste), and their son Andreas, soon to be Michael's adjutant.

In the summer months, however, all but Erich and Andreas deserted him for Beckhof, Auguste's family estate in Livonia, bought from her brother during Barclay's first summer in office.[63] Even though Barclay himself was too busy in these pre-war summers to take advantage of Beckhof, it was a source of satisfaction for him to be at last a landowner and have a proper refuge and home for his family.

One of the happiest events of this period was a reunion with his sister Christine, who came from Estonia for a long winter visit, bringing her bright little seven-year-old Christel for adoption as foster-daughter by the Barclays. Since Michael and Christine had been children together at the Vermeulens, the changes in St. Petersburg were astonishing. The granite embankments of the Fontanka had been finished and greatly built up, and it was here that Christine found the Barclays living in ministerial state, on such 'a great footing' that it seemed better, after all, that Christel return for the time being to country life with her parents. Here it was that Barclay led his niece to the window to show her how she could watch the Tsar go past every day at three o'clock. (Alexander was on his punctual way to visit his mistress, Countess Naryshkin.) And here Christel observed with a seven-year-old's scorn the general commotion involved in her aunt's elaborate dressing-up for court appearances.[64]

For Barclay, dressing up and putting in time-consuming attendance at dinners, parties, balls, were among the most onerous of his duties. His position, moreover, required him to reciprocate.[65] At such times his tall, aloof figure reigned unobtrusively in his ballroom on the Fontanka, and the foster-daughters (at least those who were old enough) whirled in delight. No one, to be sure, thought to compare a Barclay ball with those like Potemkin's which had made St. Petersburg history, but an invitation from the Minister of War nevertheless carried considerable prestige.

All Europe seemed to be dancing as the war came close and closer. In St. Petersburg and Paris, in Vienna and Vilna, the cotillons, mazurkas, and polonaises tinkled lightly over the crescendo of tramping boots, cadenced hoofs, and thudding gun carriages and wagon trains. By January 1812 hundreds of thousands of men were drawn, as if by magnet, from all over Europe in the direction of Russia's frontier.

As these armies – an unprecedented mass movement of French, German, Austrian, Dutch, Italian, Swiss, Spanish, Croat, and Polish troops – drew near, Barclay kept under steady control the onslaught of dispatches that couriers at full gallop speeded to his desk. Urgent messages flooded in from the generals, wherever in the field they happened to be – Wittgenstein in Schaueln, Baggavut in Vilna, Essen I in Slonim, Prince Bagration in Zhitomir. An avalanche of alarming intelligence reports piled up from Russian embassies abroad and listening outposts near the Polish border – from Colonel Turskii in Białystock and the Marquis de Laizer in Kovno. Queries and conflicting counsels poured in. Chernyshev, in one of his last long reports from Paris, urged Barclay to adopt the tactics of Fabius and Wellington.[66] Count Lieven, Russian Ambassador in Berlin, reported (16/28 March 1812) the approach of Marshals Ney and Oudinot, and the even more alarming news that Marshal Davout's Corps was pushing on and had already reached the Oder. Lieven also warned of the imminent arrival in Berlin of the Administrative Section of Napoleon's headquarters.[67] This staff (about 400) was headed by Count Mathieu Dumas, the Intendant General of the Grande Armée. During the Directory terror, Dumas had been sentenced to deportation to Cayenne but had managed to escape to Southern Dithmarschen in the Duchy of Holstein, where he met the famous explorer of Arabia, Karsten Niebuhr, and became warm friends with the family. On arrival in Berlin in March 1812, therefore, Dumas promptly looked up Karsten Niebuhr's son, Barthold Georg, whom he had not seen since the latter had become friendly with Barclay in Memel. A main topic, as they dined, was the great war which was about to break out. Niebuhr was pessimistic: 'Never since the crusades and the barbarian invasions have such enormous masses been pitted against each other.'[68] Dumas discussed some of the French plans, and Niebuhr in turn told of his talks with Barclay and all the details, 'perfectly remembered', of his plan for 'combined retreats'. For Dumas, Barclay's plan was a terrifying revelation: 'The Russian general hoped to lure this formidable French army into the heart of Russia, even beyond Moscow, exhausting it, removing it far from its operational line, making it use up its resources and *matériel*, whilst husbanding Russia's reserves until, aided by the rigours of the climate, he could take the offensive and deal Napoleon a second Poltava on the banks of the Volga.'[69]

Though convinced that Barclay would put his plan into execution, Niebuhr nevertheless felt that Russia did not have a chance. He thought that no 'soberminded person' could entertain any doubts about the outcome of the war, and he had put on paper that he expected it to be a very short one.[70] His opinion was shared by many in the Prussian King's entourage who, remembering Austerlitz and Friedland, considered the Tsar weak, his generals incompetent, and his army unreliable. But Dumas was deeply impressed by Niebuhr's account of Barclay's intended strategy, and passed on the warning as fast as he could: 'This was a fearful and faultless prophecy; it seemed to me so plausible and so momentous that, on rejoining Imperial Headquarters, I did not neglect to inform the Prince of Wagram [Marshal Berthier] of it. I could not doubt that the Prince reported the matter to the Emperor; but there was no further mention of it to me and I cautiously refrained from repeating these sinister predictions...'[71] Despite his fears, Dumas was not a man to insist. He was never to know the tenuous reasons which, as will appear, induced Napoleon to make light of these 'sinister predictions'.

Suddenly, command in the field became a more critical matter than running the Ministry of War. Alexander abruptly named Barclay Commander-in-Chief of the First Army (the larger of the two figuring in Phull's plan), in place of Essen I. After arranging for his household to follow him to headquarters at Vilna, Barclay rushed first to Riga to inspect its fortress, spending a few minutes with his cousin, Baron August Wilhelm von Barclay de Tolly, and the other members of the 'dear, good Barclay family' there. On 31 March/12 April 1812 the new Commander-in-Chief arrived in Vilna.

He left as deputy to run the War Ministry Lieutenant-General Prince Andrey Gorchakov, who inherited a well-ordered, effective organization. Although the urgent pre-war demands of the times precluded sweeping innovations, in Barclay's two years he had reformed the Ministry, reorganized combat leadership, introduced sorely needed new army regulations, and mobilized all available resources, both human and material, for the decisive encounter with Napoleon. His accomplishments, along with his championship of the common soldier and his attack against brutality, place him as the worthy precursor of Dmitri Miliutin.

The Tsar, who had spent a very great number of hours in these two years leaning forward with his 'good' right ear to catch Barclay's words, knew that the man he had chosen as Minister of War in 1810 had proved to be an 'extraordinary administrator and organizer',[72] not the least of whose achievements, as Beskrovnyi has pointed out, was making it possible for the Russians to mobilize and move their troops rapidly for deployment along the western frontier.[73]

CHAPTER IX

RETREAT

Confirming what Xenophon, what the Duke of Parma, and what Moreau had practised, . . . *retreats* in the presence of a *superior force* are not necessarily races . . . *conduct*, and not *speed*, can alone *prevent* inglorious disasters, more ruinous and fatal than the enemy's fire.

Sir Robert Wilson, Brief Remarks on the Character and Composition of the Russian Army . . .

The command situation Barclay faced at Vilna, and after, was the cause of a good number of his and Russia's trials. He was Commander-in-Chief of the First West Army. Bagration – who now scorned him and his ideas – was Commander-in-Chief of the Second West Army. The Tsar had lacked the courage to name either one of them Supreme Commander, knowing he would thus offend the other, and in any case Alexander really saw only himself in that role.* Moreover, his sister the Grand Duchess Catherine and Prince Bagration had been very close earlier on and Catherine at nineteen had written compromising letters to the dashing General, who thus became someone to be treated gingerly. Bagration had the reputation of being Suvorov's heir, he was a man men followed, a mythic hero to his underlings, as brave, wild, and strong as Hercules. But Barclay, though encumbered by his reputation as an 'honest and heavy German' and lacking Bagration's swagger, had nevertheless prepared this war and shown forethought and common sense, qualities truly uncommon near the throne. Barclay was four years the older but Bagration had seniority in rank and never let Barclay forget the fact; the Tsar's compromise appointments pleased neither and settled nothing. Barclay's First Army of over 100,000 men was roughly three times larger than Bagration's Second Army of 35,000 or so.† Barclay, moreover, was still Minister of War and thus entitled to issue orders to all the armies, and to all the high-born generals senior to himself. So in an undefined way he had the responsibilities of a supreme commander without the title, without the true power, and with the crucial limitation of being subject in all his words and actions to his thirty-five-year-old master the Tsar, eager as ever to make his name as a great military leader.

---

* Confusion between the terms 'commander-in-chief' and 'supreme commander' – which is common not only in Western writing about the 1812 campaign but also in Russian sources – stems in part from the frequent use of *glavnokomanduiushchii* for both, instead of invariably preceding this word by *verkhovnyi* ('supreme') when referring to the latter.
† Estimates of First Army strength at the outset of hostilities vary roughly from 100,000 to 130,000, and, for the Second Army, from 35,000 to 48,000. The lower estimates are probably more accurate, but precision appears to be impossible.

When Barclay left Riga for Vilna he sent a courier speeding back to St. Petersburg urging the Tsar once again to take the initiative – at least to let Barclay put the frontier provinces from Vilna to Kiev on a war footing.[1] But his pleas fell on deaf ears: St. Petersburg chose for the moment not to believe after all in the imminence of attack. Barclay of course, and the Tsar, were fully informed of the massing of Napoleon's might in the north-east corner of Poland, the Grand Duchy of Warsaw. It was clear that the corps of Marshals Davout, Oudinot, and Ney, and Murat's cavalry were gathering for invasion. Without an explicit order from the Tsar, however, the commanders-in-chief could not make a move along Russia's borders lest it be interpreted as signifying war – and the prerogative for that decision rested with the Tsar. Alexander, to ensure Barclay's passivity, sent him a copy of Napoleon's treaty with Austria, pointing out that a single Russian step over the border would make war 'inevitable'. So determined was Alexander to avoid even the appearance of provocation that he left the armies without contingency orders. 'My commanders still do not know the limits to which an approach of the enemy can be tolerated,' Barclay wrote to the Tsar on 9/21 April.[2] To avoid giving Napoleon any excuse for accusing Russia of belligerency, no border defences were allowed, no artillery was positioned on the Neman''s right bank at crucial places around and south of Kovno, and no boundary forces stood in waiting for the invader. In fact no real border precautions were taken at all. Even the collecting of intelligence appears to have faltered.

Trying to allay Barclay's anxieties, the Tsar wrote soothingly that as soon as he reached Vilna, 'we shall determine our definitive further actions'.[3] Eagerly, therefore, Barclay cantered out on Palm Sunday, 14–26 April (two weeks after his own arrival in Vilna), to welcome Alexander and escort him and his large suite into town. Their entrance, to pealing church bells and earth-shaking cannon salutes, brought tumultuous cheering from a nearly ecstatic population. The simple presence of the godlike Tsar seemed sufficient to guarantee safety and joy. Immediately the balls, receptions, and parades began, while the 'thorough examination of what is to be done next', which Alexander had promised Barclay, seemed to lose its urgency.[4] According to the Yellow Book 'Regulations' the monarch, now at army headquarters, was officially Supreme Commander, but he and all his retinue and indeed all Vilna seemed to be overwhelmed by a general impulse to flee reality. The Lithuanian nobility, though it had historical reason to be anti-Russian, fêted Alexander with feverish extravagance. Half a millennium earlier the Lithuanian grand dukes had made Vilna their capital. They had proceeded eastward, annexing Russian territory, taking Smolensk. For protection against Russian revenge the Grand Duchy of Lithuania – one of the largest states in Europe during the Middle Ages – then merged with Poland, but in the end was swallowed up by Russia in the course of the three partitions of Poland. Despite this history and despite the fact that the large estate owners had been suffering ever since Tilsit from the loss of western markets (as a result of Russia's adherence to the Continental System), the Roman Catholic aristocrats of Lithuania nevertheless fawned upon their Russian Tsar in the spring of 1812. Outweighing all other factors was their panic fear, shared by almost all Russian landowners, that Napoleon would free the serfs as he took over and occupied their lands. Therefore they outdid themselves in entertainments, and for two months Russian officers revelled in Lithuanian hospitality with hardly a thought of war.

By this time Barclay had realized that the moment for pre-emptive strikes was long passed. All the Russians consistently underestimated Napoleon's forces, however. Barclay and Phull judged their total at 200,000 to 250,000; Bagration's maximum was 200,000; Colonel Toll estimated 220,000; and Bennigsen, 169,000. Former French marshal Bernadotte misjudged worst of all: 150,000.[5] Actually the French advantage was colossal despite the inroads already made by typhus. In round figures Napoleon had 675,000 men poised for invasion, of whom he was to use about half a million to cross into Russian territory while keeping 226,000 in reserve east of the Oder.[6] The forces he took into Russia thus outnumbered Barclay and Bagration together – and they were not together – by almost four to one.

What consensus there was at the top, among the Tsar's advisers, was limited to the principle that the war should fall into two phases, the first phase consisting of defensive warfare on home territory, and the second, after the rout of Napoleon's armies, consisting of carrying the war to central and western Europe. Along with this there was also some agreement that the war should be dragged out and war production accordingly geared for a three-year period.[7] But as to how to get through the first phase, opinions diverged. There was no proper, authoritative General Staff to devise policy and impose it. Instead, as Thiers remarked, the Russian generals formed a military oligarchy. Schubert, an observant young staff officer, described the disorder: 'In the Tsar's entourage everyone was bent on getting himself noticed and showing off his importance. From every side advice and campaign plans were proposed and it took all of Barclay's steadiness not to lose his head while warding off all the fresh projects and the budding intrigues against himself . . .'[8] The Tsar, Supreme Commander on whom everything hinged and without whose at least implicit approval nothing could be undertaken, listened affably to all ideas, making every advocate feel that he alone had gained ultimate sanction. Thus Alexander daily increased the confusion inherent in the command situation. He was 'too weak to govern and too strong to be governed', as Speranskii had found.[9]

Phull's and Barclay's opinions carried the most weight with the Tsar, but since there was no real agreement between them and their policies had no real relation to each other – something which the Tsar did not grasp – a gap between plans and execution was the inevitable result. Phull's proposal, though unofficially accepted by the Tsar, had had no bearing at all on the war preparations undertaken by Barclay with the full knowledge and assent of the Tsar. The Drissa site, uselessly off on the periphery of the strategic approaches to Smolensk and Moscow, had been chosen only in August 1811. It was not even among the places Barclay had been fortifying and it was not until the last minute, April 1812, that work on the entrenched camp began. Barclay had seen no reason for rushing to divert manpower to a scheme which could succeed only if his First Army had nearly equalled the whole of Napoleon's army. None of the commanding generals in the field seems to have had knowledge of the Drissa scheme. No mention of it appears in any of the instructions Barclay sent them in April, May, or June 1812. What these orders did emphasize was that decisive battles with a superior enemy were to be avoided, while, on the other hand, in the course of a slow retreat, inferior enemy forces were to be engaged and if possible annihilated. Barclay also laid great stress on actions by 'irregular' troops (mostly Cossacks): they were never to lose sight of the enemy and were to harass him day and night in his flanks and rear, disrupting his movements and supply lines. And from the start Barclay laid down in detail a scorched-earth policy, essential to a strategy of withdrawal. As invasion drew near and still campaign plans proliferated at headquarters, he rushed specific instructions to the men in the field, for example telling General Tormassov, Commander-in-Chief of the Third Army, exactly what steps to take at the outbreak of hostilities: 'Tear down everything, especially hospitals, that may serve the enemy; rob him of every chance to lay hands on provisions or conveyances; burn and destroy bridges, boats, and magazines . . . ; carry off or wreck all available carts and harness; leave the inhabitants only what they need for their own sustenance . . .'[10]

Despite the differences between Barclay and Phull and despite all the rest of the disagreements and confusion at headquarters, it has nevertheless been argued, notably by Pugachev, that there did finally emerge a fundamental Russian strategy for the coming campaign and that it consisted of three elements: the withdrawal of the First Army to Drissa, the junction of the two main armies as early as possible, and the avoidance of any major battle with a superior enemy.[11] To be sure, Barclay and Bagration were against the first element while Bagration and many others failed to grasp or support the third. The untidiness of the genesis, diffusion, and application of this policy has led some historians to the belief, best countered by Pugachev, that the Russians simply improvised in mere reaction to Napoleon's moves without having any basic strategy of their own. The real trouble, however, as Beskrovnyi has pointed out, was the existence at headquarters of not one but two operational plans.[12]

It was in the very early hours of 12/24 June that, as Barclay wrote, 'the great tempest broke'. There had been no feeling of a storm in the air as, earlier on, the Tsar was dressing in Semenovskii Lifeguard uniform for a grand ball at Bennigsen's sumptuous estate at Zakret on the outskirts of Vilna, even though at the same time, less than a hundred miles away, Napoleon was impatiently watching his sappers throw three bridges across the Neman' in record time. Only some pickets of a Lifeguard Cossack regiment observed the first columns of Marshal Davout's Corps cross over into Russian territory. Only then did a courier speed off to Vilna as fast as Cossack horse could ride.

Under the same full moon that lighted the crossing of the Neman', Alexander opened the Zakret ball with his hostess, Baroness Bennigsen, dutifully danced the second dance with Barclay's wife and then, forsaking obligation for pleasure combined with politics, partnered Countess Tyzenhaus, an effervescent fourteen-year-old Polish-Lithuanian. At that moment the dispatch rider arrived at Vilna headquarters and in no time the Minister of Police, Balashov, was whispering the news to the Tsar. Alexander's discreet withdrawal marked the end of the ball and the beginning of consternation. Soon another messenger arrived bringing word that Napoleon had already reached Kovno, only sixty miles away. The jolt into reality had occurred.

Instead of a declaration of war Napoleon simply issued a proclamation to his soldiers announcing the beginning of 'the second Polish War', accusing Russia of provoking it, and promising to end 'the arrogant influence which Russia had exercised for fifty years on the affairs of Europe'. (His oratory never failed to produce the desired effect on his troops.) Naturally he made no mention of having decided ten months previously to wage this war (announced at his St. Cloud Council of State, 17 August [N.S.] 1811) and of having even fixed upon June 1812 for the invasion date. Alexander, on Rumiantsev's advice, had a last futile try at dissuasion in a letter he entrusted to Balashov for delivery to Napoleon. But at the same time, and more realistically, Alexander issued an order of the day which announced the war to his troops and denounced the unprovoked aggression. After reminding his soldiers that the blood of valorous Slavs flowed in their veins, he ended with an exalted and characteristic parallel: 'I am with you. God is against the aggressor!'

Barclay's own order, as Minister of War, surpassed even the Tsar's in patriotic rhetoric: 'You were born, you were raised, and you shall die with the splendid traits which distinguish you from other peoples . . .'[13]

Barclay correctly supposed that what Napoleon was seeking was another Marengo, Jena, Wagram, another Austerlitz or Friedland: a quick, smashing victory followed by a quick, smashing peace treaty. If, however, these plans for an immediate decisive battle were somehow not realized or if Alexander was not ready for a prompt surrender, Napoleon at this point saw Smolensk as his ultimate objective for 1812. The Grande Armée would live comfortably in winter quarters, an enormous, fat army of occupation, and would finish off the Russians in the first thaw of spring: 'We shall see which of us will tire first: I of feeding an army at the expense of Russia or Alexander of maintaining it at the expense of his own country . . . The affair is a question of time . . .'[14] But Napoleon did not really believe that he would need time as his ally. Just before crossing the Vistula he wrote to Marie-Louise to expect him home in three months.[15] And just before crossing the Neman' he told Caulaincourt that Russia would sue for peace in less than two months. Knowing his (unmerited) reputation as a liberator of serfs, he added sagaciously, 'The great landowners will be frightened and some of them ruined. Emperor Alexander will be in very deep water . . .'[16] With his far superior forces, Napoleon's aim had to be to conquer quickly before the divided Russian forces could unite.

Echoes of the polonaises at Bennigsen's ball had not yet died down when Alexander hurriedly called an improvised war council. At the end of this meeting Barclay's adjutants rode off to the points along a 120-mile stretch where the command posts of the five corps of the First Army were situated. They carried Barclay's orders to withdraw according to plan. The first step, the first element, was Drissa, and the Russian forces were commanded now to act out Phull's plan, even though the arrangements were those of an unpractical theorist and the isolation of the armies seemed to offer a perfect opportunity to Napoleon to fight his one great battle and be done. Thus Barclay's First West Army, headquartered at Vilna, had orders to withdraw to Drissa; Bagration's much smaller Second West Army, south of Volkovysk, was to smash any force Napoleon sent against it and then, with Ataman Platov's Cossacks who were stationed just north of the Second Army, attack the rear of the Grande Armée as it followed Barclay to Drissa; and Tormassov's Third West Army, still forming south of the Pripet Marshes, was to hold off the Austrians.

Barclay had placed his First Army in a slender north–south curve from Rossieny to Lida. Northernmost was Wittgenstein, then Baggavut, with Uvarov (cavalry) to their rear, making up the First Army's right flank. The centre, resting on Vilna, consisted of Tuchkov and of Grand Duke Constantine's Imperial Lifeguards. The left flank, south of Vilna, consisted of Shuvalov – succeeded almost at once by Ostermann-Tolstoy – with Korff (cavalry) to his rear. The left flank was protected by Dokhturov, who had been detached from Bagration's Second Army.

All these corps now began responding smartly to Barclay's prearranged orders, retreating by and large in a north-easterly direction towards Drissa, while *fel'djaeger* messengers also speeded to Bagration and Platov to initiate their planned moves. The Tsar's own next move, though part of the agreed-upon plan, was carried out with a singular lack of style. After hearing how speedily Murat's cavalry was advancing towards Vilna, the monarch and his military and diplomatic staffs made a frantic exit. Barclay witnessed their unseemly departure for Sventsiany and tried to counteract the impression it made on officers and troops by delaying his own departure until his rearguard – formed by the Cossack Lifeguard regiment – was in sight. Until then he busied the troops in methodically firing the vast depots of equipment and supplies impossible to load and transport quickly enough and too precious to be left to the enemy. Refusing to be hurried, he ordered the systematic packing up of the municipal archives of Vilna (and of all Lithuanian towns still unconquered) and he evacuated the public officials. This done, instead of mounting his horse as he would normally have done, he walked slowly to his carriage and deliberately seated himself, while fumes rose all around from the burning stores, adding their heat to the torrid day. His timing had been very nicely calculated. Looking back, he could see the whirling dust clouds announcing the approach of his Cossack rearguard squadrons, while the last of these squadrons, farther off, were already fending off attacks by a squadron of French *chevau-légers* (light cavalry). The French, commanded by Colonel Octave-Henri de Ségur (elder brother of Philippe, chronicler of the 1812 campaign), clashed with the Cossacks just outside abandoned Zakret. The Cossacks were victorious, the wounded Colonel de Ségur being one of their three hundred prisoners and the first prisoner of rank in the war of 1812.[17]

Within hours of Barclay's measured departure, Napoleon entered silent,

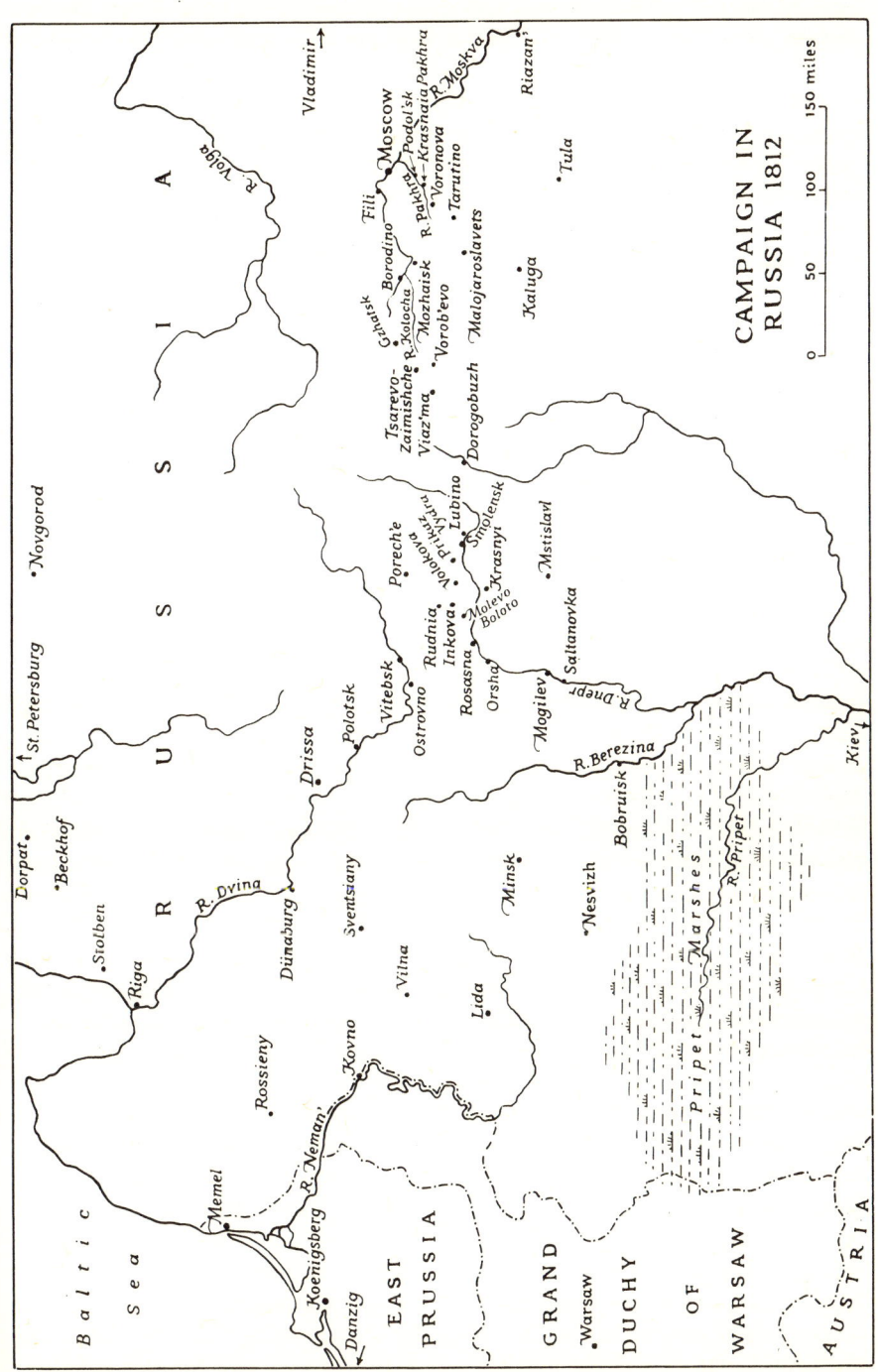

heat-drenched Vilna under a still smouldering sky (16/28 June). Frustrated and furious at finding no defending army to be conquered, he supposedly ranted to the Tsar's envoy, Balashov: 'I am not acquainted with Barclay de Tolly but, judging from the start of this campaign, I am forced to think he has but little military talent. None of your wars has begun in such disorder. How many depots have been burned and why? Why were they built if you weren't going to use them properly? Did you think I had come just to look at the Neman' and not to cross it?' Napoleon continued to berate Barclay, as Balashov much later recalled the scene: 'Aren't you ashamed? Never since Peter the First, since Russia became a European power, has an enemy penetrated your lands; but here at Vilna I have conquered a whole province without fighting. You should have defended Vilna, if only out of respect for your Emperor . . .'[18] Napoleon was expressing the view of most Russians as well, and Barclay's name at once became associated with national shame. Admiral Shishkov, close to the Tsar, successor to the ousted Speranskii as State Secretary, spoke tearfully for many: 'How can this be? To lose Vilna five days after the start of hostilities? To flee, leaving all those acres and villages to the enemy, and yet boast of a good beginning? What more does the adversary need? He has only to enter our two capitals without finding an obstacle in his way! . . .'[19]

Shishkov's 'hot tears' show how little was the basic strategy of the war known and accepted even in the highest circles. The understanding between Barclay and the Tsar that no major battle be engaged until the First and Second Armies joined seems, almost incredibly, to have been kept almost secret (though Arakcheev and Volkonskii were privy to it). At any rate the Tsar made no loud claims of responsibility for the retreat now in progress; even in these first days he was silent when it came to backing up Barclay publicly for carrying out the withdrawal to Drissa. While accepting Barclay's basic objective of preserving Russia's forces until they could equal the enemy's strength, the sovereign was not ready to shoulder the consequences. Barclay was prepared to surrender as much land as necessary; but the Tsar could accept this only up to a point, especially since most of Barclay's fellow generals were foolhardily crying for immediate battle. In the circumstances, so Pugachev contends, Barclay resorted whenever necessary to dissembling, in order to pursue the only plan which could save Russia.[20]

The wretched two months Barclay had spent in Vilna had convinced him that he was ill served both by his Chief of Staff, the clumsy General Lavrov, and by Mukhin, his Quartermaster-General, who, though a splendid draughtsman and cartographer, was totally inadequate as chief of operations: in the Russian army of this time, the chief of staff took care of administration and personnel, while the quartermaster-general looked after military operations. Barclay replaced Lavrov with, on a hint from the Tsar, Marquis Paulucci, who had achieved some distinction in the wars against Persia and Turkey.[21] Despite his high backing, Paulucci, a cynic and a mocker, lasted only ten days as Chief of Staff before Barclay turned him out in favour of a serious soldier, the outspoken General Alexei Ermolov, Bagration's friend. Ermolov was a powerful-looking thirty-five, packed with energy and drive, a high-spirited bully whose wit would get him into trouble with three Tsars and who would boast, as a conqueror of the Caucasus, that the terror of his name was more potent than fortresses, his word more irresistible than death.[22] Only on arrival in Drissa did Barclay eventually find a successor for the map-loving Mukhin: an upright, tactless Livonian, Colonel Friedrich von Toll, also thirty-five, who made a competent quartermaster-general.

On the question of overall command, the Tsar had moments of realizing that the existing uncertainty was not helping the war. From temporary imperial headquarters at Sventsiany on the Sunday following the invasion, he dispatched a rider to catch Barclay en route from Vilna with the welcome word that confusion was at an end: 'I shall give no order whatsoever, so as not to cross your directives . . .'[23] The Tsar also wrote that he had ordered Wittgenstein, Baggavut, Dokhturov, Platov, and Bagration to send their reports directly to Barclay, though with copies for information simultaneously to himself. Even while announcing these excellent decisions, however, the Tsar mentioned that he had ordered Bagration and Platov to make certain moves. And indeed the Tsar's promise remained pretty much of a dead letter, as orders continued to flow from imperial headquarters to cause repeated muddles in an atmosphere already charged with tension.

Matters came to a head when Barclay found out that His Majesty had replaced Count Shuvalov at the head of the First Army's Fourth Corps. Barclay had not been consulted, and he reacted with startling irritability. His letter to Alexander has not been preserved, but its tenor can be gauged from the Tsar's immediate, exasperated reply:

General, I received your letters of yesterday with, I confess, a feeling of affliction. How can it be that after having made a point of proving to you my esteem, attachment, confidence and, permit me to add, giving you every mark of distinction – for on every occasion I have put you even ahead of the members of my own family – how then can it be that you take pleasure in being unfair to me, and this at a moment when each should have no thought other than the salvation of the State? Allow me to tell you, General, with that frankness which my friendship for you authorizes me to have with you, that I do not recognize you in this action and that I prefer to attribute it to a moment of aberration. The facts themselves will convince you, I am sure . . .[24]

The facts were that General Shuvalov was ailing and had asked the Tsar to be relieved of his command and, as luck would have it, General Count Ostermann-Tolstoy had suddenly become available. The Tsar appointed him without consultation 'because there was not a moment to lose'. Born a Tolstoy, and having inherited the 'Ostermann' and the title from childless relatives of German extraction, this most slavic young General was provocatively patriotic, maintaining for instance that Russians would do well 'to be no better acquainted with the language of foreigners than would be sufficient for communication or common courtesies'.[25] He had not hidden his opinion of Barclay's German accent during those Finnish days when he had been in the group fiercely opposing Barclay's promotion; while Count Shuvalov, he too of a prestigious, powerful family (which had reached the height of its influence under Empress

Elizabeth when in 1749 she took Ivan Shuvalov as a lover), had taken Barclay's side.

It was not, however, out of personal pique that Barclay had reacted with such touchiness: he thought well of his old comrade-in-arms and stalwart new Corps leader. It was the knotty situation at imperial headquarters, undermining all authority for waging the war and producing an extraordinary potpourri of inconsistent directives, which Barclay found so baneful. To his wife alone he could write freely: 'I am hardly ever at the Tsar's headquarters; it is a real wasps' nest of strife and intrigue, disposing our admirable Monarch to indecision and distrust . . .'[26]

A motley crowd of self-seekers and unscrupulous intriguers, without any precise assignment, had the Tsar's ear. They spent their time squabbling, criticizing, and for ever proffering inopportune advice. Among the leaders were Count Armfelt, an erstwhile Swedish diplomat and general who had played a part in creating the Grand Duchy of Finland and was now one of the Tsar's adjutant-generals; Marquis Paulucci, ever caustic and subversive, seething since Barclay had found him wanting as chief of staff; and General Bennigsen, whose one ambition at sixty-seven was to take Barclay's place at the head of the First Army. There were others, too, who for less opportunistic reasons were critical of every one of Barclay's moves. While Shishkov and many like him reproached Barclay for not giving battle at Vilna, Phull, on the contrary, even charged him with 'disobedience' for retreating so slowly that Napoleon, he said, might beat him to Drissa. Time and again Phull sent his adjutant, Carl von Clausewitz (then thirty-two years old and a first lieutenant), to tell Barclay to hurry. Returning from these missions Clausewitz would report that he found Barclay imperturbable and 'unwilling to sacrifice by a hasty retreat the measure of self-confidence his officers and men had gained in skirmishes with the enemy'.[27] Napoleon's ironical comment to Balashov in Kovno had come close to the truth: 'Phull proposes, Armfelt contradicts, Bennigsen deliberates, and Barclay, with whom the execution rests, does not know what conclusion to draw . . .'[28]

From the wasps' nest there even issued stings for proud Prince Bagration, though in general his popularity with the headquarters swarm vastly outsoared Barclay's. The distances separating the Russian armies naturally created serious communication problems – and sometimes enabled each Russian general to pursue his own course of action independently.[29] Thus, during the first five days after the invasion there was practically no information from Bagration and none at all from Platov, the idolized Ataman of the Don Cossacks. Bagration's first reports did little to quell the Tsar's anxiety and much to inflame the antagonism between the two commanders-in-chief. The Tsar, forwarding Bagration's messages to Barclay, deplored the Prince's time-wasting failure to withdraw as ordered.[30] Barclay's reactions were more heated: 'Sire, it is extremely disagreeable that Prince Bagration, instead of immediately executing Your Majesty's orders, is losing time in futile discussions, communicating them to Platov and addling the head of this poor general who is not very intelligent to begin with and quite uneducated . . .'[31] Bagration in turn refused to believe that the orders he received came from the Tsar; he was convinced that all his orders were written by Barclay (whose right to command him he tacitly refused to recognize) and that Barclay was deliberately and falsely passing them off as the Tsar's. The only person who could clarify the situation, the Tsar, remained silent, though military authority was disintegrating and military operations were threatened with chaos. In the midst of all this tension and discord, the lack of information added to the general apprehension. With still no clear idea of how Napoleon was developing his campaign, Alexander had to enquire desperately of Barclay whether any news of the enemy had come in from 'Sanglen and his spies'.

Frustration and the weather strained the Tsar's nerves, and he reacted with impatience and harshness to every vexation. The torrid June heat wave had broken a day after Barclay had left Vilna, and the next five days' march was through mud, rain, and chill winds, followed again by unbroken, debilitating heat. All the armies, friend and foe, paid a cruel toll, though the vast Grande Armée had by far the more serious supply problems, fatal to thousands of horses and fatal as well to their popularity with the Lithuanians whom they were forced to plunder. No windfalls left from the passage of the Russians aided the enemy's plight: Barclay had ordered that all superfluous objects the troops had accumulated in peacetime be not only discarded but destroyed. Travelling relatively light, the Russians had no trouble keeping well ahead of Murat. But when Barclay stressed that the forced marches the Tsar demanded of him were needless and were giving rise to murmurs of complaint in the ranks, Alexander replied dryly that forced marches which tire the troops tire the enemy too. In all circumstances 'our soldier must never grumble', he said; it was up to the leaders to see that no grumbling occurred, 'repressing severely' any that could become serious.[32] Nor was this the last time that the Tsar would call for greater severity against his own troops than Barclay was ready to apply.

While Barclay continued obediently, then, in the direction of Drissa, he also continued to tell the Tsar how Phull's plan would not serve: 'I cannot fathom what we are supposed to do with our whole army in the fortified camp of Drissa. After such a precipitous retreat [to get there], we lose sight of the enemy altogether and, being confined inside the camp, we shall have to await him on every side and in the end have to push a large corps outside to know where the enemy is . . .'[33] After putting forward various proposals on how to make the best of a bad situation, Barclay concluded with exasperated resignation: 'That, Sire, is the opinion frankly stated . . . of a soldier who has taken the firm resolution not to get involved any further in advice and counsel, but to die for the cause of his Sovereign.'[34]

Three days later he was in Drissa (27 June/9 July), with Murat's cavalry not yet in sight behind him, but while he was still on his way a false alarm stirred imperial headquarters at Drissa: Napoleon was believed to be attempting to outflank the camp from the left. The hollowness of Phull's concept became clear: it depended in the first place on the enemy's playing the game. In a hurriedly convened war council Phull was asked to propose counter-moves, but he had nothing to offer. Although the alarm proved false, it was obvious that Phull was finally losing the Tsar's confidence. Clausewitz cannily suggested to his superior that he persuade the Tsar to make Barclay supreme commander, thus at least giving unity and cohesion to the Russian movements. Clausewitz told Phull he 'did not consider Barclay capable of leading a large army successfully against Napoleon', but nonetheless Barclay seemed 'a calm and determined man and a competent soldier who increasingly enjoyed the Tsar's confidence'.[35] Thus Phull could save face, and some solution be found for the extreme confusion existing in the Russian high command. But there is no evidence that the mortified Phull ever followed this suggestion.

Meanwhile Bagration realized perfectly well that he could not, with his insignificant forces, play the role assigned to him by Phull's plan without being annihilated. A plan for his annihilation was in fact just then being set in motion by Napoleon, using the ablest of his generals, forty-two-year-old Marshal Davout – whose baldness and whose austerity matched Barclay's own – and the Emperor's youngest brother Jerome, King of Westphalia since 1807. Jerome's job was to push Bagration into Davout's arms; Davout's, to cut off Bagration and crush him. Thus would Napoleon confound the Russians and 'bring them to their knees in less than a month'.[36] Davout as ordered did quickly block Bagration's route to Drissa, while Jerome slowly and irresolutely approached from the rear. Together at this time they outnumbered Bagration three to one and the trap looked foolproof.

Not realizing what threats were hanging over the Second Army, Alexander in his ignorance was outrageously harsh on Bagration. Complaining about his moving 'so slowly and so timidly', the Tsar had sent one of his adjutants, a disreputable young fellow named Benckendorff, to explain to the courageous, experienced Commander-in-Chief, proud scion of old Georgian kings, exactly 'the kind of war [he was] expected to wage'. That is, as the Tsar told Barclay, he counted on Benckendorff's arrival to bring Bagration 'back to his senses and make him march at once against Davout's rear'.[37]

At the very time that Alexander was putting this absurdity on paper, causing Bagration incorrectly but not unnaturally to suspect Barclay's hated hand, the Commander-in-Chief of the Second Army – who from now on would derisively refer to the Commander-in-Chief of the First Army only as 'the Minister' – was writing to Arakcheev (26 June/8 July) and spitting out his rancour and distrust while showing clearly that he understood nothing at all of the basic war policy agreed upon by Barclay and the Tsar. 'It's not my fault,' exclaimed Bagration, always convinced of being the world's cynosure: 'They stretched my troops like a bow-string, and when the enemy walks in without firing a shot, they start retreating without [anybody] knowing why. You won't be able to prove to anyone in the army, in the whole country, that we haven't been betrayed. I cannot all by myself defend all Russia. The First Army must at once and without fail march on Vilna; what does it have to fear? I am encircled . . .'[38] Constantly pushing Arakcheev to intervene with the Tsar, Bagration's every letter showed his total distrust of Barclay, his conviction that betrayal alone could explain a strategy of retreat: 'I pray you to start the offensive . . . One simply must not trifle with the country . . . It is not for Russians to flee . . . We have become worse than the Prussians . . . It's shameful. I feel anguish, God knows I don't live for myself, I would be happy to do everything, but others have no conscience or justice . . .'[39] As Bagration interpreted the situation, the only explanation that would make sense would have to be treason, not incompetence, since he had conceived a very keen respect for Barclay's military talents during the campaigns of 1806 and 1807, when Barclay had been his subordinate.[40]

On the day that Bagration and Alexander were thus writing their ill-founded judgements, Bagration had reached Nesvizh and was resting his troops, Davout had arrived in Minsk and was likewise resting his, Platov was beating off Uhlans, while Barclay was about to enter Drissa (the Tsar was already there); and Napoleon was still lingering in Vilna.

Two weeks from the day of the invasion Barclay could tell Auguste that he had 'led without a hitch, at the Tsar's behest and contrary to [his] own judgement', 70,000 foot-soldiers and horsemen and 350 pieces of artillery into the Drissa camp (which was about two and a half miles long and nearly two miles wide).[41] To guard against surprise he had placed the reliable Wittgenstein's First Corps to the north and the dutiful Dokhturov's Sixth Corps to the south. Except for these two corps, all the First Army was in Drissa by 29 June/11 July. But as Barclay discontentedly wrote home, he was now simply 'waiting to see what is to be undertaken next' – and meanwhile please to be so kind as to send some wine.[42]

While waiting, Barclay received and adopted an original proposal put forward patriotically by two professors, eager to help Russia's cause, from the University of Dorpat.[43] These professors proposed that a mobile printing press be installed at First Army headquarters to turn out propaganda.[44] Barclay had the University supply two presses equipped with latin, gothic, and cyrillic type faces and twelve typographers, and soon a French-language leaflet found its way to Grande Armée outposts, telling the French that despite all their personal bravery they had not a chance of winning: they should lay down their arms and go home.[45] This leaflet sent Napoleon into a rage. Barclay himself signed a leaflet printed for the German soldiers harnessed to Napoleon's war machine: he promised them asylum in Russia if they deserted. Another propaganda effort was drafted by the tenacious and influential Freiherr vom Stein, the former Prussian prime minister now an exile in Russia, who pressed the scheme, first mooted by General Scharnhorst in St. Petersburg the year before, for a German Legion on Russian soil. In Barclay's name an official proclamation offered German warriors a choice between joining the Legion or settling on land they would be given in 'the sunny climes of southern Russia'.[46] But these efforts had poor results. At fault was the bad Russian treatment of prisoners, which moreover made no distinction between French and Germans; the passive resistance of local Russian administrators; and above all the still high morale of the invaders. Scharnhorst, suddenly overcome by loyalty to his King, refused at the last minute to assume command of the Legion. The appeals netted only two small units from the Württemberg Army and some individual German soldiers; few officers – who were especially needed to form cadres – heeded the call; and the Legion thus never took shape on Russian soil.[47]

The Tsar meanwhile, with his gift for unhappy timing, had issued a proclamation announcing the end of the retreat and the imminence of a glorious new Poltava. Then three days after the First Army's arrival in Drissa, on 1/13 July, he summoned a council of war to discuss the next moves. Oudinot, attacking Dvinsk, had been repulsed by Wittgenstein, but it could not be long now before the action reached Drissa, so Barclay once again repeated his objections to Phull's overall scheme and criticized the specific weaknesses of the Drissa position. On this point he was now seconded by Oppermann, Bennigsen, and above all by Colonel Michaud, a Frenchman in Russian service and a specialist in fortifications whose judgement carried great weight with the Tsar. Barclay also argued forcefully that if the two main Russian armies were ever to join forces, it was urgent that he should move his army towards Bagration's. In the end reason prevailed and it was decided to abandon the Drissa camp forthwith. The next morning the army began to strike camp, demoralized and grumbling at Barclay's orders coming so soon after the Tsar's inspiring 'Poltava' proclamation and being so contrary to it. The 10,000 men of the Drissa garrison were sent as reinforcements to Wittgenstein's Corps.

Bagration had no news of these events, no notion of Napoleon's strength in the north, and no idea that Barclay was trying to join up with him as a necessary condition for giving battle. Misconceiving the situation as always, the fire-eating Georgian continued to hurl bitter appeals for the First Army to go into action to relieve the pressure on himself. On the day the decision to leave Drissa was being made, Bagration was writing once again to the Tsar: 'If only your Imperial Majesty would firmly order the First Army to attack the enemy. He would without doubt be defeated and I would be receiving reinforcements . . .'[48] And to his close friend Ermolov, Barclay's own Chief of Staff, Bagration began the abuse – 'the uniform Barclay has covered with shame' – which he continued to hurl until almost the end of his days:

I am ashamed to wear the uniform – it kills me . . . What an imbecile! . . . The Minister Barclay flees while ordering me to defend the whole of Russia. We were brought to the frontier, then scattered about everywhere like pawns, then they stayed there, mouths wide open, and, having shit all the length of the border, off they fled . . . It all disgusts me so much it's driving me crazy . . . God keep you; as for me, I am going to swap my uniform for a peasant's blouse![49]

Stifling heat raised tempers but slowed the pace of the huge effort needed to get a whole disgruntled army on the march again, and several days were required for the complete evacuation of Drissa. On 5/17 July, just beyond Drissa in a temporary command post set up in a convenient barn, Barclay, while watching his regiments file past on the road to Polotsk, received a surprise visit from the Tsar.[50] Alexander had suddenly driven back from his new Polotsk headquarters. The two remained closeted tête-à-tête for more than an hour. The monarch appeared dejected. Giving up Drissa meant giving up an illusion. And now a greater sacrifice had come. He could no longer ignore the concerted pleadings of the Arakcheev, Balashov, Shishkov triumvirate, following upon those of his beloved sister Catherine. Having realized that the imperial presence in the field led only to friction and hindered the war, very tactfully they petitioned him to leave the army. They emphasized that Alexander's role was to be at the helm of his Empire and cautioned him that remaining at the front would inevitably make him responsible for errors and military setbacks. Let the blame fall on the generals, Catherine had argued: if they make a mistake they can always be punished.[51]

Essentially the Tsar had come to inform Barclay of his decision and to bid him goodbye. There was no eavesdropper to record their meeting, but it must have become quickly evident that though the Tsar was leaving the field, he had no intention of following the new Field Service Regulations and divesting himself of the supreme command. There was no question of transferring the title to Barclay. Alexander's vanity, and his fear of upsetting Bagration (and thereby Catherine as well), precluded the move.

Before parting, the Tsar and Barclay agreed on various pressing decisions. It was probably at this time that they determined to order a general levy (over and beyond the three already completed that had been scheduled while Barclay was at the Ministry), and to form recruits into a new corps, under General Miloradovich's command. There could no longer be any doubt that Russia would need all the manpower she could summon in order to match forces eventually with a thinned-out enemy. On strategy, Alexander's main point (nothing new) was that Barclay was not to accept a general battle without being sure of winning. In Barclay's presence it was easy for the Tsar to think in such terms, but unwavering consistency was not his way. That same day, while Barclay's influence was still fresh, Alexander instructed Bagration that their chief objective must be to gain time and protract the war, but as time went on Barclay would find it frequently necessary to remind the Tsar of his basic policy injunction; his Chief of Staff, Ermolov, afterwards remarked that Barclay made no secret of the precept he had received.[52] Later, Bagration ironically alluded to it as well, in a letter to his good friend Rostopchin, appointed Governor-General of Moscow at Catherine's insistence: 'Barclay says that the Tsar forbade him to give a decisive battle and that is why we keep on running away. I take this to mean that His Majesty would not mind having all of Russia occupied by the enemy . . .'[53]

When Barclay and his Supreme Commander finally stepped out of the 'wretched barn', the Tsar embraced Barclay under the eyes of Major Loewenstern, duty officer of that day. The Tsar's significant final words, spoken from his carriage, were: 'Farewell, General, farewell. I hope to see you again. I entrust you with my army; do not forget that I have no other one; this thought must never leave you.'[54]

This thought did not leave Barclay, ever. The Tsar's meaning seemed quite clear, unlike his thinking: first of all, that to save the army was to save Russia – as Barclay had been telling him for years. But also, since the Tsar could not have been forgetting the existence of the Second and Third Russian Armies, it would seem therefore that when he said, 'I entrust you with my army; . . . I have no other one', he could only have meant that he was holding Barclay responsible for all the Russian forces ranged against Napoleon. Alexander's letter to Barclay three weeks later seems to confirm this interpretation: 'I have placed the safety of Russia in your hands, general . . .'⁵⁵ The entrustment, however, was a private understanding. From his autocratic heights the Tsar, like a fairy-tale emperor, assigned a task with impossible conditions, and it was up to the hero unaided from above to save the empire. The command situation was, if anything, more confusing than before, as shown by another letter from Bagration to Count Rostopchin: 'Yes, that's the way things are, but, between us, I have no power over the Minister even though I am older than he is [i.e. senior in rank, though younger in years]. When the Tsar departed, he did not leave any instructions as to who should be in command in case the two armies join, and hence Barclay, ostensibly because a Minister . . .'⁵⁶ Bagration did not finish the sentence.

Unravelling none of this tangle, the Tsar and Supreme Commander issued two more rousing proclamations from Polotsk and departed for Moscow via Smolensk. Accompanying him were Rumiantsev, Arakcheev, Balashov, Shishkov, and the usual large retinue. Left behind were the meddlesome Bennigsen, Armfelt, Alexander Duke of Württemberg, the utterly discredited Phull, and a gaggle of other previous habitués of the Tsar's antechambers. Now they crowded the waiting-room at Barclay's headquarters which earlier they had shunned. Politely, Barclay bade them stay one day's march away from his army. Some took offence and went off altogether. But at least Barclay had recovered his famous equanimity. Now finally he could dispose, always in keeping with the Tsar's last orders, according to what he thought tactically sound. The General's first letter to Alexander, written a full week after they parted – as if Barclay had needed this breathing-space in order to savour his (relative) independence – carried assurances that he would always be mindful of the need to spare and preserve the army's strength.⁵⁷

The evacuation of Drissa happened just in time. It thwarted still another of Napoleon's strategic plans: to nail Barclay down at Drissa with a large flanking movement, and then march on to Smolensk to threaten Moscow or, a less likely alternative, to push a damaged First Army to within only a few days' march of St. Petersburg, where Barclay would have to make a stand and be demolished. On the day before leaving Vilna in pursuit of Barclay, the French Emperor had reiterated his intention of turning the Russians at Drissa.⁵⁸ But he had lingered too long over administrative matters in Vilna – one of the worst mistakes of his career according to Jomini and most historians after him.⁵⁹ By the time Napoleon set out from Vilna, near midnight on 4/16 July, Drissa was already more than half drained of bread and powder, of massive twelve-pounders drawn by team after team of eight or even ten straining horses, of the lighter field pieces with four-horse teams, and of thousands upon thousands of men pouring out in a mighty flood upon the road to Polotsk and the east. By 6/18 July Drissa was empty, save for the debris and wastes of man and horse. And on Napoleon's way the cottages and manor houses also stood ominously abandoned and vacant.

Bagration, pushing forward only to have to retrace his steps, trying desperately to dodge Davout, had been driving his troops in debilitating forced marches. At the crucial moment when the Russians should have been caught, however, the irresolute Jerome failed to spring the trap. The Commander-in-

Chief of the Second Army was able to bring his worn and footsore soldiers dragging through sandy roads – first under devastating downpours, then in the same oppressive heat which was so severely trying all the armies of this campaign – to the safety of Bobruisk, one of the fortresses Barclay had had constructed. Luckily, for as Buturlin stated, '. . . if that fortress had not existed, Davout could have blocked Bagration's crossing [already at] the Berezina.'[60] Here Platov, who had been covering Bagration's rear, joined him. The gruff Ataman was in high spirits. Twice his Cossacks had checked and driven back the Polish Uhlans of Jerome's advance guard, inflicting losses and taking three hundred prisoners.

After Drissa, the First Army bivouacked at Polotsk, an intersection of ways leading north to St. Petersburg and east to Vitebsk on the Smolensk–Moscow road. Here Barclay received intelligence that Napoleon's main thrust was developing towards the east. The Commander-in-Chief's immediate reaction was to send Uvarov and his First Cavalry Corps towards Vitebsk and to give Wittgenstein a free hand to protect the St. Petersburg road as he judged best, if the need arose. Next Barclay quickly formed his other men into two immense columns, deployed them on either side of the Western Dvina river, and sent them marching the sixty miles – about a four-day trek – to Vitebsk. He reserved General Dokhturov's Sixth Corps, and the Second and Third Cavalry Corps, to bring up the rear. Still without news from Bagration, he hoped fervently that the Second Army could join him at Vitebsk. Making no bones about the precariousness of the situation, Barclay, en route on 9/21 July, hastily summed it up for Auguste: 'The enemy with his superior strength has now advanced between the First and Second Armies in order to open up the way to the heart of Russia. With God's help I hope this can be prevented . . . I am now, my dear wife, on a slippery path where all depends on good fortune. If heaven will give me luck . . . I shall rightly deserve the gratitude of the fatherland . . .'[61]

Alarming news of Napoleon, offset by encouraging news of Bagration, greeted Barclay on his arrival in Vitebsk (11/23 July). Signalling the approach of the Grande Armée, enormous clouds of dust from Murat's cavalry were reported rising near Polotsk; moreover, Marshal Oudinot's corps of some 40,000 was pressing hard against the outnumbered Wittgenstein. But balancing these threats was a heartening message that Bagration's advance guard had entered Mogilev: the convergence of the two armies seemed at last to be drawing near. Barclay instantly planned to hasten the meeting by marching his army to Orsha, half-way between Vitebsk and Mogilev. He sent some of Tuchkov's forces ahead to clear the way to Orsha, and dispatched a message to Bagration to meet him there. In all ranks of the First Army – which 'looked with amazement at the constant retreat' and exaggerated every rumour of success elsewhere – spirits began to rise.[62]

These spirits were dashed, however, almost immediately: the news about Mogilev proved to be false. Now again Barclay was in the dark – blacker than ever after this unexpected turn. His repeated appeals to Bagration to speed their meeting had been to no avail – though whether because the Prince could not or would not, Barclay did not know. He readily accepted the offer of his closest aide, the German-born Colonel Baron von Wolzogen – a jocular, well-educated fellow, according to Clausewitz – to go off in search of Bagration wherever he might be and set him on the road to junction with the First Army. Wolzogen took off that very evening after a careful briefing in which Barclay emphasized Bagration's extreme touchiness about the deference due to his seniority.[63]

Barclay now moved his Fourth Corps under Ostermann-Tolstoy towards Ostrovno to ward off a surprise attack on the First Army as a whole. On 13/25 July a *fel'djaeger* was dispatched to Bagration with a letter smoothing the way for the expected reunion: 'At the thought that the defence of the fatherland has been entrusted to us at this decisive time, all other considerations and everything that under normal circumstances would influence our acts must be silenced. The voice of the fatherland commands us to work in harmony . . .' Pointing out that 'even the greatest heroes' were defeated by internal dissension, Barclay urged: 'Let us join together and crush Russia's enemy. The fatherland will bless our accord . . .'[64]

While Barclay was thus pleading for co-operation between the two armies and their commanders-in-chief, at Ostrovno, or rather two miles from this village, Murat's cavalry came upon Ostermann-Tolstoy's Fourth Corps and attacked it with pent-up fury. The engagement lasted all day, with the Russians managing despite unequal forces to withstand the assault and even to gain some ground. Losses were heavy on both sides. Ostermann-Tolstoy, seeing so many of his men falling to French grapeshot, was forced to the words, 'We have no choice: let us stand and perish!'[65] From Prince de Beauharnais came reinforcements for the French, who thus kept their numerical superiority even though Barclay committed an 8,000-strong infantry division of the Third Corps under General Konovnitsyn, as well as the First Cavalry Corps. Ostermann-Tolstoy was enabled to retire and regroup his forces while Konovnitsyn led the continuing fight. Barclay ordered the defenders to hold on until Dokhturov's Corps could reach Vitebsk, but the Russians were forced to yield step by step and had to fall back on the third day.

Both French and Russian armies now felt that the war was really beginning. Russian prisoners taken by Murat provided the French with the welcome information that the First Army was settled in at Vitebsk. There was every sign that Barclay was at last seeking battle, and Napoleon saw himself on the eve of great events, sure that the First Army – one-third the size of his own at this time – was at his mercy. On his side Barclay realized that large enemy forces were nearby and that he would therefore risk exposing his right flank to heavy attack if he turned south, as planned, to Orsha. If, however, he could retard the advance of the Grande Armée and rivet its attention on himself, he saw a chance to facilitate Bagration's approach. Despite the disadvantageous terrain deplored by both Clausewitz and Ermolov, Barclay maintained unshakeably that his chances of victory were good: not all Napoleon's marching columns had yet arrived on the scene, and the Russian troops' valiant conduct during the last forty-eight hours was the 'best guarantee' of success.[66] Again the whole army stirred with anticipation.

Only a few hours later, Barclay's 'guarantee' may have seemed to be wearing thin, as Ostermann-Tolstoy and Konovnitsyn straggled back, bowed and battered, in the early hours of the night; but still Barclay showed no weakening. By dawn on 15/27 July he had lined up his First Army in battle formation; whereupon Napoleon, who was viewing the scene from some convenient raised ground, exulted that at last his hour of triumph had come. With so bright a prospect, it would be prudent, he decided, to wait one more day in order to have his complete army on hand. In the Russian camp, however, a new factor changed the general outlook once again. Bagration's aide-de-camp Prince Menshikov arrived, falling from his horse with exhaustion. Bagration had not been able to get through at Mogilev, and was making a long detour north-eastwards.

At last Barclay and his staff were able to learn what the Second Army had been doing. After a breathing-space in the safety of Bobruisk fortress, Bagration, still eager for battle, drew some fresh troops from the Bobruisk garrison and decided to go on the offensive. He sent Platov and Raevskii to dislodge Davout's well-entrenched troops at Saltanovka just south of Mogilev. The Cossacks and the Seventh Corps quickly overturned Davout's screen of light troops but were then solidly blocked, unable to make the final push through to Mogilev and the north. Bagration, unaware that Davout disposed of only two divisions at that point, did not dare commit his entire army in the operation. Thus, when for once the Russians faced a numerically inferior enemy, they missed their chance. Instead Bagration ordered a general retreat south along the Dnepr, and Davout, glad to be able to hold on to Mogilev, did not pursue. At Novy Bykhov, while Ostermann-Tolstoy and Konovnitsyn were battling the French outside Vitebsk and Barclay was still counting on an imminent meeting at Orsha, the Second Army, unmolested, crossed the river. Bagration's evasion of Davout was proclaimed as a victorious breakthrough and was generally hailed throughout Russia as a splendid triumph, despite the failure to break a passage northwards through Mogilev.[67] Twenty-four hours later Platov succeeded in skirting Davout's rear and traversed the Dnepr at a more northerly point whence he made for the First Army at the rate of thirty miles a day.

On 13/25 July, just as the first elements of the Second Army were filing across the river, Wolzogen had caught up with Bagration in his headquarters on the Dnepr's left bank. Bragging and boasting, the Prince and his Chief of Staff, the French-born Count de Saint-Priest, welcomed Barclay's aide. In view of the new developments and because Orsha was clearly blocked by Davout's presence at Mogilev, Wolzogen took it upon himself to suggest that Bagration make towards Mstislavl on the road to Smolensk, and he also brought up a promise he claimed Barclay had made to exercise jointly with Bagration the overall command of the converged armies. If one can believe Wolzogen, Bagration showed no enthusiasm at all for linking-up and instead proposed taking his 'triumphant' army to the rich fields of the Ukraine for refurbishing and to pick up new recruits. Wolzogen, although claiming old acquaintanceship, seems to have had little experience of the Prince's habit of throwing out wild threats and extravagant statements, fully believing them at the time. Losing both his composure and his memory of Barclay's warnings about Bagration's amour-propre, Baron Wolzogen on his side began to use words like insubordination, irresponsibility, and disobedience, thereby destroying any good effect of Barclay's own plea for harmony. In the end, however, Bagration, who may possibly even have decided on Smolensk at the time he had sent off Menshikov, blandly announced that he would be leaving the next day for that proud and ancient city, expecting to arrive nine days later on 22 July/3 August. Wolzogen believed himself to be responsible for bringing Bagration around, but perhaps all he had accomplished was to add fuel to Bagration's hostility to Barclay.[68]

It was not until 18/30 July that Wolzogen was to rejoin Barclay, but meanwhile, on 13/25 July, the latter, on receipt of Menshikov's breathless report, had hurriedly called a war council. Except for Duke Alexander of Württemberg, military governor of Vitebsk Province, all present were agreed: abandon Vitebsk, beat the French to Smolensk, and rendezvous there with Bagration.

At dawn on the following day (14/26 July) the Grande Armée advanced in full battle order only to find it had been outwitted.[69] The camp-fires the Russians had purposely left burning through the short summer night of their hushed withdrawal had completely deceived the French. 'One cannot imagine the Emperor's disappointment when it was ascertained the Russian army had vanished,' wrote Caulaincourt.[70] Another eyewitness invoked the masterful execution of the manœuvre: 'We were astonished at perceiving the perfect order with which Barclay de Tolly had evacuated his position. We wandered in all directions over an immense plain without perceiving the faintest trace of his retreat, not a single carriage, not a single dead horse, not even a solitary vehicle, indicated the road that the enemy had taken . . .'[71] It remains a mystery how it was possible for a huge army like this to disappear undetected without a trace within just a few hours. It is impossible that Barclay had ordered the withdrawal in advance: that fact would have been known. The silence of the evacuation, the uncanny degree of discipline, was the more remarkable in view of the army's reluctance to retreat. To be sure, distant rumblings might have been felt in the French camp as men, horses, artillery carriages, and all the enormous paraphernalia of a great army thudded eastwards through the night, but one must conjecture that their meaning simply had not registered with the French, so positive were they that battle was at hand.

Even more puzzling has been the question of Barclay's intentions at Vitebsk. The usual view is that, all set to make a stand, he changed his mind, saved by Napoleon's delay, when he learned that Bagration would not join him and must instead be joined before Davout could again separate the two armies. Indeed, to the Tsar four days later, this is how Barclay justified his failure to engage the enemy: 'The direction taken by Prince Bagration's army, too much to the right, drove me to despair. In order not to leave Marshal d'Avout's way open from Mogilev straight to the heart of Russia, there was no choice for me but to reach Smolensk by forced marches . . .' After explaining that he had changed routes because he was exposed to 'the eyes of the whole enemy army', he stated: 'In the circumstances, to fight at Vitebsk would be for nothing. Even a victory, unless it resulted in the destruction of the enemy forces, would be useless. Just think, if Marshal d'Avout arrives in the meantime in Smolensk, the state of the war will be more critical than at the beginning. That, Sire, is the reason for my making for Smolensk . . .'[72]

Barclay's explanation to the Tsar makes perfect sense. But it leaves out, for good reason, an essential point: Barclay had been shamming. In the post-war document entitled 'Justification by the Commander-in-Chief Barclay de Tolly of his Actions during the Patriotic War with the French in 1812', Barclay recapitulates the background he gave the Tsar, but the ending is completely different:

My uppermost objective being to converge with Prince Bagration and perceiving that for this purpose I had to facilitate his movements, I decided to draw the full attention of the army on myself. I met the enemy with my advance guard twenty versts outside Vitebsk. Throughout three days the battle raged there and finally *I drew up the First Army in battle formation near the town and gave the impression and had it rumoured that I intended to give battle there* . . .[73] [emphasis supplied]

On this particular step of the slippery path where all depends on good fortune, heaven clearly gave Barclay the luck he had prayed for. His ruse was immeasurably facilitated by Napoleon's one-day delay – but that very delay was after all inspired by Barclay's tactics. Nevertheless, even had Napoleon not waited, there is every indication that the withdrawal would still have taken place, though differently, with skirmishes and diversions to hold off the enemy – not without losses. As soon as he saw that Napoleon was postponing the action, however, there can be little doubt that Barclay swiftly worked out the series of orders that would be required to effect the perfect evacuation of Vitebsk, once the enemy slept. He confided in no one, not only to prevent the slightest possibility of his intentions reaching the enemy but also to protect his strategy from his own people. Although Ermolov disapproved of the Vitebsk terrain, he was as contemptuous as Bagration of Barclay's retreats and would have stirred up rumours and conflicts had he known Barclay's plan. Only Menshikov's arrival with the Second Army news permitted Barclay to withdraw by war council consensus and without having to show his hand. Even to the Tsar, surrounded by backbiters and starved of good news, Barclay dared not hint at the truth at that moment, but could only promise victories to come. And dissembling then, Barclay could not afterwards admit outright that he had deceived his sovereign and Supreme Commander. At later moments of the campaign, however, in every direct or indirect reference to Vitebsk, Barclay's letters to the Tsar clearly implied that the whole action had been intentional: the 'Vitebsk affair', Barclay called it, whereby the enemy's purposes had been frustrated and the two Russian armies enabled to join.[74]

Many of Napoleon's entourage now counselled him to halt for the year and resume the campaign in 1813. The losses in men and horses through heat, sickness, hunger, and exhaustion had been enormous. The road behind was littered with rotting corpses, including those of 8,000 horses. As many as 100,000 men had already dropped out of the Grande Armée or were straggling.

Fearing that the Russians, like their Scythian predecessors two thousand years before, might resort to a total scorced-earth policy, the State Secretary-General Daru was gravely concerned about supplies, already painfully meagre. Caulaincourt, too, advised against marching on, mindful of Alexander's telling him, 'I would rather pull back to Kamchatka than cede provinces and sign treaties . . .'[75] Taking the same view, more timidly, was Marshal Berthier, who had indeed transmitted Barclay's prediction made long ago in Memel that Russia would win, if invaded, by withdrawing into her endless depths. But because that warning had been made to a Prussian, Napoleon was convinced it was not to be trusted: 'All the jabber about the supposed project concocted by Barclay to lure us deep into Russia is a story, not by a French narrator but by the Prussian officer of whom he was the echo . . .'[76] Although granting most of the dangers urged by friends and staff, Napoleon nevertheless reasoned that once Barclay and Bagration met at Smolensk, they were bound to give battle. His decision was made; long wars did not suit his temperament. He would give the tired troops a rest and then push on to Smolensk.

From the beginning of hostilities, both the Tsar and Barclay had bent their efforts to remedying that separation of the two main Russian armies which was at the heart of Phull's plan. And yet that separation, senseless as it seemed, proved in reality to be a major cause of Napoleon's ultimate undoing. The fact that the two armies were not able to join until Smolensk, only 230 miles west of Moscow, led in practice to carrying out that very scheme of withdrawal which Barclay had thought out in 1807. If the two armies had been closer at the beginning, the temptation and the clamour to give battle would have been irresistibly overwhelming. The greatly outnumbered Russians would surely have been crushed, instead of being able to withdraw virtually intact during the first seven weeks of the campaign.[77]

CHAPTER X

'ALL BARK AND NO BITE'

> Fabius knew perfectly well that his delaying tactics were by now unpopular in Rome as well as in the army; none the less he remained inflexible . . . and robbed Hannibal of the hope of the battle he so eagerly desired.
>
> Livy, *The War with Hannibal*, Book XXII (*translated by Aubrey de Sélincourt*)

The dispersal of well over a third of a million fighting men across wide spaces came to an end during the first half of August (N.S.) 1812. From north, east, and south, the bulk of the opposing armies gradually converged upon an area of roughly seventeen square miles in the vicinity of Smolensk. First to arrive (20 July/1 August) were Barclay and his staff. They set up headquarters in the Smolensk governor's house in a suburb called St. Petersburg, situated on the northern or right bank of the Dnepr outside the crenellated walls of Smolensk. Nearby, a single bridge connected the northern suburbs with the gate giving access to the medieval town. The entire First Army, now reinforced by Platov's Cossacks, bivouacked in the fields stretching northward beyond undulating hills.

Two days later, at ten in the morning of 22 July/3 August, Bagration arrived punctually on the date promised to Wolzogen. Barclay, forewarned of the approaching cavalcade, stepped quickly out to greet Bagration, who came heavily escorted by a procession of aides and corps commanders. Barclay marked his respect for the other Commander-in-Chief's seniority by wearing parade uniform complete with medals, sash, and sword, with plumed bicorne in hand.[1] The meeting was brief but genial. Each voiced criticism of the other's operations, but in civil terms quite unlike the angry reproaches in their letters to third persons. Bagration, impressed and pleased by the deferential reception, was surprised to discover that the minister showed no signs of wishing to impose his will. Barclay was clearly living up to the conciliatory words he had sent Bagration before the meeting: we may both be in the wrong, let us forget everything, let us stop recriminations and start co-operating.[2] In this atmosphere the Prince termed the First Army's withdrawal 'faultless', while Barclay complimented Bagration on his skill in evading the French Emperor's trap. Before they parted, the Prince swallowed his pride and gallantly volunteered to subordinate himself to the other. Thus at last, by the grace of Bagration, Barclay found himself briefly acknowledged as Commander-in-Chief of both armies. Their *entente cordiale* was made visible the following day when they rode out to inspect the First Army in its bivouac and Barclay repeatedly reached over and warmly grasped Bagration's hand. Officers and men cheered.

Both commanders hastened to report to their Supreme Commander. Bagration sent somewhat reluctant assurances that he would strictly obey orders from his superior, 'whoever he might be', because he realized 'a single overall command' was called for to save the fatherland.[3] Barclay's assurances were altogether innocent and unreserved, describing his relations with the Prince as 'the best in the world', praising him wholeheartedly for his loyalty and noble patriotism, and rashly holding out a future of 'perfect harmony'.[4] In the Tsar's reply, in one well-balanced autocratic sentence, he unequivocally acknowledged that he had put Russia's safety in Barclay's hands – 'and I like to hope that you will justify all my confidence in you.'[5]

Confidence in Barclay had in fact been growing more and more shaky, but now that the two armies were finally joined, expectations for a change in Russian strategy ran high among the troops and in St. Petersburg. The withdrawal through Lithuania, though far from popular, had been reluctantly accepted in view of the enemy's great numerical superiority. But the main front now ran across ancient Russian soil and thoughts of a further retreat became intolerable. Barclay was aware of the persistent decline in morale caused by steady withdrawal over hundreds of miles. Remembering his own policy of providing explanations to the soldiers, he now issued an order of the day designed to re-establish confidence and zeal. Twisting the truth by blaming the 'cunning enemy' for the avoidance of battle at Vitebsk, he professed his own impatience to come to blows with the invaders. He promised the soldiers that the enemy would soon find out how perilous it was to intrude on Russian land, and he exhorted the troops to order and obedience, vowing that victory would be theirs.[6] The good effect of these words was greatly enhanced by news spreading through Russian ranks of exploits at the two outlying wings. In the north, Wittgenstein's First Corps had snatched a victory (but mourned brave General Kul'nev, killed in battle); and in the south, Tormassov's Third Army had turned a small but not negligible action to its advantage. All augured well for the weeks to come.

It was to chart the next moves that the two Commanders-in-Chief met on 25 July/6 August in a council of war. They were joined by the Grand Duke Constantine, Colonel Wolzogen, and the chiefs of staff and quartermasters-general of the two armies. The flat-nosed Grand Duke, condemning any thought of a further retreat, argued with great intensity for immediately attacking the Grande Armée. Intelligence reports revealed that the enemy forces were still strung out, some of their troops resting in cantonments and others still moving up from around Mogilev. Colonel Toll thought that the situation created by this dispersal of Napoleon's army while Russian forces were concentrated corresponded exactly to what his idol Baron Jomini had envisaged in his theory of 'interior lines', and therefore advocated undertaking forthwith a major attack at the enemy's centre and then crushing his scattered forces piecemeal. To the restive Tsar, still unappeased after Vitebsk, Barclay had already written that he was resolved, in agreement with Bagration, to take advantage of the enemy's dispersal by 'falling with all the mass of my forces on his left wing'.[7] Now, all the others endorsed Toll's more ambitious scheme – except Barclay and Wolzogen. For Bagration and Ermolov, amazed, no alternative was thinkable, and Barclay's attitude appeared inexplicable, or rather it confirmed their previous judgements. Wolzogen, invited by the Grand Duke to give his opinion, said that his thorough surveys of the terrain had convinced him that its woods and marshes were unsuitable for a massive manœuvre, and besides, he argued, the Grande Armée still outnumbered the Russians (actually by three to two: 185,000 as against 116,000). Once Napoleon became aware of the Russian deployment, he would certainly strike back and sever Russian lines of communication with Smolensk. Instead, Wolzogen advised keeping the Russian troops concentrated near Smolensk, and losing no time in repairing the town's obsolete fortifications.[8]

Despite his previous agreement with Bagration, and despite the heavy pressure from the others, Barclay now refused to commit himself on the spot. Referring again to the Tsar's parting admonition to preserve the army above all, Barclay voiced his scepticism about the outcome of the venture. But he well knew the army's need for forward action and he was not immune from the reasoning of the majority. He did realize the advantages of trying to forestall the full concentration of enemy forces and also of keeping the enemy pinned down to give time for more Russian troops and arms to be assembled in the interior. It was possible that success might give the war a new and advantageous turn. But if the operation failed? The others argued that in that case the possibility for a further withdrawal remained open. But Barclay's qualms were great, and finally even greater regarding the possibility of an initial success. Success was credible during the operation's first phase, but then army and public clamour for continued victories would ultimately lead to a decisive showdown, facing superior forces in unfavourable circumstances. (Speaking of Barclay's 'justified fears', the French Marquis de Chambray agreed, as he later wrote, that 'a success would not rid him of the enemy and a reverse could hurl Russia into the abyss'.)[9] Barclay determined to postpone his decision until he could go over all the factors, and he instructed Toll, the originator of the scheme, and Bagration's Saint-Priest to prepare immediately a thorough operational plan.

Their plan, more rushed than thorough, was in Barclay's hands the same evening. Isolated, and overwhelmed by the pressure which had been mounting from the whole fatherland since the beginning of the war; faced by the solidarity binding the Tsar's brother, Bagration, and his own top staff; mindful, after his unconsidered concurrence with Bagration and premature statement to the Tsar, that both would consider a change of mind as a breach of faith; and, most of all, yielding to the imperious need for unity, for that harmony he had so long been urging on Bagration, and knowing that his veto would create instant discord and chaos, Barclay gave his assent, reluctantly and with a heavy heart, but also with the strict proviso that the bulk of the army remain never farther than three days' march from Smolensk.

Coming to a decision did not lighten his spirit, however. On the contrary, he felt the full crushing weight of his responsibility for Russia's fate.

Loewenstern, his aide-de-camp, who had never seen him in such a state of emotion, said that 'it was obvious that he was not at peace with himself': 'On the one hand, he was aware of the possible gains from the manœuvre, while on the other, he saw the dangers of attacking . . . a far superior force . . . and of engaging, so to speak, in a manœuvring match with that pastmaster Napoleon . . .'[10] As events would show, Barclay had made up his mind too hurriedly, and he remained plunged in an irreconcilable mental conflict. After making the necessary dispositions for the march of the various army components, he galloped off before dawn on the following day (26 July/7 August) to the advance guard of Count Pahlen's Third Cavalry Corps. There, in the front lines, he hoped to regain his equanimity and direct the operations.

The Russians advanced to the west in three parallel columns on a twenty-mile front. The right, or most northerly, column was commanded by General Tuchkov and was composed of three infantry and two cavalry corps. In the centre, under General Dokhturov, were two infantry and one cavalry corps, with Platov's Cossacks operating ahead of them. Lastly, on the left, across the Dnepr, was Bagration's Second Army. Detached from it, General Neverovskii's reinforced 27th Infantry Division took up position near Krasnyi, about thirty miles south-east of Smolensk, to guard against surprise attack from the south. Only one infantry regiment was left at Smolensk.

A first contretemps almost brought the operation to a halt in its early hours. Apprised of the presence of large numbers of enemy troops under Eugène de Beauharnais near Porech'e, due north of Smolensk, Barclay feared to have his right flank turned. He reacted by having Tuchkov's column veer more to the right in order to cover the Porech'e–Smolensk road. Next he deployed the central column around Prikaz-Vydra, except for Count Pahlen's cavalry which he had already ordered to advance towards Rudnia to support the Ataman Platov. It was this move which unexpectedly produced the first and only victorious engagement of the offensive.

Platov's value was confirmed, as it happened, just when the Tsar was approving a cantankerous request from Barclay that the Ataman should be removed from the front: Barclay had lashed out, describing Platov as an egotistical sybarite, ignoble in character, and a poor commander to boot.[11] But on the second day of the otherwise faltering advance (27 July/8 August), at Molevo-Boloto, a short distance from Rudnia, seven regiments of Platov's Cossacks fell upon a division of light cavalry forming Marshal Murat's advance guard. The fury of the Cossack assault wrought havoc on the enemy and as their Ataman reported to Barclay, 'the enemy [troops] did not ask for mercy and the raging Cossacks slaughtered them.'[12] According to Platov his men were roused to frenzy by the sight of villages ravaged by the invaders' raping, plundering, and torturing, sparing not even churches or clergy. These undisciplined troops consisted of Poles, Prussians, and Württembergers, all lumped together by Platov as 'French', whom he thus nicely accused of all the savagery usually ascribed to the Cossacks. Platov was given credit for the victory, though it was in fact the arrival of Pahlen's hussars which decided the French divisional commander, General Sébastiani, to order an immediate retreat. Hotly pursued to the gates of Rudnia, the invaders lost several hundred in prisoners alone, including ten officers.

In Sébastiani's hastily abandoned quarters at Molevo-Boloto, the Russians found a number of documents. Among these, to their consternation, they discovered a message from Marshal Murat accurately alerting Sébastiani to the Russians' proposed offensive. At once the search was on to find the traitor: clearly someone privy to the decision which followed upon the Smolensk war council; and the deep-seated Russian aversion to Germans in high places quickly narrowed the field. To name Wolzogen was almost to name Barclay, as Constantine and Ermolov, the chief accusers, knew. Wolzogen was always close to Barclay, serving as walking atlas and reference book, thanks to his topographical expertise and his phenomenal memory. He had come out at the war council against the offensive and, most sinister, he and Barclay were always speaking German together: Wolzogen could speak no Russian, and French came less easily than his mother tongue. His German jocularity could not pass the language barrier and he was regarded by Russians as 'a fat poisonous spider'.[13] As was to be expected, Barclay stood up for his trusted German assistant, but better than that was the backing of the Tsar, who staunchly ignored demands for Wolzogen's head after Freiherr vom Stein personally vouched for Wolzogen's loyalty. To reinforce his support (rather than to recognize any particular merit), Alexander a short time later awarded Wolzogen a decoration of Germanic origin, the Order of St. Anne Second Class. Wolzogen remained an object of suspicion to his accusers and all their party, however, and Ermolov is alleged to have asked the Tsar for 'promotion' to a German, since the Germans were receiving all the awards.[14] It was six full years before it came out that, after overhearing Toll, a Polish prince, Lubomirski, one of the Tsar's aides-de-camp still in Barclay's headquarters, had written his mother a warning to flee the coming bloodshed, and the letter had been intercepted by Murat.[15] But meanwhile 'the Germans' at Barclay's headquarters were viewed as an untrustworthy, despicable lot. The bull-necked Chief of Staff continued, moreover, with the complicity of the Grand Duke, to inflame spirits. Soon the whole army had heard the story of Ermolov's entering Barclay's antechamber to ask the assembled aides whether one of them could just possibly speak Russian, to announce him to the General.

Even Barclay's efforts to stop further leakages were criticized. Trying to break up the clique of gossips he suspected of being, probably inadvertently, conveyors of secrets, he sent away a number of headquarters officers known for embroidering publicly every scrap of information which reached their ears, including Prince Lubomirski. As Barclay predicted to the Tsar, this measure did not endear him 'to some persons close to Your Imperial Majesty'.[16] He revealed the seriousness of the rift with the Grand Duke when he added: 'If I had the right, I would gladly have removed certain individuals of higher rank . . .'[17]

Just a few days later, but when all attention should have been concentrated on exploiting Sébastiani's flight, Ermolov and the Grand Duke chose a new victim close to Barclay: his Livonian adjutant and protégé Waldemar von Loewenstern, who was often observed in rapid German conversation with Barclay and Wolzogen. A question of discipline and status had suddenly occasioned new friction. Colonel Krüdener, a Balt with a 'Germanic' sense of discipline, commander of the Tsar's favourite Semenovskii Lifeguard Regiment, had punished a subordinate who was a scion of one of Russia's most distinguished families. As penalty for absence from his post, Krüdener had made Prince Golitsyn march on foot with the regiment, as Krüdener himself always did. Ermolov backed the clamorous high-born objection to this 'demeaning' punishment, and Loewenstern intervened on behalf of his fellow Balt by informing Barclay.[18] Again a feud of pure-blooded Russians against those of foreign stock divided the staff and poisoned the air. For Barclay, the meaning was exasperatingly clear. The Smolensk campaign, accepted to a large extent to preserve Russian unity, was turning into a shabby series of divisive intrigues, nettling and distracting, sapping his authority and energy, and endlessly complicating his already difficult task. Worst of all, the entente with Bagration was breaking up. 'I just cannot get along with the Minister,' Bagration wrote to Arakcheev only a week after the Smolensk reconciliation scene:

For God's sake send me anywhere, perhaps to take charge of a regiment in Moldavia or the Caucasus; I cannot remain here; the whole of headquarters is filled with Germans, a Russian cannot breathe here, and besides there is no sense in anything [they are doing] ... I swear to God, they drive me mad with their changes every few minutes ... I truly wanted to serve the Emperor and the Fatherland, but what it amounts to is that I serve Barclay, and I confess this does not suit me at all ...[19]

Bagration's accusation of 'changes every few minutes' was only slightly exaggerated. It seemed to observers that Barclay had lost his head. Vacillation and doubts beset him, and orders and counter-orders, marches and counter-marches reflected his state of mind ever since his unwilling decision to launch the offensive. His only firm conviction lay in the rightness of his long-term strategy; as if the war council agreement had never been, he wrote to Bagration that it would be very good and helpful to retain Smolensk, but not at the expense of the basic objective: 'to preserve the army and prolong the war'.[20] Meanwhile provisions were running short, pillaging increased, the weather had turned, and roads deep in mud exhausted the rain-drenched soldiers slogging to and fro to no effect under the command of officers openly scornful of Barclay's orders. Generals and colonels no longer referred to Barclay de Tolly except by a derisory pun, *Boltai da i Tol'ko*, 'all Bark and no bite' (literally, 'all talk and nothing more').[21] The sobriquet filtered down to the lower ranks and brought a gleam of relief to the hard-driven soldiers. They savoured the contrast with the nickname admiringly attached earlier to Bagration: *Bog rati on*, 'god of the army'. Clausewitz, one of the few on the Russian side who would have approved Barclay had he refused to order the advance, sadly observed the Commander-in-Chief's dismal state of distraction.[22] His manner became even stiffer, his taciturnity gave the lie to 'all talk', his isolation was almost complete. Even his devoted adjutant Loewenstern could not think well of his superior at this time.

While the Russian advance bogged down, Barclay seemed to be compensating by needless bustle. Overwrought and lonely, he wrote to Auguste: 'I remain on horseback for days on end and use the nights for writing my reports; I am often so weary I can hardly manage to hold up . . .'[23]

Misjudging Napoleon's design and still believing the enemy's target to be his right flank, Barclay led more divisions to the Porech'e–Smolensk road. While on the march there, he heard that the French had vacated Porech'e. He countermanded orders and moved back towards Rudnia. Here he hoped to crush Marshal Ney's forces before they could join up with other groups. The gap thus created at the centre of the Russian line was to be filled by the Second Army. He invited Bagration to move up to Prikaz-Vydra. Bagration obliged. But forty-eight hours later, without prior co-ordination with Barclay, Bagration abandoned Prikaz-Vydra. In a high-handed message notifying Barclay of the *fait accompli*, the 'god of the army' made no pretence of submissiveness or even of co-operation: 'I cannot agree with the reasons for your change of earlier dispositions . . . If we forever believe that our flanks are in danger, we shall never find a suitable position . . . The state of my army requires me to take up positions near Smolensk on the road to Moscow. There is neither water nor provisions here; the roads are rain-soaked and sickness is rife . . .'[24]

Finally the Russians learned from freshly captured prisoners that Napoleon had at last left Vitebsk and was heading for the Smolensk area with his Imperial Guard. There was still no way of knowing how he meant to approach nor how he planned to manoeuvre, but Barclay, determined to bar his way, decided to make a stand at Volokova. Summoning Bagration from Smolensk, Barclay asked him to bring the Second Army to positions just south of his own. While the Prince was heading for this new rendezvous, however, Neverovskii, guarding the southern approach to Smolensk, sounded the alarm (3/15 August): the French had slapped pontoon bridges across the Dnepr at Rosasna and Murat's cavalry, closely followed by Ney's IIIrd Corps, were driving towards Krasnyi. Neverovskii had slowed them down, but had not been able to hold them off. His 7,000 men courageously withstood forty successive cavalry charges but, outnumbered two to one, were forced to give way, withdrawing in exemplary fashion – 'une retraite de lion' – towards Smolensk.[25]

Neverovskii's news ended Russian perplexity. For Barclay, Napoleon's general design of envelopment was now clear: 'By his surprise move he wanted to cut us off from General Tormassov's army, from all of Russia's southern provinces, and even from Moscow . . .'[26] Both Barclay and Bagration reacted instantly, whipping back towards Smolensk. Bagration, who was closer, speeded Raevskii's Seventh Corps on ahead to set up defences and strengthen Bennigsen's garrison, while Barclay pushed his First Army forward in an unsparing forced march. The weather was dry again, and movement rapid. In the course of the next day (4/16 August), while Raevskii was already fending off the enemy, both Russian armies reached their destination on the right bank of the Dnepr. The intuitive wisdom of Barclay's ruling to keep the armies within a three-days' march of Smolensk was now proved, partially offsetting his previous error in misjudging the menace to his right flank. Napoleon, too, had miscalculated. His celebrated plan for Smolensk, generally agreed to have been one of his masterpieces, was foiled: he did not expect Barclay's and Bagration's return, which thwarted his threefold objective of taking the town by surprise, cutting off the 'Moscow boulevard', as Napoleon called the Smolensk–Moscow road, and attacking the Russians in the rear.[27]

In a rare moment of concord, the two Russian Commanders-in-Chief agreed that safeguarding the road to Moscow was their first priority and a task for the Second Army. Early the following day (Monday, 5/17 August), while the sun was just beginning to glint on the city's domes and towers, Bagration withdrew to his new position astride the 'boulevard', six miles east of Smolensk, preparatory to moving farther eastwards; there he was joined by Raevskii's Seventh Corps, falling back after having successfully beaten off the first French assaults. The defence of the Old City, the medieval inner core lying within outgrowths of new suburbs, Barclay assigned to Dokhturov's Sixth Corps, reinforcing it with two infantry regiments from Tuchkov's Third Corps.

The momentary agreement between Barclay and Bagration hid, as so often, a disagreement. Of one mind on the strategic importance of Smolensk, they differed in assessing the sacrifice to be consented to for its defence. Bagration, temperamentally incapable of thinking unheroically in terms of delaying tactics, was for defending the town to the last drop of blood: not, as Napoleon subsequently claimed, because Smolensk was a holy city – it was not – nor because the Tsar had repeatedly ordered them to fight to the end – he had not – but out of sheer blazing patriotic fervour. In Barclay's long view, the loss of a town or of additional ground had no bearing on the ultimate outcome of the war. He realized that the surrender of Smolensk would cause an unprecedented uproar, but he neglected to foresee that the uproar was bound to weaken the Tsar's faith in him.

Smolensk, like Vilna, had about 20,000 inhabitants. General Sir Robert Wilson, the British observer who had just arrived on the scene, described it as a small and uninteresting town, while Napoleon, for home consumption, called it one of the beautiful cities of Russia. Its crowded wooden houses were dwarfed by the spires of a dozen churches and by some thirty more or less dilapidated and not very high towers, punctuating the immensely thick stone walls which stretched four miles to enclose the Old Town. On its highest point, facing west, was a crumbling earthen fort misnamed the Royal Bastion. Numberless huts and stalls hugging the outside of the walls offered good cover for an attacking force and greatly hindered the defenders. In every century since it was founded in 882 the town had faced attack, and rarely had its defence been successful. In the opinion of an 1812 eyewitness, Smolensk was a vulnerable position which could not possibly withstand a resolute assault for more than three days.

A few hours after relieving Raevskii, Dokhturov undertook a successful sortie. He was able to drive the enemy out of their shelters beneath the outside walls and out of two suburbs infiltrated by the French during the night. Dokhturov then positioned his troops at critical points within and without the Old Town. Barclay meanwhile had assembled batteries of eight- and twelve-pounders on the heights of the Dnepr's right bank, aimed at the western and eastern approaches. He also threw two pontoon bridges across the river to relieve dependence and congestion on the one stone bridge. Along the Porech'e road he spread out the bulk of his army in depth.

Napoleon had deployed his overpowering mass of troops in a semicircle facing Smolensk. It was clear that his units had not been too dispersed and strung out (as Toll and others of Barclay's assailants at the war council had maintained) to prevent their rapid concentration. All Napoleon's marshals were poised for the attack, except for General Junot who had lost his way and arrived late. But the French Emperor hesitated, in the mistaken belief that Dokhturov's foray meant that Barclay was ready to give battle on the narrow plain outside Smolensk. It was only at two o'clock in the afternoon that Napoleon recognized his error and had three rockets sent skywards to signal the opening of the attack. Almost immediately two hundred cannonballs and innumerable canisters of grapeshot smote the Old Town. For the next seven hours, in searing heat, cannon on both sides thundered relentlessly, drowning the screams of the wounded and dying. The Russians defending the suburbs had to fall back into the Old Town after putting up a desperate resistance. Dokhturov called for support and Barclay sent him the Fourth Infantry Division under twenty-four-year-old General Eugen Prince of Württemberg, together with the Lifeguards' Jaeger Regiment. Twice the three corps of Marshals Ney, Davout, and Poniatowski tried to storm the town and were beaten back. Conceding their failure, Napoleon ordered his howitzer batteries into action, pitching explosives and incendiary grenades high over the walls. The wooden houses flamed instantly and very soon the Old Town was a fiery mass. Napoleon exulted: 'The spectacle Smolensk offered the French was like the spectacle an eruption of Mount Vesuvius offered the inhabitants of Naples . . .'[28]

In this volcanic tumult, discipline faltered, and Barclay, doing his utmost to maintain order and prevent excesses despite deteriorating co-operation from his officers, ordered seven offenders shot. The execution made an 'impression', as he wrote to the Tsar, responding to Alexander's repeated demands: the Tsar was particularly exercised about pillage on Russian soil (looting in Lithuania had concerned him little) and he had written to Barclay that 'a few examples of maurauders shot would have a great effect'.[29] At the same time, Barclay ordered a rescue operation to preserve the two legendary icons of Our Lady of Smolensk, the original and its equally potent miracle-working copy. It was these venerated objects which conferred 'holiness' on the town, and Barclay optimistically believed that removing the icons under army escort to safety would mitigate criticism on the loss of the so-called 'sacred city'.[30] Dokhturov meanwhile grimly held on and Barclay dispatched two more Jaeger regiments to assist him, but as dusk fell the Commander-in-Chief decided that the flaming ruins of Smolensk did not warrant a further sacrifice of men. Despite the warning concealed in a formal rescript (30 July O.S.) from the Tsar, indicating that he was withdrawing his backing for additional cession of territory and expressing 'sorrow . . . that the retreat continued to the very town of Smolensk', Barclay now ordered the evacuation of the town (except for Württemberg's division) and the burning of the bridges.[31] Notwithstanding the massive destruction, the French, according to Chandler, 'had little to show for their pains apart from 10,000 casualties'.[32] Nightfall did not end all activities, however; in the early hours of the morning (6/18 August) the French 'began creeping like mice through every breach in the wall'.[33]

Three specific considerations, beyond his overall Fabian strategy, prompted Barclay's order to abandon the burnt-out rubble of Smolensk. In the first place, he deemed the battle of the 5th/17th to be, in the circumstances, a Russian triumph: all enemy assaults had been repulsed; moreover his rearguard under Württemberg had orders to stand firm and did in fact remain in place throughout the night. Secondly, holding on to Smolensk would involve replacing the defenders with fresh units, thus gravely depleting the First Army which he was pledged to preserve; Raevskii and Dokhturov between them had already lost some 10,000 men, about one-third of their effectives. Thirdly, Bagration was nearing Dorogobuzh, about fifty miles east of Smolensk, thereby leaving a perilous opening for Napoleon at last to drive a wedge between the two armies.[34] Certainly this is what Napoleon should have done – as Chandler points out, Napoleon 'delayed the final advance on Smolensk, then indulged in useless and piecemeal assaults on the city instead of pressing on to cut the Moscow road' – and Barclay had every reason to expect his great opponent to take advantage of the Russian separation if the First Army stayed in Smolensk.[35] It seemed to Barclay unthinkable to risk leaving the small Second Army alone to face Napoleon on the Moscow road. Furthermore, the separation of the Russian armies, under their independent Commanders-in-Chief, led to a dangerous lack of co-ordination. After withdrawing from Smolensk, in fact, Barclay discovered with stupefaction that Bagration had ignored his pressing demand to have sizeable Second Army rearguards posted along the Moscow road. What Bagration had spitefully ordered was a mere screening force, which was commanded to fall back at the first sight of approaching First Army units. Again Barclay realized that concerted action was impossible as long as there was no real unified command.

The uproar caused by Barclay's decision to evacuate Smolensk was much greater than even he had anticipated. Just before he issued the order he was handed an urgent message from Bagration, who urged him 'not to quit Smolensk and to hold on to the position there with every ounce of strength. . . . You will then be in a condition to hit the enemy in the rear when he retreats.' And Bagration warned that withdrawal 'would be very harmful and not please His Imperial Majesty or the Fatherland'.[36] (In the same breath the Prince inconsistently asked Barclay to lend him an entire infantry corps to make up for Raevskii's losses which had weakened the Second Army.) The contents of this supposedly private letter were spread rapidly through Barclay's headquarters. There was nothing in Bagration's message, however, to change Barclay's mind, nothing to alter his realistic assessment of consequences. But it stiffened the opposition of Barclay's generals. The first to argue with him was his great favourite, the popular twenty-eight-year-old Count Kutaisov, commander of Barclay's artillery, who spoke now in the name of a group of senior officers.

Barclay listened attentively to his plea to revoke the order and replied kindly, firmly, and not very satisfactorily for his petitioners, 'Let everyone mind his own business and I shall mind mine.'[37] Sir Robert Wilson, fresh from soundings at the Old Town battle stations, then returned to report pleadingly to Barclay that Dokhturov and especially Württemberg desired to remain where they were, and that all the generals at the different posts had assured him 'they could hold out for ten more days, if supplied with provisions, for not the slightest impression had been made on the defenders'.[38] For the fiery Englishman thousands of Russian casualties apparently did not count nor, according to Toll, did Dokhturov's fears that his exhausted men could not hold out much longer. Wilson was followed, unbidden, by the raging Grand Duke and by Bennigsen, who had assembled Ermolov, Nicolas Tuchkov, and some of the other generals happening to be nearby, to confront the Commander-in-Chief as a group. Without the leadership of the Tsar's brother, these others would hardly have dared take part in a scene which bordered on mutiny. But the Grand Duke's imperial insubordination was sanctioned by scarred old Count Bennigsen, damaged by months of corrosive envy, whom Barclay had come to regard as 'a veritable pest to the army'.[39] Crackling with fury, Constantine insisted that Barclay annul his 'cowardly' order and take Bagration's advice. It was treason to abandon Smolensk. Only someone serving Napoleon's interests could even think of it. Quite carried away and convinced by now that he was the voice incarnate of Russia in the very act of dramatically reversing the fortunes of war for his country, Constantine, surrounded and supported by the others, imperiously and irresponsibly demanded an immediate attack on the enemy. The moment for Barclay to give way had arrived. But with icy confidence he simply gestured to the Grand Duke, granting permission for him to finish. Then, gathering about him all the mystique of discipline, conveying command in every muscle, the Commander-in-Chief tersely announced to all present that he would call upon them individually if ever he needed their advice. Ignoring their calumnies, not stooping to explain or defend, Barclay dismissed the now silent generals with a caustic reminder that the gratuitous proffering of opinion was contrary to service discipline.[40]

There was every reason on every side not to spread news of this confrontation. But word that Barclay would not rescind his order immediately became common knowledge. Wilson wrote in his journal: 'I cannot express the indignation that prevailed. The sacrifice of so many brave men; the destruction of an important town unnecessarily; the suspicion that Buonaparte directed Russian counsels; the sight of the holy city in flames, etc., etc., worked strongly on the feelings of the Russians . . .'[41] Using as pretext the sending of urgent confidential dispatches to the Tsar, Barclay succeeded in getting the Grand Duke off to St. Petersburg, though not without Constantine bitterly resenting his being treated as a common messenger, a *fel'djaeger*.[42] Bennigsen also was sent back to the capital. But even without these two ringleaders, the opposition to Barclay in his own army, the hatred among those who remained, now swelled to a climax.

Letters and reports streamed constantly from the field to St. Petersburg and

Moscow, recording the rebellious dismay of the generals. Clamour grew for the appointment of Bagration, or even Bennigsen, in Barclay's place. The quartermasters-general of the two armies, Toll and Saint-Priest, were exceptional in remaining within the bounds of objective criticism. Ermolov and Bagration charged like bulls. Almost daily they exchanged inflammatory letters egging each other on to the overthrow of 'the minister and his clique'. At the same time they bombarded Arakcheev and Rostopchin with messages intended for the Tsar or for the Grand Duchess Catherine and her circle, great friends of Moscow's military governor. Bagration managed to envisage Barclay at once as a military fool and as a sly fox. Two days after the battle of Smolensk he wrote to Arakcheev (7/19 August): 'Your minister may be good at ministerial affairs, but as a general he is not only bad but simply worthless . . . I am truly going out of my mind from grief . . .'[43] The following day another Bagration outcry went to Arakcheev, containing even an allusion to executing Barclay for treason: 'I held out for more than thirty-five hours with 15,000 men and I was beating them, whereas he did not remain even for fourteen hours. It is disgraceful. It is a blot upon our army and as for him, I consider that he should not stay alive . . . It is not my fault if the minister is a feeble, cowardly, muddle-headed dawdler – everything that is worst. The whole army weeps over it, and condemns him out of hand . . .'[44] In a note in Bagration's hand to Rostopchin (14/26 August), expletives (roughly: blackguard, scoundrel, and fool), probably considered unfit for Catherine's eyes, were indicated by initial letters and dashes:

That b_____ s_____ f_____ Barclay gave away an excellent position. I personally begged him and wrote him in all seriousness not to withdraw, but I had hardly reached Dorogobuzh when he came dragging after me . . . I swear we had Napoleon in the bag, but Barclay never agrees with my proposals and does everything that serves the enemy. I can positively tell you that we would have covered Napoleon with shame if only the minister had held fast . . . All the French prisoners tell me that he [Murat] was saying that once he vanquished Bagration he could take on Barclay with his bare hands . . .[45]

Dokhturov, disgusted and ready to quit the army, wrote to his wife: 'You cannot imagine, my friend, what a stupid and loathsome man Barclay is: he is irresolute, sluggish, and not capable of commanding any section, least of all an army. The devil only knows what got into him . . . leaving so many wounded in the hands of the enemy. My heart bleeds when I think of it . . .'[46]

The disaffection, however, was not quite as complete as Bagration and others wished to convey. One case, for example, was that of Fiodor Glinka, whose originality was apparent in poetry – rare religious verse with startlingly martial metaphors – and in politics (he later became a Decembrist): he refused to be carried away by majority opinion about Barclay. In his campaign diary he wrote: 'But when I behold the features of this leader of Russian forces and I see him, calm, unperturbed, serene, I am ashamed of my doubts. Then I think, no, a man who has not a thought-out plan and a right purpose cannot have such an unshakeable presence of mind . . .' Glinka took heart from the example of Columbus, who completed his task despite the discontent of his men: 'That is how . . . General Barclay de Tolly led our armies with unusual care from the Neman' until now without having even the smallest unit cut off, practically without losing a single cannon or vehicle; this sensible leader will in the end see his scheme crowned with the desired result . . .'[47]

While Russians, with the exception of men like Glinka, were ashamed of the retreat and embittered against Barclay, French generals were filled with admiration for his skill and steadfastness. To be sure, Napoleon, frustrated once again, railed against him: 'How shameful for Barclay to have yielded the key to old Russia without battle! . . . All he lacked was resolution . . .'[48] But officers around Napoleon thought otherwise: 'Among us, [Barclay] was praised for having maintained this wise defensive, despite the clamour of a vainglorious nation . . .'[49] Ségur summarized opinion at French headquarters:

He had forestalled Napoleon . . . his resistance had been proportionate to the time and the place; . . . this fragmented war and the losses it entailed had been only too much to his advantage, each one of his steps backward increasing the distance from our reinforcements and decreasing the distance from his. He had done everything properly, whether risk, defence, or abandonment.

And yet he had brought on himself general animadversion. But this was in our eyes the greatest praise. We approved of him for having disdained public opinion . . .[50]

The admiration of the enemy was useless as well as unknown to Barclay. Also unknown to him was the fact that already, while he was still fighting the battle of Smolensk on 5/17 August, the Tsar had convened a special commission to choose a supreme commander superior to the commanders-in-chief of all the Russian armies. Nor could Barclay at this moment be sure that history would record his long retreat and repeated abandonments of towns and territory as 'a great military success', as a leading Russian historian, Platonov, was to write more than a hundred years after Smolensk.[51] But what Barclay did, perhaps, suspect was that 'more often than not nations are saved in spite of themselves'.[52]

CHAPTER XI

CROSSFIRE

> The enemy is coming fast,
> Farewell Smolensk and Russia!
> Barclay's fighting days are past,
> He's heading towards Siberia.
>
> *'Songs of a Glorious Epoch, 1812–1814, Sung by Russian Officers', Russkii Arkhiv (Moscow 1887)*

Barclay's evacuation of Smolensk proceeded smoothly through the night and he rested his army a mere two miles beyond the St. Petersburg suburb, near the junction of the Moscow and St. Petersburg roads. Having burnt the bridges and left General Württemberg (reinforced by units from Korff's cavalry) to stave off the pursuers, Barclay, still hoping to keep Napoleon in doubt as to whether the First Army was heading for Moscow or St. Petersburg, split his troops into two columns and started them off via different detours towards the rendezvous with Bagration at Dorogobuzh. Half-way there the two First Army columns were to meet at the Dnepr. This excellent plan, however, broke down in execution.

Württemberg managed to repulse Ney's men all day (6/18 August), withdrawing only at six in the evening when the French had enough pontoon bridges in place to start crossing the Dnepr *en masse*. But in the ranks of the two First Army columns, dawdling, darkness, and default combined to produce chaos. Units in the second column lost contact with each other and several regiments took off in the wrong direction. For some of the first-column troops, a night's tramping through damp woods brought them nearly full circle, almost back to the St. Petersburg suburb where an irresolute Ney, receiving inconclusive reports from his patrols, had stopped for the night instead of pushing on towards Moscow. The Russians Ney sighted in the morning (7/19 August), therefore, he naturally assumed to be only some rearguard remnants not worth a serious action, and thus they were able to slip away after only a skirmish, and proceed as planned.

Meanwhile Barclay had prudently sent ahead, directly along the Moscow road, a mixed detachment of some 2,400 Jaegers, hussars, and Cossacks under General Pavel Tuchkov (Tuchkov III, younger brother of Nicolas Tuchkov, commander of the Third Corps). This body had reached a point six miles east of Smolensk, near Lubino and Valutina Gora, when Tuchkov, hearing the approach of enemy cavalry, turned about and beat off a first assault. For the second time that day the French misjudged the situation, this time believing they were engaging Barclay's main army. Ney's and Murat's troops together with one of Davout's infantry divisions under General Gudin flung themselves against the modest Russian detachment. A new hazard was developing at the same time on Tuchkov's left flank: Junot's corps had crossed the Dnepr at its southward bend, and was ready to fan out. Barclay, seeing the danger, brought Tuchkov's strength up to 8,000, thereby enabling him to stand his ground for another three hours before retreating behind the small stream called Stragan'. Here one of Barclay's columns was to debouch on the Moscow road; it was thus a point to be held at all costs until then, and Tuchkov and his men stood firm.

By lateish afternoon the number of troops engaged had swollen to some 50,000 French and 22,000 Russians, but still the Russians were not to be dislodged. Barclay, once again in his element as field commander, sloughed off in action the bitterness of his disputes with the Grand Duke, Bennigsen, *et al*. The Commander's leadership in battle remained as unquestionable as ever, inspiring Wilson to change his tune to one of fervent admiration:

Overwhelmed with shells, shot and musketry, [the Russians at one outpost] flew back to seek shelter behind the crest of the hill; but General Barclay . . . opportunely arrived at this moment and seeing the extent of the danger to his column galloped forward, sword in hand, at the head of his staff (including myself) . . . and rallying fugitives, and crying out 'Victory or death! We must preserve this post or perish!' by his energy and example reanimating all, recovered possession of the height. . . .

The storm of fire was heavy; but, so help me God and my sword hereafter, I would rather have died with Barclay than have quitted the ground . . .[1]

More prosaically Clausewitz confirmed Barclay's radiant example of 'perfect calmness . . . steadfastness and personal courage', as well as his skill in the utilization of troops and seizure of 'reasonably good terrain' to give 'partial battle'.[2]

Luck was on Barclay's side. Napoleon, dismayed that 'the hands of the Grand Army had met upon Smolensk and clasped the air', had cantered out to Valutina Gora expecting at last a major battle.[3] When informed – misinformed, rather – that only Tuchkov's detachment was involved, the Emperor readily believed that Barclay had eluded him once again. Disheartened, Napoleon turned back to smouldering Smolensk, missing by yet another mistaken judgement the bold stroke which could have ravaged half the First Army.

And still Barclay's luck held: Junot refused to co-operate with Ney and Murat. At dusk the French were still trying desperately to overrun Tuchkov. Leading their last attack of the day, General Gudin fell and, on the Russian side, Tuchkov himself was wounded and captured despite heroic attempts to rescue him. The twelve-hour combat, moving from steep stream bank to stream bank (called by the French the battle of Valutina Gora; by the Russians, Lubino), had cost the Russians 5,000 to 6,000 casualties, the French 7,000 to 9,000. By midnight the last of the debouching First Army column had safely reached the Moscow road, and four hours later, unpursued, it was on the march to join the other column and thence to rendezvous with Bagration. Thus ended the fighting around Smolensk, the watershed of the war, and thus a new phase of the campaign began.

In the days that followed, reconsiderations were forced upon the principal protagonists, Napoleon, Barclay, Bagration, and eventually Alexander. The greatest change was in Bagration, who suddenly began advocating a measured strategy closely resembling Barclay's own and even viewed with some respect the past conduct of the campaign. The former proponent of incessant attack was now recommending offensives 'when conditions are favourable' and emphasizing the importance of defence and manœuvrability.[4] Bagration had certainly had time for reflection, during his days of comparative inactivity while Barclay had been plunged in battle, and it is probable that the expectation of responsibility had given a more sober turn to his thinking: there must have seemed every likelihood that Barclay was going to be removed and Bagration appointed to command the two armies.

As for Napoleon, back in Smolensk, he was again under heavy pressure from some of his commanders who were begging still more urgently than at Vitebsk for a pause. Murat, his brother-in-law, is said to have gone on his knees. Using the excuse of answering an enquiry from Barclay about the captured Tuchkov's health, Napoleon did actually make a small peace gesture consisting of compliments via Barclay to Alexander, with assurances that war could not alter Napoleon's esteem and friendship for the Tsar.[5] But Alexander did not take the bait. And in the end the very difficulties of replenishing the Grande Armée in manpower and supplies pushed Napoleon on: he was convinced that only an advance could keep the army from disintegrating. As on similar occasions, when hemmed in and in a difficult situation, Napoleon chose, daringly, to flee forward ('la fuite en avant').[6] Besides, the immense Russian sacrifices in the defence of Smolensk seemed proof that the enemy would seek at all costs to bar his way to Moscow: battle and therefore victory seemed assured.

Barclay, on his side, was realizing that a battle had to be fought before drawing much closer to Moscow. The Grande Armée had now melted to some 156,000 men and the approach of General Miloradovich's reserve corps meant the Russians could at last confront an enemy not greatly superior to themselves. In spite of some reluctance in St. Petersburg to arming the peasants, Barclay also counted on support from the population. 'Fall upon scattered enemy units,' he directed the people, calling for armed harassment before and behind his lines; 'catch and destroy enemy patrols and bands of marauders.'[7]

He therefore instructed his Quartermaster-General to search out an advantageous terrain for battle, and on 9/21 August Barclay and Bagration met at Umol'ia to inspect Toll's choice. But now it was Bagration's turn to worry about an unprotected flank – which his army would have to guard – and he rejected the position outright. He had another site in mind, one mile closer to Dorogobuzh. This position was 'abominable' according to Clausewitz, and Barclay, who found it faulty on four counts, resolved on a further search and further withdrawal.[8] The two disheartened Russian armies fell back on the Moscow road beyond Dorogobuzh on 12/24 August. As Barclay was passing a marching regiment, a soldier's voice was heard: 'Look, look, there goes the traitor.'[9] Bagration, in contact as always with Rostopchin, warned his fellow Commander-in-Chief: 'Our retreat to Dorogobuzh has thrown everybody into a state of excitation. We are both unanimously accused, and if it gets known that we are approaching Viaz'ma, all Moscow will rise against us . . .'[10] Barclay quickly assured the Moscow Governor that the fatherland would be saved: 'With the Almighty's help, we and Prince Bagration will be giving a general battle . . .'[11] But it was only beyond Viaz'ma that Barclay and Bagration finally found a position they could agree upon – at Tsarevo-Zaimishche, one day's march west of Gzhatsk and hardly more than a hundred miles from Moscow. Although Barclay was not altogether happy about the absence of natural protection at either wing, he and Bagration both knew that a better position could not be found at a safe distance from the capital. The two armies at once began throwing up earthworks and preparing for battle.

Alexander's decision to appoint a supreme commander and bypass Barclay was made, as has been seen, even before the abandonment of Smolensk. On returning from a visit to Moscow where the intensity of patriotic fervour had thrilled him, the Tsar's immediate impulse had been to rush to the front, reassuming the supreme commandership he had relinquished after Drissa but which *de jure* was still his. Grand Duchess Catherine tartly dissuaded him, telling him to appoint a leader 'in whom the troops would have complete trust, and on that score, you inspire none whatsoever'.[12] This letter was quickly followed by a message hand-carried to the Tsar from General Count Shuvalov, Barclay's erstwhile defender now blaming him for every ill including bread and fodder scarcities, warning that Russia was lost unless the armies were put at once under a single command.[13] These urgings coincided with the arrival of the letters from Bagration and others criticizing Barclay's irresoluteness during the Rudnia episode before Smolensk. In St. Petersburg as at the front Barclay was being called a traitor, or out of his mind, or at best a fool; in any case, he was wrecking Russia.[14] Alexander, who had accepted every calumny against Speranskii six months earlier, was quite untouched by the attacks on Barclay's loyalty and unshaken in his belief that Barclay's course of action in general was the only possible one. But reasons of state restrained the Tsar from further shows of either trust or faith. The army's confidence in Barclay had been eroded and finally shattered, and an army which lacked confidence in its leadership could not be counted on. Barclay was there to be blamed for the long and frightening withdrawal. As the Tsar later wrote to him, 'We had to expect this disapprobation and I was prepared for it.'[15] The Tsar was always prepared to throw bodies to the wolves.

Stung by Catherine's sisterly assessment of his military virtues, Alexander chose to ignore her and her consort's recommendations in favour of Bagration. The Tsar also had second thoughts about offering the overall command to Bernadotte, an odd notion fleetingly entertained before a meeting with the new Crown Prince of Sweden. Many general officers favoured the Livonian General, Count Peter Pahlen, banned from St. Petersburg as the arch-conspirator against Tsar Paul, but Alexander refused even to consider this 'perfidious and immoral' man who in any case had not seen active duty for twenty years.[16] The selection narrowed down to Kutuzov, who was the popular favourite though not, as Clausewitz confirms, the unanimous choice of the army. Some of the generals saw

Kutuzov more as a wily and greedy courtier than as a field commander, and some remembered that what Suvorov had most appreciated in him besides his courage was his foxiness. According to Clausewitz, cunning was the only attribute he still retained at sixty-seven.[17] He was obese, debilitated, and decayed. Moreover, the Tsar continued to detest him, still blaming his 'sycophant character' for Austerlitz, and holding him responsible for negotiating poor peace terms with the Ottoman Empire and failing to swing the Sultan against Napoleon.

Nevertheless the choice of Kutuzov was a sheer necessity at this moment. He was Russian to the core, and no other name could so effectively rally the anxious patriots, reassure the xenophobes, and turn the war into a national crusade. Rather than name him outright, however, Alexander interposed a nominating committee, though its choice was a foregone conclusion. To avoid any mixing of signals and with a flourish of imperial hypocrisy, he gave an unmistakable hint to the Special Commission, just before its sitting, by conferring on Kutuzov the hereditary title of Prince – for his 'advantageous' conclusion of the Turkish war.[18] The Commission duly met, therefore, for three and a half hours (5/17 August), duly studied the various complaints in private letters from Bagration, Saint-Priest, Toll, and Shuvalov, and some of Barclay's official dispatches to the Tsar, agreed on the necessity for a single commander, reviewed the formal candidatures of Dokhturov, Tormassov, Bennigsen, and Bagration, and called for the immediate appointment of Kutuzov.

But the Commission went further and ruled that 'it was inappropriate for the Minister of War to be at the same time a commander-in-chief and hence able to influence the actions of other commanders-in-chief who enjoy seniority in rank.'[19] It was therefore recommended that Barclay be stripped of his ministerial post. That humiliation was intended was made entirely clear by the Commission's offer of a choice for Barclay between remaining with the First Army in the field or returning to St. Petersburg but even then not as Minister of War.

For three days after receiving the Commission's recommendations the Tsar could not bring himself to sign the ukase appointing Kutuzov. Only after getting the news of the fate of Smolensk did he send out rescripts transmitted by Kutuzov to each of the commanders-in-chief of the four armies of the West: Barclay, Bagration, Tormassov, and Chichagov:

Various grave complications coming after the two armies met have impelled me to appoint one Commander above all others. I have chosen for this post the General of Infantry, Prince Kutuzov, under whose command I place all four armies . . . I am confident that your love for the Fatherland and your devotion to duty will clear the way for new exploits by you which I shall be only too pleased to recognize with befitting rewards . . .[20]

Barclay received his copy on 15/27 August while his army was passing through Viaz'ma still in search of good terrain for a battle. It was one thing for the Tsar, as Barclay had implored him, to appoint a single leader, a popular figurehead; it was joltingly different to receive a demeaning official notification out of the blue, unsoftened by a single personal word from the Tsar; especially just when Barclay's strategy was at last showing results and Napoleon's superiority in numbers was beginning to even out. Stoically Barclay assured the monarch of his 'real happiness' and his desire to prove by the sacrifice of his life his 'eagerness to serve the country in whatsoever post or assignment'.[21] Realizing that it was feeding time for the wolves, but not yet informed of the Commission's recommendation in this respect, Barclay himself brought up the question of his Ministry. He suggested that the Tsar should not allow feelings of generosity to one 'who once enjoyed His entire confidence' to interfere with naming a new Minister of War if such was required for the good of the country.[22] Only at the end of Barclay's letter did a note of chagrin seep in: 'Had I been motivated by blind and reckless ambition, Your Imperial Majesty would perhaps have received quantities of reports of battles fought and nevertheless the enemy would be at the gates of Moscow without encountering sufficient forces able to resist him. . .'[23] It was still too soon for Barclay to feel the full impact of the event. On the same day he wrote to Auguste that what mattered most of all was that the Tsar should not take command into his own hands, 'but God only knows whether the choice [of Kutuzov] is a good one'. For comfort he added: 'As for myself, I am too much of a patriot to feel any bitterness, besides I have only contempt for the petty intrigues which must have played a role. My conviction of having served the Tsar with greater loyalty and fervour, and perhaps even with greater courage than anyone, remains undiminished. Our ultimate triumph will prove it . . .'[24] In a very brief note dated 24 August (O.S.) the Tsar notified Barclay that in view of the General's 'momentous and manifold' preoccupations at the front, he had given the duties of Minister of War to Prince Gorchakov.[25]

The injury Alexander felt he was doing to Barclay no doubt increased the monarch's anger. He was angry with Barclay and Bagration, and angry that he had no choice but to name Kutuzov. To his sister Alexander wrote an exasperated and contradictory explanation of why he had appointed Barclay in the first place, why he thought Barclay was superior to Bagration, how he knew of no one better than Barclay, and how 'Rostopchin told me that all Moscow considered both Barclay and Bagration incapable of command and wanted to see Kutuzov take over': 'And at this point Barclay, as if on purpose, committed blunder upon blunder near Smolensk, and thus there was nothing I could do but give in to the unanimous clamour and name Kutuzov . . .'[26] Meanwhile, in a brief but courteous message accompanying the rescript, Kutuzov notified Barclay of his imminent arrival at the front.

Barclay, with equal courtesy, immediately informed Kutuzov of the battle preparations under way at Tsarevo-Zaimishche, and as soon as Kutuzov arrived on the scene on 17/29 August Barclay lost no time in taking the new Supreme Commander on a tour of inspection of troops and terrain. Flat, unobstructed land, a rarity in that region of groves and thickets, stretching for many miles in front of the hamlet of Tsarevo, made it impossible for the enemy to approach by stealth; behind the village, softly rising ground gave the Russian artillery a commanding position on the ridge; and beyond lay a safe road across dried marshes for withdrawal towards Gzhatsk in case of need. Kutuzov – who, like

Barclay, had promised both the Tsar and Rostopchin to protect absolutely the approaches to Moscow – was quick to appreciate the useful features of the terrain, and proclaimed the position to be 'wholly advantageous'.[27] He directed the speeding up of field fortifications and showed, by dismissing Barclay's precautionary scheme of preparing a fall-back position just beyond Gzhatsk, that he had no intention of being routed from the site.[28]

Thus Barclay had reason to feel some satisfaction. There was seemingly to be a change in personnel but not in policy. The dispositions he had taken to defend the fatherland were not going to be reversed, and Russia's 'ultimate triumph' would still be his vindication. In any case it was Russia's triumph, not his own, that was his deepest concern and, writing after midnight to Auguste, Barclay uttered his sincere relief that at last the armies had a single leader. The thunderous welcome the troops had given this leader, however, must have had something to do with Barclay's 'ardent longing' for the day when he could renounce all pursuits to live happily in seclusion with his family.[29] Apart from Kutuzov's approval of the Tsarevo battle site, Barclay had indeed no reason to be happy. He cannot have enjoyed Kutuzov's hearty comment to the honour guard: 'How can one retreat with such splendid fellows!' More serious, more devastating, was the prompt reorganization of staff. Kutuzov simply snatched Colonel Toll for himself and transferred to Supreme Headquarters the quartermaster corps of both the First and Second Armies, with their engineering staffs of pioneers and sappers and all their pontoons and equipment. (Toll was delighted: from his cadet days he still retained his admiration and respect for Kutuzov, who had then been head of the Cadet Corps; and Kutuzov still paternally called him 'Karl'.) The new Chief of Staff responsible for these rearrangements was old Bennigsen, whose totally unexpected reappearance filled Barclay with forebodings. The durable ex-Hanoverian, eight months Kutuzov's senior, had been making his way in ignominious disfavour to St. Petersburg when he learned of Kutuzov's appointment and his own elevation to Chief of Staff (by recommendation of the Special Commission); hurriedly he retraced his steps in order to join Kutuzov's retinue in time to be 'welcomed' back by the man who had just sent him away. In what happened next Barclay saw Bennigsen's hand.

Overnight, Kutuzov changed his mind. On 18/30 August Barclay and Bagration were ordered to abandon the 'wholly advantageous' terrain of Tsarevo and withdraw their armies to Gzhatsk.

The explanation of this sudden volte-face is still controversial. Kutuzov himself gave two main reasons for it: a numerical deficiency he had noticed in several regiments (along with the extreme exhaustion of those men who had been repeatedly in battle); and the need to await reinforcements from Moscow. In respect of the first point, Toll has claimed categorically that the losses in both Barclay's and Bagration's armies were fewer than might have been expected – between 16,000 and 17,000 men.[30] Kutuzov, doubtless briefed by one of Barclay's critics, explained the deficiency not so much by battle loss as by desertion to marauding bands, claiming that 2,000 marauders had been caught in a single day.[31] The implication of course was that Barclay had been lax in maintaining discipline. Here again Toll, despite his devotion to the old man, contradicts Kutuzov. Deserters and marauders there certainly were in great numbers but Eugen of Württemberg supports Toll's view, judging that the squabbles at headquarters had not impaired the spirit of the rank and file and that discipline and order remained intact.[32] Kutuzov himself wrote to his wife: 'The morale of the army is extraordinary . . .'[33] As for Kutuzov's second point, what he expected in the way of reinforcements was unrealistic. On 19/31 August he knew that General Miloradovich had brought to Gzhatsk fewer than 16,000 hastily gathered men – just about enough to fill the gaps he had noticed. He also knew than no other regular troops were available anywhere nearby. The *opolchenie*, or people's militia, of which up to 75,000 had been promised by the boastful Rostopchin, was the only other source of manpower. Kutuzov was thus apparently exchanging a good defensive position for the promise of some ill-trained militiamen. (When 10,000 – not 75,000 – of these irregulars in their drab kaftans did reach the eventual battle site, they were mostly put to work on entrenchments.)

So clearly did Kutuzov originally plan to stay at Tsarevo and so unconvincing were the reasons proffered for precipitously changing his mind and dangerously narrowing the distance to Moscow that it is not to be wondered at that Barclay and others believed personal rather than military factors to be involved. Bennigsen was boasting freely of having spotted better battle positions beyond Gzhatsk, and in every way he was instigating moves to cripple Barclay and Bagration. Now the rearguard of the First Army was taken away from Barclay and placed directly under Bennigsen. And the Commanders-in-Chief of the two armies were relegated lower and lower in the hierarchy of power as Kutuzov decreed that orders from Bennigsen and from Colonel Kaisarov, the opinionated twenty-nine-year-old *général du jour*, were to be considered as if coming from the Supreme Commander. It soon emerged that Toll and Kutuzov's pampered son-in-law Colonel Prince Kudashev were also giving orders in Kutuzov's name and without, so Barclay claimed, Kutuzov's knowledge. In fact the Supreme Commander seemed to Barclay to be so in name only, while his assistants acted as they saw fit.[34] The suspicion arose that the two young colonels, Kaisarov and Kudashev, had convinced His Serene Highness that a victory won in a position of Barclay's choosing would diminish Kutuzov's merit in the eyes of his countrymen. As Tolstoy put the matter, blandly enough: 'Kutuzov did not wish to occupy a position he had not himself chosen . . .'[35]

Yet it may finally be that the whole episode of accepting the position and then refusing it was simply a matter of dissemblance, for Kutuzov, to a greater degree even than Barclay, did not divulge his innermost thoughts. After a thorough analysis of Kutuzov's words and deeds the independent Soviet historian Tarlé has concluded that Kutuzov, like Barclay before him, did not wish to oblige Napoleon with a pitched battle before Moscow.[36]

CHAPTER XII

BORODINO

> Why was the battle of Borodino fought? There was not the least in it for either the French or the Russians. Its immediate result for the Russians was, and was bound to be, that we were brought nearer to the destruction of Moscow – which we feared more than anything in the world; and for the French its immediate result was that they were brought nearer to the destruction of their whole army – which they feared more than anything in the world.
>
> Leo Tolstoy, *War and Peace*, translated by Louise and Aylmer Maude

The halt at Gzhatsk was short, and so was the next one, at the high-towered Kolotskii monastery. Here, after Kutuzov's armies had moved past, Murat's relentless vanguard caught up once again with the Russian rearguard (now under Konovnitsyn), and they fought for thirteen hours. The third day's march brought the first Russian units, on 22 August/3 September, to the outskirts of the village of Borodino on the Kolocha river, seventy-two miles from Moscow. In the next two days the two Russian armies took up battle positions according to Kutuzov's directives, Barclay's troops occupying the right and part of the centre, with Bagration on their left.

The site, first spotted and praised by Bennigsen, had been surveyed and approved by Toll. The soundness of the choice has been questioned by military experts, including Clausewitz, but, so Kutuzov explained to the Tsar, it was one of the best defensive positions to be found in that flat region (after the 'wholly advantageous' terrain of Tsarevo-Zaimishche had been eliminated). Hedged in by the New Smolensk Road in the north and the Old Smolensk Road in the south, the battle terrain was bordered a couple of miles to the east by the steep banks of the Moskva river. (In order to impress his countrymen and convey a dramatic though false impression that he was fighting 'under the walls of Moscow', Napoleon named the battle fought on this terrain 'the battle of the Moskva', although that river had no role in the action.) The four-mile frontage was unobstructed to the west. On the left, the Old Smolensk Road ran through a large wood and past an ancient burial mound or *kurgan*. The entire area, except for a narrow, three-mile-long ridge running from south of Borodino to north of Utitsa, was intersected by half a dozen brooks and as many ravines, with several hamlets nestling among hills and knolls and woods of various sizes: Tolstoy's Pierre Bezukhov was not alone in seeking vainly to discover a proper, recognizable battlefield in these surroundings.[1]

Arriving on the scene with his advance guard, Barclay reconnoitred the sector assigned to his army, and gave orders for improvements where natural protection was inadequate. The following day, 23 August/4 September, Barclay accompanied Kutuzov on an inspection of Bagration's sector to the south. The Georgian Prince had good reason to complain: his left flank was exceedingly exposed and could easily be turned. To help remedy this situation, three arrow- or V-shaped entrenchments with embrasures – the 'Bagration *flèches*' – were being hurriedly dug on three neighbouring hillocks in front of Semionovskoe village. Barclay, finding these precautions insufficient and perceiving that the deployment chosen by Kutuzov's staff over-emphasized the right at the expense of the left, proposed to move all of his corps leftwards, leaving the protection of the right flank to a screen of Jaeger battalions and Cossacks. Kutuzov seemed to agree, but then instead had the idea of placing the pike-bearing Moscow *opolchenie* to the rear of the left flank to mislead Napoleon into over-estimating Russian strength there. (Kutuzov's idea did work at the beginning, but as the battle unfolded Barclay's proposal was perforce adopted.)

A full mile to the west of the *flèches* stood the pentagon-shaped Shevardino Redoubt in precarious solitude, requiring for its defence a good third of Bagration's army; and one mile to the north of the *flèches*, on a plateau, the engineers had set up the Great Redoubt, also called the Raevskii Redoubt; its eighteen twelve-pounders dominated the approaches to the Russian centre.

Kutuzov and Barclay differed in their conjectures as to what strategy Napoleon would adopt. The Supreme Commander, as evidenced by his reports to the Tsar and to Rostopchin, at first expected a large flanking movement.[2] At some point later on Kutuzov appears to have changed his mind and expected a frontal attack against the centre in an endeavour to smash through to the New Smolensk Road. Barclay, on the other hand, firmly believed that the French Emperor, while tying down the Russian forces at the centre, would attempt to overrun the vulnerable Russian left with a large enveloping movement.[3] As it turned out, however, Napoleon thought that an extensive flanking movement of this sort – which could have been devastating to the Russians – would make him lose too much time and deflect him from his objective. Therefore he incautiously turned a deaf ear to Davout's plea to join his own force with Poniatowski's beyond the Russian left and with this mass of 40,000 troops roll up the Russians from left to right and put an end at once to 'the Russian army, the battle, and the war'.[4]

On 24 August/5 September the Grande Armée was sighted, with Beauharnais heading for Borodino village; Davout, Ney, Junot, and Murat for the Shevardino Redoubt; and Poniatowski for Bagration's left flank. Napoleon's disposable force was now reduced to 135,000 men and 587 cannon. Facing him a mile away Kutuzov lined up 126,000 men (including the raw Moscow and Smolensk irregulars) and 640 pieces of artillery.* Napoleon's superiority – owing to the Russian Fabian strategy – had shrunk to a matter of six to five.

---

* Estimates among reliable sources vary between, for the Russians, a minimum of 120,000 (Zhilin) and a maximum of 132,000 (Wolzogen); for the French, 130,000–135,000 (Zhilin) and 156,000 (Chandler). Only regarding artillery numbers is there general agreement.

Losing no time, the French Emperor ordered the immediate assault of the Shevardino Redoubt. The foredoomed struggle for this Redoubt continued without interruption all afternoon. Time and again it changed hands, but even Bagration's appearance at the head of a grenadier division could not affect the ultimate outcome. At seven in the evening, after Neverovskii had lost half his brave and battle-proven division, Davout's equally stubborn troops took firm possession. Four hours later, at eleven o'clock at night, Kutuzov finally ordered Bagration to fall back with all his men to the main defence line. Barclay was indignant about the useless sacrifice of some 6,000 valiant men.[5] And even Ermolov, in the past always quick to take issue with Barclay, concurred in condemning the wastefulness of this whole episode.[6] Barclay's disapproval of the conduct of operations was soon fed by other incidents. After losing Shevardino, Kutuzov and Bennigsen realized that resistance to Poniatowski's Polish–French forces on the Old Smolensk Road could never be assured by six Cossack regiments and green *opolchenie*. Without informing Barclay, Kutuzov sent Toll to Tuchkov with orders to rush his First Army's Third Corps on to the Old Smolensk Road. When Barclay discovered this breach of command and asked for an explanation, the Prince shrugged it off as a mistake and promised it would not happen again. But a more dangerous mistake followed: Bennigsen, not knowing of Kutuzov's scheme to keep Tuchkov's Corps hidden in the Utitsa woods for a surprise strike, ordered it out into the open.

These incidents, coming after the degradation already suffered, increased Barclay's bitterness. Kutuzov wisely told Barclay and Bagration to proceed freely, and they were therefore able to display valuable initiative in combat, but their low opinion of the aged Kutuzov as a tactical commander, along with distrust of his motives, prevented them from recognizing their debt to him as they went into battle. Barclay, who had never shunned responsibility, could not appreciate the rare opportunity of fighting Napoleon without having to bear ultimate accountability for the outcome. Instead he dwelt critically on the ineptitude, confusion, and blunders of the Supreme Commander and his staff: a natural reaction, in view of his discovery that the Tsar was being told, in order to increase Kutuzov's merit if he proved successful, that Barclay had handed over the army in deplorable shape.[7]

The full measure of his bitterness appears in the letter – in effect, a semi-suicide note – he sent the Tsar that evening, in the expectation of full battle the next day.[8] At last Barclay shows his wounds – those 'shattering the interior of my soul' – inflicted directly or indirectly by the Tsar, and comes out openly about 'the disgrace . . . the disdainful manner in which I am treated!' He rises up against the Tsar's two rescripts, the one which named Kutuzov Supreme Commander and insultingly promised Barclay 'befitting rewards' for 'new exploits', treating him, as Barclay says, like a 'venal poltroon', and one to Kutuzov which disapproved operations under his predecessor. Time will tell whether his own conduct of the war was right, he said, but for the present he saw no point in trying to justify himself: 'the way they treat me here, it is as if my sentence was signed.' Almost worse, he was not allowed to do 'anything' and he felt utterly useless. The fact was that he was being given no part in decisions and Ermolov confirms that 'nobody even asked his opinion'.[9] 'Afflicted in spirit', Barclay therefore made a 'last' appeal: 'This is why I dare beseech Your Imperial Majesty to rescue me from this miserable position and dismiss me entirely from Your service. I dare be this frank, Sire, since we are on the eve of a bloody and decisive combat where I shall perhaps succeed in fulfilling my utmost wish . . .'[10] To make it clear that his 'utmost wish' is for death in battle, Barclay pleads for the granting of 'this unique and perhaps last of my prayers': 'I ask for nothing; I desire nothing except to pass the sad rest of my life, if I cannot sacrifice it for you, Sire, on the field of honour, in an isolated corner of Your Empire and if possible forget the past . . .'[11]

Having relieved himself of these dark thoughts, Barclay remained his vigorous and commanding self the next day, 25 August/6 September, during which only minor skirmishes took place, mostly on the Russian right flank where Napoleon tested the solidity of Barclay's lines. But the probers, though insistent, were warded off and Barclay could report to Kutuzov that his troops had not flinched during the assault and 'carried out to the letter my orders to stand fast at all costs'.[12] Most of the day, however, was spent by both sides in perfecting their field fortifications and boosting the morale of their troops. The salvaged icon of Our Lady of Smolensk was paraded through the deeply bowing Russian troops by censer-swinging priests, while French officers and the Imperial Guard were shown a new portrait of Napoleon's son, the infant King of Rome. Napoleon proclaimed: 'Here is the battle you have so ardently desired . . . Let it be said of you, "He was in the great battle under the walls of Moscow!"'[13] Kutuzov, in his little drozhki, drove from regiment to regiment giving encouragement to the men and enjoining the commanders to be chary of committing their reserves too early: 'The general who still has some reserves left is not vanquished.'[14] This sensible warning was repeated by Barclay and Bagration. Bagration also urged his corps commanders to provide the troops with hot kasha gruel and wine. Barclay informed all First Army generals that during the battle he could be found between Ostermann-Tolstoy's Fourth Corps and Dokhturov's Sixth Corps. (Actually he did not stay there but was everywhere.) He ordered his commanders 'to restrain their men from banging off with their muskets to no purpose, and to get their gunners to economize as far as possible on their ammunition. A rapid harmless fire may astonish the enemy in the beginning of a battle, but soon loses its power to impress.'[15]

Barclay, General Kutaisov, and Colonel Zakrevskii spent the night before the battle in a peasant hut. Kutaisov, twenty-eight, was Commander of the First Army Artillery; Zakrevskii, twenty-six, was head of Barclay's field staff. The two young men were subdued by Barclay's sadness. The Commander spent most of the night writing, and only towards morning sealed and pocketed what he had written, and dozed off for a little while.[16]

After a clear summer night during which each side observed the other's campfires, a morning mist rose above the Kolocha.[17] It was just past five o'clock of 26 August/7 September when Barclay rode up to the crest of Gorki hill accompanied by his staff. He was dressed not in his usual battle gear but as conspicuously as possible in full uniform, three stars and all his medals on his chest, and his general's bicorne flourishing its plumage. His aides were startled, but his manner told them nothing, expressing only serenity and confidence. He had hardly reached the concealed battery on top of the hill when hundreds of French cannon opened fire all along the front. The Russian guns at once replied, and thus began the deafening, suffocating cannonade which was to last for twelve unimaginable hours.

No sooner had he reached his destination than he was handed a pressing message from Colonel Bistrom. This courageous commander of the Lifeguard Jaeger Regiment – posted, against Barclay's will, on orders from Kutuzov and Bennigsen, in forlorn isolation beyond the Kolocha – had seen the rapid movement of a large French force towards the village of Borodino. Bistrom's four battalions were no match for the sixteen battalions of Delzon's 13th Infantry Division now approaching inexorably to double-time drum beat. In the first fifteen minutes Bistrom lost half his force, and thirty of his officers were put out of action. Borodino village fell to the French. Barclay sent Loewenstern to help Bistrom extricate his men, but the retreat of the Jaegers across the Kolocha bridge turned into a stampede under 'murderous fire': 'We were so cramped that not a single enemy musket shot was wasted.'[18] As the French pressed forward across the bridge, Barclay, seeing the danger of any enemy bridgehead on the Russian side of the Kolocha, sent in Colonel Vuich, whose Jaeger Brigade of the 24th Infantry Division was nearest, to mount a bayonet charge. Vuich had only eight battalions but they were intact, and the French were thrown back with heavy casualties. Barclay's sappers immediately blew the bridge.[19]

This first phase of the Borodino battle lasted a deadly hour and a half. Had Barclay had his way, only a small detachment for observation purposes would have been stationed in Borodino village: he was cruelly aware that the dismemberment of an élite regiment could have been avoided.

After thwarting this first French attempt to cross the Kolocha, Barclay and his aides cantered off through falling shot and fallen bodies towards the Raevskii Redoubt where cannonballs were crashing like hail. Among those riding at Barclay's side was the future Decembrist leader A. N. Murav'ev, who described the 'unprecedented savagery' with which the combatants were cut down by 'cannonballs, canister shots, grenades, fired by more than a thousand guns on both sides, not to mention 200,000 muskets, bayonets, and other weapons'.[20] On the French side alone 60,000 artillery shells and 1,400,000 musket bullets were fired that day.[21] While dead and wounded fell all around, 'their bodies crushed by gunwheels and horses' hoofs racing across the fallen', Murav'ev, hearing that his younger brother, not yet sixteen, had been hit, charged off to the Redoubt with Barclay's unhesitating blessing to try to find him.[22] Loewenstern, soon himself to be wounded, takes up the narrative of Barclay's cavalcade as it passed before the Preobrazhenskii and Semenovskii Guard Regiments, who were not yet committed but were waiting in impeccable formation: 'These fine fellows impassively saluted Barclay. Already their rows were being thinned by cannon fire, but they stood stoically as before, their muskets at their sides, and calmly closed ranks when one or more of them was felled . . .'[23] The reason for such scenes, and ultimately for the enormous losses, was mainly the choice of terrain. Because the battlefield at Borodino was so compact, 'the second line of infantry stood no more than two hundred steps behind the first line, the cavalry three hundred to four hundred steps behind the infantry, and the reserves no more than a thousand steps behind the cavalry; hence, not only both lines of infantry and the cavalry, but even some of the reserves were exposed . . . even when not in action, to crossfire from strong enemy batteries.'[24]

Barclay rode rapidly from place to place, wherever danger was the greatest, calmly giving the necessary orders, imperturbable even when his horse was shot from under him, as happened three times in the day, and then moving on to the next danger spot. Improvising in the heat of battle, both Barclay and Bagration, stirred by a new spirit of solidarity, dispensed with formalities, no longer held to their allotted sectors, or strictly observed their separate chains of command; victory was all. Eyewitnesses testify to the extraordinary impression Barclay made that day on all beholders. It was as if the struggles of the whole campaign were washed away, as if he had found the solution to an impossible problem. It was said that he became 'the soul of the army at Borodino'.[25] The Prince of Württemberg, who himself had four horses shot beneath him, recognized that Barclay's commanding presence inspired confidence as did no other, radiating a marvellous composure amid the chaos.[26] Württemberg was reminded of the 'noblest knights of old'.[27] Glinka, the soldier–poet, describes how Barclay's white horse stood out against the dark smoke of battle, how his brow gleamed like a target, and 'his honest face, his calm features, his eyes full of good sense expressed his self-possession'.[28] To Loewenstern, Barclay seemed a towering figure who 'appeared to have grown by several inches while, in the sweeping tumult which shook the ground all around us, he unflinchingly and with heroic composure tried to assure the outcome of the battle'.[29] Württemberg noted that Barclay's presence was a mixed blessing in that 'it seemed to draw increased fire from the enemy; three of his orderlies were killed; one of his adjutants, Lamsdorff, had his head blown off; and still another one, Klinger, had a leg torn off.'[30] Loewenstern and Seslavin, who later joined the irregular forces that harassed the retreating French, were among seven others in Barclay's entourage who were wounded.

Although no sign could be read in his face, Barclay's conduct, according to Glinka, was interpreted by nearly all as suicidal. 'I myself', Glinka says, 'overheard officers and men saying, "He is seeking death!"'[31] Tarlé describes how 'Barclay, who apparently was searching for death, went off ahead and stopped in a place where the fire was particularly intense.' Not to be outdone, Miloradovich then went even deeper into enemy fire, dismounted, sat upon the ground, and announced that he would lunch there – or so Tarlé recounts.[32] But, as seems clear from his letter to the Tsar, Barclay was serious; he was indeed putting his life at hazard, with death not a certainty but a strong possibility, and the outcome beyond his control. Every soldier risks his life, but to seek out consistently the places of highest risk is a form of attempted suicide, submitting oneself to the judgement of the gods. Now his mourning for the 'loss' of the Tsar, and for his own reputation, was translated into simple courage; and by drawing enemy fire like a beacon, he was threatening the Tsar – the little father of all the Russians – with the loss of a tried and loyal soldier, making a 'final' appeal, protesting his innocence, provoking remorse, and demonstrating the purity of his intentions: he would die as he had lived, for Tsar and country. The pattern was deep within him, perhaps from the time of his first experience of being forsaken. At Ochakov in 1788 he was 'in all the most perilous places', in Finland in 1790 in 'all the most dangerous spots'. At Hof in 1807: 'I considered it my duty to sacrifice myself with my entire regiment' in order to save the army. At Preussisch-Eylau, crossing the Kvarken – he had never shunned danger nor shrunk from sacrifice. This pattern was repeated and intensified at Borodino.

The main impact of Napoleon's attack, as Barclay had anticipated, was aimed at the Russian left centre, against the *flèches* and the Great Redoubt, and Barclay's greatest concern during the first four hours of the battle was to redeploy forces piecemeal to assist Bagration and Raevskii. The Second Army had regained the *flèches* after a first French attack at six o'clock and Bagration – on his own or with Kutuzov's consent – had already drained off some reserve forces from Raevskii and Tuchkov. With French guns again concentrating their firepower on him, Bagration, hard pressed, was obliged to appeal to Barclay, who responded at once by moving Baggavut's entire Second Corps to the *flèches* plus three élite Lifeguard regiments (Ismailskii, Litovskii, and Finliandskii) and various cavalry units. But he knew it would take Baggavut some two hours to traverse the whole length of the position – hours which would not have been wasted had Kutuzov listened in earnest when Barclay had proposed moving the entire First Army to the left, thereby also avoiding this gobbling up of reserves early in the morning. 'Eyes blazing,' Barclay hastened up to Kutuzov's observation post near Gorki village where it appears he expostulated with the Supreme Commander on the question of the reserves, since Loewenstern saw Kutuzov seemingly trying to mollify Barclay and, as they rode back into the thick of battle, Barclay told Loewenstern, with some satisfaction at having penetrated Kutuzov's lethargy, 'At least they won't be scattering the rest of the reserve.'[33] But returning to the centre of the Second Army, Barclay found that everywhere reserves had already been committed. There was no point in recriminations, and in any case it was quite clear that the Supreme Commander, though keeping himself informed through the ubiquitous Colonel Toll, was pinned to his observation post and in no way seriously directing operations: 'Kutuzov, decrepit and exhausted, was unwilling or unable to make use of the channels of communication and the system of staff support that Barclay had worked out in his *Yellow Book*. The scamperings and inspirations of a person like Colonel Toll were no substitute for the work of a body of trained and trusted staff officers . . .'[34]

The already blood-soaked *flèches* were changing hands about once an hour, each· French assault being followed by raging counterattacks with Bagration throwing everything into the attack. By ten o'clock, thanks to reinforcements and the concentrated fire of three hundred guns, Bagration had retaken the *flèches* for a third time, but Barclay saw that more help would be necessary and called Ostermann-Tolstoy and his Fourth Corps into position between the *flèches* and the Redoubt.

At this point the 26th Infantry Division of Raevskii's Corps on the Redoubt was still intact, having repulsed a first cautious thrust at the rampart; on the Russian far left, Tuchkov had stopped Poniatowski near Utitsa, before being killed (and being replaced by Baggavut). Suddenly Beauharnais's Corps, having crossed the Kolocha on pontoons, began a murderous bombardment of the Redoubt. Raevskii's men, being attacked from both sides, fled in disorder through low-hanging clouds of whitish-grey smoke. Barclay, who was returning from Gorki, saw the smoke but could not see through it, and sent Loewenstern ahead to investigate, while Ermolov, coming upon the scene, brilliantly rallied the fleeing soldiers and turned the tide. Having commandeered a battalion from the Tomsk Regiment, Loewenstern helped recapture the battery. Barclay meanwhile ordered flanking attacks, and the French were pushed down the slope. The reversal took only ten minutes, but the costs were high, 'no fewer than 3,000 casualties' for the French by Barclay's estimate. Among the Russian casualties, Ermolov received a canister shot in the neck, Loewenstern was sent to the dressing station with a superficial but disabling arm wound, and Barclay's favourite among all the younger generals, Kutaisov, the Commander of Artillery, who was as gifted in music and poetry as in war, was killed.

The moment the Redoubt was back in Russian hands Barclay re-formed the lines around it. He pulled out the exhausted, depleted 26th Division and replaced it with Likhachev's 24th Division. Countermanding an order from Toll, he directed the Prince of Württemberg to plug a gap to the left of the Redoubt with part of his 4th Division. While these moves were going on, fighting in the whole sector had started up again more hotly and more confusingly than before. Barclay, Miloradovich, Raevskii and their staffs were suddenly almost overrun by enemy cavalry and had to resort to hand-to-hand fighting, only saving themselves by slipping inside a defensive square formed by one of Württemberg's battalions.

Meanwhile at the *flèches* at about the same time, shortly after ten o'clock, Bagration was mounting one of his inspiring counterattacks to break up the gathering enemy forces when his left shinbone was smashed by a shell. Bleeding profusely, he lost consciousness and was carried to the dressing station. Upon coming to himself he recognized Loewenstern who was having his arm seen to. Bagration beckoned him over and gave him a message for Barclay. 'Tell the General', said Bagration 'that the fate, the preservation of the army is in his hands; so far all is going well, but let him look after my army, and may God help us all.' Barclay, who had only just been informed of the Prince's injury, was 'startled' when Loewenstern delivered this message.[35] It marked a turning-point: not all the rescripts in the world could mask the fact that Barclay was the effective leader of the Russian forces and had the fate, the preservation, of the army in his hands. There could be no shirking responsibility; there could be no suicidal self-sacrifice. From now on he faced death in a different mood.

To the consternation of his troops Bagration was evacuated from Borodino and he died three weeks later, at the age of forty-six, having taken part in twenty campaigns and wars and more than 150 skirmishes and battles. Twenty-seven years later the remains of 'the god of the army' were brought back to Borodino and buried there.

A degree of confusion was engendered by Kutuzov changing his mind several times about who was to be Bagration's successor, but he finally appointed fifty-six-year-old Dokhturov, one of the oldest generals on the field. The Supreme Commander also sent Toll to take a look at the situation of the Second Army, telling him, 'Karl, whatever you say, I'll do.'[36] But there was not much that could be done, beyond sending in more reserves. It took Napoleon's troops two more assaults before the *flèches* were definitely in their hands at eleven-thirty and the defenders had to withdraw behind the Semenovskii ravine.

Barclay, galvanized by Bagration's message, set about saving the Redoubt, the last, the crucial Russian bastion. The French marshals had already moved more guns to the *flèches* and the Redoubt was caught in crossfire from left and right. It would not be long before Napoleon would order the ultimate assault.

But a timid diversionary action against the French left flank across the Kolocha – proposed by Platov, seconded by Toll, and authorized by Kutuzov – though it ended in failure, sufficiently distracted Napoleon to give the defenders of the Redoubt some respite. They hastily assembled ammunition supplies, and Barclay drew up units of the Fourth and Sixth Corps supported by Lifeguard Regiments, cavalry, and 100 cannon. By two o'clock the 150 French guns concentrating on the Redoubt had begun another full-scale bombardment, but Barclay was encouraged to see that his infantry and Jaeger regiments, changing from battalion column formation to defensive squares, 'withstood the terrifying fire with remarkable fortitude'.[37] Barclay and Miloradovich and their staffs were themselves caught in the cannonade, but escaped without injury.

Soon after three in the afternoon the assault itself began, not with a frontal attack of the French infantry, though they had been the first to set out, but with wave after wave of French, Saxon, and Polish cuirassiers, supported by light cavalry, bearing down on the flanks. Young Auguste de Caulaincourt's cuirassiers were the first to break through Dokhturov's infantry on the right of the Redoubt, leaving their commander, the brother of Napoleon's Master of Horse, dead on the field. On the left, the cuirassiers of Latour-Maubourg, followed by Polish Uhlans, outflanked the Redoubt. From the front came the Saxon cuirassiers rushing across the breastwork and through the embrasures, silencing the great battery. Attacked from the rear, from the sides, and from the front, the outnumbered Russians held on heroically. Over and over Russian cavalry – Korff's dragoons and Kreutz's hussars – counterattacked until, as an eyewitness recorded, 'in the end their troops formed an entangled mass as usually happens after repeated cavalry charges'.[38] Schubert recalls that Paskevich, commander of Raevskii's 26th Infantry Division, or what was left of it, 'was tearing his hair in despair . . .; Barclay, whose horse [the third one] was shot under him, calmly tried, afoot, to restore order.'[39] Barclay personally brought the Horse Guards into line to hold the Redoubt while he sent for reinforcements: 'My cavalry being already exhausted to the very limit I sent for the 1st Cuirassier Division in the belief that it was still in the place I had assigned, for I had intended to save it for a decisive blow; but unfortunately some one, I don't know who, had moved it to the extreme left flank; all my adjutant found were two regiments of Lifeguard Cuirassiers . . .'[40] 'Figuratively speaking Barclay was beating off the enemy with one hand and groping behind him with the other for reinforcements from the reserve; thanks to Kutuzov's sporadic interventions there were at least two occasions when that hand closed on empty air.'[41] Barclay therefore reassessed the desperate situation: 'I already saw our fate sealed; my cavalry was too weak to stop the enormous enemy and I did not dare lead it against the enemy for fear it would be overthrown and pressed down on our infantry. I pinned all my hopes on the brave infantry and artillery, for they had proved themselves immortal that day. They met my expectations: the enemy was stopped . . .'[42]

With excellent timing the two reserve Lifeguard Cuirassier regiments (under General Shevich) now arrived, and Barclay threw them in to the attack at once. He reinforced them with two hussar and three dragoon regiments and, eventually, a reserve regiment apiece of more hussars and dragoons. As cuirassiers clashed against cuirassiers through unremitting artillery barrages from both sides, there began, in Barclay's words, 'a protracted cavalry battle such as was never fought before'.[43] Seen from the Gorki observation post, the setting sun flashing on the metal of cuirasses, helmets, and arms made a 'dreadful yet majestic picture'.[44] At the height of the noise and confusion, Wolzogen reports, 'Barclay and his staff got into the thick of the struggle. A French cuirassier had already lifted his sabre to split Barclay's head, but was shot dead by Barclay's groom.'[45] (A little later his adjutants saved Barclay from the spears of Polish Uhlans.)[46] The Prince of Oldenburg's adjutant, rich in experience of Marengo, Austerlitz, and Preussisch-Eylau, thought the charge of the Russian cuirassiers 'the most magnificent' he had ever seen – though his report loses in authority when he adds that 'the echo of a single Russian blow on the enemy cuirasses made the enemy scatter like chaff in the wind'.[47] With a great deal more than a single blow the Russians nevertheless did rout the French cavalry altogether, leaving it in a state from which it did not recover for the rest of the campaign: a Soviet writer goes so far as to state that 'Napoleon's cavalry found its grave at Borodino.'[48] But now it was the enemy infantry that came swarming into the Redoubt from all sides. Even as they were pushed back, new Grande Armée columns poured over the corpses choking the ravine and took up the charge. Russians and French stabbed each other and fell together. In the end it was the French who had the extra ounce of strength to hold on to the smoking mound after its defenders, with 'unflinching, blind, and resigned courage', had perished almost to a man.[49] 'Whatever dreadfulness our imagination can produce was surpassed here,' shudders the Polish Captain Heinrich von Brandt. 'Men and horses, alive, mutilated, or dead – lying six or eight deep – covered the approaches far and wide, filled the ditches, and were piled up inside the Redoubt.'[50]

Through the lengthening shadows the cannonade continued, though less strongly than before, while on the Russian left Baggavut was still stubbornly fighting Poniatowski and Junot. In vain Barclay tried to rally a few battalions to retake some of the Redoubt cannon, but the general prostration and disarray were too great. Only around 13,000 still remained, in untouched regular units, of the original 126,000 troops, and these units were scattered all over the field of battle. Some 15,000 *opolchenie*, still fairly intact but unarmed except for their pikes, brought the grand total of usable manpower up to 28,000. Napoleon disposed of just about the same number of fresh troops: 20,000 Old Imperial Guards – whom he adamantly refused to commit, although they could possibly have tipped the scales – and some regiments of Delzon's division. The Russian line, dented but unbroken, had been pushed back roughly fifteen hundred yards – a small achievement for the enormous effort made by the Grande Armée.

Reeling with fatigue, Barclay held himself together by downing a glass of rum and a bite of bread. The day was ending. It was time to get Kutuzov's opinion. He sent Wolzogen to give a complete report to the Supreme Commander and request orders for the next phase, and he reminded Wolzogen to get all instructions in writing 'because with Kutuzov one must be careful'.[51] Wolzogen found the Prince about half an hour's ride beyond the rear, with a retinue big enough to make up an auxiliary corps, though a closer look showed it to be a collection of rich young sons of noble Russian families. These able-bodied officers who 'had taken no part in the horrifying seriousness of the day' were surrounded by champagne bottles and were feasting on all sorts of appetising delicacies. Somewhat aggressively Wolzogen launched into his report, detailing in his heavy Prussian accent the position and condition of the army, recounting with feeling what he himself had observed. But Kutuzov, suddenly awake, interrupted him, shouting furiously: 'What low-down sutler woman have you been getting drunk with that you dare give me such an inept report? I am the one who knows best how the battle is going! The French attacks have been victoriously repulsed everywhere and tomorrow I shall put myself at the head of the army and drive the enemy from Russia's holy soil!' Whereupon, comments Wolzogen, Kutuzov 'looked defiantly at his corps of attendants who all nodded their enthusiastic approval'. Wolzogen swallowed his anger, interpreting his 'outrageous reception' and Kutuzov's 'cunning, self-serving motive' as proof that His Serene Highness did not dare to repudiate before his entourage the jubilant bulletin which was already prepared, claiming a glorious victory. Remembering Barclay's stipulation, Wolzogen asked for a written order either for the resumption of the battle or for whatever else should be undertaken. Kutuzov stepped away from the crowd to confer with Toll, who stopped munching a capon long enough to prepare a note for Barclay which the Prince then signed, handing it disdainfully to Wolzogen. (An identical note went to Dokhturov for the Second Army.) It read: 'I can see from all the movements of the enemy that he is as weakened as we are and hence, having already engaged him in battle, I have decided to put order into our army during the night, supply our artillery with more ammunition, and continue the battle tomorrow. To withdraw in the present disarray would bring about the loss of the artillery.'[52]

By the time Wolzogen reported back to Barclay the sky was dark except for a red bruise over Borodino. Wolzogen claims that Barclay shook his head over the message, saying that the troops were so exhausted and hungry that a new battle the next day would be out of the question.[53] But Barclay had spent the whole day coping with impossible situations and he was not stopping now, whatever he may have said. Long before Wolzogen's return Barclay had been issuing orders and arranging the army for battle the next morning. To keep the lines straight and facilitate movements, fires were lit at regular intervals. Miloradovich was to spread out his Sixth Corps from the Gorki hillock in a straight line to Semenovskoe village. The Fourth Corps was to take up position next to the Sixth. A second line was to be formed by the two Cavalry Corps with the Fifth Corps in reserve. To Dokhturov he proposed that the Second Army, reinforced by units from the Fourth Corps, take up position between the Fourth Corps and Baggavut. Baggavut was to move forward to the position he had last defended. Two thousand *opolchenie* were to dig a new lunette on the Gorki hillock. After a reconnaissance of the Raevskii Redoubt showed that only a few enemy units were still there and even these were scrabbling their way out, Barclay ordered Miloradovich to send several battalions and a battery to occupy the Redoubt at dawn. 'All these measures I reported to Kutuzov; he thanked me for it, approved everything and told me he would come to my camp where he would await dawn and renew the battle . . . Everyone was cheered by our victory and eagerly awaited the morning.'[54] Barclay surely exaggerated the victory and the eagerness; nevertheless the fact that Napoleon had abandoned terrain from which the Russians had been unable to dislodge him must have signified to Barclay that the Grande Armée had suffered terrible losses and was therefore vulnerable.

After checking that all his orders were being carried out, Barclay and his few remaining aides threw themselves for the night on the straw-covered floor of a peasant's hut at Gorki. However inconclusive the military results might prove, it had been a day of destiny for Barclay. Not only would the Russians 'certainly have been lost without the dedication of Barclay', but also, as Glinka saw, it had been a day of self-liberation:[55] 'Two challenges confronted Barclay de Tolly at Borodino, and he seems to have met both triumphantly. The second one, when he triumphed over his own feelings, was the most important . . .'[56]

Meanwhile Wolzogen's sobering report to Kutuzov had after all disturbed the Supreme Commander, and alarming news was trickling in from various unit commanders as well. The Prince ordered Toll to go and see for himself the condition of the Second Army and the left wing in general, and what Toll saw surpassed even Wolzogen's gloomy assessments. The Second Army was a shambles. It had lost some 20,000 men, three-fifths of its strength. Indeed, not counting the irregular units, the two combined armies had been reduced by 36 per cent, with the dead, wounded, and strayed totalling 44,000.[57] A complete inventory was of course impossible, but Toll proceeded by spot-checks. Thus, encountering a smallish unit, he asked its colonel to identify the regiment and was told, 'They are the Second Division' – the remnant, that is, of twelve battalions and not, as it seemed, of two.[58]

The only heartening note was that the Grande Armée had left the field and withdrawn behind the west bank of the Kolocha. Napoleon's army had suffered perhaps as much as Kutuzov's – estimates vary from 30,000 to 50,000 dead and wounded, and the leadership loss was staggering: 14 lieutenant-generals, 33 major-generals, 32 staff officers, 86 aides-de-camp, and 37 regimental colonels.[59] All in all, many more men fought at Borodino than at Preussisch-Eylau or Waterloo, and many more men died there. Napoleon, who (unlike Kutuzov) had spent at least three hours on the field towards the end, was overwhelmed by 'a great sadness', according to Ségur: 'this victory, so hardily pursued, so dearly bought, was incomplete . . . The losses were immense and out of all proportion to the results.'[60] For the first time Napoleon found the price of glory to be too high, according to his Prefect of the Imperial Palace, who observed that Napoleon's 'colour was flushed, in contrast to his usual appearance, his hair dishevelled, and his whole appearance tired' – but 'be that as it may, victory was complete.'[61] The Prince of Württemberg, at least after the event, showed clearer judgement: 'In all honesty, Kutuzov had no more reason to let Alexander in St. Petersburg celebrate with a Te Deum, than had Napoleon grounds for victory reports to Marie Louise . . .'[62]

After Toll returned to headquarters with his devastating account of the army's condition, Kutuzov reluctantly laid aside the long, glowing report Toll had previously drafted for the Tsar. Though still convinced on the basis of the French withdrawal that he was the victor of Borodino, Kutuzov now decided against continuing combat in the morning. He ordered a four-mile fall-back behind Mozhaisk. His justification for the move was sent to the Tsar the next day in a revised and very brief dispatch on Borodino: 'It is not a matter of the glorious battle just won, but that our main objective remains the destruction of the French Army . . .'[63] There is no direct evidence that the Tsar noted how Kutuzov was now using Barclay's language. What he did, however, with the dispatch was to pencil in extensive editorial changes, delete all references to the new retreat, command Te Deums, and send 100,000 rubles and a field-marshal's baton to Kutuzov, 50,000 rubles to the wounded Bagration, and St. George stars, second class, to Barclay and Bennigsen. (Surviving soldiers got five rubles each.)

At midnight Barclay was sleeping soundly when a lieutenant tracked him down to the hut at Gorki and startled him awake with Kutuzov's orders for withdrawal. The First Army artillery was to leave at once, the infantry and cavalry at 2 a.m. Barclay sprang to his feet and called for his horse. He would see Kutuzov and persuade him to change his mind. But when told that Dokhturov was already carrying out orders and retreating towards Mozhaisk, Barclay subsided: 'The only thing left for me was to obey with a heavy heart,' although 'the reasons for the retreat were kept from me.'[64]

It has been truly said that 'in regaining the army's confidence [Barclay] won one of his proudest victories'.[65] After so long and desolate a time when the troops had not even been saluting him, 'at Borodino from every regiment there rang out "hurrah!"'[66] A highly coloured phrase, no doubt, but indicative. Thus encouraged, Barclay had looked forward to leading these men in battle in the morning; yet it is likely that what the Barclay of Borodino desired was not necessarily what Barclay in supreme command would have ordered.

CHAPTER XIII

'THE OFFENDED FATHERLAND'

The people you had always saved from danger
Have mocked your name as if you were a stranger.
And he whose subtle mind discerned your heart,
To please the multitude, with cruel art
Condemned your cause.

Alexander Pushkin, 'The Commander' (translated by David Walters)

Those who were able to, about seventy thousand, left Borodino with their guns and baggage, abandoning to their fate countless dying or gravely wounded comrades. Kutuzov marched his exhausted forces eastwards in four straggling columns on and beside the New and Old Smolensk Roads, the rear being well protected by cavalry and Cossacks under the command first of Uvarov and then of Miloradovich. A halt for the day was made at Mozhaisk, but there was no question of remaining there for another pitched battle. Most of the infantry regiments were seriously disorganized and many were led by junior officers, their elders having perished. There was no sign of reinforcements or ammunition supplies or fresh horses or even the shovels and axes Kutuzov had urgently requested of Rostopchin 'in order to save Moscow'.[1] Kutuzov therefore ordered the continuation of the retreat, and thousands more of the wounded (the Marquis of Chambray speaks of 10,000), who had made their way that far but could go no farther, were again left behind, huddling on the main square, or in churches and houses, only to be driven out the very next day when the French made room for their own disabled.[2]

The condition of the retreating survivors was deplorable, especially as the weather had changed, temporarily turning almost autumnal with chill rains. Most official and patriotic Russian writers would have one believe that the withdrawal was carried out in perfect order, always in battle readiness. The theoretician Clausewitz, who saw soldiers as stereotypes rather than as men, wrote that he saw 'no trace of disintegration'.[3] More plausible, however, is Barclay's description of the retreat being executed 'in the greatest disorder'; no preparations of any kind had been made, and the soldiers just 'tossed themselves into the mud for the night'.[4] Chambray, a usually reliable witness, reported that the Russian infantry 'was in such disorder that it formed a tangled mass unfit for combat'.[5]

Barclay, too, was suffering from the aftermath of Borodino. The recurrent chills which had afflicted him ever since the crossing of the Kvarken now struck him again and high fever kept him out of the saddle. The exemplary calm of

Borodino gave way to irritability, and he felt subjected to 'hourly vexations and insults'.[6] His opinion was not sought and in this decisive phase of the campaign he was being kept in the dark even as to what choices were being considered. But it was not Kutuzov's habit to disclose his thoughts, and Barclay was not the only one to worry over the Supreme Commander's intentions as the army now approached the ancient capital of Muscovy.

Doubts soon disappeared, however. Bennigsen had once again discovered what he believed to be a good defensive position. It stretched between the low hill of Salutation and the Sparrow hills, between the villages of Fili and Vorob'evo, on the western outskirts of Moscow. On 1/13 September, after five marching days, the army encamped near Fili. Barclay, justifiably distrustful of Bennigsen's judgement, insisted upon mounting his horse again despite fits of shaking and rode off to inspect the position. What he saw was a 'cobweb' of narrow, in some places impassable, gullies and gorges. Through one of these flowed a stream; another was sixty to a hundred feet deep, its banks rising steeply just behind where the first line of infantry would be. Units would be separated from one another without means of communication. The left flank at Vorob'evo would be entirely vulnerable, yet beyond the reach of reserves because of the terrain; and to the rear lay the sprawling streets of Moscow where, in case of retreat, the pursuing enemy could destroy the whole army 'down to the last man'.[7]

Spurring back to headquarters, Barclay met Bennigsen, to whom he described the flaws in the position, asking him whether it had really been decided 'to bury the army in that spot'.[8] Bennigsen had obviously not reconnoitred the area seriously, and in the face of Barclay's criticism felt obliged to promise that he would soon take a look himself at the left wing – but he did not find it urgent to do so.

With the help of a sketch he had made, Barclay reported on his observations to Kutuzov. According to Barclay's account, the Supreme Commander appeared 'horrified'. Toll, present at Kutuzov's side, entirely subscribed to Barclay's report and added that he himself would never have chosen this site. Kutuzov then asked Ermolov what he thought, and Ermolov's condemnation of the 'untenable' position was so blistering that Kutuzov felt his pulse and asked him whether he was quite well. Seemingly unnecessarily – except for the record – Kutuzov ordered Ermolov, Toll, and a Spanish colonel newly arrived from the Peninsular War to return to the area and reconsider it. (Meanwhile the deployment of troops on the left wing was to be delayed.) When the three came back with nothing positive to say about the position, Kutuzov, who a few minutes earlier had confided to Prince Eugen of Württemberg that 'in the present case I must rely only on myself, whatever I may be, whether wise or simple-minded', summoned his corps commanders to a council of war at his modest quarters in a peasant hut later to be known as 'Kutuzov's *izba*' or cottage.[9]

Ermolov, who had reported back to Barclay, accompanied him to the council of war. The tension between the two men had disappeared after Borodino. Each had been impressed by the other's performance during the battle and Ermolov

Barclay de Tolly. Portrait by George Dawe. In the background, the Russian camp outside Paris in 1814. This portrait inspired Pushkin's poem, 'The Commander'.

(Left) Auguste Barclay de Tolly, *née* von Smitten. Probably painted between 1813 and 1815.
(Right) 'Christel' – Auguste Christine Anna von Lueder, Barclay's niece and foster-daughter. Wife of General Wilhelm Peter von Weymarn and mother of the first Prince Barclay de Tolly-von Weymarn.

Stolben. The Livonian estate, north-east of Riga, that Barclay bought six months before his death. Lithograph by H. Mützel after the drawing by J. F. Krestlingk.

Tsar Alexander I and his wife, the Empress Elizabeth. Pair of portraits given to Barclay by the Tsar.

Barclay de Tolly in 1816. Drawn from life and engraved by Carl August Senff in Dorpat. Dawe's portrait of Barclay was painted from this engraving.

Field-Marshal Prince Kutuzov, who took over from Barclay de Tolly and was named supreme commander in August 1812. Engraving after a drawing by Hopwood.

Colonel Count Zakrevskii, who saved Barclay from a lynching in 1812. Portrait by George Dawe.

General Prince von Wittgenstein, a stalwart Westphalian, who served Russia soberly and well. Portrait by George Dawe.

Major Baron von Loewenstern, Barclay's candid Livonian adjutant. Engraving by Alexander Albeth.

General Platov, general of cavalry and ataman of the Don Cossacks. The commander of these greatly feared troops had little in common with Barclay. Portrait by George Dawe.

General Prince Bagration. He commanded the Second Army in 1812 and would gladly have taken over Barclay's First Army as well. Engraving by Vindromini.

Colonel Davydov. A hussar colonel and partisan leader in 1812, he inspired the character of Denis Denisov in Tolstoy's *War and Peace*. Portrait by George Dawe.

Lieutenant-General Ermolov. A friend of Bagration, he was Barclay's Chief of Staff in 1812. Portrait by George Dawe.

The War Gallery of the Winter Palace (Hermitage), Leningrad. The Gallery houses 332 portraits of Russian heroes of 1812–1814 painted by the English George Dawe and his Russian assistants Alexander Poliakov and Vasily Golike between 1819 and 1828.

The Russian army at the Battle of Smolensk, 1812. Because of Barclay's determined evacuation of Smolensk Bagration called him 'a feeble, cowardly, muddle-headed dawdler' and 'simply worthless'.

The Russian army at the Battle of Borodino. Painting by Denis Dighton. An idealized view: in reality the battle grounds were far less spacious and open.

The Council of War at Fili, before the retreat through Moscow in 1812. Painting by A. D. Kivschenko, 1882. Left to right: Kaisarov, Kutuzov, Konovnitsyn, Raevskii, Ostermann-Tolstoy, Bennigsen, Barclay, Uvarov, Toll, Dokhturov, Ermolov.

Cossacks stripping a body in the Grimma suburb of Leipzig, after the battle in 1813. Barclay was intolerant of indiscipline and brutality but even as Commander-in-Chief he could not maintain the humane army he dreamed of.

Barclay's conquest of Paris, 31 March (N.S.) 1814. Bronze bas-relief on the socle of a monument in the Barclay de Tolly Mausoleum, Beckhof, Estonia by Vassili I. Demuth-Malinovskii, 1823. Barclay has paused at the approaches to Paris before Montmartre to view his army marching into the city.

could no longer suspect Barclay of cowardice or treachery. At the same time, Ermolov had become disillusioned with Kutuzov. As Barclay and his Chief of Staff headed towards the *izba*, Barclay explained why he believed a further withdrawal was unavoidable. 'His reasoning', wrote Ermolov, 'was most lucid, sound, and irrefutable; never had I heard Barclay argue so sensibly.'[10] Only in the matter of which direction the retreating army should take did Ermolov at that moment disagree with his superior.

The small oil lamp in the icon corner glanced upon the faces already crowded around the rude table: Kutuzov and his aides Toll and Kaisarov, the Generals Dokhturov, Ostermann-Tolstoy, Konovnitsyn, and Uvarov. Bennigsen had been inspecting the left wing, as he had promised, and was late. Raevskii also was late, having had to make his way from the rearguard.

It was seven o'clock when Bennigsen strode in and immediately challenged the group without waiting for Kutuzov to open the meeting: '. . . whether it is better to give battle before the walls of Moscow or to abandon the town to the enemy? . . .'[11] Kutuzov roughly interrupted his Chief of Staff: it was necessary first to expound all the relevant factors. The Supreme Commander spoke with marked seriousness and proceeded slowly to enumerate the shortcomings of the terrain as Barclay, corroborated by Ermolov and Toll, had indicated. Again echoing Barclay almost word for word, Kutuzov affirmed: 'As long as the army remained in existence and as long as it was in condition to oppose the enemy, hope remained to finish off the enemy in the end; but once the army was destroyed, not only Moscow but all of Russia would be lost . . .'[12] The Supreme Commander then put the question in a significantly different way from Bennigsen: 'Should one wait to be attacked in a disadvantageous position, or cede Moscow to the enemy? . . .'[13] Kutuzov turned to Barclay, who restated the theme he had been so stubbornly defending ever since the invasion occurred: the primacy of saving not a particular city but the whole fatherland, and for that, the necessity of preserving the army. In straightforward fashion he added four other points:

The position is disadvantageous and the army undoubtedly risks being demolished.

In case of defeat, everything that was not lost to the enemy on the field of battle would be destroyed during the retreat through Moscow.

To abandon the capital is painful, but if we do not lose courage and if we conduct operations energetically, the seizure of Moscow could bring about the enemy's ruin.

Abandoning Moscow will not come as a surprise to our Sovereign and he would no doubt approve the withdrawal.[14]

No one seems to have challenged Barclay's soothing assumption of the Tsar's approval, which was based on nothing more, it would seem, than his parting remarks after Drissa. Although at this point in the war Alexander's approval would not be the controlling factor in an important military decision, Barclay's assurance gave encouragement to those leaning towards withdrawal.

Barclay's own proposal was for a withdrawal through Vladimir in the direction of Nizhnii-Novgorod in order to protect communication with St.

Petersburg and with the bases in the Nizhnii area which were organizing for the continuation of the conflict. (This proposal turned out to be impracticable, however, because of autumnal flooding of the Oka, which would have severed the army from the rich southern provinces.)

Bennigsen rose to his feet. He was much the same age as Kutuzov, senior by a decade or more to all the others – in some cases by more than three decades. He intended his voice to be the voice of experience and wisdom. Also, he had not forgotten Barclay's dismissal of him after the Smolensk confrontation, and he meant to be the victor in this one. His arguments against the evacuation of Moscow touched on many points: the immense losses to the crown and to a host of individuals; public opinion and the effect this would have on the continuation of the war; the difficulties and dangers of rushing the army through Moscow with the enemy at one's heels; the shame of abandonment; the loss of credibility, for how could the public believe in the Borodino victory if losing Moscow was its only result; and the effect on foreign opinion. He also doubted whether the army would be better organized after an evacuation of Moscow. Finally he thought an immediate attack on the French would be successful because the Russians, unlike the enemy, had received some reinforcements (three regiments had just arrived), and because they were still the same Russians who had fought so bravely on so many occasions; though they were disorganized and weakened since Borodino, the enemy was in like condition. In conclusion Bennigsen called attention to the latest reports about Napoleon's attempt to outflank the position on the right and proposed a gathering of all Russian forces towards the left wing during the night and a strike at dawn at the enemy's centre.[15]

Barclay replied only to Bennigsen's tactical proposals, pointing out that they came too late. To carry them out, the troops would have to be deployed accordingly: in the morning when he had first spoken to Bennigsen about the faults in the position, there had still been time for redeployment. Now at night it was impossible to identify all the units, hidden as they were in deep valleys, and before they could be disentangled they risked being smashed by the enemy.

Although Kutuzov's opening statement leaves no doubt that he favoured abandoning Moscow, he had cannily left the question open for discussion, and it was Barclay who had come out with a clear proposition. According to Ermolov, 'Kutuzov was enchanted because he was not the first to propose the abandonment of Moscow and he could now put the blame on someone else'.[16]

Ostermann-Tolstoy, Raevskii, and Toll also spoke in favour of giving up Moscow. Siding with Bennigsen were Dokhturov, Uvarov, possibly Konovnitsyn, and, in the end, Ermolov – who spoke passionately, however, against giving defensive battle at such an untenable position and instead proposed attacking the enemy where he was and at once. Toll suggested a retrograde flanking movement along the Old Kaluga Road but found no adherents for his plan since it would expose part of the army to Poniatowski's already advancing corps. Ostermann-Tolstoy asked Bennigsen whether he could be answerable for the success of an action at Fili, a question Barclay found unreasonable but which had the merit of silencing Bennigsen. Kutuzov brought the discussion to an end. After a brooding pause he stated solemnly: 'I am aware of the responsibility I am assuming, but I sacrifice myself for the good of our country. I hereby order the retreat.'[17]

As the generals filed out into the black night to carry out this order, no one ventured a comment. Some feared that Kutuzov was risking his command and that Bennigsen, who had played his cards well, might gain the Tsar's support and take Kutuzov's place. Barclay, having seen that Kutuzov, Ostermann-Tolstoy, Raevskii, and Toll shared his views, had no inkling that he alone would be considered responsible for the decision.

The baggage trains and the reserve artillery were ordered at once towards Moscow, and the infantry, cavalry, and the main artillery departed at two in the morning. Immediately following the war council Barclay sent a rider galloping to Rostopchin to inform the Governor-General of Moscow with 'deep-felt sorrow' that the army would be marching through the streets of the city. Barclay enjoined him 'to take all precautions for keeping the remaining people of Moscow calm and quiet . . . to post policemen in all streets to prevent . . . house-breaking or breaking ranks . . . and to place at the army's disposal as many guides as possible with good knowledge of all the main and secondary roads.'[18]

It was a sleepless night for Muscovites as the endless rumble of horse-drawn guns, caissons, and carts trundling through the city from the Dorogomilov barrier told the inhabitants that the army Rostopchin had repeatedly sworn they could depend on – as Kutuzov 'by the white hair of his head' had sworn to him up to the very last minute – was leaving them behind to the mercies of Napoleon. On the west bank of the Moskva river thousands of men with jostling horses and artillery stumbled in the dark and crowded the approaches to the only bridge, wooden and in disrepair. Kutuzov, caught in this chaos with his staff, sent Wolzogen to discover the cause of the delay – the bridge had by now broken – and to take appropriate measures. Seeing the artillerymen searching for shallows to ford the stream, Wolzogen told the others to do likewise: 'The *opolchenie* took off their boots, rolled up their trousers, and like the children of Israel waded safely across.'[19] The bridge was soon repaired and Kutuzov and staff rode across, losing themselves in side streets, 'probably', thought Wolzogen, 'to avoid the eyes of the people'.[20] Barclay, however, had quickly reached the other side of the town, stopping near the stone bridge across the Iauza, where the road to Riazan' began. It was this road, midway between the road to Nizhnii (Barclay's choice) and the road to Kaluga (Toll's choice), that Kutuzov had cleverly chosen.

Rostopchin, busy with many other matters (such as collecting all Moscow's fire-fighting equipment), paid as little heed to Barclay's request for policemen and guides as he had to Kutuzov's request for shovels or Barclay's own urgent demand the day before for fresh horses ('through voluntary donations by Moscow's merchants and residents – or any other means').[21] The dismal result was that 'there were no guides posted for the troops, none of the quartermaster officers was on hand, and those who were supposed to be repairing roads and bridges were mostly just blocking the way.'[22]

With no help from Rostopchin, then, Barclay rode through the streets from barrier to barrier, striving to keep order among the thousands of troops, characteristically taking comfort in the thought that without his 'unsparing efforts, the army would have found it difficult to get out of Moscow'.[23] And it is true that most of the other senior commanders showed little initiative in this difficult withdrawal. Many, like Prince Golitsyn, were so struck down by 'unfathomable grief' that they were incapable of serious leadership.[24] Though Barclay was still burning and shivering with fever, and the weather was again extremely hot, he remained in the saddle for eighteen hours.

He sent out his adjutants, each with a strong Cossack escort, to police the streets, hurry the thirsty troops along, and gather up stragglers. These Cossack escorts were especially effective in swooping down and confiscating plundered vodka and other liquor, breaking the bottles with their lances before the arrested looters' regretful eyes. Loewenstern, who was on this round of police duty, said that 'it was due to such rigorous measures that General Barclay saved the army from disaster'.[25] When the rumour spread that soldiers were pillaging the main bazaar, the *Gostinnyi Dvor*, Barclay sent off a remaining aide who reported back that the proprietors themselves had invited the soldiers in, rather than have their goods fall into enemy hands. Naturally the soldiers had broken ranks and were helping themselves, not only in the *Gostinnyi Dvor* but by breaking into unguarded shops and mansions whose owners had fled. Foreign shops were favourite targets of the vandals. Feeling ran high against all foreigners and it was enough to be heard speaking any language but Russian to be insulted and molested. In greatest danger from the soldiers were the 3,600 French people then living in Moscow. Of these, only forty-three of the most fiercely patriotic – among them actors and artisans, traders and tutors and stewards, forming in Rostopchin's words 'la canaille de la canaille' – had been shipped away to Saratov on the Volga.[26] But Barclay's resources in adjutants were limited: he had not enough aides to pursue every dispersing miscreant or even every group of looters. Altogether some six thousand soldiers were lost to the army in the dusty streets of Moscow. (With few exceptions they were to fall into the hands of the French.)

Another problem of the withdrawal, particularly after the sorry experience of Mozhaisk, was to see to measures for the protection of wounded and sick soldiers, of whom considerable numbers remained in the city. Kutuzov's aide Kaisarov therefore made some proposals in a letter to Marshal Berthier, Napoleon's Chief of Staff. Miloradovich, who by virtue of leading the rearguard was nearest to the enemy, delivered the letter and as a result he and Murat, with Napoleon's consent, came to an understanding about a short truce: it was agreed that the French would not enter Moscow until seven o'clock of the following morning, 3/15 September. It was therefore possible to evacuate all but the most serious cases among the sick and wounded.

Except for the rearguard, all the troops had left Moscow, speedily and for the most part in amazingly good order, and Barclay was ready to follow them. He was joined at the Iauza bridge by Count Rostopchin, dressed in a military frockcoat. According to popular invention, Barclay asked the meaning of the carts he had seen pass by loaded with pumps and fire-hose; and Rostopchin portentously replied, 'I have good reasons for this.'[27]

The army's new resting-place was some ten miles to the south-east on the Riazan' road. Here the whole army settled in with exemplary speed, craving sleep above all. Barclay set up quarters in a nearby village. Wolzogen, billeted close by, was awakened an hour before midnight with the news that Moscow was burning. 'We stepped out into the field and saw . . . the fire, which already covered almost the entire northern horizon with a red glow.'[28] During the next five days this glow dominated the vision and the thoughts of every soldier on either side.

Since Kutuzov's Borodino 'victory' report, the Tsar had had no official news from the front. It was from his sister Catherine that he learned of the fall of Moscow, and it was a whole week later before he received Kutuzov's explanations. The Supreme Commander sent his report, dated 4 September (O.S.) and reaching the Tsar four days later, with one of his aides, Colonel Michaud, who he was sure would present his case favourably in St. Petersburg.[29] The Colonel also carried a letter to Arakcheev from Bennigsen, giving his version of the Fili war council and recording his opposition to the decision taken.

Kutuzov's report to the Tsar, which Barclay did not hear about until weeks later, emphasized three reasons for abandoning Moscow: one, the disarray of the army after the bloody though 'victorious' battle of Borodino; two, the enemy's entry into Moscow would not entail the subjugation of Russia and Kutuzov's removal of the army a short distance beyond Moscow would enable him to await the enemy on a 'firm footing'; and three, His Majesty 'would graciously concede that these consequences are closely related to the loss of Smolensk and the complete state of disorganization in which I found the army'.[30]

The third point of course accuses Barclay. That Kutuzov should defend himself to the Tsar was natural, but to repeat the lie about the condition of the army and shift to Barclay the entire blame for Moscow's surrender was treacherous and base. Kutuzov was able to get away with this only because of the nearly universal amnesia regarding Smolensk's defensibility. Apparently by common consent it was forgotten that there could be any question about the matter. Naturally, no importance was to be attached to the opinion of young Lieutenant Clausewitz who thought that the whole region of Smolensk was 'basically not at all suitable for defensive deployment', and the town itself so disadvantageous that it would have had to be transformed and armed at an unrealistic cost and even then could not have held out long enough to make the attempt worthwhile.[31] But no one discussed these questions: reality was no longer a factor in people's views about Smolensk. And thus it seemed that only stupidity, timidity, or treason could explain Barclay's failure to hold the city, and holy Russia's problems could all be traced to this one crucial fault.

Kutuzov's action was of course particularly disloyal just after the perilous withdrawal through Moscow which Barclay above all had successfully managed for him, avoiding what could have been catastrophe. Commenting on this withdrawal, Loewenstern had noted how 'Barclay and Miloradovich were vigilant; Field-Marshal Kutuzov could depend on them.'[32] Any expectation that Barclay could depend in turn on Kutuzov's honesty was clearly mistaken. After Barclay's selfless performance at Borodino, Kutuzov saw in him the only possible rival for the glory of saving Russia, a glory he was not prepared to share with anyone.

Bennigsen's letter to Arakcheev which went by the same messenger heaped more accusations on Barclay. He was described as being by far the most vigorous advocate at Fili for the abandonment of Moscow, and he was also belaboured for asserting that the Tsar would approve the retreat. 'Time will tell to what extent such an assurance was well founded,' growled Bennigsen,[33] though at least he did not resort to lies.

The Tsar, far from satisfied with Kutuzov's report, called for a meeting of his Committee of Ministers. The fourteen members met on 10/22 September and decided unanimously that Kutuzov be asked to submit the protocol of the Fili war council and in future to submit detailed information on everything he was doing. The Committee insisted, however, that this request should not be interpreted as a rebuke to the Supreme Commander. But Alexander himself imputed full responsibility to Kutuzov. In a later rescript demanding that operations be speeded up, the Tsar bluntly told him: 'Remember that you still owe an explanation to the offended fatherland for the loss of Moscow . . .'[34]

No official minutes had been kept of the Fili council and it was therefore a makeshift summary that was prepared at Kutuzov's headquarters for St. Petersburg. The author is unknown. In this protocol, a model of disinformation, the names of Raevskii and Uvarov do not appear, and Ostermann-Tolstoy is strangely linked with Konovnitsyn and Ermolov as disapproving Bennigsen's choice of defensive terrain, urging instead an immediate attack on the enemy.[34] This left only the two Livonians, Barclay and Toll, in favour of surrendering Moscow.

After covering eighteen miles on the Riazan' road, the army abruptly turned west in a flanking movement to the south of Moscow. It recrossed the Moskva on 4/16 September and, keeping to the left of the river Pakhra which protected its right flank, it stopped near Krasnaia Pakhra, fifteen miles due south of Moscow. This countermarch had the advantage of safeguarding Tula with its arms factories, Kaluga with its large warehouses, and of keeping communications open with the 65,000 men of Tormassov (Third Army) and Chichagov (Army of Moldavia) in the south-west. The move confounded Napoleon and his marshals for several days. It was Kutuzov's master stroke (though probably it owes much to Toll's suggestion at Fili for a withdrawal on the Old Kaluga Road). Barclay was pleased with the manœuvre, 'the most important and most propitious move since the arrival of the Prince'.[36]

Barclay was certain that Napoleon was doomed. 'This certainty was for me so soothing that it sustained me in my ailing condition,' he affirmed.[37] Unwell and uncomfortable, ignored or denigrated, he reached for every possible support.

On 7/19 September he toured the bivouacs, handing out (with Kutuzov's permission) medals and promotions for Borodino, and rousing the soldiers for the offensive action which would now crown the months of withdrawal. By telling each regiment the story of how Peter the Great had lured the King of Sweden all the way to Poltava and there royally defeated him, he left the soldiers somewhat enlightened about national strategy and looking forward to a quick end to the campaign.[38]

But these high hopes came to nothing during the next few days, and Barclay felt he had been made to seem a liar in front of the whole army.[39] Although the Russians were about to achieve numerical superiority in all sectors and Kutuzov's main army now outnumbered the Grande Armée in and around Moscow by 10,000 or 15,000 men, no really serious operations were undertaken. Barclay's proposals for vigorous action went unheeded as did those of Bennigsen, Wilson (who had just returned to the front), and others. The army crossed and recrossed the Pakhra, and moved back and forth between Krasnaia Pakhra, Podol'sk, and Voronovo, recalling Barclay's indecisive manœuvres between Smolensk, Rudnia, and Porech'e eight weeks earlier. Reports of French forces south of Moscow were exaggerated: only Murat was active in this area, and an opportunity to defeat him soundly was passed over for lack of determination. Barclay could count one success, however, with his proposal to send the grim-featured cavalry General I. S. Dorokhov to operate partisan-fashion in the rear of the Grande Armée. On 12/24 September Dorokhov's hussars, dragoons, and Cossacks cut the road between Moscow and Mozhaisk, ambushing and capturing to a man a detachment of fifteen hundred French *chasseurs* Napoleon had sent out expressly to destroy him.[40] Finally, the Russians retreated farther south and encamped at the fortified position of Tarutino, forty-six miles from Moscow.

Ever since Borodino, Barclay had been sending short messages to Auguste, but at last on 11/23 September a secure way of communicating privately suddenly presented itself. A courier was about to leave for St. Petersburg with Sir Robert Wilson's reports to the British Ambassador, and Barclay was able to enclose his letter in an envelope marked for the Ambassador, Lord Cathcart.[41] His hopes, complaints, and criticism tumbled out in a hasty jumble: 'Our affairs here have at present taken such a turn that we can hope to terminate the war happily and honourably, but we should be operating altogether differently and with more enterprise . . . It seems they avoid me and hide much from me. Whatever the result, I still am convinced that I did everything necessary to preserve the state, and if His Majesty still has an army which threatens the enemy with ruin, it is owing to me . . .' Showing how cruelly he felt the inventions being spread about him, he continued insistently, defensively: 'I handed the army over to Prince Kutuzov . . . in a condition such that it could match itself against any enemy force. I handed it over to him at the moment when I was firmly resolved to await the attack of the enemy in an excellent position where I was sure to win. I do not know why we pulled back from this position and why we are wandering about like the children of Israel in the desert.' Coming back to the subject of Borodino, he wrote what he would never say so openly to any other person: 'If the army was not completely demolished in the battle of Borodino, it is owing to me, and this conviction will give me consolation in the last moment of my life.' But quickly he told Auguste to keep silent about this: 'Everything I write you here is a secret and I pray you to keep it well.' Meanwhile, by the very same pouch on the very same day, Bennigsen was writing to Baroness Bennigsen – also claiming credit for Borodino: 'It is certain that the disposition of the battle of the 26th [Borodino] was due to me and if they had wished to listen to me entirely, it could have become more decisive for us and with much less loss . . .'[42] Finally, in a sad echo from before Borodino, Barclay ended: 'The only grace that I implore is to be delivered from here and I don't care in what way it happens . . .'

Meanwhile, even before he reached Tarutino, Barclay's health took a turn for the worse, while he found less and less reason to go on surmounting his ills. Continuing slights, ever more blatant, were wearing him down. At one point the place assigned for First Army field headquarters was completely separated from the headquarters area of the others. Wolzogen quipped that 'they kept him beyond the outposts in the hope he would be snatched up by the French'.[43] At about the same time Barclay got wind in a roundabout way of the fact that Miloradovich, still under his command, had departed for some unknown destination for an unknown operation at the head of 25,000 troops. Worst of all, he saw the administration of the army disintegrating under Kutuzov and Bennigsen as if the Yellow Book had never been written, and watched helplessly the results of his tenacious strategy being frittered away. He saw repeated lost opportunities for striking at the enemy, though he continued always to maintain that the greatest by far of lost opportunities was Tsarevo-Zaimishche. Contradictory orders were flying about, issued without clearance by nearly a dozen people who seemed to have assumed overall command. Kutuzov's headquarters staff was much given to detaching First Army contingents without notifying their Commander. Sometimes Barclay could not locate them even when he enquired of the Prince's duty officer. Platov himself was unable to help him find the First Army Cossacks. The quartermaster corps was completely disorganized, with no one person in charge (Toll at this point was only one of several). There was no proper direction of troop movements, no planning of road and bridge repairs, no co-ordination of supplies. 'Transports cross each other, the Kaluga ones going to Riazan' and the Riazan' ones going to Kaluga – while the army had no food for several days running.'[44]

On 16/28 September Kutuzov ordered the amalgamation of the First and Second Armies, but left their titles, now meaningless, to Barclay and his Chief of Staff Ermolov.[45] Barclay was Commander-in-Chief – of nothing, and Ermolov's position was even more absurd. Both had been shorn of all authority and responsibility. Ermolov at once and repeatedly begged Kutuzov to relieve him formally of his non-existent duties. 'But Kutuzov quite naturally did not respond to these requests, since by abolishing the duties of the First Army's Chief of Staff he deprived Barclay of the last reason to call himself Commander-in-Chief, reducing him to the level of all the other subordinate generals, and at the same time prevented Barclay from having an excuse later to say he had been removed from the army . . .'⁴⁶ So well did wily Kutuzov manipulate the situation that very little was made of this amalgamation at the time it happened, or by later historians. Curiously, even Barclay does not utilize it when he is importuning the Tsar with an endless series of self-vindicatory letters. In any case, Kutuzov's manœuvre was successful: two days later (18/30 September) Barclay asked for sick leave. He attached to his application an extraordinary document in which he itemized his complaints against the way he had been treated and against the way the army was being run. Blinded to the effect his scathing words would necessarily produce, he wrote: 'In these decisive times . . . you will permit me, Prince, to speak to you with full candour and to call your attention to the bad things which have surreptitiously crept into the army either without your accord or without your noticing. The leadership of the army which had been soundly established, at present no longer exists . . .'⁴⁷ Kutuzov, with quite uncharacteristic swiftness, granted the application, informed the Tsar, and informed the troops. Making no mention of the amalgamation, he told the Tsar that he had taken Barclay's duties upon himself 'until such time as Your Imperial Majesty will graciously name a new commander of the First Army'.⁴⁸

Once the momentous decision was taken, Barclay made his preparations in a tranquil spirit. One by one, he called in all but two of his adjutants to bid each a calm and kind farewell, taking the trouble to find out confidentially their wishes for reassignment in order to make helpful recommendations. Loewenstern asked for, and got, a transfer to Kutuzov, whose goodwill he had always enjoyed. (Barclay's adjutants risked their lives daily, Loewenstern remarked, whereas all Kutuzov's adjutants at war's end 'were fresh and had a rosy colour'.)⁴⁹ According to Loewenstern, who described their leave-taking as 'an unforgettable conversation', Barclay told him:

The present is against me and I must yield to it; I foresee calmer times, times when consideration of what has happened will do justice to me. I have pulled the wagon uphill, and it can roll downhill by itself with only a little steering. I do not grudge the Prince the merry descent, however, and I would gladly have joined in, if only as the modest commander of my Jaeger regiment, if this were at all opportune. But I see clearly that my remaining here will stir up discord and dissension in the army. Therefore I must leave . . .⁵⁰

Once more Barclay referred to having left a 'well-kept, well-provided, combat-ready army' – he called it his 'monument' – and again he stated that the enemy was 'in disarray, in despair, they are clay in our hands'. With a final blessing – 'God be with you, dear Loewenstern' – Barclay gave him the agreeable news that his promotion to lieutenant-colonel, 'because of that day at Borodino', had just come through.⁵¹ (Presumably nephew Andreas Barclay de Tolly was also among the adjutants who were left behind.⁵² Since shortly after Vitebsk this young man who had just left school, too callow and inexperienced to provoke jealousy, had had the sinecure of handling his uncle's secret correspondence with the Tsar.)

Among those who claimed to have had interviews with Barclay before his departure was Clausewitz. The Tsar had ordered his transfer to the still unconquered fortress of Riga. Clausewitz recounts his visit to Barclay in the early days of October (N.S.) to obtain from the 'Minister of War' his official travel orders. Barclay allegedly told him and several other officers on that occasion: 'You may thank God, Gentlemen, that you are called away from here; nothing sensible can come of this whole thing . . .'[53] But these words, in amazing contrast to those cited by Loewenstern, are not very credible. The conversation with Clausewitz must have occurred before 22 September/4 October, the date of Barclay's departure. He was no longer Minister of War. Clausewitz, moreover, elsewhere ascribed the same pronouncement to General Phull, a seasoned pessimist, in November 1812: 'Believe me, nothing sensible can come out of this whole thing.'[54] Even though Barclay had no confidence at all in the leadership of 'the two feeble old men', Kutuzov and Bennigsen, the tone of these words seems to fit Phull much better than Barclay, who was completely confident of Russia's victory.*

The actual moment of departure was surprisingly moving. All the generals accompanied him to his carriage and many, according to Loewenstern, were visibly affected. Ermolov, in that Russian gesture mixing affection and respect, embraced Barclay on both shoulders.[55] General Wilson, the Englishman, was rather less affected: '[In] General Barclay we lose a brave executive officer, who greatly distinguished himself at Borodino; but his departure will do good by removing a spirit of dissension . . .'[56] Sir Robert also wrote to the Tsar in much the same equable spirit, partly because he still had full confidence in Kutuzov, whom later he would criticize in the strongest terms.[57]

Some people, however, blamed Barclay for leaving his post before the end of the war. One of Bagration's generals who had been wounded at Borodino thought that 'Barclay is acting badly in asking to be relieved; his services are necessary both for the State and for his own good.'[58] This general, Michael Vorontsov, showed a keen understanding of Barclay's plight: 'A series of difficult events have brought him vexation. This will pass as soon as everything calms down, and justice will be done to him on many accounts. But in retiring he plays into the hands of his enemies, and to them he will appear even more culpable.'[59] On the very day of Barclay's departure Vorontsov was saying, 'Believe me, in the end people will think less of Drissa, of the abandonment of Smolensk, but only of how much they owe him for having preserved the strength of the army . . . At the front and in the councils Barclay would be helpful to the fatherland at a time when nobody should leave his post.'[60]

The days were shorter, crisper, and it was in waning light on 22 September/4 October that Barclay left Tarutino for Kaluga, the first stop in the long roundabout homewards journey which was to take two months out of his official six-months' leave. Wolzogen left headquarters a few days later; he was still aide-de-camp to the Tsar, from whom he had to seek his new assignment. Bennigsen, the inveterate schemer, constantly intriguing against Kutuzov, was sent away some weeks later. The Supreme Commander also got rid of his two

* Clausewitz's death prevented him from going over his draft; final revision was done by his wife Marie.

meddling aides, Kaisarov and Kudashev, who were sent to forward units where they could collect medals and send home glowing accounts of their deeds.

Accompanying Barclay on his journey were a doctor named Batalin and two aides, Major Reitz and Colonel Zakrevskii. Barclay had first known the latter in Finland where this scion of an old, impoverished, noble family had been young Kamenskii's aide. Zakrevskii had been close to Barclay all through the present campaign and throughout the battle of Borodino. The Commander treasured him for his disinterested patriotism, and praised unstintingly his merit, courage, zeal, and 'real military talents'.[61] Prophetically – since Zakrevskii rose to high positions including Governor-General of Finland and Minister of the Interior – Barclay promised that his young aide would eventually give great and important services to the state.

Through most of the tedious journey Barclay was sullen and preoccupied, remaining indifferent to everything around him. He left all arrangements to Zakrevskii. Whether or not Zakrevskii showed him Vorontsov's letter accusing him of 'acting badly', Barclay must have been a prey now to the voices of duty and obedience. He knew well enough that his health was an insufficient reason for leaving. When he applied for leave, everything without exception had been pushing him to get away. To be delivered had been the seemingly unattainable 'only grace' he had implored. But how easily it had been done, after all, and now that he had obtained satisfaction of his immediate desire, qualms assailed him and he had also to ask himself if the Tsar would think he had been 'acting badly'. As the carriage swung and jolted, leaving the army behind, General Barclay thought of himself in turn as a frustrated and unacknowledged saviour and as a sorry failure, a man disgraced, whose public career – once so gloriously promising – was finished at the age of fifty, after some forty years of service.

On arrival at Kaluga Barclay finished and sent off a letter he had started to the Tsar.[62] To vindicate himself he presented another detailed indictment of Kutuzov's and Bennigsen's mismanagement of the army and showed his own untenable position there. He argued that these considerations alone, quite apart from questions of health, would justify his departure 'in the eyes of any impartial judge' – hardly a diplomatic phrase to send to an autocrat.[63] The tone of this letter and those to follow was testy and unsure. Except for one or two scraps of formality including the hurtful announcement of Kutuzov's appointment, the Tsar, who used to write to Barclay sometimes twice a day, had not sent him a word since Smolensk. Barclay's letters to him therefore suffer particularly from being written into a vacuum. There is no doubt that what he craved more than anything was just one message of reassurance from the Tsar.

On 30 September/12 October Barclay and his companions reached Tula. His carriage needed mending and he planned to sell some of his horses. He had been doing much practical thinking. 'I am not counting on anything any more,' he wrote to Auguste, telling her to prepare herself for an extremely simple, frugal life.[64] It was not an easy letter to write to the *General'sha*, the expansive St. Petersburg hostess. 'Sell everything that in your judgement is superfluous,' he insisted, 'but do not dispose of my library, my map collection, and certain papers in my desk.' (She would know he meant especially letters from the Tsar.)

Knowing how difficult the first reaction would be, he gently preached that 'human beings do not need much and can be happy in straitened circumstances such as ours as long as their hearts beat steadily and they have the courage not to miss some of the things they have become accustomed to'. It is clear, however, that he wished Magnus, now past fourteen, to escape contamination from his ill fortune. Barclay hoped Auguste had not brought him home because of any fears for the capital: Magnus should remain in St. Petersburg in the Corps of Pages. As for Napoleon, he was finished and if he did not depart soon he would find it impossible to return at all: Barclay's tone despite himself suddenly became cheerful.

From Tula the journey went first east and then north to Vladimir province where Zakrevskii had his country home. Vladimir, like all the *guberniia* surrounding Moscow, was overrun by refugees, merchants and noblemen and their families, and their enormous disrupted retinues of servants of all kinds. The heads of these refugees were crammed with Rostopchin's rousing proclamations, their hearts heavy with loss and insecurity. The legitimate patriotism which at the beginning inspired the young sons of the aristocracy to set off enthusiastically to fight Napoleon, had now turned into a braying chauvinism.

Vladimir province seethed with hatred of the French and the foreign, and it was here that an ugly incident marked Barclay's journey. The day was a holiday, the people idle and drunk. Hearing that Barclay was in the relay station a mob gathered, muttering, shouting, clamouring for 'that traitor', and threatening to lynch him. Fortunately the horses were already harnessed and Zakrevskii, sword in hand, cleared the way and ordered the coachman to use the whip.[65] Barclay maintained his famous composure, but the incident confounded him. He knew nothing of Kutuzov's unscrupulous charge that the loss of Moscow was due to Barclay's having lost Smolensk. By this time most of Russia knew, however, since the Tsar had let Kutuzov's letter be featured in the Government's gazette, *Severnaia Pochta* (*The Northern Mail*), on 18 September (O.S.) and copies had by now reached almost every part of the empire. The old suspicion of Barclay's treachery seemed to be officially confirmed by the Tsar, and became a national conviction. The Russian people felt righteously unified by their hatred of Barclay, their adoration of Kutuzov. Barclay's sister, not known to everyone as such, had to hear her brother casually denounced by a stranger (a Herr von Engelhard): '"We did have a man on whom our hopes rested . . . but he is a traitor who has lured the enemy into our land."'[66] Even Pushkin, Kuechelbecker, and the other pupils of the new *lycée* at Tsarskoe Selo, who knew little enough of what had been going on at the front, had no doubt that Barclay was a traitor.[67] They had heard the 'hue and cry of hate' which fastened on his 'name's outlandish sound for bait'.[68]

Barclay's fever broke out again and it took a serious turn when he finally learned of Kutuzov's infamous gambit and read the unbearable accusation in the government press; his heart was 'shattered'.[69] Slowly Dr. Batalin nursed him back, at Zakrevskii's house, but when the convalescent started to venture out again he was met by jeers. Smolensk – Moscow: everyone now had a handy explanation for what had happened, attributing it, said Barclay, to his 'want of courage . . . various weaknesses and shortcomings . . . treachery and betrayal'.[70] To himself, to Zakrevskii, to Auguste by letter, he reiterated his steadfast conviction of having acted rightly, in the only possible way 'to prepare the ground for the enemy's inevitable downfall'.[71] More profitably, he used his convalescence to write a concise explicative summary of the campaign, and finally, on 25 October (O.S.), more than three weeks after his arrival in Vladimir, he sent it to the Tsar, asking him to have it published in the public gazettes, to let the 'truth in all its nakedness . . . silence the malicious tongues'.[72] The Tsar did select a few extracts for the newspaper, but then decided firmly against publication. He needed, and the country needed, Barclay in the role of scapegoat. Kutuzov's accusations therefore went unchallenged in public.

This was a pity, because the 'Obiasneniia . . .' or 'Explanations . . .' were admirably dispassionate.[73] They began with the preparations for war and described the moves of the two Western Armies from the day of the invasion to the battle of Borodino. Barclay showed clearly and convincingly how each move had led to the next in a continuous effort to reduce Napoleon's superiority in numbers and increase his distance from his supply bases, while preserving the Russian armies' strength, order, and organization, 'without which the terrible battle [Borodino] could never have been fought'.[74] No aspersions were cast on Kutuzov, no direct criticism. Publication might well have cleared Barclay's reputation, for, as he himself concluded: 'Discerning people will appreciate the strength of my arguments; for the mistrustful I have perhaps not sufficiently justified myself, but time will do it for me; the prejudiced, cloaked in their unfairness, will have to deal with their own consciences; and as to the thoughtless, they could, out of pity, be left to their delusions because for them even the most telling arguments carry no weight . . .'[75]

Meanwhile, Wolzogen arrived in St. Petersburg on 7/19 October and was received the next day by the Tsar, who asked for a detailed description of everything that had happened since he, the Tsar, had left the army. The German Baron's testimony is the only serious evidence there is concerning Alexander's thoughts and feelings about Barclay at this time. One cannot forget, however, that Wolzogen was biased in Barclay's favour and that the Tsar was suggestible, changing opinions fairly easily according to the persuasiveness of his interlocutor. Wolzogen seems to have been very persuasive, not only in putting Barclay into the best possible light but Kutuzov into the worst:

When I got to the description of the battle of Borodino and Kutuzov's comportment during the battle, the Tsar interrupted me with the words, 'that _____ (swearword) [sic] who commands my army at present has not written me of all these details, but has reported nothing but lies . . .'

I continued, by his order, and never omitted to praise appropriately the merits of Barclay, and in the end I asked the Tsar not to withdraw his mercy from Barclay. The Tsar replied: 'You know that Barclay is somewhat heavy-handed and sometimes does not really understand me, but that he is an honest and efficient man who devotes all his strength to me and to the Nation, this opinion I still hold to this very day, and I also know that as a person he excels by far the dissolute Kutuzov. I shall always hold Barclay in high esteem and shall again appoint him when the time is right [Wolzogen was perhaps using hindsight here]; but for the time being he must remain in exile, that is how the general public considers his retirement; even the all-powerful Monarch is obliged to put imperative circumstances above personal sentiments.

Finally, showing some slight appreciation of Barclay's distress, Alexander suggested: 'If you should have a secure occasion to inform the General of my views, then do it, although I must ask you not to mention anything to anybody about the contents of our conversation . . .'[76]

But if the Tsar had any thought of facilitating a meeting between Barclay and Wolzogen, all was forgotten when the news reached the Winter Palace that Napoleon had left Moscow.

On 6/18 October Kutuzov, with fresh reinforcements and a reorganized army, defeated an unwary Murat near Tarutino. In Moscow, closed in on three sides by ever-growing masses of *opolchenie*, Napoleon, worn down by thirty-five days' vain waiting for a response to his overtures to the Tsar, stirred himself at last when he heard of Murat's defeat. On 7/19 October he and most of the Grande Armée evacuated Moscow. He meant to give battle to Kutuzov, fight his way through to Kaluga, and thence retreat to Smolensk. But after a whole day's bloody battle at Malojaroslavets on 12/24 October, the 120th day of the campaign, the Grande Armée began its wretched retreat, retracing its steps through Mozhaisk, Borodino, and Viaz'ma. Hindered by its own booty-crammed carts and wagons, constantly harassed by partisans, shadowed by Kutuzov's main army, the demoralized Grande Armée was in essence already defeated even before the first snow eddied about its pitiful ranks.

When he began to feel well enough to travel again, Barclay intended to go to St. Petersburg to attempt a reconciliation with the Tsar. But still no word came from the sovereign, not even a reply to Barclay's request to proceed to St. Petersburg on the pretext of convalescence. He decided to return home to Beckhof via Novgorod. In Novgorod he completed a thirty-page confidential narrative or 'tableau' of the operations of the First Army, entitled 'Izobrazhenie . . .', which has been used as an important source for this book.[77] Barclay worked at this with enormous care, checking constantly for accuracy with Zakrevskii, who had been handling his paperwork all through the campaign. Barclay sent the 'Tableau . . .' to the Tsar on 9/21 November with a letter warning him that it contained matter (particularly, critical remarks about some of his fellow generals) 'intended for Your Majesty's knowledge only'.[78] By now Barclay had learned of Napoleon's retreat and diplomatically gave all credit to the Tsar: 'The affairs of war have at present taken the turn which Your Majesty foresaw in tracing the overall plan for this campaign.' Barclay felt that his own affairs, also, would be able to take a new turn, now that Russia was coming out of the cloud of defeat for which he was blamed. Delicately, indirectly, he offered his services again: 'Your Majesty is approaching the moment when He will become the arbiter and the sovereign of oppressed Europe. I congratulate You, Sire. But if You can find subjects who will serve You with more zeal, fidelity, and sincere devotion than I have done, I shall congratulate You still more . . .'.⁷⁹ Although 'having no longer the right to involve myself in these affairs', Barclay could not resist urging the Tsar to prepare now for the next campaign in the spring. He reminded him that the army was suffering a breakdown in administration, making it 'like a body without a soul'. It kept going now on pure patriotism because it was defending Russian soil, but once over the frontier it would be a different story. A lot of preparation would be needed, especially since there would be 'nations to protect and tranquillize, fortresses to be taken . . .'. Barclay sounds in fact as if he can hardly wait.[80]

On or about 12/24 November Barclay, still accompanied by Zakrevskii and Dr. Batalin, reached Beckhof. He had last seen Auguste in Vilna on the day Napoleon crossed the Neman', and he had not been in Beckhof for almost a whole year. Life in his 'little village' was going on as if there had never been a war and Beckhof was a 'safe haven' after his having battled for so long 'a stormy and raging sea'.[81] The flames of Smolensk and Moscow and the corpses of Borodino seemed to belong to another life, and St. Petersburg to another world. Barclay continued to tell everyone that his one desire was to obtain final dismissal from the army, forget the past, and settle down to the life of a countryman, like his father. Nevertheless, almost as soon as he reached home he was writing to a St. Petersburg friend, the assessor Alexander von Maier, to ask him to supply him with *The Petersburg Gazette*, *The Northern Mail*, and *The London Courier*.[82]

A few days later he was enjoying a taste of country and family life at their most attractive, on a visit to his sister Christine and her amiable husband Major Magnus von Lueder, a man who delighted in writing rhymed verse for family occasions. Barclay was absorbed in meeting his five little nieces, especially in renewing acquaintance with the second eldest, Christel, his nine-year-old foster-daughter, when finally the event he had despaired of came to pass, changing his whole outlook: he received a letter from the Tsar. This letter has never been found,[83] but Christel later recalled that it contained 'a vindication of his [Barclay's] actions and heartfelt expressions of appreciation'.[84] The Tsar possibly asked Barclay, as he had asked Wolzogen, to keep his views confidential. According to the account left by Barclay's niece, her uncle, being a 'high-minded man did not wish to see this letter at any time compromise his Emperor; and although it would have been very valuable for him to possess such a document, he nonetheless had a smallish iron box made in which he returned the letter to the Tsar, most certainly with a letter of gratitude.'[85] The letter of gratitude exists, fawning and ecstatic:

Sire! You have restored peace to the man most devoted to Your Sacred Person, whose heart has been grieving over the very idea of having lost the benevolence of the best of Masters, of the beloved and idolized Monarch. I find no better answer to all the favours with which Your Majesty has deigned to honour me than to throw myself at Your feet as early as possible and I hope to prove to all of Russia that You did not bestow Your confidence on an unworthy object . . .[86]

It was Zakrevskii who took these effusions to the Tsar, no doubt along with the smallish iron box, and probably the Tsar did then destroy his own letter.

Significantly, Zakrevskii had no difficulty at all in approaching the monarch, who received him particularly graciously. The Tsar in his own hand answered Barclay at once with a very long letter which, he said, it took him several days (with interruptions) to write.[87] With right royal hypocrisy he claimed that he had not for a moment ceased to show friendship and esteem for Barclay, and chided him for having hesitated to come to St. Petersburg without permission:

> I was even waiting for you, since my heart's desire was to explain myself *viva voce*. But since you did not wish to do justice to my character, I shall try in a few words to instruct you as to my true way of thinking about you and about events. . . . The campaign plan we adopted, the only one, I still believe, which could succeed against an enemy like Napoleon . . . necessarily had to meet with lots of disapproval and denigration . . . One had to expect this disapproval, and I myself was prepared for it. But at the same time one had to avoid carefully anything which could attract justified criticism, and there, General, is where I have some reproaches for you . . .

The Tsar went on to list these criticisms. Barclay had not got rid early enough of the excess baggage carried by Lithuanian regiments. Barclay had not seen to it that all the bridges were in proper repair. Hospitals were not properly evacuated (a fault all too characteristic of the times). 'There you are, General, those are frankly the wrongs I reproach you with.' It is not enough, Alexander added, to order the right things to be done; one must check and verify constantly that every detail has been properly executed.

This picayune list of errors was followed by mention of 'the very grave faults committed by Prince Bagration', and then by a flat judgement that Barclay would have done better to fight at Smolensk instead of waiting for Tsarevo-Zaimishche. Smolensk, after all, was 'the first truly Russian city' and the soldiers would have defended it with ardour. After the abandonment of Smolensk, popular feeling was too strong, 'and since unfortunately the faults I mentioned above were in everyone's mouth, I was accused "of sacrificing the safety of the country to *amour propre*, wishing to uphold my choice of your person".' Moscow and St. Petersburg called for Kutuzov. 'In giving in to their opinion I had to impose silence on my own feeling.' Alexander then put it that Barclay should never have left the army, that he had been well on the way to regaining everyone's esteem.

In this strikingly selective review of events, the Tsar omitted any reference to Kutuzov's calumnies and the lynch mood in the country after their official publication. There was no acknowledgement of Barclay's arguments in favour of abandoning Smolensk. There was of course no apology for ignoring all Barclay's pleas, for giving no private sign of the continued friendship the Tsar pretended to have felt. But the monarch knew his man: whatever Barclay's objections, they must have dissolved when he read these concluding words:

> Never shall I forget the essential services you have rendered to the country and to me, and I like to believe that you will render more of them, even more eminent . . . The struggle is not over and it will offer you every possibility of drawing attention to your military qualities, which are beginning again to be generally recognized.
>
> I shall have published a kind of explicative justification of your conduct drawn from the materials you have sent me. [This promise was not kept.]

Believe me, General, that my personal sentiments for you will never vary. Yours entirely . . .[88]

Barclay, accompanied by Dr. Batalin, left his arcadia at once, rushing to stay at Alexander von Maier's house in St. Petersburg in the happy knowledge that the 1,886 doors of the Winter Palace were no longer closed against him. He arrived just in time for the Tsar's birthday, 12 December (O.S.) – one day before his own – and hurried in his most resplendent uniform to the reception, only to discover that Alexander was already in liberated Vilna where Kutuzov had set up headquarters. Not only that, but silence and chill descended on the guests, many of whom pretended not to recognize him. When the Empress Elizabeth made her entrance, however, she walked straight to Barclay, greeting him warmly; and now the courtiers, all smiles, crowded round him. As soon as the Empress withdrew, Barclay, grim-faced and grim-hearted, marched out and hastened back to his 'little village'.

CHAPTER XIV

APPOINTMENTS IN GERMANY

> The alliance of Russia, Prussia and Austria against Napoleon – this was the combination which it had hitherto been impossible to produce. This, however, and the rising of the peoples appeared as a sequel to the retreat from Moscow . . .
>
> Butterfield, *Napoleon*

Returning by sledge from the Winter Palace to Beckhof, Barclay was attacked once again by chills and fever, but with the care of Dr. Batalin and Auguste he was beginning to recover by early January 1813. He longed to start rendering those 'eminent services' the Tsar had mentioned, and see the stain removed from his reputation. His restlessness was probably sharpened by hearing that Alexander himself up to his very departure for Vilna had been impatiently enquiring whether Barclay had yet arrived in St. Petersburg.[1] By mid-January there was no holding him back. Bundled under layers of furs he set out for Plock on the Vistula. As the runners of his sledge creaked hour after hour on the fresh snow, there was time to remember the Plock he had known in 1806, the dismal little Polish-speaking town where he and his soldiers had fought against famine in the cruel winter of his first Napoleonic campaign, and to imagine it now as the new imperial headquarters of the Russian advance, where reappointment and recognition surely awaited him. Auguste, who had decided that her place was near her husband, followed a day or so later, determined always to be within reach in case he should have another relapse. Whether Barclay had any choice in the matter is not known.

While Barclay had been ill events had been moving fast. Already, on 23 November/5 December, Napoleon had abandoned the suffering remnants of his once grand army, turning command over to Murat who quickly disposed of it to Eugène de Beauharnais. The Russian army, after a short rest at Vilna, were soon at the Neman', which they crossed despite Kutuzov's reluctance and only because of the Tsar's insistence. Kutuzov, like his ragged army – of which only one-third survived after Tarutino – bore the marks of the campaign. He considered that his mission had been to rid the fatherland of the invaders and that this had been accomplished. He had no desire to take his tired army of only 40,000 ill-equipped men to foreign parts, nor did he at his age yearn after 'nations to protect and tranquillize, fortresses to be taken'.

Prussia showed signs of independence after the signature of the Tauroggen Convention which involved a remarkably bold decision by General Yorck to lead his 17,000 men and 60 guns out of Macdonald's XIth Corps into neutrality. Yorck had been swayed by Russia's General Diebitsch (whose connection by marriage with Barclay was still in the future), with assistance from Clausewitz. It was the first defection from the ranks of Napoleon's vassal armies.

At the southern end of the front, the Austrian General Schwarzenberg did not immediately follow Yorck's example – Metternich, wary of Russia, saw to that – but on 18/30 January he did sign a Convention with Kutuzov and with the Tsar's political emissary, Baron Anstedt, stipulating that the Austrian army would vacate the Duchy of Warsaw within two weeks. The first step had been taken in Austria's withdrawal from the alliance with Napoleon, despite the buttresses of marital bonds.

On 22 January/3 February Alexander and Prussia's King Frederick William signed the Treaty of Kalisch making their countries allies against Napoleon. It had been a long time since Alexander had forsaken Frederick William at Tilsit; even longer since the two of them with the late Queen Louisa had sworn eternal friendship in Frederick the Great's crypt at Potsdam. Now Prussia was to surrender to the Tsar most of the territory she had obtained in the second and third partitions of Poland, in return for which the Tsar vowed to continue the war until all other Prussian possessions were restored.

At Russian headquarters word seeped out from the Tsar's entourage that Barclay and Bennigsen would be returning to the front, but no pronouncement was made. Barclay arrived to discover that his situation was still ambiguous. Wilson, who had been glad to see Barclay go and was glad enough to see him return, conveys the atmosphere of whispers and uncertainty: 'Yesterday General Barclay rejoined the army. All is hocus-pocus in the Russian counsels. Russia, however, has a very brave officer again in employ. She will need every hand very soon to repair the want of a head . . .'[2] The meeting with the Tsar failed altogether to fulfil Barclay's hopes; on the contrary, it 'oppressed [his] heart'.[3] Despite Alexander's promise, nothing had appeared in print to refute Kutuzov's allegation. The atmosphere was so forbidding that Barclay found it too difficult to explain himself in the Tsar's presence and took again to letter-writing: 'My sullied reputation prevents me from being useful as long as my Sovereign does not find it right to come out in support of my political and military conduct . . .'[4] The Tsar, however, who had trouble enough making Kutuzov continue the advance westwards, was staying mum, knowing he could count on Barclay's patience and loyalty in any event. As if to test him, Alexander handed him command of the Third Western Army, in replacement of the incompetent and unpopular Admiral Chichagov, and Kutuzov announced Barclay's appointment 'with all rights and advantages' prescribed by the Yellow Book, on 6/18 February.[5]

Whatever Barclay may have felt about this appointment, it overjoyed the Third Army which had long felt unappreciated. General Langeron, a Frenchman over twenty years in Russian service and a corps commander in Chichagov's Army, witnessed the welcome Barclay received on his surprise arrival at Third Army headquarters in a small village north of Plock. Chichagov had already left, 'pursued by the curses and hatred of his whole army'.[6] Langeron wrote: 'In

General Barclay's arrival the army saw the fulfilment of its long-standing wish; for all of us the day became an occasion for celebration' . . .'[7]

The paper strength of the Third Army consisted at that point of 11,000 foot soldiers, 4,000 mounted troops including 1,000 Cossacks, a battalion or so of engineers and sappers, and 120 pieces of field artillery serviced by 1,500 gunners – altogether some 17,000 men. But almost a third of this force had been detached by Kutuzov for various purposes – with Barclay's agreement and with the maintenance of customary civilities, for relations between the two were now scrupulously correct. As Barclay told the Supreme Commander, the Third Army was more a contingent than an army. And it was in dire need of ammunition, boots, and shirts.

Barclay's November prediction about 'fortresses to be taken' had been to the point. After the last of the French invaders had recrossed the Neman' and evacuated northern Lithuania, there were still a dozen fortresses in French hands at key points in Poland and Prussia, their garrisons totalling 200,000 men and their supplies enormous. Barclay's first assignment was to invest one of these, the fortress of Thorn on the Vistula. His main problem was a lack of heavy batteries. The nearest were in Prussian Graudenz and he had to wait for them to be put on barges and hauled upstream, a time-consuming operation, hampered by ice. During this waiting-time he had an expert team of engineers, including his old friend General Oppermann and the French Colonel Michaud, to help him with siege preparations. Finally, on 30 March/11 April, he opened the bombardment of the fortress – and five days later saw the white flag hoisted on the ramparts. The French general in command, Morillon, and 3,000 Bavarians (including twelve generals) surrendered. Barclay left it to his own Frenchman, General Langeron, to dictate terms. One thousand of the Bavarians were sick or wounded and were kept in hospital, the other 2,000 were allowed to go home on condition that they would not again take up arms against the Russians or Russian allies during the rest of the year. Fifty-seven cannon, plenty of ammunition, and a good year's supply of foodstuffs came into Russian hands at a minimal cost of dead and wounded on the Russian side. Barclay (via Kutuzov) sent Alexander the keys to the fortress and recommended the award of St. George medals Fifth Class and twenty-five rubles to a list of common soldiers.

In itself it was a modest victory, but nevertheless it was the first success of Russian arms on foreign soil since Napoleon's invasion. It brought Barclay back into prominence and gave both Kutuzov and the Tsar opportunities to make certain gestures. Kutuzov, realizing there had been a change of wind, publicly saluted Barclay by ordering all the armies to celebrate a solemn thanksgiving service for the capture of Thorn.[8] As for the Tsar, he sent Barclay the diamond insignia of the Order of St. Alexander Nevski, a fabulous red-enamelled star covered with sizeable brilliants, and the sum of 50,000 rubles; a gesture which evidently cost him less than publishing selections from Barclay's 'Obiasneniia' or 'Izobrazhenie'.

While the Russian columns and a revived Prussian army pressed on to Saxony, Napoleon arrived on 13/25 April in Erfurt, where he and the Tsar had last met in 1808. Napoleon had raised a new army in France, mostly of raw recruits, had called back some seasoned troops from Spain, and had collected several new German and Italian contingents. With these, along with the survivors of the Grande Armée (and not counting the garrisons in Prussia), he now commanded some 225,000 men, giving him a more than two-to-one advantage over Russians and Prussians combined. The Allies meanwhile had advanced too far, to Dresden, Leipzig, and Berlin, and their armies were too far apart – on the right Wittgenstein, at the centre an ailing Kutuzov (whom Barclay had joined after the fall of Thorn), and on the left Blücher – to present a solid combined front. As Napoleon had foreseen, discord was the rule among the Allied leaders. What he had not expected and had hoped to forestall was the landing in Pomerania of Crown Prince Bernadotte with a Swedish force of 12,000. And what surprised him above all was the total transformation of Prussia. Led by Stein, Hardenberg, Scharnhorst, Gneisenau, and Yorck, nurtured in part by the *Tugendbund*, all of Prussia had become imbued with a fervently patriotic, even revolutionary, spirit, eager for revenge for the humiliation suffered in 1806.

Three days after Napoleon's return, on 16/28 April, Kutuzov died in Bunzlau, Silesia, after a brief illness. His embalmed body was transported with all pomp and military honours to St. Petersburg where it was buried in the Cathedral of Our Lady of Kazan'. The last weeks of the Field-Marshal's life were not happy ones. He was opposed to his Sovereign's policy and allegedly went so far as to warn Alexander that 'Russia will never forgive you'.[9] The Tsar treated his opinions as worthless and raided his staff, abstracting Toll, now a Major-General, to serve as Quartermaster-General of the Tsar's own staff, of which Prince Volkonskii was Chief of Staff and Ermolov was named Chief of Artillery. Now that the Tsar was back in the field he meddled in everything and assumed *de facto* supreme command (which was his *de jure*, as stipulated in the Yellow Book) without, however, actually taking public responsibility for the course of events.

As Kutuzov's successor the Tsar's choice of the enterprising and straightforward Wittgenstein, dubbed with some exaggeration 'the Saviour of St. Petersburg' after defeating Oudinot at Kliastitsy in July 1812, did not go down well with some of the generals claiming seniority in rank, notably Tormassov and Miloradovich. As in Finland in 1809, the Tsar paid no attention to these claims, but did pacify the claimants by allowing Tormassov and Miloradovich direct access to himself. Thus, typically, he created an untenable situation. There is no evidence one way or the other as to the reaction of Barclay to the promotion over his own head of his former First Corps Commander, but it is reasonable to assume that he was biding his time and was not eager to take on his shoulders the weary, disorganized, and again thoroughly outnumbered Russian armies. Besides, he had repeatedly told the Tsar that he was ready to serve his country in any capacity.

Barclay, as ordered by the Tsar, was marching his small army some 220 miles from Thorn to Bautzen, north-east of Dresden. He therefore missed the first encounter, the battle of Lützen, fought between Napoleon's new Grande

Armée and the Russo–Prussian forces of Wittgenstein (20 April/2 May).[10] Wittgenstein was the loser and Napoleon with habitual hyperbole proclaimed the battle to be more important than Austerlitz, Jena, Friedland, or Borodino.[11] For Alexander and Frederick William in any case it was a more than ordinary defeat: it put at risk Austria's decision to join the alliance. And for the Tsar, Wittgenstein's feeble performance was deeply disappointing.

Barclay reached the headquarters of the main army on 5/17 May. The following day, about ten miles to the north near Königswartha, Russian observers spotted strong French forces they believed to be Lauriston's approaching the Russian right flank in an obvious attempt to turn it. If the attempt succeeded, they would also cut off Russian and Prussian supply depots in Silesia. The Tsar therefore ordered Barclay to meet the enemy. Besides his own Third Army, Barclay took Yorck's Corps with Raevskii's Grenadier Corps acting in support, and advanced with his usual three-column formation (the veteran General Chaplits on the left, Langeron with Barclay himself spearheading the centre, Yorck on the right). The plan was to attack Lauriston before Ney, whom they knew to be one day's march behind, could catch up. Wittgenstein promised Barclay that he would supply diversionary action against the French left wing as soon as the attack was launched; but as it proved, no preparations for such action were undertaken.[12]

Masked by surrounding woods, the Russians' arrival before Königswartha surprised an Italian division (of General Bertrand's IVth Corps). The Italians were mauled, losing 2,800 out of their 9,000. Four generals and 750 men were captured and seven cannon taken. But the surprise was also Barclay's when he discovered that he had not engaged Lauriston's Vth Corps of 19,000. It was Yorck's bad luck to have run into the forward elements of this Corps and, although Barclay sent him as many reinforcements as possible, the Prussians lost 1,100 before Yorck managed to retreat after nightfall. Nevertheless, Napoleon's plan to turn the Russian right flank seemed foiled for the day.[13] Yorck rejoined Barclay at Klix on the river Spree, where they received orders from the Tsar to return to Bautzen.

No sooner had Barclay and his men arrived in Bautzen (8/20 May), however, than the Tsar ordered them to retrace their steps, and only a few hours later the small, footsore contingent was back in the vicinity of Klix. Their objective was to bar the northern approaches to the very hilly territory just west of Bautzen. After stringing out his meagre forces over some two miles and sending reinforcements to his advance guard under Chaplits, Barclay had only 5,000 men left. Behind him at some distance were the three Prussian corps of Blücher, Kleist, and Yorck, in that order. Farther down the line, facing the Spree and its uneven banks, were Wittgenstein's Russian forces, with Miloradovich and Württemberg at the far left. Across the Spree, from his vantage point on some rising ground, Napoleon was waiting for Ney to bring four corps from the north before giving the signal to the four corps already massed in front of Bautzen to cross the river. With the forces Ney was bringing, Napoleon would have 200,000 men altogether. Some four miles away as the crow flies was the Tsar on his own viewpoint, with Frederick William nearby. The Tsar had taken into his

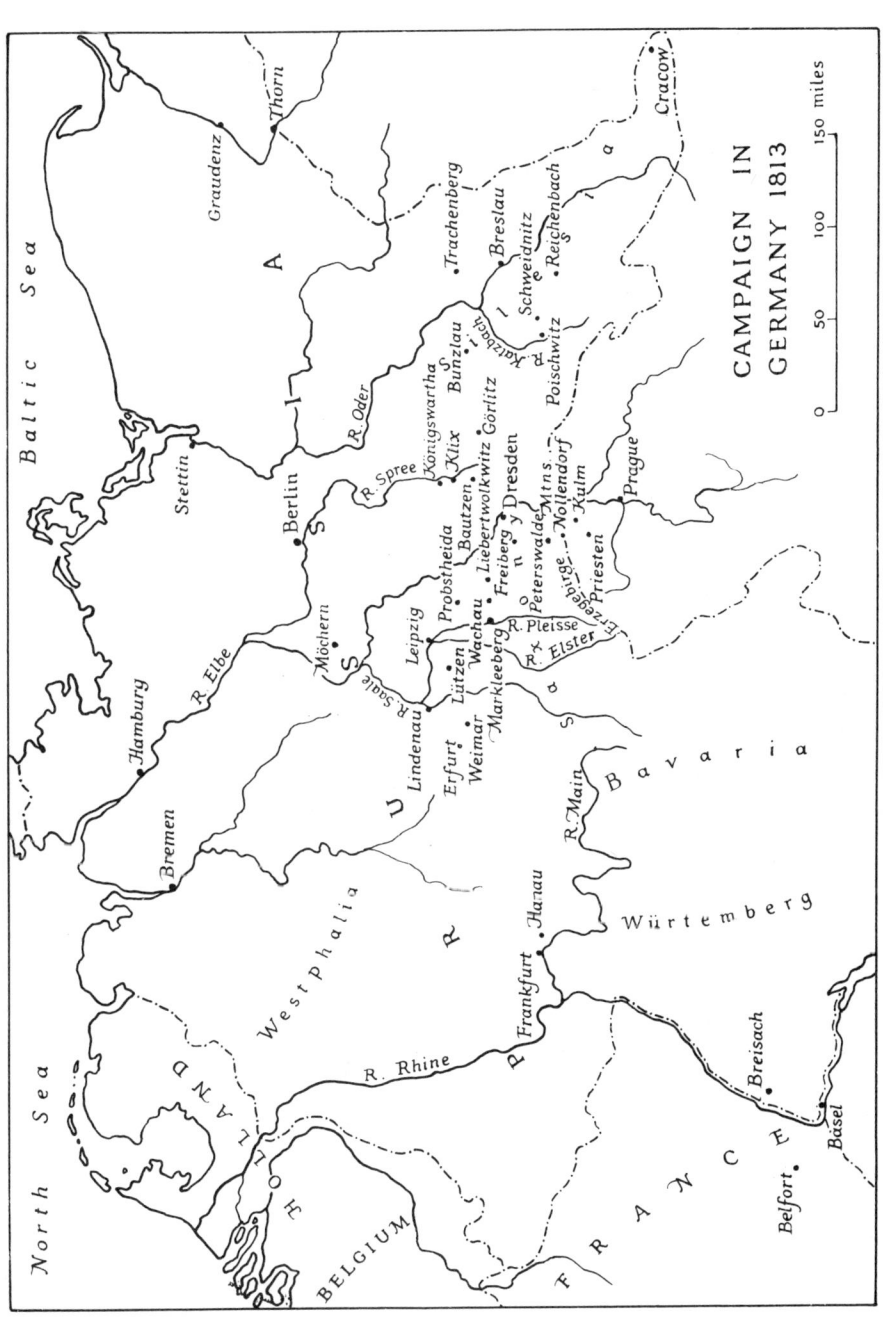

own hands the direction of the 96,000 Allied forces, seeking advice mostly from the Prussian General Knesebeck, while Wittgenstein, who had no real say in the matter, though he was consulted from time to time, dozed or pretended to doze under a tree.[14]

When Napoleon finally launched his attack that afternoon at the centre and left of the Allied position, he aimed at pinning down the Allies and thus preventing them from reinforcing their right wing where he planned eventually to deliver his final blow. The gambit was successful. He gained a further advantage when Oudinot rapidly pushed back Miloradovich. The Tsar responded by sending in reserves and completely ignored the possible threat from the north which had loomed large in his mind all the day before. Neither Barclay nor Blücher could count on reinforcements and they were left to their own devices. When night fell, Napoleon's forces were solidly entrenched in the space between the Spree in their rear and the main Allied position, while in the north Ney was getting ready to pounce upon Barclay, and Lauriston was preparing to move past Barclay against the Allied rear. In a hastily convened council of war during the night the Allies, not fully realizing the precariousness of their situation, decided against taking advantage of the dark for an immediate withdrawal. They hoped to regain the lost terrain in the morning.

For a time in the early hours of the morning of 9/21 May it appeared to have been a correct decision: Miloradovich, having been reinforced by fresh regiments, succeeded in turning the tide in his sector. But in the north, Ney's 18,000 men were now a real threat to Barclay's small force which had to fall back in stages until it was in line with Blücher's position. With Lauriston about to outflank Barclay on the right, Barclay turned to Blücher for some of the latter's reserves. These, however, were already fully committed in an effort to ward off the assault of the French IVth and VIth Corps. Barclay therefore attacked Lauriston's left flank on his own and brought to a standstill the attempt to turn his own right flank. But the Tsar was annoyed that Blücher and Barclay did not mount major and decisive attacks and he did not understand why Barclay had given up his first position which had seemed so secure. It was afternoon before Alexander could finally be persuaded by Knesebeck of the need to withdraw. And it was then that the Tsar suddenly remembered the existence of Wittgenstein, telling him, 'I have no wish to be a witness to this discomfiture; you order the retreat.'[15]

The withdrawal eastwards towards Görlitz was executed in two columns in perfect order. Not a single gun or vehicle was lost (not even a wheel, according to the Tsar's account).[16] Barclay was among the last to leave the field. After adding another division to Chaplits's rearguard, Barclay took command of one of the two retreating columns as they were moving away. Wittgenstein headed the other column; in its midst were the Tsar, the King of Prussia, and their staffs.

As soon as the march got under way Wittgenstein, disheartened by Alexander's sporadic interferences, asked to be relieved of his post. He recommended that Barclay, his senior, be appointed Commander-in-Chief of the combined Russian and Prussian forces, adding generously, 'It will be my pleasure to serve under him again.'[17]

On 14/26 May, even as the withdrawal continued, the Tsar sent word to Barclay to turn his column over to Blücher and present himself for 'a personal explanation'.[18] The substance of this explanation was made known on 19/31 May when the Tsar signed the order appointing Barclay 'Commander-in-Chief of All Armies'. Thus at last, four months after his return to the army, Barclay could feel he had received the ultimate sign, far surpassing rubles and diamonds, of the Tsar's trust, which is what he valued more than anything else in his life. Time, events, and his own unshakeable loyalty had worked in his favour, enabling the Tsar to right a wrong at no cost to his own dignity.

On the same day as the interview, Alexander wrote to his sister, preparing the way for the announcement, assuring her that 'everyone' was in the best possible humour and disposition, and this after Lützen and Bautzen. His pen transformed the latter into a Russian triumph: 'Our troops have covered themselves with glory. On the 7th, General Barclay totally defeated Lauriston at Königswartha . . . [!]'[19] The enemy's attempts to dislodge the Allies were utterly futile, according to Alexander's dishonest recital, and 'our left had meanwhile put to flight the French right. Nevertheless Wittgenstein thought it prudent to order the retreat. As for me, I was of the contrary opinion . . .'[20] Undaunted by the falsity of his own words, the Tsar went on to say how impressed he was by the troops' drill-ground precision during their retreat and to claim that 'not a single battalion was in disarray, not even during the two days of the most terrible and obstinate combat, even three days for the troops who were fighting with Barclay . . .'[21] The way was now paved for Catherine's and Moscow's receiving the news of Barclay's nomination through official channels. Nor was it only the Tsar who credited Barclay extravagantly with great deeds at Bautzen. Thus Rostopchin from Moscow, singing a tune much changed from the days when he and Bagration used to exchange imprecations about 'the Minister': 'They write from the army – and everyone here says it publicly – that at Bautzen our army was saved by Mikhail Bogdanovich [Barclay], which pleases me . . .'[22] Suddenly it was fashionable to be pro-Barclay and to exaggerate and distort his accomplishments at Bautzen.

The resolution of his problems with Barclay and with his new appointment was not the only reason for the Tsar's 'best possible humour and disposition'. More important, Austria was mobilizing and he had been visited by an emissary from Vienna and had seen – and had even stiffened – the proposal for peace that Metternich was to take to Napoleon. The terms would be quite unacceptable to the temporarily victorious French Emperor and it was clear how Austria intended to act when Napoleon rejected them.

There is insufficient evidence to determine whether Barclay made his acceptance of his new appointment conditional on the Tsar's agreement to a pause in operations. Despite certain indications to that effect, it seems very improbable that Barclay went that far. But he did expound to the Tsar the extremely critical condition of the Russian army – the tired survivors of some 2,000 kilometres of marching and of almost an entire year of incessant warfare – and he did insist that it was not possible to restore the condition of the army while it was fighting.

Infantry regiments had shrunk from three battalions to one, and cavalry regiments from eight squadrons to only two or three. On paper, the number of formations was still impressive, but at Bautzen they had added up to hardly more than 55,000 men (the rest were Prussians). Some Prussian participants in the campaign, like Blücher's Quartermaster-General von Müffling, were speaking disobligingly of the Russian army 'heading straight for total disintegration'.[23] There were severe shortages of food and ammunition, and no transportation for either was in existence. Notwithstanding the Tsar's praise for the troops, there was a marked decline in discipline and morale. Marauding and theft were not confined to the Cossacks, though they were the most blamed. Gneisenau, Blücher's Russophobe Chief of Staff, noted with indignation that 'it is vexing to see our own wounded stripped of their belongings on the battlefield by our friends'.[24]

To the astonishment of the Allied leaders, and to the relief of Barclay, Napoleon was eager for an armistice. With superior forces, he had thrown the Allies out of Saxony, conquered half of Silesia, reached the Oder, and taken Breslau, but he, too, felt the need for a pause. Bautzen had shown him that no decisive victory was possible without building up his weak cavalry, and he also needed time to deal with Austria's ominous hostility which presaged a new and wider coalition against him.[25] Most historians agree that this consent to a ceasefire was the greatest mistake of his career.

On 21 May/2 June hostilities were suspended for thirty-six hours and on 23 May/4 June a formal armistice was signed at Poischwitz (or Pleiswitz), to expire on 8/20 July (later extended to 29 July/10 August), with six days' notice to be given before resumption of hostilities. Desultory peace negotiations were begun.

Barclay issued an order of the day to the Russian forces calling for intensive use of the armistice period to re-equip themselves, restock with ammunition and weapons, bring health and discipline back up to standard, carry out basic training for new recruits, and 'in short, raise to perfection the efficiency of every unit . . .' The soldiers themselves were exhorted to total obedience, in almost Biblical tones: 'Our Tsar is among us; He will observe your exploits and will reward each of you according to your deserts . . .'[26]

This was well and good, but Barclay created an uproar at Prussian headquarters by insisting on taking the main Russian army back into Poland, there to reorganize and refurbish it in all tranquillity and integrate the reserves already forming there. All the Russian generals, with the sole exception of Diebitsch, backed Barclay's idea, which also had the Tsar's tacit approval. The Prussian generals, however, with Gneisenau as spokesman, called for a new battle to be fought at once in the Schweidnitz area bordering on Austria, and accused the Russians of pusillanimous, self-interested appeasement. Baron vom Stein, while granting that Barclay himself was 'courageous, upright, experienced in war' (and in any case better than Wittgenstein), still damned him as 'narrow-minded, not very enterprising, and hence', said he, against all evidence, 'more inclined towards peace'.[27] Loewenstern described German tongues clacking all over Prussia and Germany spreading 'fulmination, lament and a portrayal [of the armistice] as a supreme misfortune'.[28] General Knesebeck told General Müffling: 'I know Barclay from the years 1806–1807, he is a man of iron will; he will not give up his plan to withdraw to Poland, especially since from a military view there is much that speaks for it . . .'[29] But whatever the military merits of the plan and however unyielding Barclay's will, the Russians finally gave in to the pressure, recognizing their Allies' legitimate fear of being left alone within Napoleon's reach, and solaced by Prussian promises to supply all the ammunition they needed. Barclay withdrew the Russian army, therefore, only to the southernmost corner of Prussian Silesia, around Reichenbach.

Energetically and methodically, Barclay set about his task: to provide new boots and uniforms for everybody, fresh horses for the cavalry and artillery, plentiful stocks of provisions and fodder. During the two months at his disposal he could see before his eyes the soldiers regaining their vigour; it was as if 'the whole army had been resuscitated'.[30] By the end of July, when the Tsar inspected the main army, he found it 'in a highly satisfactory condition, with some units positively resplendent'.[31] General Wilson, never tempted by understatement, remarked in his *Journal*: 'No man ever beheld such guards and such artillery. Infantry, after two successive seasons, is rarely in similar order; and the cavalry is in as high a condition as if it had never marched more than five versts a day, and never encountered a cold or wet night . . .'[32] With a new army of 60,000 that was being prepared under Bennigsen in the Grand Duchy of Warsaw and a reserve army of 85,000 under the soldier-diplomat Prince Lobanov-Rostovskii, the Russians by themselves, without their allies, could field a force of 350,000 men against Napoleon.

Barclay also set to work to form his own new General Staff. Making a fresh start, he surrounded himself in large part with people he had not worked with in his First Army days. In fact, most of the staff members came from the former staffs of Chichagov and Wittgenstein. Barclay simply took over in their same capacities Diebitsch, Wittgenstein's Quartermaster-General, and Sabaneev, Chichagov's Chief of Staff and a veteran of Suvorov's campaigns. Among all the newcomers Barclay was gratified to welcome back to his staff Colonel Zakrevskii, on loan from the Tsar's throng of aides-de-camp. It seems that Alexander had been impressed by Zakrevskii's fidelity to Barclay when the latter was out of favour.[33] This loan was therefore a friendly gesture towards the new Commander-in-Chief. Zakrevskii's job was to relieve his superior of the chore of putting in writing everything Barclay deemed the Tsar would want to know about. Diebitsch and Zakrevskii were eventually to achieve great eminence, but another man on Barclay's new staff was destined to rise even higher: Count Capodistria, now thirty-seven years old, who later became Alexander's Minister of Foreign Affairs and later still the first President of Greece. He had entered the Russian diplomatic service in 1809, gained an excellent reputation for his expert knowledge of Balkan politics, and had become head of Chichagov's diplomatic chancery when the Admiral had replaced Kutuzov on the Danubian front. After Barclay had replaced Chichagov, Capodistria had met the new Commander under the ramparts of Thorn and the two had hit it off so splendidly that the Greek soon claimed to have become 'the repository of his confidence'.[34] Apart from Capodistria's own declaration there is no evidence of his having really broken through Barclay's reserve, but there is no doubt that the Count did have a way with him. He tells how the Tsar, on a visit to field headquarters, came across him working at Barclay's side, asked for his name, remembered who he was and, all affability, suggested he be used for oral reporting to the Tsar to save the trouble of written reports.[35] There could have developed a rivalry between Capodistria and Zakrevskii, and their staffs, but they worked out amicably the contradiction in their assignments, especially since Capodistria was canny enough not to want to be messenger-boy for a flood of uninteresting communications.

In search of agreement on a common strategy, Alexander, Frederick William, Bernadotte, and their aides met at Trachenberg Castle north of Breslau on 30 June/12 July. From many plans, the one that was retained had been worked out by Toll, with modifications by Barclay, in collaboration with Austria's Chief of the General Staff, Field-Marshal Radetzky. This Trachenberg Operational Plan was adopted a whole month before Austria declared war on Napoleon. It was agreed to create three separate armies containing various mixtures of Allied forces and named respectively the armies of Bohemia, of the North, and of Silesia. These armies were to converge on Saxony after the armistice expired, with Leipzig their main target. The Army of Bohemia – the strongest, consisting of Austrians and of Barclay's Russo–Prussian army – would be placed under a commander who would at the same time become the supreme commander of all Allied forces. The Army of the North, under Bernadotte, totalling 127,000 men, would consist of more than one-half Prussians, one-third Russians, and the rest Swedes. The Army of Silesia, under the septuagenarian Blücher (after the Tsar had vetoed Frederick William's tentative proposal of Barclay), would total 100,000 men: 62,000 Russians and 38,000 Prussians. Finally there was a fourth army: Bennigsen's 60,000 men in Poland, now named the Army of Poland.

Since Russia at that stage contributed by far the largest number of troops it was not surprising that the Tsar was the obvious first choice for supreme commander. In a way he coveted the post despite his memories of Austerlitz. Shil'der, Alexander's foremost biographer, denies this, but it is safe to say that Alexander must have been in two minds about it, torn between thirst for glory and dread of criticism for bungling.[36] While many diplomatic soundings were being taken in the various camps, it may have come to seem finally more attractive to the Tsar, after relinquishing the title for himself, to defer magnanimously to an ally rather than yield first place to one of his own generals, as if admitting that he himself was not equal to the task. In any case, the only plausible Russian candidate would have been Barclay, the most senior in rank except for Bennigsen whose star was fading; and Barclay, though he would not have been able to refuse had the Tsar insisted, and though indeed he may have been tempted momentarily by the glory, had only to recall recent experience to quench all desire to serve as a so-called supreme commander when royalty was in the field. Six weeks as Commander-in-Chief of All Armies had been enough.

In the end, Austria's Prince Schwarzenberg, experienced in both war and diplomacy, was charged with that thorny supremacy, handling it expertly enough to deserve Blücher's post-war toast to 'the Commander-in-Chief who had three monarchs at his headquarters and still managed to beat the enemy!'[37]

The Tsar's generals, however, still felt slighted by the appointment of three non-Russians to command the three main armies. After all, it was the Russians who had just defeated Napoleon in Russia, and the Prussians and Austrians who had repeatedly been trounced. This injury to patriotic pride would be one of the causes for the bad blood between Barclay and Schwarzenberg that was noticeable from the beginning.

Five days before Austria declared war and with three days of the armistice still to go, Barclay's army was already on the march to a rendezvous in Bohemia with the Austrians. Leading the principal Russian contingents were the experienced Wittgenstein, Miloradovich, Gorchakov, Württemberg, and Pahlen; Raevskii was in command of the Grenadiers, Ermolov led the Lifeguards, and Grand Duke Constantine the reserves; Ostermann-Tolstoy, wounded at Bautzen, would soon rejoin the party. The Prussian Corps was under the command of General von Kleist. On 30 July/11 August, four days after starting out, the troops arrived in Bohemia, moving towards Budin where the Austrians awaited them. Barclay, accompanied by Diebitsch, reported at Schwarzenberg's headquarters north of Prague. The Supreme Commander had been warned to expect Barclay to be, 'like the Tsar himself', someone strong-willed and outspoken. At this prickly first meeting Barclay's manner, stiff but co-operative, came as a surprise, and Count Stadion, the Austrian plenipotentiary to the Russians, could only attribute it to a blanket order from the Tsar for Barclay to conform to all of Schwarzenberg's requests.[38]

On 10/22 August the entire Army of Bohemia began advancing on miserable roads across the high crests of the convoluted Erzgebirge separating Bohemia from Saxony. During the difficult passage the Allied commanders were cheered by the news of Wellington's decisive victory at Vittoria and by Marshal Oudinot's failure to take Berlin. But neither the Allies nor Napoleon correctly guessed the other's next move. The Tsar had two respected new advisers, both formerly in Napoleon's service: after having spent nine years in exile in the United States since plotting against Napoleon, the famous French General Moreau came to Russia at the Tsar's own invitation; and the Swiss General Jomini, in the future a great authority on strategy, had deserted the French out of personal pique. When dispatches from the Silesian front revealed that Napoleon, trying to crush Blücher, had taken his main force away from Dresden, these two advisers had little trouble persuading the Tsar to move against the Saxon capital instead of Leipzig. Schwarzenberg, always polite and never especially firm, assented; Toll dissented, and so did Barclay. The latter put his objections in writing to the Supreme Commander and suggested that the Army of Bohemia continue its march to Freiberg, midway between Dresden and Leipzig, deciding once there which way to move. But Schwarzenberg, among other reasons, stressed concern for Wittgenstein – he and the whole right wing would be at Napoleon's mercy – and maintained the Dresden plan. One of Barclay's adjutants remarked cuttingly that nevertheless 'the main reason was surely the fear of an invasion of Bohemia by Napoleon'.[39] Such was the brotherly love prevailing among the Allies.

On 14/26 August, on orders from Austrian headquarters, the Army of Bohemia successfully attacked the outskirts of Dresden. The city itself, however, was well fortified and Napoleon had left some 20,000 men behind for its defence under Marshal Gouvion St. Cyr. There was a division of views, therefore, about going on to storm the city. The Tsar, on Moreau's advice, wanted immediate action, whereas Schwarzenberg decided to wait for the rest of the Austrian forces. Wittgenstein went to Barclay for permission to assault the city that night, at once, but Barclay had to turn him down on the basis of orders from above. On the following day, however, Barclay had reason to regret his obedience: Napoleon and his main forces were back, and the Allies suffered a humiliating defeat.[40] In the two days of 14/26 and 15/27 August they lost one-third of the 30,000 men committed to battle, and thirty Austrian cannon. Moreover the Tsar had to mourn General Moreau, killed before his eyes so soon after his return to Europe and to war. Despite protests by the King of Prussia, who was eager to dethrone the King of Saxony, orders were given for the Army of Bohemia to return to Bohemia. This move conformed belatedly with the Trachenberg Operational Plan to attack Napoleon's marshals but to refrain from attack when Napoleon was present in person.

In dismal weather on slippery, rain-soaked roads – three separate ones, for safety's sake – men and horses scrambled back again in small groups over the craggy passes of the Erzgebirge. The bitterness of the defeat and the exceptional difficulties of the retreat increased the disharmony in the high command and the grumbling at all levels against other nationals. The army was struggling through hazards posed by the enemy, the topography, and the weather; so torrential was the rain that the muskets frequently failed to go off. In the chaos Schwarzenberg could not always be found, and the Tsar and once or twice even Frederick William took matters into their own hands. In one such case the Tsar ordered Austria's Divisional Commander Count Colloredo to rush his cavalry to the rescue of the hard-pressed Prince of Württemberg. But Colloredo, quite unceremoniously rebuffing the Tsar, refused to depart from Schwarzenberg's previous orders. Luckily Count Metternich could be found and, though loath to involve himself in military matters, he obliged Alexander by giving the necessary order, and the wrangle was more or less smoothed over.[41] Schwarzenberg eventually became exasperated by this sort of interference and complained to his Emperor that the Tsar never left him alone, not even in the heat of battle, and was always pestering him by passing on the complaints and remarks of subordinate generals. The Supreme Commander further complained that Barclay had 'no sense of obedience, nor for affairs, and besides he is terribly envious'. Finally Schwarzenberg implored Emperor Francis to persuade the Tsar to quit the army, to remove Barclay, and to place Kleist's, Wittgenstein's, and Miloradovich's corps directly under Schwarzenberg's own command.[42] After nothing came of this wild plan, Schwarzenberg next tried an approach in line with Metternich's apprehensions about Russian territorial expansion. The new stratagem would engage Russian troops in a diversionary action away from Bohemia, in Upper Lusatia in Saxony. But the Tsar saw through this scheme immediately and put a stop to it, and a stop to premature exultings at Austrian headquarters.[43] Meanwhile the pattern was set for the whole campaign, a pattern of 'everlasting arguments' as Knesebeck described it: 'One order follows upon another, and nobody knows who is cook and who is butler.'[44]

These differences between the Russians and the Austrians reflected a deep malaise. Metternich was apprehensive about the arrival of the Russians on the banks of the Danube. On the Russian side there was some fear that Emperor Francis, meek as he was, might influence events in favour of his son-in-law Napoleon. And Barclay and other Russian generals could not easily forget that Schwarzenberg had, less than a year before, led the Austrian Corps in Napoleon's invasion of Russia. True, on orders from his government, he had not been particularly active and did not penetrate very deeply into Russia, but still his presence had been a real threat.

The muddles multiplied as more and more discrepancies appeared between headquarters' orders and the complicated reality of moving hundreds of thousands of men through near-impossible mountain passes in the midst of enemy ambush and pursuit. Of the roads assigned to the three retreating columns, for instance, one was already in Murat's hands, one was blocked by mud-slides, and the one assigned to Barclay, the new Peterswalde road, was that which had been taken, with a two-day start, by the French Marshal Vandamme and 40,000 men. Barclay, ever prudent, refused to risk his main force being trapped between Vandamme in front and Marshals St. Cyr and Marmont pursuing from behind. Despite all his devotion to discipline, the foremost Russian commander was not going to chance losing an army on the orders of an Austrian. When Schwarzenberg saw Barclay's columns emerging on a different road, he was furious. Toll, who was alleged to have earlier slipped Barclay a scribbled note in Russian authorizing him to act as he saw fit, was also alleged to have denied all when confronted by Schwarzenberg's fuming Chief of Staff and to have declared that Barclay 'deserved to have his [severed] head laid at his feet'.[45] The mystery of the slip of paper has never been solved. If, as may be, the Tsar had empowered Barclay to find his own solution, Barclay would have been the last man to embarrass his sovereign.

Confusion and conflict continued on down the line of command. The order to retreat which Barclay gave Ostermann-Tolstoy was sufficiently vague to cause a dispute between that general and Eugen of Württemberg. The order read: try the Peterswalde road but only if conditions there are favourable. Since Ostermann-Tolstoy was told that the road was blocked farther on (by Vandamme's troops) and since moreover he was responsible for the safety of élite Guard regiments under his command, he therefore chose a different route. But Württemberg nevertheless insisted that he would fight his way through on the assigned road, even if he had to proceed alone. After a heated debate during which Württemberg rallied the support of Wolzogen and Ermolov, Ostermann-Tolstoy gave in and agreed to follow Württemberg. As predicted, the Russians soon encountered a sizeable enemy force belonging to Vandamme. In the ensuing battle Württemberg's Corps was reduced to a little over 2,000 men, but the Guards hardly suffered. The rest of the road was unobstructed.

Vandamme sent Napoleon a message that 'the enemy' had been defeated on the Peterswalde road – without specifying that the enemy in question consisted of Württemberg's Corps. The French Emperor, thus misled (and falling ill besides, according to his apologists), retired to Dresden, and his Marshals St. Cyr, Marmont, and Murat stopped their pursuit. Vandamme was left without assistance on the Bohemian side of the mountains and there had to face Ostermann-Tolstoy and important Russian and Austrian reinforcements brought up and quickly deployed by Barclay. At the right Barclay placed Count Colloredo, in the centre Miloradovich, and at the left Raevskii, keeping the Guards in reserve under Grand Duke Constantine. All through 17/29 August the battle raged around the villages of Priesten, Kulm, and Nollendorf. Towards evening the real hero of the day, Ostermann-Tolstoy, had his left arm torn off by a cannonball and had to leave the field. The next morning Kleist, who had been following (with a 1721 map) the route Barclay had assigned to him, unexpectedly emerged from the mountains, his Prussian artillery shelling Vandamme's rear. The fate of the outnumbered French 1st Corps was sealed. Despite desperate resistance, Vandamme – a man thoroughly hated for his harsh and arrogant conduct during the French occupation – was taken prisoner, along with his Chief of Staff, many superior officers, and 10,000 of his men. French standards, ammunition, and eighty-four cannon fell into Russian hands. It was the first, and much needed, victory for the Allies since Napoleon's return, deemed of great 'brilliancy', and the previous mood of discouragement now gave way to boundless joy.[46] All the disobediences and confusions, and notably Barclay's part in them, could very well have led to an enormous Allied catastrophe, but had turned out undeservedly well. Barclay himself called the defeat of Vandamme 'the greatest victory over the French ever achieved' and thanked kind Providence for granting it to him.[47] A Te Deum was held in the open field and Russian and Prussian Guards paraded in front of the Allied monarchs. 'It was incredible', said Wolzogen, 'to see these troops, after the exertions and losses during the previous days' retreat and although some had lost their shoes [in the mud], performing a march that outdid in *grandezza* all other brilliant comedies of this kind . . .'[48]

Barclay, whose army was responsible for the victory, received from the Tsar the highest of all decorations for military distinction, the Order of St. George First Class. In addition, the Austrian Emperor awarded him the Commander's Cross of the Knighthood of Maria Theresa. To soothe Schwarzenberg, whose orders had been so thoroughly overlooked, ignored, and disobeyed, the Tsar gave him in turn an Order of St. Andrew. No one was really mollified, however. Barclay wrote to his wife that he would gladly trade back his Maria Theresa Cross for 'a better conduct of operations' and 'everything would be much better if only our Commanding Field-Marshal, Prince Schwarzenberg, were more capable and more resolute.'[49] In the same letter Barclay admitted that he had 'got into real hell with the Austrians and there is nothing I desire more fervently than to get away from them'. As time went on he complained more and more to Auguste of Schwarzenberg's 'insufferable slowness' and 'clumsiness', saying that 'his slowness and irresolution have brought me on several occasions to the brink of desperation. I have had many a scene with him and his patronizing petty courtiers.'[50] Bohemia was a land he despised and as for the Austrians, 'coarse and insufferable', he repeatedly attacked their laxity, describing them, much as he described Schwarzenberg, as self-seeking, slow, irresolute, and lacking both in energy and in patriotism, unlike 'the brave Prussians'.[51] The antagonism was clearly mutual and petty retaliations were the order of the day: 'Even the Tsar and myself do not get forage – the Austrians want everything for themselves . . .'[52]

The Vandamme disaster, along with Macdonald's defeat by Blücher at Katzbach and Ney's failure to break through to Berlin, marked the turning point of the German campaign. What the Allies needed now was a major victory to bring the campaign to a close, but such an event was still some miles and many lives away. Napoleon could count on few fresh troops, but Austria's forces were constantly being reinforced and Bennigsen had at last brought 57,000 men and 200 guns from Poland. Two-thirds of this new army was in very good condition. (One-third was made up of *opolchenie*, many of whom were still armed only with pikes; their officers led or, rather, drove them with curses and knouts.) Nothing could please Barclay better than this gathering of forces presaging an imminent Allied offensive. He was impatient for the next appointment with Napoleon, frustrated by the failure to follow up quickly the victory over Vandamme. The time seemed quite long enough, as he wrote home in a rare ironical vein, to have taken the waters at Teplitz, 'which would have been good for my health'.[53] Instead the time was filled by keeping Wittgenstein and his rearguard supplied, attending countless planning meetings and troop inspections, and dutifully preparing for the celebration of the twelfth anniversary of the Tsar's coronation on 15/27 September. After an Orthodox service of thanksgiving attended by the three monarchs, there followed a gala parade and a huge banquet given by the officers of the Russian Imperial Foot Guards for the monarchs, their suites, all the Russian and Prussian generals, and all the officers of the Prussian Guards.[54] The glamour of royalty touched even the lowest of *opolchenie*. Invincibility was in the air.

In high feather, the Army of Bohemia took up its march again at the beginning of October (N.S.) 1813, its destination Leipzig. Converging on Leipzig as well were Bennigsen's Army (now also under Schwarzenberg's command – except for 20,000 men diverted to blockade Dresden); the Army of the North; the Army of Silesia; and a Bavarian Corps, since Bavaria had become the latest defector from the French. Altogether 300,000 Allied troops with almost 1,500 cannon were closing in upon Leipzig, where Napoleon had a hurriedly gathered 200,000 with 916 guns. The Battle of the Nations was to last from 4/16 to 7/19 October 1813.

Schwarzenberg deployed his enormous army in a semicircle stretching from Lindenau (west of Leipzig) to Fuchshain in the south-east. Barclay's responsibility was the southern sector situated to the east, or on the right, of the river Pleisse, his left wing verging on marshland covered with underbrush. Following a 'monstrous idea' of Schwarzenberg's adviser General Langenau, who was no strategist but was determined, according to Wolzogen, that the victory be secured by Austrians, the Supreme Commander placed the élite of the Austrian troops in the swampy area next to Barclay and a mix of Allied troops everywhere else: 'All this was done so that, if a brilliant coup took place in any sector, the fame would at least be shared by the three nations, while the major coup would be carried out by the Austrians alone . . .'[55] Barclay's forces, augmented by a strong contingent of Austrians and Prussians under Generals Klenau and Ziethen respectively, were thus deployed in five separate columns placed inconveniently far from one another in order to cover the entire front of six miles. Klenau (later superseded by Bennigsen) was at the extreme right. Gorchakov and Württemberg were in the centre, with Pahlen's cavalry just behind them, and these Russian forces formed a corps under Wittgenstein's overall command. Kleist's Prussian Corps held the left wing. The approximate total of these forces including some reserves was 72,000. They were to be reinforced by 24,000 Russian Guards and Cuirassiers whom the Tsar had, after some argument, extricated from Schwarzenberg.

Napoleon had originally planned to defeat Bernadotte and Blücher before the Army of Bohemia arrived on the scene.[56] He miscalculated; it was Schwarzenberg who got there first. Napoleon accordingly changed plans and moved some 95,000 men, almost half the forces at his disposal, to the south, around the villages of Markkleeberg, Wachau, and Liebertwolkwitz. The troops, an imposing array, were those of Marshals Augereau (IXth Corps), Macdonald (XIth Corps), Victor (IInd Corps), Oudinot (Young Guards), and Generals Prince Poniatowski (VIIIth Corps), Lauriston (Vth Corps), and Sébastiani (cavalry). In reserve were the Old and New Guards under Marshal Mortier and Murat's three cavalry corps.

Once the mist had cleared at eight o'clock on the cold, rainy morning of 4/16 October, Württemberg attacked Wachau. His troops easily took the village but could not hold it, and in the course of the next three hours Wachau changed hands time and again in bitter close-quarter fighting, ending up finally in the enemy's possession. Immediately following the bugles which sounded Württemberg's initial advance, the rest of Barclay's forces went into action. Kleist and Klenau at the two wings were at first successful in taking Markkleeberg and Liebertwolkwitz, but Gorchakov and Pahlen could not withstand the dense artillery fire and had to give ground. Even veteran French gunners, according to an eyewitness, had never seen such concentrated fire.[57] Eighty thousand shots were fired by Napoleon's artillery.[58]

From two opposite hills facing each other some three miles apart, Alexander and Napoleon watched the attacks and withdrawals by their sodden troops. The development in the centre alarmed Barclay. He galloped up the hill and together with Wolzogen, Toll, and Jomini obtained the Tsar's consent to request Schwarzenberg to move some of the idle Austrian reserves over to the right side of the Pleisse. Schwarzenberg made no difficulties and Barclay's official *Journal* lauded the harmony that prevailed that day among the various nationalities involved, 'all guided by the same spirit and all having but one goal, that of honour and glory'.[59] These Austrian reinforcements were very much needed since Bennigsen and Colloredo had not yet been heard from despite urgent messages sent to speed up their march.

Shortly before midday Napoleon noticed that Allied pressure was slackening and ordered the counterattack. The French surged forward all along the line. Resisting stubbornly, the Allies were nevertheless slowly pushed back to the positions from which they had started. Their losses were heavy, but their vigour and morale were unimpaired. Whenever they could they counterattacked. When Barclay ordered the Imperial Mounted Guard and the Cuirassiers forward against the French Cuirassier division which had just sabred its way through Württemberg's infantry, they fought brilliantly and threw back the enemy. The fighting continued all afternoon, but at nightfall, when only sporadic shots still resounded in the sudden stillness, it was clear that the first day of the battle had ended in stalemate. For Napoleon, who had prematurely announced a decisive victory in the south to the King of Saxony, the day's conclusion augured ill. Already Blücher's Army of Silesia had broken through in the north, by defeating Marmont at Möckern, and was at the gates of Leipzig.

The next day, Sunday, the foul weather continued and the guns were silent. Bennigsen and Colloredo finally arrived, their rain-soaked troops worn out by forced marches. Bernadotte, on the other hand, was lagging. Schwarzenberg called off a new attack until Monday. Napoleon, too, was in no mind to take the offensive and the French spent most of the day digging in.

Early on Monday, 6/18 October, the battlefield was again shrouded in thin autumnal mist. At seven, the Army of Bohemia began advancing in three main columns, the Austrians on the left, Barclay in the centre, Bennigsen on the right with Platov on the extreme right. The positions for which such a furious battle had been fought two days earlier were quickly passed and Barclay's forces continued on towards the enemy's key position at Probstheida, over two miles north of Wachau. He stopped his contingents just short of the entrenched enemy to wait for the other two columns to draw even: Bennigsen, whose assignment was to outflank the French left, had the longest way to go. Again at eight the mist lifted, this time leaving the field bathed in sunshine. The Allied artillery, greatly reinforced during the previous twenty-four hours, began their bombardment, round upon round, while the French gunners for the first time in all of Napoleon's campaigns were told to economize on their ammunition. The King of Prussia and the Tsar had now moved forward, too, and Alexander impatiently ordered Barclay to assault the French position. The moment was not auspicious, since Napoleon had just reached Probstheida and his presence always galvanized his troops. Kleist and the Second Russian Grenadier Division attacked and gained a foothold inside the village but were beaten back. A second attack also failed, and so did a third by Württemberg. But the enemy suffered greatly and Napoleon sent in Lauriston's Corps to relieve Victor's. When the Russians received good news of Allied progress in other sectors and of the defection from Napoleon first of some Saxon and Württemberger units, then of two full Saxon brigades and a battery of twenty-two twelve-pounders, the Tsar agreed not to sacrifice any more of Barclay's men. (Napoleon would use these defections – though the Saxons numbered fewer than 4,000 – to maintain that treachery had lost him the battle, just as he had blamed the winter for his defeat in Russia.) Barclay remained on the defensive during the rest of the day, contenting himself with preventing an enemy breakthrough while keeping the French under constant artillery fire.

Already in the morning evidence had started accumulating that some of Napoleon's army was withdrawing over the causeway at Lindenau. At four in the afternoon a number of French cavalry corps were observed leaving Leipzig; they were followed by some of the artillery. By early evening there was no longer any doubt of the Allies' victory. While Napoleon spent a dejected night in Leipzig's Hôtel de Prusse, the jubilant Allied armies bivouacked all around Leipzig, and their campfires and the blaze of burning villages encircled the still-occupied city in a ring of flame.

'Thus ended that memorable day of 6/18 October,' recorded Barclay's military *Journal*; 'our successes were that much more glorious because our reserves did not have to be committed. Our officers and soldiers surpassed themselves.' Barclay generously singled out the Grand Duke Constantine, praising him for having given 'unequivocal proof of admirable steadiness and valour'.[60]

To be sure, Leipzig still had to be taken. All through the morning of 7/19 October furious fights raged at the various gates leading into the town, but by one in the afternoon the end came. Napoleon's forces were not spared an added catastrophe when in the confusion of their retreat the only bridge giving access to the Lindenau causeway was prematurely blown by one of their sappers. Thousands of French troops were trapped and had to surrender. Others tried to swim across the Elster, many reaching the other bank but just as many drowning, and among these was Prince Poniatowski whom Napoleon had just named Marshal after the battle of Wachau on 4/16 October.

The Russian losses in this Battle of the Nations were enormous – 800 officers and at least 20,000 other ranks, far surpassing the losses of the Prussians and almost three times those of the Austrians, while Swedish losses were only 300. The French may have lost 38,000 in killed and wounded, and 15,000 in prisoners, including Lauriston, Reynier, and thirty-four other generals.[61] The Russian losses led Barclay to write to Auguste: 'May God give us peace soon, otherwise our gracious Monarch will have to shed more of his brave soldiers' blood to no purpose.'[62] Barclay had always kept from Auguste harsh details of war. At the end of the Battle of the Nations, however, he had a battleground event of a different kind to write to her about:

I am writing this on the battlefield on which after three days of combat we have forced the enemy into full flight . . . His Majesty the Tsar has honoured me by naming me a Count and this on the very battlefield. I am about to march off with part of my army to bar Napoleon's way to the Saale . . . I shall write again soon; having spent the best part of three days on horseback, I am as tired as a post-horse . . .[63]

After the victory parade in the market-place where the victors received a tremendous welcome, Barclay had one other piece of urgent business in Leipzig before setting out after Napoleon. Auguste had asked him to keep a lookout for some velvet, and in Leipzig he found what he was sure would please his Countess. He was able to buy her twelve ells of 'cosmos'-coloured velvet and twelve ells of dark green.

CHAPTER XV
GLORY

Loyalty and Patience
Michael Barclay de Tolly

The victors of Leipzig failed to catch up with Napoleon. The only attempt to bar his way was by a mixed army of 30,000 Bavarians and Austrians coming up from southern Germany, and this was promptly worsted, at Hanau, just east of Frankfurt. Before the Allies could reorganize, Napoleon was safely across the Rhine on 2 November (N.S.) 1813, two weeks after his retreat from Leipzig. The confusion of this French withdrawal was, according to Marshal Marmont, just as harrowing as the retreat from Moscow, and not more than 70,000 relatively fit troops were salvaged, only two-thirds of them with arms.[1] Once more Napoleon abandoned sick and wounded by the thousand, and he also left behind some 100,000 men scattered in various isolated fortresses. As time wore on these garrisons surrendered one by one, except for Marshal Davout's sizeable force in and around Hamburg which held out successfully and was eventually permitted an honourable return to France. Napoleon's crossing of the Rhine marked the end of his last campaign in Germany and signalled the collapse of one of his prime political structures, the nine-year-old Confederation of the Rhine. That assemblage of German kingdoms and grand duchies, seven in all, had provided him with many soldiers who now began to swell the Allied ranks.

For the Allies' march to the Rhine, the Supreme Commander, Schwarzenberg, had carefully selected two routes: a convenient one for the Austrian forces and an inconvenient one for Barclay's Russians and Prussians. The idea was that the Emperor Francis should be the first to arrive in the ancient city of Frankfurt, appearing as the unrivalled great liberator of the German states. Alexander, however, alert to Austrian wiles and fairly wily himself, took from Barclay four Russian cavalry divisions and one Prussian brigade of Horse Guards (to represent Frederick William, who was in Berlin), and with these 10,000 splendid horsemen he sped off, making a fine, majestic entry into Frankfurt at midday on 5 November (N.S.) under the startled eyes of Schwarzenberg and amid the jubilant applause of the inhabitants. Emperor Francis arrived a full day later.

Throughout November Frankfurt was the hub of Allied diplomatic and military bustle. The questions of whether, when, and where to attack Napoleon divided the Allies and split each national headquarters as well. The basic cleavage into war-party and peace-party factions became evident at the Allied council of war on 8 November (N.S.), and prevented it from coming to an agreement. In the Prussian camp one extreme supported Gneisenau who insisted on immediate pursuit of Napoleon, while the other extreme shared Knesebeck's alarm at the idea of crossing the Rhine and thus 'tempting the gods'. The Austrians on the whole still wished to believe in the possibility of success for their peace overtures to Napoleon, whereas the British representatives favoured bringing about Napoleon's downfall by force. Among the Russians, the Tsar remained determined not to stop half-way to Paris, but most of his generals were hesitant. Barclay, as he had written to Auguste, was praying for peace, for the avoidance of useless bloodshed. Besides, he and his colleagues were keenly aware of the terrible problems of logistics. Napoleon's experience in 1812, and the empty larders they had found in Leipzig, were fresh in their minds. Their armies were already very far from their borders and there was no desire to repeat Napoleon's mistakes. But the Tsar's judgement was decisive.

The day after the inconclusive war council the Tsar, manœuvring quickly and expertly, set out in his own hand a plan (owing much to Gneisenau and Langenau) which was then accepted by the Prussians and the Austrians. Broadly it laid down what was to be the future Allied strategy, and as usual involved some renaming and reorganization. The Army of Bohemia, now referred to as the 'Main Army', was to operate through neutral Switzerland. Even though Napoleon had been violating Swiss neutrality for many years, this decision did not come easily to the Tsar, who had to fight down the intense opposition of his old Swiss tutor Laharpe and his Swiss adviser Jomini. At the same time the Main Army would keep under observation two possible Rhine crossing-places at Kehl and Breisach in case of a French counterattack. The chief object, however, was to reach the high plateau of Langres by the shortest possible route, which was through the Belfort gap. To the north, part of Blücher's army was to cross at mid-Rhine and another part at Cologne, to cut off Holland. Meanwhile Bernadotte was to use one of his corps to liberate Holland, while most of his forces would be keeping Davout in check around Hamburg. A number of individual corps, including Bennigsen's, would besiege those German and Polish fortresses still in French hands. And lastly, the Austrian army in Italy would attempt to link up with Wellington in the south of France.[2] Altogether the Allies had more than 600,000 men under arms and, along with this overpowering force, they had what the statesman–historian Alphonse Thiers called 'that fervent and sincere passion which is the only substitute for genius'.[3]

More than half the Main Army was now made up of Austrians, and it also included several German corps composed of Bavarians, Württembergers, Hessians, and others. Wittgenstein's Corps now came under Schwarzenberg's direct command. To the Main Army belonged also a supporting force which was placed under Barclay de Tolly. It consisted entirely of élite formations: Constantine's Foot and Horse Guards and the Grenadiers, all with their artillery, three Cuirassier divisions, a Guard Cossack regiment, Prussia's Foot and Horse Guards, and reserves – in all, some 32,000 men. In the coming campaign Barclay's main task was to assist any unit suffering a major enemy attack. Theoretically, therefore, Barclay might play a decisive role. But it was the Tsar's eagerness to keep this select force intact and in sparkling condition for a grand entry into Paris – his revenge for Moscow – that had made him choose Barclay, knowing he could rely on him (unlike Constantine) to avoid costly glory-hunting at the expense of his men. In addition, though the Tsar's wishes prevailed, Barclay was nominally Commander-in-Chief of all Russian contingents and in this capacity paid particular attention to organization and supply.

Towards the end of November (N.S.), while peace negotiations dragged on in Frankfurt, the Main Army moved forward in nine columns towards the Swiss border. The first forward units crossed the Rhine by the Basel bridge in the last week of December (N.S.), and one of these, under the Austrian General Bubna, moved rapidly towards Geneva to threaten Lyons. Barclay's force crossed the Rhine in the first days of January (N.S.) 1814, just twelve months after the Russians had crossed the Neman' in their pursuit of Napoleon through Germany. Farther downstream Wittgenstein and Blücher were also over into France. Everywhere the crossing went smoothly (by pontoons except at Basel) despite snow and rain and alternating frost and thaw. Setting foot in France was accompanied by Allied proclamations assuring the population that the war was being fought not against the French nation, whose greatness was unquestioned and honour unsullied, but only against Napoleon.

After successfully bypassing the strong defensive line of the Vosges, Barclay and his élite forces reached the 1,600-foot-high plateau of Langres; only 170 miles remained until Paris. Barclay wrote to his friend Alexander von Maier in St. Petersburg, declaring somewhat hastily: 'Thus we are almost at the end of our labours. May God grant that we reach our goal soon because we are all much in need of rest.'[4] Believing that the final reckoning was almost due, Barclay also disclosed to this one friend how much the old injury to his name still smarted: 'I would like to know what they are saying now, those people who, in ignorance of my guiding motives, permitted themselves to condemn me so loudly and brazenly? . . .' After this outburst, however, Barclay's thoughts soared to the future, envisaging Russia emerging from the great struggle 'as if reborn, reaching a pinnacle of greatness and might, for which she will be indebted to the Tsar and to his immeasurable patience and indefatigable solicitude'.[5] This vision was vague enough and patriotic enough to carry him along indefinitely.

Barclay's expectation of a quick end to the war was not, at that moment, unrealistic. The Allies' progress in France was at first 'nothing but a military promenade'.[6] They bypassed all fortified places, leaving behind small forces to contain enemy garrisons, and by the end of January had deployed most of their troops between the Marne and the Seine, reaching Bar-sur-Aube without encountering any serious opposition. As they advanced into French territory, some 46,000 enemy troops were falling back, and to the right of Schwarzenberg's army Blücher was advancing so fast that Parisians were beginning to panic. Napoleon was still busy in Paris raising contingents of very young, totally inexperienced conscripts; hundreds of thousands fled into the forests to avoid service. He did not reach the field until 26 January (N.S.) 1814 and then with only 85,000 troops at his disposal and only half of these under his immediate command. Muskets and horses were insufficient and there was hardly any bread. Marauding Cossacks and Prussians were remorselessly pillaging all villages within reach. The Allies were perforce living off the land.

In a first clash with Blücher at Brienne on 29 January (N.S.), however, Napoleon gained an important victory. It sent Blücher's army reeling back towards Schwarzenberg's approaching forces. Three days later (1 February), two miles south of Brienne at La Rothière, the Allies took their revenge and triumphed in an eight-hour battle fought out in fog and blizzard. The control of all Allied forces had been put in Blücher's hands for the occasion and it was perhaps the only time when absolute harmony prevailed among the Allies. The Tsar, the King of Prussia, Schwarzenberg, and Barclay were all on the scene. Without interfering, for once, they watched through rain and snow as Blücher directed not only his own army but the reinforcements supplied by Schwarzenberg and the support Barclay provided from his Grenadier Corps and two of his Cuirassier divisions. The event was unusual enough to inspire the Tsar's aide-de-camp Mikhailovskii-Danilevskii, the future military historian, to record gratefully how Schwarzenberg and Barclay 'showed no sign of resentment': 'One cannot pass over the noble spirit displayed by the other two Commanders-in-Chief . . .'[7] The Tsar was happy enough at this first triumph over Napoleon on French soil to give each of the three Commanders – Blücher, Schwarzenberg, and Barclay – a gold sword encrusted with diamonds. The next day a council of war was held at Brienne-le-Château, where thirty-five years earlier Napoleon had attended cadet school. The Allies decided to drive straight for Paris and young Allied officers made luncheon appointments for a week thence in the gardens of the Palais Royal.

But Napoleon was far from beaten. While deceptive peace negotiations were continued in the Congress of Châtillon by the diplomatists of both sides (notably Lord Castlereagh and Metternich for the Allies, and Caulaincourt, who was now France's Foreign Minister), a new phase in the campaign began. In an incredible burst of energy, and with all his customary determination and brilliant strategy, Napoleon went after Blücher's army. Even the stupendous numerical superiority of the Allies seemed not to count against Napoleon's master strokes. Blücher had imprudently divided his forces into four separate columns, and allowed the distance between them to widen constantly. Day after day, moving with remarkable speed, Napoleon took maximum advantage of his 'interior lines' and fell upon Blücher's dispersed forces, almost annihilating them piecemeal. Blücher, a complicated personality containing various unstable elements (like his lifelong fear of giving birth to an elephant), now became desperate and suicidal. Day after day Napoleon sent jubilant letters back to Paris, to Marie-Louise and his elder brother Joseph, ex-King of Spain, telling them to publish the good news everywhere. By exaggerating the number of enemy losses of all kinds, Napoleon hoped to raise morale in Paris and impart a sense of his invincibility to his young soldiers. On 11 February (N.S.) he boasted to Joseph that he had completely routed Blücher: 'The Silesian Army is no more.'[8]

Despite ever-increasing evidence, Schwarzenberg remained unconvinced that Napoleon's immediate objective was the destruction of the Silesian Army. Also, not realizing the extent of this Army's dispersal, Schwarzenberg was unable to imagine that Napoleon's young recruits could seriously injure it. Therefore he was deaf to all arguments to relieve it. The Tsar and his counsellors, on the other hand, favoured a forceful diversionary offensive in Napoleon's rear to lighten the pressure on Blücher's embattled forces. But, as the Tsar's headquarters informed the Allies, 'His Imperial Majesty could not prevail upon Prince Schwarzenberg.'[9] The Prince, with the backing of the Emperor Francis, held on stubbornly to his own plan for moving the Main Army in cautious steps in the direction of Fontainebleau, farther and farther away from Blücher's unfortunate troops, among whom the Russian corps were suffering most.

It was only after a reconnaissance in force behind Napoleon's lines was undertaken by Diebitsch at the Tsar's prompting and on Barclay's orders that Supreme Allied Headquarters became aware of the extent of Blücher's defeats, and great was the consternation. With 120,000 men of the Main Army now poised along a twenty-five-mile stretch north of Troyes, and forward units only forty miles from Paris, the Allied leaders were in a quandary about what to do next. Jomini, thoroughly disliked by the Austrians and of late neglected by the Tsar, was once again consulted. He promptly replied that if it were up to him, he would immediately march the 120,000 men to Paris while Napoleon was still chasing after Blücher. Knesebeck thought this preposterous: 'It was for wanting to march on Paris that Blücher was beaten. What need have we to see the Paris Opera!'[10] Nor did Jomini's counsel please a Supreme Commander already being driven half mad by the Tsar's incessant meddling. For Schwarzenberg, Blücher and Gneisenau had been 'trampling underfoot the very rules of war' with their 'childishly furious drive on Paris' – Gneisenau being more to blame than 'good old' Blücher who was 'merely lending his name'.[11]

Jomini's advice came anyway too late. Napoleon abandoned for the time being his pursuit of Blücher in order to turn his attention to the Main Army, so frighteningly close to Paris. On 15 February (N.S.) he began a forced march, 'one of the swiftest marches of his career', according to Chandler, using requisitioned wagons to cart some of his infantry and covering forty-seven miles in thirty-six hours.[12] The Allied advance units at Mormant and Nangis were routed by Marshals Victor and Oudinot while Macdonald pushed through to the centre of the Main Army's line. In his panic Schwarzenberg proposed a ceasefire. This sign of weakness immediately fortified Napoleon and he indignantly rejected the overture. To Joseph he branded Schwarzenberg a coward and ridiculed the Allies as 'wretches who fall on their knees at the first setback', and he assured his brother: 'I shall never accept an armistice until this land is purged of all the enemy . . .'[13]

The retreat of the Main Army began, first to Troyes, then to Bar-sur-Aube, and by 1 March (N.S.) Barclay and his troops were back in Langres. New developments were, however, changing the balance of forces. On 9 March (N.S.) the Allies formed a Quadruple Alliance including England and signed the Treaty of Chaumont. They vowed to continue the war for twenty years if need be and to keep 150,000 men each under colours. Meanwhile Wellington had entered Bordeaux, strong reinforcements for Blücher arrived from Bernadotte, and a major levy was undertaken by the German states, large and small. Napoleon, on the other hand, had to swallow the bitter pills of his brother-in-law Murat's defection in Naples and his stepson Eugène de Beauharnais's refusal to obey orders, while suffering the alarming inefficiency of Marshal Augereau who did not move out of Lyons. But it was Blücher's initiative in late February that actually brought about the decisive turn in the war.

With Napoleon's attention elsewhere, Blücher, empowered to proceed on his own, began marching north on 25 February (N.S.). On 1 March (N.S.) the Silesian Army crossed the Marne by pontoon bridges at La Ferté-sous-Jouarre, forty miles east of Paris. Once over the river Blücher joined forces with Wintzingerode's newly arrived Russian Corps and Bülow's Prussian Corps, a link-up Napoleon had sought to prevent. Hearing this good news, Frederick William intervened with Schwarzenberg, demanding action in support of Blücher. A decisive move towards the Marne was also what Barclay and Diebitsch were recommending, so Schwarzenberg finally gave in and called a halt to the increasingly unpopular withdrawal. Turning about, the Russians under Wittgenstein, Wrede's Bavarians, and the Württembergers under their Crown Prince took Bar-sur-Aube on 2 March after a hard-fought battle with Marshal Oudinot. Two days later the Allies re-took Troyes, and their leading units were pushing ahead both to the north and to the west.

But when these troops reached the Seine they halted again. Several possibilities were open to Schwarzenberg, among them a vigorous march west to Paris or a decisive attack northwards against Napoleon's rear.[14] But these possibilities were not even contemplated. The best evidence that Schwarzenberg did not plan an offensive is the fact that he kept Barclay's Guards and reserves at Langres and Chaumont until 12 March (N.S.). It was only on 13 March that the Supreme Commander finally gave orders for a general advance and moved Barclay's force up to Bar-sur-Aube. The reason for Schwarzenberg's sudden activity lay in Blücher's achievement. After meeting up with Wintzingerode and Bülow, Blücher's rearguard suffered a defeat at Croanne, but on 9 and 10 March (N.S.) his forces gained a major victory over Napoleon at Laon.

Schwarzenberg's two weeks of immobility had angered the Tsar and he now habitually referred to the Austrian high command as 'these gentlemen'. 'These gentlemen', he told Barclay, 'have given me a lot of grey hair.'[15] The Tsar's feelings were shared by his own senior officers and by the Prussian commanders. Judging by the last few weeks, they believed that nothing much could be expected from the Main Army and the Supreme Commander. By default, the role of a main army thus fell to Blücher's Silesian Army. A complete split in the Allied high command was narrowly averted by Schwarzenberg finally dropping his idea for Austrian unilateral action and agreeing to launch a general offensive.[16]

Just as this offensive was starting, two important changes were made in the Russian command. Wittgenstein, wounded at Bar-sur-Aube while leading a cavalry charge, left the army and was replaced as head of the Main Army's Sixth Corps by Raevskii, until then commander of the Third Grenadier Corps in

Barclay's formation. Platov's case was different. The other leading officers, especially the Prussians, wanted his removal, incensed at his inability or unwillingness to keep his impulsive Cossacks in check. The Cossacks' whole tribal style was anathema to the Prussian spirit, and Platov was considered to embody all the worst Cossack features, being a degraded, dim-witted old fellow, no fit companion in arms for the other commanders. Barclay, too, found him temperamentally uncongenial and in the early days of the war had judged him ignoble and dilatory.[17] The Tsar, however, was fond of his oldest active general, and though he reluctantly agreed to replace him with the more polished Kaisarov, thirty-two years Platov's junior, he kept Platov on his own staff.

Napoleon, now driven, as Marmont saw him, 'by a blind passion and giving way to rash manœuvres', turned from Laon towards Reims.[18] Here he surprised and overwhelmed a mixed corps of Russians and Prussians led by Saint-Priest, the French expatriate who had been Bagration's chief of staff. (The leg wounds Saint-Priest collected during this short battle proved, like Bagration's at Borodino, to be mortal.) Next, Napoleon set out to defeat the Allied Main Army before Blücher could close in on him from the rear. He hurried his tired troops – 30,000 to 40,000 boys and men – through Épernay and Fère-Champenoise to Arcis-sur-Aube. Here he hoped to turn Schwarzenberg's right and, by attacking the various enemy columns one by one, to drive the Allies back to the Rhine. Exhilarated by the easy victory at Reims and encouraged by the peasants' response to his appeal to arm themselves and harass the invader – in pale imitation of what he had seen happen to his Grande Armée in Russia – Napoleon was convinced that he had only 'to say "boo" to send Schwarzenberg reeling backward'.[19]

Schwarzenberg, however, was determined and this time the Allies would be first to attack. The terrain turned out to be propitious around Arcis-sur-Aube. From the south or left bank of the Aube, a rolling plateau stretched for about three miles before it rose in a gentle slope. It was ideal ground for large-scale cavalry charges. If Napoleon crossed over at Arcis, his forces would suffer the disadvantage of having to fight with the Aube at their back. Schwarzenberg deployed a sizeable number of his 90,000 men along a fifteen-mile front facing the river, with the rest ready to move up from Troyes, and placed Barclay's Guards and reserves in readiness to the rear on the top of the slope. The Tsar, having made it his habit to be close to Barclay's headquarters in moments of crisis, remained nearby. He needed reassurance: suddenly, after urging an offensive, he found himself not at all happy about Schwarzenberg's offensive plans.

At one o'clock in the afternoon of 20 March (N.S.), after the French cavalry had crossed the Aube, Schwarzenberg, despite last-minute hesitations, gave the starting signal, a cloud of smoke accompanied by three detonations of twelve-pounders. Kaisarov's Cossacks and Frimont's Austrian Hussars opened the charge and quickly forced the outnumbered French cavalry into flight back to Arcis. A complete rout was prevented only by Napoleon's brisk and courageous intervention, setting an example to his flagging troops while braving death from a howitzer shell which killed the horse beneath him – and by the arrival of his

Old Guards. To the right, at nearby Torcy-le-Grand, Wrede's Bavarians, supported by Barclay's reserves, launched attack upon attack against Ney's infantry. The battle raged throughout the afternoon, and the struggle was fierce and evenly balanced. 'It was as if all art of warfare had ceased,' wrote the eyewitness Plotho. 'There was room only for savage killing.'[20] As the sun was about to set, the bulk of Barclay's Guards, Grenadiers, and Cuirassiers attacked down the slope with a tremendous flourish. The Tsar and King Frederick William came down with them, defying the fire of enemy artillery,[21] but still the French, though vastly outnumbered, managed to hold on to Arcis and Torcy. That night the Allied troops, to prevent any new attack, bivouacked on the field of battle. Barclay slept among them, as he had throughout the campaign.

At six the next morning, the Allies took up battle position according to Schwarzenberg's plan, in the expectation of Napoleon's attack. But Napoleon finally realized that what was facing him was not just a few corps, as he had fooled himself into thinking, but the solid mass of the whole Main Army. Though he gave orders for his troops to advance, he almost immediately countermanded them. Through the morning's fateful hours the two armies stared at each other in dramatic suspense, their leaders undecided whether to attack, hold still, or withdraw. At last, about noon, the tension broke: the French were seen falling back across the Aube and beyond. Napoleon had lost. Leaving Sébastiani's cavalry and an assortment of cavalry and infantry under Oudinot to defend Arcis and cover his retreat, Napoleon, still living in his illusions, believed that by joining up with the garrisons in Alsace and Lorraine and by fanning revolt among the shocked and starving population he could in the end drive the Allies out.

As after the battle of Leipzig, the Allies were slow in organizing pursuit of the enemy. Schwarzenberg kept his corps commanders in what was meant to be a short conference, 'eine kurze Besprechung', which lasted long enough to allow the French to escape and blow up the bridge at Arcis after them. Besides, the Allies were not sure in which direction Napoleon was withdrawing, though they were soon enlightened by a message he had carelessly sent by unescorted courier to Marie-Louise. The courier was captured and the message informed the interceptors that Napoleon had decided to move towards the Marne, 'in order to push the enemy farther away from Paris and bring me closer to my fortresses. I shall be tonight in St. Dizier' (123 miles from Paris).[22] Soon after, while the Allies were moving northward towards St. Dizier, Cossacks intercepted a whole batch of confidential letters to Napoleon from high functionaries in Paris. These letters described the general dissatisfaction with everything, the anxiety, and the open hostility to the Emperor prevailing among large numbers of Parisians. Reading these letters gave keen satisfaction to the Tsar and his immediate staff.

On 24 March (N.S.) at Sommepuis, while the King of Prussia and Schwarzenberg were already heading towards Vitry-le-François, only eighteen miles from St. Dizier, the Tsar called a meeting of his personal Chief of Staff Prince Volkonskii, and Barclay, Diebitsch, and Toll. Standing in front of a map of northern France, the Tsar asked for their opinion: whether to pursue Napoleon with the whole Allied force or whether to march directly on Paris, while masking their intention of doing so. The Tsar broke his generals' long silence by turning to Barclay, who then spoke up in favour of not missing this long-awaited opportunity to smash Napoleon and his remaining army once and for all. Diebitsch proposed a variant, to detach 40,000 to 50,000 troops for a march to Paris and with the rest go after Napoleon. Toll was of the opposite opinion: he wanted to send a small force to follow Napoleon, but also, with the combined Main and Silesian Armies, to hurry by forced marches to Paris. Since the Allies and Napoleon would be moving in opposite directions, it would mean that each day's march would add two days to the distance between the armies and so, once Paris was taken, there would be plenty of time to deal with him if he chose to retrace his steps towards the capital.

The Tsar was thoroughly pleased with this last proposal and already saw himself riding into Paris at the head of his army. Diebitsch quickly sided with His Majesty, but Barclay was still not convinced that it was the right move. When at last Barclay had to give in, the Tsar, taking Toll and the map with him, galloped off after Frederick William and Schwarzenberg.[23] News of a first link-up between the Main and Silesian Armies made it easy for the Tsar to be convincing. A message was sent to Blücher to meet the Main Army at Meaux on 28 March (N.S.). Wintzingerode's Corps of 15,000 was given the task of following Napoleon and warding him off. Meanwhile, on 19 March (N.S.) the Châtillon Congress had broken down.

After fighting off stubborn resistance by the forces of Marshals Marmont and Mortier, the Allies reached the outskirts of Paris on 29 March (N.S.). There, on the eastern approach to the city at the Château of Bondy, a war council was convened that same evening. Even more than before, the Tsar dominated the meeting. He made all major decisions, and then entrusted Barclay with the execution. Frederick William, out of habit, accepted everything the Tsar proposed and, out of complaisance, so did Schwarzenberg. With the end approaching, however, both Alexander and Schwarzenberg still had some fears. What if Napoleon reached Paris before it was in Allied hands? What if the struggle for Paris reduced it to rubble? To spare the city the Tsar was eager to obtain an early capitulation, though if need be he was ready to rush the city's defences. 'Europe will sleep tonight in Paris, whether in palaces or ruins,' pronounced Alexander as he sent off his dynamic aide Count Orlov, a future founder of the Decembrist movement, on the first of his missions (after midnight) to obtain a capitulation.[24] While awaiting the outcome of Orlov's embassy, the decision was taken to assault Paris in the very early hours of the coming morning in the hope of capturing the capital before Napoleon could reappear.

There were three main obstacles for the Allies to overcome in their attack on Paris: facing the Silesian Army on the north was Montmartre; facing the Main Army on the east were the easily defensible heights of Belleville and those rising between Romainville and Pantin. It would have been less difficult to get to the centre of Paris from the west but, because of the need for haste, this possibility was not considered. It was decided that Blücher should assault Montmartre at five a.m. The order did not reach him until after seven, however, as the Prussian messenger had lost his way in the dark. Moreover, the three corps that Blücher could use for this operation were still some distance away, and Blücher himself was suffering from a severe attack of fever. On the Allied left flank there also occurred a delay that prevented the Crown Prince of Württemberg, with Austria's Gyulai in support, from reaching Charenton and Vincennes until early afternoon. Thus, at the fateful hour when the dawn attack was scheduled to be launched, on 30 March (N.S.), the only Allied force ready to attack was Raevskii's, with its 19,000 men and 53 guns.

Opposing Raevskii in those early hours was Marshal Marmont, his left arm in a sling, his right hand mangled. His 14,500 infantry were well entrenched, his 3,400 cavalrymen at the ready, and he had a good number of guns trained on the Russians from the plateau of Belleville. The stone houses and walls and narrow streets of the Paris suburbs, interspersed with areas of woods and hedges, formed an almost impregnable defensive position, especially against cavalry charges. On his left Marmont had Mortier with a much smaller force of some 4,400 infantry and 2,200 cavalry. The regular forces of both marshals were augmented by miscellaneous collections of volunteers: students from the Military Academy of Artillery and Engineering; Marshal Moncey's 6,000 National Guardsmen, their day's supply of *brioche* speared on their bayonets; militia; fire brigades; other irregular skirmishers; and even a few thousand ordinary citizens. But still the defenders were outnumbered by about four to one.

As both Barclay and Marmont knew, the key to the eastern defence line was Romainville, and the fighting was intense in the struggle for this position. Eugen of Württemberg, at the head of Raevskii's Second Infantry Division, advanced to the village but found himself outnumbered there and sent urgently to Barclay calling for reinforcements. These Barclay supplied at once, sending off two divisions of Russian Grenadiers and also moving the Russian and the Prussian Guards to the vicinity of the hotly contested area. Throughout the day Barclay directed operations from the height between Romainville and Pantin. His was a judicious balancing act, sending in troops where needed while mindful of the requirement to save élite formations for the expected grandiose entry into Paris. To avoid squandering his reserves, and since neither the Prussians in the north nor the Württembergers in the south were yet in position, Barclay interrupted the assault – a pause which lasted, except for artillery duels, for more than an hour. At two in the afternoon, when the Württembergers were ready to outflank the defenders on their right, Barclay gave the signal to resume.

The short respite granted by Barclay made it possible for Marmont to regroup his forces. But the Marshal no longer had any doubt about his ability to hold out for more than a few hours. Allegedly Marmont conveyed his misgivings to Joseph Bonaparte who, as Lieutenant-General of France, was responsible for defending Paris. Joseph and his staff were on Montmartre when they saw the long, massive columns of the Silesian Army approaching across the plain of Saint Denis. Joseph took fright and consulted hastily with the members of his Defence Council, including General Clarke, Napoleon's War Minister of Irish extraction. It was agreed that the situation was hopeless. Word was sent to Marmont and Mortier authorizing them, if they could resist no longer, to seek negotiations with Schwarzenberg and the Tsar and withdraw their troops to the Loire. Joseph then left Paris to join the Empress Marie-Louise and the young King of Rome who had left the day before in accordance with Napoleon's standing instructions.

Marmont did not immediately make use of his *carte blanche* and continued his heroic but hopeless stand; by four o'clock, however, his situation became untenable. He sent three of his aides over to ask for a ceasefire and only one of them safely reached the Allied headquarters. After the onslaught of Kleist, Yorck, and Vorontsov, Mortier found himself in a similar situation and had to withdraw all the way to the barrier at Saint Denis. At about the same time Napoleon's adjutant Dejean arrived on the scene and informed Mortier of Napoleon's imminent arrival, whereupon Mortier tried to hoodwink Schwarzenberg into a twenty-four-hour truce, but Schwarzenberg did not fall for the ruse.

The Tsar responded to Marmont's initiative by again sending Count Orlov, this time with Austria's Count Paar, to negotiate a ceasefire to be followed by capitulation at nine the next morning, by which time the defenders were to have evacuated the capital, taking arms and possessions with them.

Shots still came from Montmartre, where Langeron's Russians, unaware of the ceasefire, were making a final push. Otherwise a sudden stillness engulfed Paris after the day-long cannonade: night came after a struggle which had spilled the blood of some 9,000 men on each side, of whom more than 7,000 were Russians. Looking down with Frederick William from the Buttes de Chaumont, with Paris at their feet, the Tsar performed one final task: he congratulated Barclay on his nomination to the rank of field-marshal.

Field-Marshal Count Barclay de Tolly spent the night neither in palace nor ruin, but at his headquarters in Romainville. The Tsar, too, remained on the outskirts and had already retired at the Château of Bondy when Orlov brought him the signed act of the capitulation of Paris. Alexander tucked it under his pillow and went to sleep.[25]

On 31 March (N.S.) 1814 the Parisians woke early to a mild, overcast morning and the buzzing of contradictory rumours. Many were relieved when they learned from their departing soldiers of the capitulation. Many, because of gruesome tales from the provinces, dreaded massacre, pillage, and rape by Cossacks and Prussians. The Allied leaders did everything in their power to reassure the population, issuing proclamation upon proclamation. At seven in the morning the Tsar received a deputation of the Paris municipality and told them he had taken the city under his personal protection; that museums and other public monuments would not be harmed, that citizens would not be molested, and that Allied soldiers would not be billeted in the inhabitants' homes. Moreover, the terms of the capitulation stated that the National Guard and Gendarmerie, though disarmed, would be maintained in their functions. Barclay's order of the day commanded his troops to treat 'the cultivated and peaceable inhabitants . . . with consideration and friendship, and as allies united by the same interests'.[26] There could hardly be a greater contrast to the Grande

Armée's stabling of its horses in Moscow churches, nor indeed to the pattern of atrocities committed by both sides throughout the war.

By eleven o'clock the Tsar, at Bondy, had received Talleyrand and, later, Caulaincourt; Barclay had checked and re-checked his gleaming formations; the imperial cortege had lined up, with everyone in his place; and the trumpeters blew their victorious blasts as the procession entered Paris by the Pantin barrier. After the trumpets came the Imperial Guard Cossacks in their brilliant red tunics and trousers, riding fifteen abreast. Then, flashing in the thin March sunlight, regiment upon regiment of Cuirassiers, and both Russian and Prussian Dragoons and Hussars. Next came the Tsar, riding a light grey mount said to have been a present from Caulaincourt when he was Napoleon's Ambassador to St. Petersburg. On his right the Tsar had Schwarzenberg who was representing the Emperor Francis, and on Schwarzenberg's right rode King Frederick William. Immediately after came the Grand Duke Constantine, and Blücher and Barclay with their field-marshal's batons. These were followed by the colourful cavalcade of some 1,000 generals and other officers of many nations and branches of the armies. Following them came Austrian, Russian, and Prussian Grenadiers and Guards, and bringing up the rear were forty-seven squadrons of Russian Cuirassiers. Thus was fulfilled – with a three-year delay – General Vandamme's prediction to Napoleon after Austerlitz that if the Russian Guard prisoners were returned to Alexander they would be in Paris in six years.[27] 'Despite the fact that most of these men had been in battle the day before,' said Houssaye, 'with their clean uniforms and sparkling weapons they seemed just to have stepped out of barracks in Berlin and St. Petersburg.'[28] With drummers drumming and banners high, the paraders filled the Grands Boulevards and approached the Champs-Élysées. Among the many onlookers bearing their grief in silence and hoping for Napoleon's revenge, there were enough spectators wearing white cockades for King Louis XVIII, waving handkerchiefs, and shouting 'Vive Alexandre!' and 'Vivent les Alliés, vivent les Bourbons!' to turn the entry into Paris into a celebration. 'It was the festival of Europe,' said the eyewitness Giraud,[29] and Sir Charles Stewart told Castlereagh it was 'electric'.[30] On the Champs-Élysées where the Allied sovereigns and field-marshals reined in to review the parade, Barclay must have felt deep satisfaction and pride.

Napoleon meanwhile had been making his way towards Paris in a simple wicker gig. Early on the morning of the 31st he learned of the capitulation and the imminent Allied entry into Paris. Furious and cursing, calling his brother Joseph a swine, the French Emperor finally took the road to Fontainebleau. Napoleon's hagiographers maintain that if he had only arrived in Paris the previous afternoon, he could have changed the course of events. They seem to forget the vast numerical superiority of the Allies and the reserves they could have raised, whereas Napoleon had exhausted his recruitment potential. If he and his army had intervened, it would have meant the wanton sacrifice of many thousands more lives to no purpose, and the destruction of Paris. Not that he would have been much troubled by adding to the macabre mortality list of the

Napoleonic wars, already approaching the five-million mark.³¹ Those silent bystanders on the Champs-Élysées were not thinking of the slaughter they had been spared. Nevertheless, and despite his laments and curses, one is bound to ask how Napoleon could have been so misled by Wintzingerode's small force to have wasted so many days marching his troops from St. Dizier and back. Perhaps Clausewitz was right in judging that, from the inexplicable mistakes Napoleon made in this final phase of the campaign, 'it would appear he was not inclined to expose himself to the ignominy of a defeat under the walls of Paris'.³²

After the parade, Blücher, afflicted by eye-trouble, laid down the command of the Silesian Army. The King of Prussia handed it over immediately to Barclay (five Prussian corps, and three Russian corps that had been given to him earlier). In further recognition of Barclay's merits, and of Russia's role in the deliverance of Prussia, the King, at Stein's and Hardenberg's suggestion, also proposed a substantial but rather curious reward which would have cost Prussia nothing at all while expressing Prussian indebtedness to the Tsar's men. Barclay, Prince Volkonskii, the Tsar's top aide and close friend, Count Nesselrode, the Tsar's current foreign minister, and Jean Anstedt, the Alsatian diplomat in Russian service, were all four to share some of the spoils of the defeated French generals.³³ The Tsar, who was enjoying his French reputation for clemency, agreed to this idea only after great hesitation, but nothing ever came of it. In the same grateful spirit the King addressed a long memorandum to Barclay asking him to convey to the Russian forces his 'lasting admiration'. And the King added: 'As to yourself, there is no need for me to repeat how affectionately disposed I am towards you which, I am sure, you already well know . . .'³⁴ To be on affectionate terms with the King was pleasant, but to be personally congratulated on his field-marshalship with participatory 'cordiality' by the Dowager Empress Maria Fedorovna was certainly more profoundly gratifying. Alexander's mother, native of Württemberg, wrote to Barclay in German, and the erstwhile 'traitor' with the hated accent cannot have failed to appreciate this nicety.³⁵

Barclay's wife Auguste soon reached Paris and the two were allotted as residence the Hôtel de Brienne in the Rue St. Dominique, the former house of Letitia Bonaparte, Napoleon's mother. Loewenstern, who commanded a Cossack detachment in Vorontsov's Corps, was in and out of the house, a welcome guest, and a welcome and much needed adviser on which French dignitaries Barclay should visit and similar protocol problems. With strangers, Barclay became conscious of his partially immobilized hand and arm as social handicaps. He was ill at ease, and grateful for Loewenstern's presence. Loewenstern also accompanied Auguste and sometimes the couple on their shopping tours, always aghast at their taste. What most struck the Barclays in Paris were the high prices, pushed up by the influx of military 'tourists' paying gold coin. Although the Barclays had set their hearts on a silver centrepiece with matching candlesticks for the dining-table, they found the price, 6,000 francs, outrageous. Fortunately the good Loewenstern was able to show them similar pieces made for some of the French marshals and priced at 20,000 to 50,000 francs, so the Barclays happily realized they had a bargain.³⁶

It was a pity that Loewenstern was not also in the London victory celebration party. Except for the friendly meeting with kinsman Robert Barclay, during which these two 'cubs of the same breed' are said to have discussed Towie Castle, the Field-Marshal felt awkward and uncomfortable during most of his brief stay in London.[37] From his arrival on 6 June (N.S.) 1814, he found himself on display in a never-ending tumult of entertainments totally foreign to his nature. All England seemed to have made the pilgrimage to pay homage to 'Boney's vanquishers'. The crowds overflowing the Dover–London road were, said *The Times*, 'a spectacle unequalled in its kind'. They pressed into Hyde Park, craning to watch the great Allied military review and cheering frenetically their special idols Blücher and Platov (who also received honorary degrees from Oxford). Barclay shunned attention as much as possible, though the scenes with the people were at least more congenial than the silliness of the court. His thoughts were with the army, already starting the long journey back to Russia. He had worked out carefully the order of march of both the Russian and Prussian forces and he was impatient to rejoin his soldiers.

By 30 July/11 August 1814 Barclay had reached the Vistula and established his headquarters in Warsaw. The Tsar had again named him Commander-in-Chief of the First Army, now consisting of six corps, or two-thirds of all Russian forces. Bennigsen was given command of the Second Army, containing the remaining one-third. Barclay set about at once to revive his war-weakened troops. On 22 February/6 March 1815, as the sessions of the Congress of Vienna struggled through their sixth month, and one day before the startling news of Napoleon's escape from Elba became known, Barclay issued a nine-point programme to the commanders of all units. These points dealt in order with: care of the soldiers; discipline; martial spirit; weapons and ammunition; soldiers' basic education; general rules for teaching and training; duties of commanders; cleanliness of uniforms, footwear, barracks, and billets; and explanation of soldiers' manuals. Perhaps before the war cleanliness would not have had a whole chapter to itself, but Barclay had seen the stupendous ravages of typhus epidemics during the war and knew hygiene was his only weapon against this enemy. The whole programme was an extension of the practical and humanitarian instructions that had marked his tenure of the War Ministry, brought up to date, expressed with field-marshal's authority. In a situation of legal serfdom, savage punishments, and general arbitrariness, what Barclay said was revolutionary in outlook: 'In no circumstances does [an officer] have the right to injure the self-respect of a subordinate with insulting and indecent punishment. Such acts debase an officer and are the best proof of his incompetence to lead . . .'[39] Of particular importance is the fact that Barclay made clear that these orders applied not only to commissioned officers but just as much to non-commissioned officers, who must be encouraged to develop a 'sense of propriety'.[40] Barclay had seen both sides of the coin of military paternalism. He had seen how treating soldiers as 'children' resulted generally in moral degradation and brutality. Instead, he offered a change of attitude, a concept of human dignity and rights, and effective reforms.

Ceaseless activity and a resurgence of his old Kvarken symptoms had brought him at this time to ask the Tsar for a leave of absence. Alexander could see for himself that Barclay's health was deteriorating and he readily granted the request, though with the limiting, and at the same time gratifying, proviso that the First Army 'must never and at no time be deprived of your leadership'.[41] But Barclay could not take advantage of his permission: Napoleon had escaped to France and was successfully rallying a new army.

In early April 1815 Barclay was once more in the field, leading a Russian army of over 200,000 men towards France. Again the army marched in three columns, Dokhturov on the right, Sacken at the centre, Raevskii on the left. The Tsar and soon Emperor Francis travelled in Raevskii's column, where shortly they were joined by Frederick William. (The King of Prussia immediately put his Guards and Grenadiers once again under Barclay's command.) A Bavarian Corps made up the rearguard and Württembergers protected the right flank. It was as this formidable army reached the Rhine that the news came of Blücher's and Wellington's decisive victory at Waterloo on 18 June (N.S.). The Tsar was for maximum security, however: he told Barclay it was imperative for the Allies – he meant the Russians – to have Napoleon in their hands. 'We shall press and insist on having him turned over to us,' said the Tsar in a handwritten memorandum to Barclay, dashing all thoughts of home, and adding with an imperial flourish: 'With the blessings of the Almighty, and with the help of gifted commanders like yourself and the unflinching courage of our troops, I hope to bring this war to a desirable conclusion and achieve a prosperous peace for all Europe . . .'[42]

Since the fighting seemed to be over, Barclay was particularly pleased that his path and his son's were going to cross in eastern France. Magnus, now seventeen, had just become a cornet in the élite corps of the Horse Guards. Barclay reassured an anxious Auguste, writing to her not to fret about the boy's safety in enemy territory: he told her that Russian forces were satisfactorily choking the roads of France. To cheer her further, he promised he would not fail to present Magnus to the Tsar.[43] The Field-Marshal's son surely made a striking impression in at least one respect: he was now 'almost half a head' taller than his towering father.[44] Shortly afterwards Auguste also arrived, coming from Frankfurt, and the family was for a rare moment complete.

As Barclay moved his army into France he issued an order of the day summoning the troops 'to demonstrate the moderation and calm bearing that distinguished you in the past and earned you the flattering praise of all Europe'.[45] To make sure this exhortation was heeded, with the Tsar's approval he turned one of his Dragoon regiments into a special Regiment of Gendarmes, a force that in later years grew into the Corps of Gendarmes and played a brutally repressive role under the next Tsar.

No battle for Paris was necessary this time; the capital surrendered on 3 July (N.S.). The Allied monarchs with their staffs and senior officers quickly entered the city, though it was three weeks before a token force of Cuirassiers and Grenadiers followed. Napoleon, having broken the pledge he had given on 11 April 1814 renouncing the thrones of France and Italy, could imagine what would be in store for him if he fell into the hands of the Russians, Prussians, and Bourbons. He therefore surrendered to the British, and finished his days in St. Helena embroidering new legends.

Barclay at last had time to write to his foster-mother: 'Since the year 1810 I feel a great change in the condition of my health, and the need for some rest becomes more necessary with each day; when and how it will be possible to satisfy my urgent desire for tranquillity, I do not yet know . . .'[46] Having supreme command of all Russian armed forces – not only of the large army in France but also of all troops left behind in Russia and Poland – Barclay knew it would be unrealistic to ask for leave. Luckily his mind was often distracted from ailments by the not unpleasant duty of receiving honours. His chest now displayed, in addition to its sparkling constellation of international medals, the *Grand Cordon* of the French Legion of Honour, and on 18 August (N.S.) at six in the evening the Duke of Wellington, on behalf of the Prince Regent, invested him with the Order of the Garter and gave a dinner for him.[47]

Barclay's eagerness to be away may have been partly caused also by the Tsar's strange, petulant mood, 'dull and angry'.[48] It was not simply a case of Alexander's suffering from a blasé disenchantment on entering Paris the second time round. Something very important had happened to Russia's ruler: a conversion to fervent religiosity. Depressed after the break-up of his long-standing liaison with Princess Naryshkin (who had borne him two children), he had on his way to Paris fallen under the spell of the fanatic 'Livonian sibyl', a magnetic grey-haired mystic, Madame de Krüdener, who called him 'God's Instrument to Deliver Europe'. Alexander had brought her, and some of her family and evangelical sect, under Cossack escort, from Germany to Paris and installed them close to the Élysée palace where he was staying. He visited her nightly for prayer sessions and stayed until the early hours of the day. These nightly visits, dragging out old feelings of guilt, starting from the murder of his father, brought about a drastic change in his manner. Gone was the society Tsar; gone, Alexander the gallant. Pious at night, he was utterly intolerant of even the smallest breach of discipline during the day. Fits of anger became frequent. He yelled at Ermolov, now commander of the Cuirassiers and Grenadiers, for objecting to his orders to seize and punish two colonels for a minor misdemeanour: they had stumbled on parade. He firmly believed that it was due only to rigorous discipline that 'his army was the most courageous and the most splendid'.[49]

The Deliverer of Europe now hit upon the twofold idea of showing off his courageous and splendid army, which had no more battles to fight, to all of 'Europe', and of solemnizing the occasion by a massive religious spectacle. His 'paradomania' taking hold, he acted as his own impresario, working out himself every detail of a prodigious review, and he also kept his staff frantically busy drawing up charts of where to place each unit, where each was to move, and the whole pattern of commands. Barclay, tired but dutiful, responsible for the entire military side of the show, went from unit to unit, inspecting, correcting, rehearsing. When everything was ready the Tsar ordered a grand dress rehearsal for 26 August/7 September. The immense army (minus Langeron's corps which was besieging some French fortresses that had not yet capitulated) gathered on the plain near Vertus, in the Champagne region eighty miles or so from Paris. Only the Russians, in their thousands, were present. The Field-Marshal's gaze checked over the endless ranks on horse and afoot, generals and privates each in his allotted place, all awaiting Barclay's transmission of the signal of command. It was three years to the day, he realized, since he had courted death at Borodino, when his humiliation felt too great to bear.

Three days later, in radiant late summer sunshine, the actual review was staged. The village of Vertus was transformed by colourful stalls set up everywhere by Paris shopkeepers. Splendid officers mingled with hawkers and sutler women. Large tents, gaily festooned, put up in artificial gardens by Napoleon's favourite architect Pierre-François Fontaine, served meals to Alexander's guests. These included, besides the Emperor Francis and King Frederick William and their royal offspring, an international array of princes, field-marshals, generals, and diplomats, and, in a plain dress and perennial straw hat, Julie de Krüdener, at the 'luminous pinnacle of her influence'.[50]

The Tsar, sword unsheathed, personally reported the various formations to the Emperor and the King. The troops stretched out in perfect order almost as far as the eye could see, the most distant looking like toys. Five hundred and forty guns lined the field. An earth-shaking cannon and musket salvo, twelve minutes long, signalled the start. (Actually, a considerable pause was required after this signal, in order to let the smoke clear: the army had entirely disappeared from sight.) Never before, and perhaps never since, has there been such a parade: over 145,000 men led by 87 generals and some 4,500 senior officers – 150,554 persons in all. The Tsar's young brothers, the Grand Dukes Nicolas and Michael, having made their début in active service in Barclay's First Army, each headed a unit: Nicolas, a Grenadier brigade, and Michael, a company of Horse Artillery. Dazzling the eye were eleven infantry divisions, seven cavalry divisions, three Cossack regiments, and companies of pioneers and sappers. Throughout the review not a single man or horse once stumbled.

Since voice commands could not carry over the immensity of the parade area, Barclay's initial commands to shoulder arms, present arms, and shoulder arms again were made by cannon-fire, and barked out after to the units by all their commanders. As the first of these shots roared out, the amazement of the onlookers was boundless, to see this multitude of men react as one, or rather as one machine. The second shot brought forth a mighty, thunderous hurrah from all ranks, as they presented arms. On the third shot, shouldering arms again, they formed into battalion columns, and on the fourth and last shot the columns made a gigantic square, three sides of foot soldiers and one side of cavalry. The Tsar descended from the viewing hill and rode into the centre of this square.

After the march-past, while a beaming Alexander was receiving compliments from his guests, Mikhailovskii-Danilevskii overheard Wellington saying that he had 'never imagined that an army could reach such absolute perfection'.[51] Wellington added that he had admired the Russian Cuirassiers and Grenadiers during the entry into Paris and had thought them exceptional, but now he had seen that every infantry division was their match. Also overheard by Mikhailovskii-Danilevskii was Admiral Sir Stanley Smith saying the review 'was a lesson given by Russia's Emperor to other nations'.[52]

Alexander had kept the religious part for the following day, his own name day, the feast of the warrior-saint Alexander Nevskii. Seven Orthodox altars had been set up on the field and at each a priest and archimandrites were celebrating mass. This time the soldiers were unarmed, the cavalry dismounted. One hundred and fifty thousand voices rose in the ancient Slavonic chants: 150,000 men prostrated themselves. The Tsar and Madame de Krüdener trod a stately procession after the mass, worshipping at each of the seven altars in turn. Thanking his officers and soldiers, the Tsar invoked God's blessing on them all. That night he told Madame de Krüdener, 'This day has been the most beautiful of my life.'[53]

It was without doubt an unforgettable day for everyone who was there. For Barclay and his family it marked the apogee of glory. At the end of the ceremony, when the Tsar was citing a large number of worthy commanders, he singled out Field-Marshal Barclay and named him *Kniaz'* – Michael Bogdanovich Prince Barclay de Tolly. (In Russian, the hereditary title *kniaz'* was originally reserved for a few ancient families like Bagration's, and later, unlike 'prince', was never given out freely. Peter the Great bestowed it only once, Catherine the Great only twice.)*

To Prince Michael's collection of stars and crosses were added on that same day new medals from several nations, and his collection of weapons was increased by a new English sword studded with precious stones, given commemoratively by the City of London. On the journey back from France – the fourth time he had covered the Paris–St. Petersburg route – Barclay stopped off in October in Erfurt where he was made a member of its time-honoured Academy and, in nearby Weimar, he paid his respects to Goethe, whom he had met twice before.[54]

By the time he reached St. Petersburg on 10/22 December 1815, the Tsar had lost interest in Madame de Krüdener and was giving full attention again to earthly matters. In retrospect 'the most beautiful day' was unquestionably the military-parade day, and the Tsar had not forgotten how much he owed to Barclay for making it so. An honour guard from the Tsar's favourite Semenovskii Lifeguards (the regiment which was to revolt in 1820 after a flogging incident) was, to Barclay's embarrassment, drawn up for him before a fully-equipped house (including a maître d'hôtel, kitchen staff, carriage, and another carriage promised for Auguste on her arrival). The Tsar had thought to set him up in a manner befitting a prince and field-marshal, highest-ranking officer of the Russian empire. Repeatedly describing Prince Michael as 'the most loyal', Alexander praised him over and over to his mother the Dowager Empress. Barclay wrote to his Princess: 'The Tsar embraced me, the mother was so deeply touched that she kissed me on both cheeks and then embraced the Tsar . . .'[55]

* The distinction between *kniaz'* and prince cannot be shown in translation.

Three days of celebrations followed, starting with a dinner for Barclay given by the Tsar, receptions at court, a brilliant ball, and a great regimental banquet where the Tsar, remembering it was Barclay's birthday (his fifty-fourth), drank his health. 'I felt as if in a constant delirium,' wrote Barclay to Auguste, telling her of the enquiries made for her by the Tsar, the two Empresses, and Grand Duchess Catherine. Although probably knowing it was a lost cause, Barclay asked his wife to keep all these details to herself, because 'I do not want to sound like boasting'.[56]

As *kniaz'*, Barclay had now to choose his coat of arms. Unhesitatingly he knew what his motto must be, because it had been that of his whole life: Loyalty and Patience.

CHAPTER XVI

THE LOST BATTLE AND THE LAST JOURNEY

> Thou man of greatness!
> . . . . . .
> [The] invocation of thy name
> Will rouse in thine heirs' breast exalted flames,
> And at the glowing feast posterity will dedicate to thee,
> It will be said, with tears: 'He loved his native land.'
>   *Mikhail Lermontov on Barclay de Tolly*

After a few calm weeks at Beckhof, Barclay resumed his duties as head of the Russian army and departed early in 1816 for Mogilev, a dull provincial agricultural centre, the capital of the Mogilev region. Situated on the Dnepr, 120 miles south-west of Smolensk, it was an important road junction, and for that reason, and because of its nearness to Poland, had been chosen as the headquarters of the Russian army. Here Barclay devoted most of his time to maintaining and raising the standards the army had already achieved under his leadership, promoting as far as he could his nine-point programme of 1815. The Tsar was a frequent visitor at headquarters, and parades, therefore, absorbed a good deal of time. Parades, drills, field manœuvres, and the usual desk-work – it was a life that suited Barclay well enough after years of wearing campaigns.

In this Mogilev region a few villages had been selected in 1810 for the establishment of the first experimental military settlements (or 'military colonies' as they are often, less accurately, referred to in translation). Essentially, the idea for such settlements occurred to the Tsar during a visit to Arakcheev's show-place estate at Gruzino. Alexander was thrilled, as were visitors from all over Europe, by the immaculate symmetry of the flourishing Gruzino villages where everything, including the identical and equidistant thatched roofs, seemed to be, as it were, on permanent parade. These villages seemed to prove that good management was possible; they struck Alexander as 'a model of efficiency and rational planning'.[1] If only he could replace some of the appallingly filthy, squalid, disorderly villages he knew with lovely new ones having the 'order . . . neatness . . . symmetry and elegance' that the iron-fisted Arakcheev had created.[2] With Napoleon at last subdued, Russia was left with no wars to fight and an enormous idle army eating its way through the treasury: in 1816 more than half of the entire budget was spent on the upkeep of the army.[3] Why not settle the soldiers with their families in model villages, make them self-sustaining, tilling the soil and doing carpentry when they were not at drill? (Some would be exempt from combat and be proprietors; others would 'assist' these, labouring in peacetime under their direction; the children would be brought up in special military training schools; and the sick and old provided for in village 'invalid houses' at government expense.) It was not so much 'a Chinese wall' of cannon fodder the Tsar had in mind but rather more a utopian scheme for creating 'spearheads of civilization' throughout the empire, raising living standards, improving the soldiers' lot – and creating order.[4] Arakcheev was the obvious choice for directing the project, which the Tsar would personally supervise.

Despite the small start made before the war, it was only after this interruption that Arakcheev was set to work putting the project on paper and setting in motion the whole vast enterprise. Barclay was naturally the first to be invited to comment, and the Tsar no doubt expected him fully to share his own unlimited enthusiasm and to start immediately throwing his enormous organizational talents into making the project successful. All through April 1817, however, Barclay kept silent while thoughtfully studying the proposal, weighing the merits and drawbacks. Then, in a comprehensive, dispassionate, point-by-point examination which altogether filled twenty-nine pages (in the printed version of 1861), he came to the conclusion that the idea was unsound and would do great harm.[5] His judgement was that neither the soldiers, nor the local peasants, nor the State would benefit from the plan. When the Tsar's chancery received Barclay's communication, Arakcheev laconically scribbled on the front page, 'Report from Field-Marshal Barclay de Tolly to His Majesty the Emperor about the disadvantages of military settlements.'[6]

If the Tsar had not been so carried away by the scheme, he might have realized that it would be surprising for the head of the army not to be disturbed by a proposal for the break-up of that army. The core of Barclay's objections did not lie there, however. His arguments combined acumen and farsightedness. Thus, for instance, about the peasants:

Agriculture can only be successful and produce the desired results when peasants are given complete freedom to organize their farming as they think best . . . and when they are fully convinced that the fruit of their labours will go to their kin and that no power can deprive them of that right . . .[7]

As for the soldiers, whom he knew best:

As long as the martial spirit with which, thank God, the soldiers are at present imbued, and which gives them pride in their calling, subsists, it is impossible to expect them to be good assistants to their proprietors in cultivating the soil, and impossible not to foresee hourly disagreements and quarrels. Perhaps in time they would get used to bowing to the inevitable and turn their hands from guns to the plough or sickle; but their martial spirit must then be expected to disappear completely and, from being good soldiers, they will turn into indifferent or poor farmers . . .[8]

About the officers, he pointed out again, as he had in the Yellow Book before the war, that it was difficult enough to educate them for their duties, even with senior staff devoting themselves full time to purely military service:

What will happen when they, while in military service, will spend much of their time dealing only with the colonists and have no other pursuit than agriculture? . . . We must remember that a large proportion of our officers . . . enter the army without any education and in a state of such ignorance that some of them can hardly sign their name . . . But a well-educated officer corps, imbued with a noble spirit . . . is imperative for the well-being and morality of the army . . .'[9]

Barclay also had misgivings about the independent, self-contained organization of the settlements network, answerable only to its own administration: a state within a state, a military archipelago in a civilian sea.[10]

Not to be entirely negative, however, Barclay ended his memorandum by examining the feasibility of adapting and limiting the scheme to provide permanent cantonments in state-owned settlements for *reserve* infantry battalions. This suggestion was far removed from the Tsar's expansive ideas, and nothing came of it.

To buttress his own arguments, Barclay submitted them along with concurring opinions from his nephew-by-marriage and Quartermaster-General, the future Field-Marshal Diebitsch (now the husband of Barclay's niece and foster-daughter Jenny von Tornauw).[11] But it was a hopeless battle, lost in advance. The scheme fitted too well the driving elements, both mystical and methodical, idealistic and despotic, of Alexander's character. Under Arakcheev's control there was launched what was to become 'one of the most hated institutions' in Russia.[12] Ignoring all Barclay's pertinent and remarkably perspicacious warnings, Alexander was set upon improving willy-nilly the lot of his 'beloved subjects'. But when these subjects showed resistance, Alexander's procrustean determination was unshakeable: 'There will be military settlements at any cost, even if it is necessary to line the road from Petersburg to Chudov with corpses . . .'[13]

At their peak (in 1825) the military settlements accommodated 748,519 men (not counting women and children) – an immense number compared, say, to the size of the mighty Russian army Barclay had led to France in 1815, though trifling compared to Alexander's dream of five million settlers. The settlements were abolished in two stages, in 1830 and 1859. The scheme collapsed, 'ignominiously and bathed in blood', comments Richard Pipes, 'because it was utopian and because it was forcefully imposed on a people unable and unwilling to participate. . . . It left nothing but bitter memories.'[14] And Barclay's prediction came true: the army lost in this experiment its combative spirit, its *esprit de corps*, its high morale. It paid the price of the settlements – in the Crimean War.

Barclay too was left with bitter feelings. While on a visit to St. Petersburg early in 1818 he asked for a lengthy leave to enable him to restore his health in a Bohemian spa. The Tsar granted him two years and magnanimously threw in 100,000 rubles for expenses. With such time and such money at disposal, the family travel plans expanded accordingly. The party grew and new destinations were envisaged after the spa cure. Plans were made for a European education for Barclay's favourite, Christel, now almost fifteen, pert and pretty, who arrived in April at long last to take her place in the family. In Germany she was to study sciences, in Italy music and painting, and in France and England she was to learn the languages.¹⁵ Barclay was eager to give his foster-daughter opportunities that had been closed to himself and Magnus (now nearly twenty) by their military careers. Finally, on 28 April/10 May 1818, Barclay and his party set off from Beckhof in four carriages. Travelling with Barclay and Auguste were Magnus, Christel, a nephew and niece of Auguste, a doctor, an adjutant, and servants.

The third stage of the journey brought the party some forty-five miles north-east of Riga to Stolben, an estate Barclay had bought six months earlier for 70,000 rubles.¹⁶ It was an annex of one of the oldest estates in Livonia, a property worthy of a prince, set in a lovely park where Barclay strolled briefly with Christel, stretching his cramped legs after the fatigue of the carriage ride. Beyond Stolben, as the four carriages rumbled on through Riga, Memel, and Tilsit, ever more frequent stops became necessary, to give Barclay some respite from chest pains. After two weeks of travel, on 13/25 May, on the outskirts of the East Prussian town of Insterburg, the doctor ruled that Barclay could not continue the journey. He was taken to the nearest landowner's house, and there, sitting in an armchair that same evening, he died.

First to receive the news was Frederick William, who at once sent a Guard of Honour to accompany the embalmed corpse to the Russian border. (The autopsy revealed that Barclay's heart and all his vital organs had deteriorated far beyond the usual attrition of fifty-six years.) The King also ordered a tall monument with both German and Russian inscriptions – designed by Berlin's great neoclassical architect, Karl Friedrich Schinkel – to be placed on the spot where Barclay's heart was buried (in a silver urn in a seven-and-a-half-acre plot of ground) on the hospitable Insterburg landowner's property.

At the border a Russian Guard of Honour under General Diebitsch took over, and on 30 May/11 June the cortege reached the troop-lined streets of Riga. There, after a great military funeral, with Lutheran and Orthodox clergy on either side of the coffin, Barclay's remains were given temporary burial.¹⁷

In his letter of condolence to Auguste the Tsar wrote of the esteem he had always felt for Barclay's 'eminent merit and the distinguished qualities of his heart': 'The State loses in him one of its most zealous servants, the army a chief who constantly gave it an example of highest valour, and I, a companion in arms whose loyalty and devotion were always dear to me . . .'¹⁸

A gentle tug of war ensued between the Tsar and Auguste, with Auguste the foregone winner. The Tsar desired a grand state burial in St. Petersburg's Kazan' Cathedral, which was dedicated to the war of 1812 and where Kutuzov and other heroes were interred, whereas the Princess wanted to have Barclay entombed in Beckhof, where she could eventually lie beside him, as she does today. On the Beckhof property, therefore, at the end of a long avenue of dark fir trees (now gigantic), Auguste erected a large and imposing neoclassical mausoleum designed by two famous members of the St. Petersburg Academy of Arts, an architect and a sculptor. The massive building itself – the Dôme des Invalides or the Grant's Tomb of Estonia – is surmounted by a western cross, while its entrance 'conveys the illusion of a Roman triumphal arch'.¹⁹ On the tympanum in high-relief are Barclay's arms and the 'Loyalty and Patience' motto, and the façade is decorated with sculpted branches of laurel, oak, and olive. The arms, the motto, and the branches recur throughout. In the cool white interior there is a monument four metres high in granite, marble, porphyry, and bronze, with a bust of Barclay flanked on one side by a Pallas Athene crowning him with laurel and on the other by a seated woman with urn, symbolizing 'Russia, mourning for her dead hero'.[20] A bronze relief shows an equestrian Barclay approaching Paris. In the vault lie the sarcophagi, velvet-covered and draped with banners, arms, and drums. It is, as the guidebook says, 'one of the most popular historical and architectural memorials of Estonia'.[21]

As soon as the enshrinement at Beckhof was complete, Auguste went to Stolben. Here the Tsar visited her while on his way abroad. 'He spoke to her with emotion of the deceased as "his dear friend",' remembered Christel.[22] The two Empresses also travelled to Stolben to express their sympathy: 'First came the delicate, charming, and solicitous Empress Elisabeth, and soon afterwards the splendid Dowager Empress.'[23]

Auguste, aged forty-eight at the time of her husband's death, outlived him by ten years. She spent most of this time neither at Stolben nor Beckhof but in a magnificent house in Dorpat, 'one of the noblest', near the old city hall.[24] The Princess lived in some state but surrounded herself, as she and Michael had done during his lifetime, with swarms of young people. The noble house was often the scene of balls, above all at Shrovetide when the Dorpat gentry danced by night, and by day merrily sleighed on the frozen Embach. Family and foster-families and all the interconnected Livonian network absorbed most of her attention. Erich, Michael's elder brother, blind at the end of his life, died only a year after the Field-Marshal. 'Foster' grandsons and granddaughters began to appear. The years of widowhood were filled with interest, energy, entertainment, and good deeds. She founded in Dorpat a charitable institution, for which she secured the support of Empress Elisabeth, to educate the children of the Second Regiment of Carabineers, which had been renamed the Barclay de Tolly Regiment.[25]

Magnus, also called Maximilian or Max, became an aide-de-camp of the Tsar, with the rank of colonel. At one of his mother's balls, when he was twenty-eight and resplendent in his Guards uniform, he met the seventeen-year-old Leocadie von Campenhausen and fell in love at first sight. Leocadie's father, Baron Christoph von Campenhausen, of the most ancient Livonian aristocracy, objected to the match on the grounds of Magnus's title. 'What is a prince without lands?' protested the old Baltic baron; 'let him divest himself of that title.'[26] Refusing to the end to recognize the title and always calling Magnus 'Colonel', stickler von Campenhausen finally permitted the marriage, which took place at one of his estates, Wesselshof, on 25 April (O.S.) 1825. The young couple settled at Stolben where they led a gay and carefree life surrounded by many friends: they could sleep one hundred guests! One of their earliest guests was Tsar Alexander, who visited them in the summer of 1825 just a few months before his death. What Magnus and his bride most enjoyed, however, was travelling abroad, and for this reason Magnus gave up his post. It was on one of their stays in Germany, in 1852, that Leocadie died, in Baden. Six years later Magnus (who had meanwhile sold Stolben) remarried. His second wife, née Alexandra von Kramer, was a young widow, sixteen years younger than he, whose first husband, Baron Georg von Tiesenhausen, had died in 1814. Magnus himself died in 1871, never having fathered a child.

Twelve years before Magnus's childless death, the 'Tsar-liberator' Alexander II, desiring to provide for the continuation of the hereditary princely Barclay de Tolly line, chose an heir to the title. It was a choice that would have pleased Barclay: the eldest grandson of his sister Christine and son of his dear niece and foster-daughter Christel. She had married Wilhelm Peter Jost von Weymarn in 1822. Their eldest son, Alexander Magnus von Weymarn, was forty-seven when he received the title in 1872, and the name became Barclay de Tolly-Weymarn. The Weymarns, originally called Weimar or Weimer, came from Lübeck to Courland around 1600, then moved to Livonia, and were ennobled in 1693. The first Prince Barclay de Tolly-Weymarn was a full general of infantry and well liked at the St. Petersburg court. The title descended to Alexander's son, Ludwig Alexander, also an officer in the Russian army. His son, Prince Nicolas, the last direct male descendant, was a captain of horse and still master of Beckhof until after the Russian Revolution. He died in Sweden in 1964,[27] and thus the line ended.

EPILOGUE

THE POET AND THE COMMANDER

> Is it possible that after twenty-five years of silence a poet should not be permitted to utter Barclay's name with sympathy and emotion?
>
> *Alexander Pushkin in 1836*

Barclay de Tolly's reputation has been buffeted about nearly as much since his death in 1818 as during his lifetime. He has been defamed, denigrated, or dismissed as 'merely methodical' far more often than he has been praised. The image created by Tolstoy, lumping Barclay with other unreliable 'Germans' at the 1812 headquarters and completely overshadowing him with the all-Russian Kutuzov, is the Barclay most people know – and barely remember. But just as Kutuzov's greatest monument is *War and Peace*, so Barclay's is a poem, 'The Commander' ('Polkovodets'), by Pushkin, one of Russia's finest poets but one whose qualities are notoriously difficult to convey in translation. The poem (see Appendix A) is based upon a painting (see Pl. 1).

In the sombre days of 1812 when the thirteen-year-old Alexander Pushkin was infected like nearly everybody else with the conviction that Barclay was a traitor, a first corrective was supplied by Wilhelm Kuechelbecker, a fellow poet and fellow schoolboy in the select Tsarskoe Selo *lycée*. In a letter quite clearly aimed at influencing Kuechelbecker's schoolmates, his mother, a distant relative of Barclay, chided her son for jumping to hasty and calumnious conclusions: 'Would the Tsar offer Barclay the choice between returning to his post of Minister of War and staying in the field as Commander of the First Army if there were any thought of treason or of any other fault imputable to him? What better proof is there of Barclay's love for his fatherland than his acceptance to serve in a subordinate position? . . .'[1] Pushkin was one of those influenced by Kuechelbecker's views, and it would seem that the two linked ideas of Barclay's love for his fatherland and his willingness to serve as Kutuzov's subordinate implanted themselves in Pushkin's mind.

Nevertheless in 1825 Pushkin, like most others, was still hostile to Barclay, even though there was no longer any question of treason. The posts and grades and titles that came to Barclay after 1812 had not really cleared the air, then or after. At Alexander's death, while Grand Duke Constantine was still the presumed heir, Pushkin wrote to a friend: 'As a loyal subject I am naturally grieved by the death of the Tsar; but as a poet I am happy at Constantine I's accession to the throne. There is much romanticism in him; his stormy youth, his campaigns with Suvorov, his hostility to the German Barclay, remind me of Henry V . . .'[2]

Some time before 1830 Pushkin's opinions changed. In the third quatrain of the fragmentary Chapter 10 of *Eugene Onegin* he wrote forthrightly:

> And who then came to our assistance
> When we were bowed beneath the rod
> In 1812? The folk's resistance,
> The winter, Barclay, Russia's God.[3]

Believing these verses and this chapter to be in fact much too outspoken for publication or even for the desk drawer, Pushkin left them only in code, which was finally deciphered in 1910.

Meanwhile, in December 1826, the War Gallery in the Winter Palace had been inaugurated, in commemoration of the Patriotic War of 1812. It is an immensely long hall, its crimson walls covered from top to bottom with 331 portraits, almost all of them done by Pushkin's friend, the skilful English portraitist George Dawe. Tsar Alexander had 'discovered' George Dawe and his gift for likenesses and flattery in 1818 at the Congress of Aix-la-Chapelle. All but seven of the 331 paintings are busts. The three portraits of the Allied sovereigns, Alexander, Francis, and Frederick William, are large equestrian canvases, and besides these there are four large full-length portraits – Barclay and Kutuzov faced respectively by Wellington and Constantine. Apart from the two foreign monarchs and Wellington, all the subjects were commanders in the Russian army, including a dozen or so foreign nationals in Russian service. The portrait of Barclay, considered by many to be Dawe's finest, was painted from an etching done from life two years before Barclay's death by Carl August Senff, painter, engraver, and art teacher at the University of Dorpat. Dawe idealized Barclay's features, very slightly elongating the forehead, straightening the nose and, by lengthening the lips, changing Senff's warm, kind expression into one of scorn. It was this look of contempt that especially haunted Pushkin, though he was not sure whether it was a stroke of luck on Dawe's part or whether it revealed great insight and skill. Barclay is angled against a dramatic sky and there stretches behind him 'a host encamped'; in fact the Russian encampment on the outskirts of Paris in 1814. On his many visits to the War Gallery Pushkin was fascinated by this portrayal of a noble, lofty, tragic figure:

> But of this sombre band of brothers
> One always draws my mind more strongly than the others . . .

Pushkin first visited the Gallery during the summer of 1827 on his return from exile. Later he became a frequent visitor on his way to palace duties after his appointment by Nicolas I in 1834 as 'gentleman of the chamber', an appointment Pushkin found highly offensive. The poet's interest was sharpened by a press episode which occurred at about this same time. No voice had been publicly raised in Barclay's favour for as long as Pushkin could remember. In September 1833 the *Moscow Telegraph* finally broke the silence by stating in print that Barclay had preserved the army and had, by his temporizing with Napoleon, become 'the guardian of Russia': 'Regrettably circumstances did not permit Barclay to complete his great deed which therefore is not appreciated by many as much as it should be . . .'⁴ Nicolas I threatened to close down the paper because of this 'offensive gossip'.⁵ Pushkin knew of the incident and was pained by it. His mood at this time was one of 'sadness, depression, heart-rending melancholy', and he looked at Barclay's portrait with a growing sense of identification.⁶

Pushkin had discovered a good deal about Barclay from some of the survivors of 1812 with whom he had become friendly, among them Raevskii, Davydov, Ermolov, Langeron, and Zakrevskii. From Zakrevskii he heard details of the mob attacks – in early drafts of his poem he tried out raw phrases like 'the mob barked at you' and 'the louts barked at you' – and from Davydov and Ermolov he learned of their own conversions during the 1812 campaign from being severe critics to true admirers. Ermolov even wrote to Davydov to say that 'everything Barclay said at the Fili war council should be cast in letters of gold'.⁷ Pushkin also saw Speranskii in 1834 and probably sounded him out on Barclay and heard him praised as War Minister and author of the Yellow Book reforms.⁸

On Easter Sunday 1835 Pushkin finished the final draft of 'The Commander', titled in early drafts 'Barclay de Tolly'. It passed the censors without apparent problem and Pushkin published it in early October 1836 in *The Contemporary*, the literary journal of which he was editor. Ecstatic praise and pointed abuse greeted the publication of these alexandrines. They became a great subject of controversy. 'Barclay – a delight', was the verdict passed by Alexander Turgenev, a leading opinion-maker, to the poet Prince Viazemskii.⁹ Nicolas Gogol was enthusiastic: 'Has anyone anywhere seen such felicity!'¹⁰ Nicolas Grech, the well-known journalist, lavished effusions on Pushkin – though only in a private letter: 'With this exemplary poem, exemplary also in its form, you have given proof to the world that in you Russia has a true poet, a supporter of honour, devoted to truth . . . Honour to you, glory, and gratitude! You have found the true, the real, and the only meaning of poetry! . . .'¹¹ In Pushkin's grateful reply, his admiration for Barclay's character was expressed without reticence: 'Barclay's stoic features are among the most remarkable in our history. Whether one can entirely support him in matters of the art of war, I do not know; but his personality will forever deserve wonder and worship . . .'¹² (Later, Vissarion Belinskii, one of the foremost Russian critics, called the poem 'one of the greatest works of Pushkin's genius'.¹³ And in the twentieth century, the literary historian D. S. Mirsky has judged the poem to be 'the most majestic' of Pushkin's 'elegiac meditations' of this period.)¹⁴

The first volley against 'The Commander' was fired by Login Golenishchev-Kutuzov, a naval officer and, more importantly, Kutuzov's nephew. He stumbled upon a reprint of the poem (in the *Northern Bee*, 15 October [O.S.] 1836) and was horrified by what he felt was an affront to his uncle, although he did admit to finding some of the verse beautiful. His literal mind was also upset by poetic 'lies', such as Pushkin's 'alien soil' ('To alien soil in sacrifice you brought your all'). To be sure, Login Golenishchev-Kutuzov was correct and Pushkin in error. The logic of Justine Kuechelbecker's phrase – on Barclay's 'love for his fatherland' – had not really pierced the habitual Russian reaction to a Baltic accent, a 'French' name, a faith that was not Orthodox. The assumption that Barclay was 'foreign' was probably so widespread that it may not even have occurred to Pushkin to find out the truth. In any case the factual error furnished a useful stick for beating the poet. Login Golenishchev-Kutuzov wielded it at length in a fierce letter he addressed to the Minister of Education and President of the Academy of Science, S. S. Uvarov, whose hostility to Pushkin was common knowledge. He made much also of two other verses which he felt insulted his uncle's memory: the line in which the nation is said to have been rescued by Barclay's stratagem, and that referring to Barclay's having to yield the high command when only 'half-way home'. Login Golenishchev-Kutuzov made sure that this letter was widely known by publishing the attack in 3,600 copies in pamphlet form (November 1836). He also attacked Pushkin in a more personal way by putting pressure on his cousin, Elisabeth Khitrovo, one of Kutuzov's five daughters, who was Pushkin's mistress. Elisabeth was sixteen years older than Pushkin; she was twice widowed, and she herself had a daughter, Daria, old enough to be married (to the Austrian Ambassador Ficquelmont) and to be in love with Pushkin too, though this relationship was platonic. Login Golenishchev-Kutuzov angrily told his cousin that Daria must remove Pushkin's portrait from her bedroom – after the insult of 'The Commander'. Elisabeth wrote tearfully to her lover: 'Your elegy is causing me endless trouble. I feel like a martyr, dear Pushkin, but it makes me love you even more . . .'[15]

It was Pushkin who was really having endless trouble, however, including a murky flood of anonymous letters. The St. Petersburg salons of 1836 thrived on the controversy. Society generally sided against Pushkin and against Barclay. It seemed to be taken for granted by everyone that to praise Barclay was to disparage Kutuzov.

After Login Golenishchev-Kutuzov's attack appeared, Pushkin published an 'Explanation' in the next issue of *The Contemporary* (at the end of December 1836).[16] In it he dismissed the notion that giving recognition to the one diminished the other, that his admiring and compassionate verses on Barclay could in any way lessen Kutuzov's well-established and well-deserved fame. 'Kutuzov's monument is the rock of St. Helena!' wrote Pushkin. Then again there was the business of Barclay de Tolly's 'outlandish' name: Kutuzov's 'name is not only sacred to us, but we Russians should rejoice at the Russian sound of his name'.

Pushkin proceeded to give Kutuzov his undisputed due, acknowledging that only he could have given battle to Napoleon at Borodino, only he could have sacrificed Moscow. But, 'Because Kutuzov was great, must we be ungrateful for Barclay de Tolly's achievements? . . .' Finally, Pushkin met head-on that strange and seemingly indestructible Russian literary tradition which calls writers to account for not following approved views: 'Is it possible that after twenty-five years of silence, a poet should not be permitted to utter Barclay's name with sympathy and emotion? You reproach the poet for the injustice of his complaints; you say that Barclay's merits have been duly acknowledged, appreciated, rewarded. Maybe so, but by whom and when? Certainly not by the people and not in 1812! . . .'[17] Twelve years later Viskovatov was saying the same thing, though with a touch of optimism: 'Our Government has done everything to reward the merits and to honour the memory of Barclay de Tolly; what he was lacking is only the full justice and gratitude of his contemporaries, but this debt too will be paid for them by posterity . . .'[18] Pushkin felt strongly that the debt had not been paid. He realized with a poet's sympathy that the titles and rewards later heaped upon Barclay by the Tsar did not redeem the antipathy of the Russian people – to the man and to his memory. Barclay's hope that 'impartial posterity will judge with greater justice' was still unrealized.[19] Pushkin's own hope was that 'The Commander' would be the leaven working in Russian consciousness, correcting the injustice.

But meanwhile he had to keep his balance in the controversy and spare the tears of his mistress. Very soon after the publication of his 'Explanation' he produced a poem 'To The Artist' ('Khudozhniku'), dedicated to the sculptor Galberg. Pushkin described the sculptor's studio and his entries in the St. Petersburg competition for twin statues of Barclay and Kutuzov to stand before Kazan' Cathedral:[20]

> Here is Barclay the conceiver and here Kutuzov the completer . . .

Thus, in one line of verse, did Pushkin demonstrate his impartial stance.

But this was not what was wanted either. Suddenly it turned out that the approved position was to praise Barclay in order to praise the Tsar. (As far as 'The Commander' was concerned, this would seem to mean overlooking Pushkin's lines on Alexander (unnamed), 'whose mind was shrewd enough to be exempt' from the mob's execration but 'found it more politic to join them in contempt'.) At the end of his 'Explanation' in *The Contemporary*, Pushkin had made another demonstration of his fairmindedness by printing the first three of five stanzas of a hitherto unpublished poem he had written in 1831, 'In The Shadow of The Commander' ('V teni Polkovodtsa'), the commander in this case being Kutuzov. To Pushkin's surprise, the publishing of this eulogy was soundly rebuked by Faddei Bulgarin, editor of the semi-official *Northern Bee* (11 January [O.S.] 1837), who liked 'The Commander' very much because it indirectly supported 'divine autocracy': Barclay's strategy had the approval of Alexander I and thus, ultimately, the Tsar was the saviour of Russia.[21] This casuistry probably made few converts, however.

A recent discovery has again stirred up the controversy regarding Pushkin's attitudes respectively to Barclay and Kutuzov.[22] In a private album belonging to the Grand Duchess Elena Pavlovna, the wife of Grand Duke Michael, younger brother of Tsars Alexander I and Nicolas I, Pushkin had written out 'The Commander' in his own hand. The Grand Duchess, a former Princess of Württemberg, was a cultured, intelligent woman, interested in history, science, and the arts, who, to compensate for her loneliness amidst her Romanovs, befriended the leading Russian writers of the period, including Pushkin. (Nicolas called her the family 'savante', Michael shunned all that pleased her – the only musical instrument he could tolerate was the drum – but between her and Pushkin there was a relationship of trust.)[23] In her album Pushkin had written 'The Commander' with a quatrain replacing the two lines of ellipsis marks that appeared in the published version in *The Contemporary*:

> In vain! Your rival reaped the triumph early planted
> In your high mind; and you, forgotten, disenchanted,
> The sponsor of the feast, drew your last breath,
> Despising us, it may be, in the hour of death.[24]

The first line of the quatrain is significant. Here for the first time Pushkin spoke slightingly of Kutuzov. 'In these lines,' writes I. T. Trofimov, the scholar who made the discovery, 'Pushkin's endeavour to rehabilitate Barclay reaches its apogee.'[25]

The question of which version of 'The Commander' Pushkin himself considered final is still moot, despite the attention focused on the poem by at least a dozen Soviet scholars during the 1960s. The distinguished literary critic Efim Etkind argues in favour of the printed version, principally on the grounds that the quatrain is inferior in quality to the rest of the poem. He explains the two lines of ellipsis marks as providing 'an unusually dramatic pause', an intended literary effect.[26] The main argument of the Pushkin scholar Petrunina in favour of the printed version is that the quatrain over-emphasizes the image of Barclay as victim declaiming against his fate and the people. She also believes Pushkin wanted to avoid taking sides in military matters.[27] Trofimov, who found the album, holds that the poem should henceforth be printed in its album-version entirety.[28] Although some of those involved in the dispute deny the possibility of Pushkin having dropped the quatrain in print for fear of censorship, none has made the plausible suggestion that he may have done so to spare the feelings of Madame Khitrovo.

Pushkin's noble effort to vindicate Barclay was followed in a small way by two of his noted contemporaries, the poets Vassilii Zhukovskii and Mikhail Lermontov. As proof of the unspoken taboo against Barclay, the first had written 'A Poet in The Camp of Russian Warriors' where he had named twenty-one of the heroes of 1812, with no mention of Barclay; on Pushkin's prompting he tried to repair the oversight by a new poem, 'The Anniversary of Borodino'.[29] As for Lermontov, he wrote a three-stanza poem, untitled, and unpublished for almost forty years, beginning:

> Thou man of greatness!
> No quittance here is worthy of thy valour . . .

This poem, rediscovered only recently, has been definitely identified by the Lermontov specialist Iraklii Andronikov as dedicated to Barclay.[30]

Pushkin was killed in a duel while the controversy was still seething. If he had lived it is tempting to think he might have written an epic poem where Barclay figured – a poetic counterpart to *War and Peace*: Pushkin did conceive of Barclay as 'a highly poetical figure'.[31] But by itself 'The Commander' cannot offset the effect of Tolstoy's misleading masterpiece. Waves of xenophobia again and again have washed out the chances of a true rehabilitation of Barclay among the Russian people. Between waves, however, scholars both Tsarist and Soviet have tried to render him his due, and among these there is hardly one who has not referred to 'The Commander'.

While Pushkin's poem was inspiring the polemicists' wrath, it is significant that no one seemed to be excited about the unveiling (in December 1837) of the Kutuzov and Barclay statues before Our Lady of Kazan'. Monuments in stone, as Pushkin knew, are a cold substitute for the appreciation and affection of poets and people.[32] Barclay's fate – to serve his country and his countrymen and reap disgrace, then glory, but never the heart's reward of simple recognition – is illuminated by 'The Commander' as it can never be by half a dozen monuments in stone or bronze scattered between Leningrad and Regensburg's Walhalla Hall.

APPENDIX A

ALEXANDER PUSHKIN
The Commander

One of the Tsar's palatial halls is an apartment
With neither gold nor velvet rich; here no assortment
Of coronation gems, kept under glass, is found;
But up and down, throughout its length and all around,
His ranging brush instinct with free and generous feeling,
An artist has embellished it from floor to ceiling.
No maidenly madonnas, nymphs on sylvan lawns,
Full-bosomed women, goblet-wielding fauns,
No dances, hunting scenes – instead, all cloaks and sabres,
And countenances marked by war's resolve, war's labours.
In serried throng the artist conjured up to light
The high commanders of our nation's warlike might,
All laureates of that campaign of wondrous glory,
Of Eighteen-hundred-twelve's imperishable story.
At times, astroll amongst them, as my gaze was caught
By the familiar likenesses, I idly thought
That I could hear their warrior notes ring down those spaces.
Yet many are no longer, and the rest, whose faces
In bloom of youth still grace this canvas lively-hued,
Grown old by now, incline in modest quietude
Their laurelled heads . . .
                But of this sombre band of brothers
One always draws my mind more strongly than the others;
Bemused anew each time, I stop and cannot spare
A glance elsewhere, and then, the more I brood and stare,
The more I feel my heart in leaden sadness buried.

He is portrayed full-length. Bald like a skull's, his forehead
Gleams loftily, and you would say, betrays the blight
Of some great suffering. Deep gloom surrounds the site;
The background shows a host encamped. Calm in dejection,
He seems engrossed in some disdainful recollection.
The artist either drew no more than he had seen
In choosing to portray him with just such a mien,
Or by some insight not his own it was engendered –
No matter, it is this expression Dawe has rendered.

Luckless commander! Ah, your fate was bitter gall:
To alien soil in sacrifice you brought your all.
By gaze of savage ignorance unpenetrated,
You strode alone, your mind with lofty concepts freighted,
But, fastening on your name's outlandish sound for bait,
And letting loose on you its hue-and-cry of hate,
While being rescued by your stratagem, the nation
Reviled your venerable head with execration.
And he whose mind was shrewd enough to be exempt,
Found it more politic to join them in contempt . . .
And long, your mighty heart upheld by strong conviction,
Undaunted you outfaced the cretinous affliction;
Until, but half-way home, you were compelled at length
To yield without a word the laurel wreath, the strength
Of high command, and that design so deeply pondered –
To vanish in the lines and see your glory squandered.
There, lord of hosts retired, young ensign now instead,
Who never heard before the merry hiss of lead,
You charged the firing line and sought the death you craved –
In vain! –
....
....

Ah, men! A wretched tribe, both tears and laughter worth!
Priests of the momentary, the success of earth!
How often in his passing may a man be seen
At whom a blind and hectic age will vent its spleen,
But whose exalted face within a generation
Draws poets into rapt and loving contemplation!

© Translated by W. W. Arndt

APPENDIX B

THE PRIVATE CORRESPONDENCE OF BARCLAY DE TOLLY
An Inventory

This inventory of the extant *private* correspondence of Barclay de Tolly lists seventy-six letters written *by* him – mostly to his wife Auguste, with four to his aunt and foster-mother Auguste von Vermeulen, one to his sister's husband Magnus von Lueder, and several to his friends Ludwig and Alexander von Maier, the father and son – plus one letter written *to* him by his wife. All the letters are in German, in a difficult archaic script.

The autograph originals of seventy-five of these letters are to be found either in the von Campenhausen family archives in the care of Baron Balthasar von Campenhausen in Meinerzhagen or in the von Schroeder family archives in the care of Dr. Johann Karl von Schroeder in Berlin. In two cases, however, as noted, copies of the originals are in the Schroeder collection, but the originals themselves are missing. Excerpts from one of these were published in Mikhailovskii-Danilevskii and Viskovatov, *Imperator Aleksandr I i ego spodvizhniki v 1812, 13, 14 i 1815 godakh: voennaia galereia Zimniago Dvortsa* (St. Petersburg 1848–9); from the other, in *Russkaia Starina* (St. Petersburg, October 1888).

Over half (forty-five) of the seventy-seven letters listed here can be found in published, though rarely complete, form. Seventeen, selected by Siegfried von Vegesack, appeared in *Baltische Hefte* (Hanover) in January 1959, and another twenty-four in March 1959, under the overall title, 'Die Briefe des Feldmarschalls Barclay de Tolly an seine Frau aus den Jahren 1812, 1813, 1815'. All but six of these same letters have also appeared, often in shorter excerpts, in Vegesack, *Vorfahren und Nachkommen: Aufzeichnungen aus einer altlivländischen Brieflade 1689–1887* (Heilbronn 1961). Thirty-two of these same letters, plus one not used by Vegesack, first appeared, more or sometimes less completely, presented by Otto Harnack as 'Briefe des Feldmarschalls Fürsten Barclay de Tolly aus den Jahren 1812–1815', in *Baltische Monatsschrift*, Vol. XXXV, No. 6 (Reval 1888). There is thus a good deal of overlap among these three published sources. Letter No. 25 appears not only in the three sources above but also in N. F. Dubrovin, *Otechestvennaia voina v pis'mach sovremennikov (1812–1815 gg.)* (St. Petersburg 1882). One of the letters to Barclay's aunt appears only in F. W. von Weymarn, *Barklay de Tolly und der vaterländische Krieg* (Reval 1914). The following abbreviations are used:

BH 1/59	= *Baltische Hefte*, January 1959
BH 3/59	= *Baltische Hefte*, March 1959
vV	= Siegfried von Vegesack, *Vorfahren und Nachkommen* . .
BM	= *Baltische Monatsschrift*, Vol. XXXV, No. 6 (Reval 1888)

MD-V	= Mikhailovskii-Danilevskii and Viskovatov, *Imperator Aleksandr* . . (St. Petersburg 1848–9)
RS	= *Russkaia Starina*, October 1888
FWvW	= F. W. von Weymarn, *Barklay de Tolly* . . (Reval 1914)
Dub	= N. F. Dubrovin, *Otechestvennaia* . . (St. Petersburg 1882)
inc.	= incomplete
sd	= *sine dato*
sl	= *sine loco*
Campenhausen	= von Campenhausen Family Archives
Schroeder	= von Schroeder Family Archives

D.J.

THE PRIVATE CORRESPONDENCE OF BARCLAY DE TOLLY
A. From Barclay de Tolly

No.	Date	Place	Addressed to	pp.	Publication data	Originals	Remarks
1	15.3.1796	Grodno	Aunt/Foster-mother von Vermeulen	3	Unpublished	Schroeder	
2	27.4.1809	Vasa	Aunt/Foster-mother von Vermeulen	3	Unpublished	Schroeder	
3	17.6.1811	St. Petersburg	Wife	3	Unpublished	Campenhausen	
4	19.6.1811	St. Petersburg	Wife	3	Unpublished	Campenhausen	
5	22.6.1811	St. Petersburg	Wife	3	Unpublished	Campenhausen	
6	24.6.1811	St. Petersburg	Wife	3	Unpublished	Campenhausen	
7	26.6.1811	St. Petersburg	Wife	2	Unpublished	Campenhausen	
8	4.7.1811	St. Petersburg	Wife	4	Unpublished	Campenhausen	
9	8.7.1811	St. Petersburg	Wife	4	Unpublished	Campenhausen	
10	sd.7.1811	St. Petersburg	Wife	3	Unpublished	Campenhausen	
11	30.7.1811	St. Petersburg	Wife	2	Unpublished	Campenhausen	
12	9.8.1811	St. Petersburg	Wife	3	Unpublished	Campenhausen	
13	27.3.1812	Riga	Wife	4	Unpublished	Campenhausen	
14	28.3.1812	Riga	Wife	3	Unpublished	Campenhausen	
15	19.6.1812	Sventsiany	Wife	3	BH 1/59, 92–3, inc.; vV 207, inc.; BM 493–4, inc.	Campenhausen	
16	26.6.1812	Belmonte	Wife	3	BH 1/59, 93–4; vV 207–8, inc.; BM 494, inc.	Campenhausen	
17	28.6.1812	Drissa	Wife	2	BH 1/59, 94; vV 209, inc.; BM 494, inc.	Campenhausen	
18	9.7.1812	sl	Wife	2	BH 1/59, 94–5, inc.; vV 209, inc.; BM 494–5, inc.	Campenhausen	

No.	Date	Place	Addressed to	pp.	Publication data	Originals	Remarks
19	23.7.1812	Smolensk	Wife	2	BH 1/59, 95, inc.; vV 209, inc.; BM 495, inc.	Campenhausen	
20	27.7.1812	sl (between Smolensk & Rudnia – BM)	Wife	2	BH 1/59, 95–6, inc.; vV 209, inc.; BM 495, inc.	Campenhausen	
21	16.8.1812	sl	Wife	1	BH 1/59, 96; vV 210, inc.; BM 495, inc.	Campenhausen	
22	18.8.1812	sl (Tsarevo-Zaimishche – BM)	Wife	1	BH 1/59, 96; BM 496, inc.	Campenhausen	
23	*7.9.1812	Kaluga	Wife	2	BH 1/59, 96	Campenhausen	*sd on original; supplied in BH
24	10.9.1812	sl	Wife	1	BH 1/59, 97, inc.; vV 210, inc.; BM 496, inc.	Campenhausen	
25	11.9.1812	Krasnaia-Pahkra	Wife	3	BH 1/59, 97, inc.; Dub, 128–9, inc.; vV 210–11, inc.; BM 496–7, inc.	Campenhausen	
26	12.9.1812	sl	Wife	1	BH 1/59, 98, inc.; vV 211, inc.; BM 497, inc.	Campenhausen	
27	18.9.1812	Voronezh	Wife	1	BH 1/59, 98, inc.; vV 211, inc.	Campenhausen	BH & vV omit place, which BdT writes Woronowo
28	19.9.1812	Ratchino	Wife	2	BH 1/59, 98, inc.; vV 211, inc.; BM 497, inc.	Campenhausen	
29	1.10.1812	Tula	Wife	4	BH 1/59, 98–9, inc.; vV 212–13, inc.; BM 497–8, inc.	Campenhausen	
30	8.10.1812	Vladimir	Wife	4	BH 1/59, 99–100, inc.; vV 213, inc.; BM 498, inc.	Campenhausen	

No.	Date	Place	Addressed to	pp.	Publication data	Originals	Remarks
31	9.10.1812	Vladimir	Wife	2	Unpublished	Campenhausen	
32	16.10.1812	Vladimir	Wife	4	BH 1/59, 100–1, inc.; vV 213–14, inc.; BM 499, inc.	Campenhausen	
33	16.11.1812	Beckhof	Alexander v. Maier	4	RS, 263–4, inc.	Missing; copy in Schroeder	
34	sd.4.1813	sl	Ludwig v. Maier	4	Unpublished	Schroeder	
35	26.4.1813	Pinno (?)	Ludwig v. Maier	4	Unpublished	Schroeder	
36	11.6.1813	Reichenbach	Ludwig v. Maier	2	Unpublished	Schroeder	
37	3.8.1813	Nedilastic	Wife	2	Unpublished	Campenhausen	
38	5.8.1813	Prague	Wife	2	BH 3/59, 165, inc.; vV 214–15, inc.	Campenhausen	
39	11.8.1813	Furstenberg in Saxony	Wife	1	BH 3/59, 166, inc.; vV 215, inc.; BM 501, inc.	Campenhausen	
40	19.8.1813	Teplitz	Wife	3	BH 3/59, 166–7, inc.; vV 215–16, inc.; BM 501–2, inc.	Campenhausen	
41	8–20.8.1813	Bylyn (?)	Wife	3	BH 3/59, 165–6, inc.; vV 215, inc.; BM 501, inc.	Campenhausen	
42	27.8.1813	Peterswalde	Wife	3	BH 3/59, 167, inc.; vV 216, inc.; BM 503, inc.	Campenhausen	
43	sd	sl	Wife	6	BH3/59, 167–8, inc.; vV 216–17, inc.; BM 502, inc.	Campenhausen	
44	29.8.1813	Teplitz (Kulm near Teplitz - BM)	Wife	4	BH 3/59, 168, inc.; vV 217, inc.; BM 503–4, inc.	Campenhausen	
45	2.9.1813	Teplitz	Wife	4	BM 504–5, inc.	Campenhausen	
46	5.9.1813	Teplitz	Wife	3	BH 3/59, 168, inc.; vV 217, inc.; BM 505, inc.	Campenhausen	

No.	Date	Place	Addressed to	pp.	Publication data	Originals	Remarks
47	10–22.9.1813	Teplitz/ (Brix)	Wife	4	BH 3/59, 168–9, inc.; vV 218–19, inc.; BM 505–7, inc.	Campenhausen	
48	22.9.1813	Brix	Wife	2	BM 507, inc.	Campenhausen	
49	14–26.9.1813	Teplitz	Wife	2	BH 3/59, 169–70, inc.; BM 507, inc.	Campenhausen	
50	28.9.1813	Commotau	Wife	2	BH 3/59, 170, inc.; BM 508, inc.	Campenhausen	
51	29.9.1813	Tschopau in Saxony	Wife	3	BH 3/59, 170, inc.; vV 219, inc.; BM 508, inc.	Campenhausen	
52	sd	sl (Saxony)	Wife	3	BH 3/59, 170, inc.; vV 219–20, inc.; BM 508–9, inc.	Campenhausen	
53	19/9/–1/10/1813	Brix	Wife	1	Unpublished	Campenhausen	
54	7/10/1813	Leipzig	Wife	2	BH 3/59, 171; vV 220, inc.	Campenhausen	
55	sd (early Oct. 1813)	sl (Saxony)	Wife	4	BH 3/59, 171–2, inc.; vV 220–1, inc.; BM 509–10, inc.	Campenhausen	
56	10–22/10/1813	Naumburg	Wife	3	BH 3/59, 172, inc.; vV 221–2, inc.	Campenhausen	
57	13–25/10/1813	Weimarn	Wife	4	BH 3/59, 172–3, inc.; vV 222, inc.; BM 510, inc.	Campenhausen	
58	8.11.1813	Aschaffenburg	Ludwig v. Maier	2	Unpublished	Schroeder	
59	15/1/**1814**	Langres	Ludwig v. Maier	1	Unpublished	Schroeder	
60	15.1.1814	Langres	Alexander v. Maier	3	MD-V, 89, inc.		Missing; copy in Schroeder
61	5.5.1814	Paris	Aunt/Foster-mother	2	FWvW, 170–1	Schroeder	
62	20.6.1814	Rastatt	Alexander v. Maier	1	Unpublished	Schroeder	
63	30/4/**1815**	Prague	Wife	3	BH 3/59, 173–4, inc.; vV 223, inc.; BM 511, inc.	Campenhausen	

No.	Date	Place	Addressed to	pp.	Publication data	Originals	Remarks
64	11.5.1815	Dresden	Ludwig v. Maier	2	Unpublished	Schroeder	
65	29.5.1815	Bamberg	Alexander v. Maier	1	Unpublished	Schroeder	
66	20.6.1815	Saarbrück	Wife	2	BH 3/59, 174, inc.; vV 223, inc.; BM 512, inc.	Campenhausen	
67	27.6.1815	Bissey, not far from Châlons	Wife	2	BH 3/59, 174–5; vV 223-4, inc.; BM 512–13, inc.	Campenhausen	
68	21.7.1815	Châlons	Aunt/Foster-mother	2	Unpublished	Schroeder	
69	30.11.1815	Riga	Alexander v. Maier	1	Unpublished	Schroeder	
70	14.12.1815	St. Petersburg	Wife	7	BH 3/59, 175–7; vV 224–6, inc.	Campenhausen	
71	18.12.1815	St. Petersburg	Wife	3	BH 3/59, 177, inc.	Campenhausen	
72	21.12.1815	St. Petersburg	Wife	3	BH 3/59, 177–8, inc.	Campenhausen	
73	21.6.**1816**	Mogilev	Ludwig v. Maier	2	Unpublished	Schroeder	
74	27.9.1816	Mogilev	Magnus v. Lueder	3	Unpublished	Schroeder	
75	19–21.9.**1817**	Kursk	Wife	3	Unpublished	Campenhausen	
76	9.2.**1818**	Mogilev	Alexander v. Maier	1	Unpublished	Schroeder	

B. To Barclay de Tolly

No.	Date	Place	Written by	pp.	Publication data	Original	
77	26.12.**1812**	Wieratz	Wife	4	BH 1/59, 101, inc.	Campenhausen	D. J.

NOTES AND SOURCES

CHAPTER I
'YOUR NAME'S OUTLANDISH SOUND'

1 H. F. Barclay, *A History of the Barclay Family* (London 1933), including 'The Barclays in Scotland' and 'The Russian Barclays de Tolly', being part II of a work begun by the Rev. Charles W. Barclay: *A History of the Barclay Family* (London 1924). This book is the most extensive source on the Berchelais and Barclays of Scotland and Russia.

2 William J. Watson, *The History of the Celtic Place-Names of Scotland* (Edinburgh/London 1926), 442.

3 H. F. Barclay, *A History* . . , 289. Unfortunately no documentation is given for the conversation with Sir Robert Barclay. Nor for the account (268) of Sir Robert's dealings in 1816 with heraldic authorities who told him, 'Sir Robert, these cannot be your coat of arms . . . they are the very same arms and motto as those of the Russian Field-Marshal Prince Barclay de Tolly.' 'Oh,' said Sir Robert, 'if that is all, there is nothing wrong, for we are cubs of the same breed!'

4 This paragraph is based mainly on G. W. S. Barrow, *The Kingdom of the Scots: Government, Church and Society from the eleventh to the fourteenth century* (London 1973), especially 332–4, and on a letter from Professor Barrow to the author (St. Andrews, 28 April 1975). Professor Barrow has convinced me that his conjectures and findings in early Scots Barclay genealogy must supersede most of the preceding histories. Barrow states: 'There are surely more published histories of the Barclays than of any other Scottish family. The Barclay histories published in this century are worse than those published in the eighteenth, and those in turn are distinguished for the low level of their medieval scholarship' (*The Kingdom* . . , 332).

5 The pre-Barrow Barclay story as gleaned primarily from Hubert F. Barclay, *A History* . . , and the Rev. Charles W. Barclay, *A History of the Barclay Family* (London 1924), starts with Roger, supposedly from Aumale, Normandy, being appointed provost of Berchelai manor with large holdings in Gloucestershire. His grandson, Roger de Berkeley III, sides with King Stephen against Maud, loses title to the Castle and Barony of Berkeley which were handed over to a wealthy merchant, Robert Fitzhardinge of Bristol. The Fitzhardinges afterwards assume the name Berkeley. Roger III, allowed to keep the Barony of Dursley, becomes Roger de Berkeley (Berchelai) de Dursley. One of Roger's sons, John de Berchelai, settles in Scotland, according to this version, during the reign of David I (1124–53), receives royal favours including the Towie lands, and appears as Towie I in the Towie-Barclay genealogy. John arrives even earlier in Scotland according to a legend whereby he accompanies Edgar the Atheling after the latter loses his crown to William the Conqueror, is blown off course from Hungary and is welcomed by King Malcolm Caenmore (Malcolm III) who bestows the Towie lands. Another story has John joining the Scottish court after Malcolm's marriage to Edgar the Atheling's sister, the 'saintly' Margaret. Despite these many versions, 'it has never been possible to point to a single piece of evidence which would link the Scottish and [Gloucestershire] English families', according to Professor Barrow.

6 H. F. Barclay, *A History* . . , 203–8, claims that various features of the Towie Castle great hall and oratory, with their gothic ribbed cross-vaulting and sculptured corbels, belong to the period from 1570 to 1600. The Towie Castle of the Barclays is not to be confused with the Towie Castle which belonged to the Forbes family.

7 A. Francis Steuart, chronicling *Scottish Influences in Russian History* (Glasgow 1913), reports that many Scots in the sixteenth century also became mercenaries in Russia, finding it easy to enter the country but close to impossible to get out again when they wished to return home to Scotland. Until the early eighteenth century, as now, Russians were not permitted freely to leave their country; valuable foreigners serving Russia also found usually insurmountable difficulties in leaving. In the seventeenth century many Scots, including Bruces, Gordons, Keiths, and Ogilvys, served Russia as generals, field-marshals, and admirals. Especially welcome to the imperial court were Scottish physicians.

8 H. F. Barclay, *A History* . . , 241–3, 279. Another document, however, if it does indeed refer to the same Andrew Barclay, casts doubt

on the closeness of the relationship to Sir Patrick: 'In 1588 Patrick Barclay of Towie sold some land . . . and witnesses to the charter of this sale . . . were George Barclay of Mathers, George Barclay of Syde, and Andrew Barclay servitor to Patrick Barclay of Towie. If this Andrew was the father of Peter Barclay their blood relationship with the main Barclay family would appear to have been fairly remote.' – Scots Ancestry Research Society letter to author, 23 August 1972.

9 H. F. Barclay, *A History* . . , 241–3, 279.

10 The Hanseatic League – or Hanse – which originated in Lübeck in the twelfth century and spread out from there, flourishing until the middle of the sixteenth century, was crucial for the development of Riga. Starting as a community of merchants whose object was to protect their trade with distant lands, the League became in the fourteenth century a community of city-states, a unique institution. Scarce and precious goods from as far away as Byzantium, the Far East, or fur-supplying Arkhangel'sk on the White Sea were imported to western Europe; and cloth and salt were exported, primarily to the East. Among the many factors contributing to the collapse of the Hanse, the most important was the rise of Dutch and other competition which broke the Hanse monopoly. But by then Riga's mercantilism and relative liberalism had taken root, thanks to its membership in the League, and its favourable geographical position enabled the city to continue to prosper while other more westerly ports declined. — see Philippe Dollinger, *La Hanse (XIIIe–XVIIe siècles)* (Paris 1964).

11 The *Schwarzhaüpterhaus* was the guildhall of castle wardens and mercenaries, scribes and clerks, artisans and manservants; their patron was the African St. Mauritius. — Reinhard Wittram, *Geschichte der Baltischen Deutschen: Grundzüge und Durchblicke* (Stuttgart 1939), 20.

12 Johann Gottfried Herder to Johann Georg Hamann in Rudolph Haym, *Herder* (East Berlin 1958), 95.

13 Herder, *Journal meiner Reise im Jahr 1769*, ed. Johannes Nohl (Weimar 1949), 26.

14 Francis Ley, *Madame de Krüdener et son temps, 1764–1824* (Paris 1961), 14.

15 Herder, *Journal* . . , 110.

16 Arthur Boehtlingk, *Frédéric-César Laharpe, 1754–1838* (Neuchâtel 1969), 75.

17 H. F. Barclay, *A History* . . , 279–85, 290.

CHAPTER II

THE MAN

1 Johann Karl von Schroeder, 'Michael Barclay de Tolly: zum 200. Geburtstag des Feldmarschalls', *Baltische Hefte* (Hanover 1962–3), IV, No. 2, 66. Until the publication of this essay, all biographical notices named Luhde-Grosshof as BdT's place of birth.

2 H. F. Barclay, *A History* . . , 285.

3 BdT's maternal great-grandfather, Johann Smitt, was ennobled as von Smitten by Sweden's King Charles XI. L. von Stryk, the great authority on Livonian estates, dates the acquisition of Beckhof by the von Smittens to March 1740. It is not quite clear why BdT's mother is usually referred to as heiress of Beckhof when she was one of several children, of whom the male, Heinrich Johann von Smitten, in fact inherited the estate. He left it to his eldest son, who sold it to a younger, who in turn sold it to a sister, BdT's wife. — Family archives of G. R. von Prosch (Bad Homburg vor der Höhe); *Genealogisches Handbuch der Baltischen Ritterschaften: Teil Estland* (Görlitz 1929–31); L. von Stryk, *Beiträge zur Geschichte der Rittergüter Livlands* (Dorpat 1877), 352–3.

4 Prosch, *Stammtafeln aus neuerer Zeit: Die Fürsten Barclay de Tolly* (Munich 1948), 35–43 (with subsequent corrections and amplifications in letters to author), is the source for genealogical information on BdT relatives and descendants, unless otherwise noted.

The elder brother, *Erich* Johann Barclay de Tolly ('Ivan' in Russian references), 1758–1819, a major-general in the Engineers, was decorated for bravery with the Order of St. George Fourth Class and headed a committee for the construction of fortifications in Finland. Erich and his wife, née Margarete Sophie von Lilienfeld (whose mother was a von Smitten, maternal aunt to the Barclays), had two sons, one dying in childhood and Andreas, the one who served as adjutant to his uncle Michael, who died without issue in 1847, ending this line.

The younger brother, *Heinrich* Johann Barclay de Tolly, 1766–1805, did not marry.

The sister, *Christine* Gertrud Anna, née Barclay de Tolly, 1770–1865, married Major Magnus von Lueder, master of Köllitz (in eastern Livonia), where they lived in apparent poverty. They had five daughters, of whom two married von Weymarns.

Cf. A. V. Viskovatov in A. I. Mikhailovskii-Danilevskii and A. V. Viskovatov, *Imperator*

Notes and Sources

Aleksandr I i ego spodvizhniki v 1812, 1813, 1814, i 1815 godakh (St. Petersburg 1848–9), 3; Schroeder letter to author, 25 July 1972; BdT to Auguste, Riga, 27 March (O.S.) 1812; and 28 March (O.S.) 1812, BdT Private Correspondence, 13, 14 (see Appendix B).

5 A. Bartenev, 'Pamiati General-Fel'dmarshala kniazia M. B. Barklaia-de-Tolli', *Voenno-istoricheskii Sbornik* (St. Petersburg 1912), II, No. 1, 136.

6 BdT to Auguste, Riga, 27 March (O.S.) 1812, BdT Private Correspondence, 13. The cousin (son of Michael's paternal uncle), August Wilhelm von Barclay de Tolly, 1752–1826, raised to hereditary nobility of the Holy Roman Empire by Francis II in 1792, became alderman of Riga in 1797, mayor in 1800.

7 Brigadier Georg Wilhelm von Vermeulen was born in St. Petersburg in about 1726. He, his three brothers, and one sister were orphaned at an early age and brought up in the house of the mathematician Leonhard Euler whose wife, Katharina Gsell, was their aunt. The Brigadier's maternal grandfather was the painter Georg Gsell of St. Gallen, Switzerland, who was invited to Russia by Peter the Great and there taught at the Academy of Sciences. In 1741 Euler was summoned to Berlin by Frederick the Great and took three of the nephews Vermeulen with him. All three eventually joined the Prussian army, but Georg Wilhelm 'ran away' and returned to Russia in 1750, where his advancement in the Russian army was rapid.

Sources for the Vermeulens and for BdT's childhood in following text are: Erik Amburger, 'Wer war der Pflegevater Barclay de Tollys?', *Baltische Hefte*, Hanover 1963, X, No. 4, 253–4; *Voenno-Entsiklopedicheskii Leksikon* (St. Petersburg 1838), 130; F. W. von Weymarn, 'Barklai-de-Tolli i otechestvennaia voina 1812 goda', *Russkaia Starina*, St. Petersburg, Aug. 1912, 181; Bartenev, *Biografii Generalissimusov i Generalfeld'-marshalov rossiiskoi imperatorskoi armii* (St. Petersburg 1912), 17; Prosch letters to author, 21 June and 14 July 1973.

8 BdT to Auguste von Vermeulen, Grodno, 15 March (O.S.) 1796; and Vasa, 27 April (O.S.) 1809, BdT Private Correspondence, 1, 2.

9 Germaine de Staël, *Oeuvres complètes de Mme la Baronne de Staël*, XV, *Dix années d'exil* (Brussels 1812), 232.

10 Bartenev, *Biografii* . . , 17.

11 Bartenev, 'Pamiati . . .', 136.

12 Mikhailovskii-Danilevskii and Viskovatov, *Imperator* . . , 96.

13 *Russkii biograficheskii slovar'* (I–XXV), ed. by A. A. Polovtsov (St. Petersburg 1896–1918), II, 508.

14 Mikhailovskii-Danilevskii and Viskovatov, *Imperator* . . , 96.

15 F. W. v. Weymarn, 'Barklai- . .', 181 fn 2, citing I. P. Liprandi, a Russian historian who was quartermaster of the Sixth Corps in 1812.

16 Waldemar von Loewenstern [General V. I. Levenshtern], 'Zapiski', *Russkaia Starina* (St. Petersburg), Jan. 1901, 124. See note in bibliography.

17 F. F. Vigel', *Zapiski*, ed. by S. Ya. Shtraikh (Moscow 1928; reprint Cambridge 1974) I, 96.

18 BdT to Auguste, Tula, 10 Oct. (O.S.) 1812, BdT Private Correspondence, 29; Mikhailovskii-Danilevskii and Viskovatov, *Imperator* . . , 96. BdT's library has been destroyed, making it impossible to know with certainty what his reading consisted in, but it is inconceivable that a military man with a reputation for studious habits should not have read the leading military literature of the day: Vauban, Frederick the Great, Count de Guibert, von Bülow. Ermolov, BdT's Chief of Staff in 1812, confirms that BdT, a 'patient' and 'thoughtful' man, habitually used his spare time for reading. — A. P. Ermolov, *Materialy dlia istorii voiny 1812 g* (Prilozheniya), (Moscow 1863), 69.

19 Friedrich von Toll, *Denkwürdigkeiten aus dem Leben des Kaiserl. Russ. Generals von der Infanterie, Carl Friedrich Grafen von Toll*, ed. by Theodor von Bernhardi (Leipzig 1865), I, 268. Toll was Quartermaster-General under BdT in 1812.

20 Friedrich von Schubert, *Unter dem Doppeladler: Erinnerungen eines Deutschen in russischem Offiziersdienst, 1789–1814*, ed. with an introduction by Erik Amburger (Stuttgart 1962), 94. Schubert – only son of the astronomer Theodor Schubert, who left his native Pomerania for St. Petersburg where he became a member of the Academy of Sciences – served in various capacities and in several campaigns under BdT.

21 Mikhail A. Fon-Vizin, *Zapiski Fon-Vizina, ochevidtsa smutnykh vremen Tsarstvovanii Pavla I, Aleksandra, I, Nikolaia I* (Leipzig 1859), 107. Fonvizin (Fon-Vizin) was later one of the Decembrists. His high regard for BdT stemmed in part from their common concern for the common soldier and their outrage over needless brutalities.

22 Toll, *Denkwürdigkeiten* . . , I, 268.

23 Mikhailovskii-Danilevskii and Viskovatov, *Imperator* . . , 96–7.

24 Helene *Auguste* Eleonore Barclay de Tolly, *née* von Smitten, 1770–1828, born at Beckhof, died in Dorpat. Her father, Johann von Smitten, master of Beckhof, was BdT's uncle (his mother's brother), and her mother was Renata von Stackelberg of an important Livonian family. — Prosch, *Stammtafeln*.., 39.

25 Loewenstern, 'Zapiski', Dec. 1900, 554.

26 L. A. A. Comte de Langeron, *Mémoires de Langeron, Général d'infanterie dans l'armée russe: Campagnes de 1812, 1813, 1814*, ed. by L. G. Fabry (Paris 1902), 185.

27 Auguste to BdT, Wieratz, 26 Dec. (O.S.) 1812, BdT Private Correspondence, 77.

28 BdT to Auguste, St. Petersburg, 24 June (O.S.) 1812, BdT Private Correspondence, 6.

29 BdT to Auguste, sl, sd [September (O.S.) 1813]; and Drissa, 28 June (O.S.) 1812, BdT Private Correspondence, 52, 17.

30 BdT to Auguste, St. Petersburg, 17 June (O.S.) 1811, BdT Private Correspondence, 3. BdT was having to steady himself with his partially paralysed right hand because he was saluting with his left hand – the proper form at the time.

31 Concerning other possible BdT offspring, Schroeder notes ('. . Geburtstag . .', 84): '"From this marriage, fate left him one son, Ernst *Magnus* August." From this remark by his biographer and secretary Alexander von Maier, and a hint in his letter of 15 March 1796 to his aunt and foster-mother Vermeulen, we learn that other children were born to them but died early, so that only this son remained.' The letter referred to (BdT to Auguste von Vermeulen, Grodno, 15 March [O.S.] 1796, BdT Private Correspondence, 1), written two years before the birth of Magnus, states only: 'My wife, who is expecting in a few weeks at the most, is still, thank Heaven, quite well, and I hope that kind Providence will give her a happy accouchement this time.'

BdT's son, Prince Ernst *Magnus* August Barclay de Tolly, 1798–1871, died without issue. He married, first, Leocadie von Campenhausen, 1825; second, Alexandra von Cramer, widow of Colonel Georg von Tiesenhausen.

32 BdT to Auguste von Vermeulen, Grodno, 15 March (O.S.) 1796, BdT Private Correspondence, 1.

33 Alexander to Grand Duchess Catherine, 9 July (O.S.) 1810, in Nicolas Mikhailovich (Nicolas Michaïlowitch), *Correspondance de l'Empereur Alexandre Ier avec sa Sœur la Grande-Duchesse Catherine, 1805–1818* (St. Petersburg 1910), 32.

34 *Lina*: Caroline Elisabeth von Helffreich, 1794–1865, born at Reval, daughter of Estonian country gentleman, parents divorced; in 1812 married a favourite of the Tsar, Lieutenant-General Christopher von Reutern.

Catherine: Catherine Murav'ev-Apostol, 1795–1849, daughter of State Councillor Zachary Murav'ev-Apostol, Russian nobleman, and Baroness Elisabeth Posse (daughter of Erika Johanna von Smitten, sister to BdT's mother, and to Auguste BdT's father); in 1816 married Georg Ludwig von Kankrin, formerly secretary to BdT in War Ministry, who became Minister of Finance and member of the Imperial Council, named Count Kankrin in 1839, with rank of lieutenant-general at death (1845). (Catherine's brother Artamon was a famous Decembrist, exiled to Siberia.)

Jenny: Johanna Wilhelmina von Tornauw, 1798–1830, daughter of Georg von Tornauw, a retired officer, chief provincial postmaster of Riga, and of Johanna von Smitten (daughter of Heinrich Johann von Smitten who was brother to BdT's mother, and father of Auguste BdT); in 1815 married General Hans von Diebitsch, BdT's Chief of Staff 1815–18, named count in 1827, and field-marshal with honorific addition of Zabalkanskii to his name in victory celebration. (Jenny's husband under Nicolas I was active in repressing Catherine's Decembrist brother and cousins.)

Christel: Auguste Christine Anna von Lueder, 1803–1887, born in Reval, second of five daughters of Major Magnus von Lueder, master of Köllitz, and of Christine Gertrud Anna Barclay de Tolly (BdT's sister, Auguste BdT's cousin); in 1822 married Wilhelm Peter von Weymarn, master of Kaskowo, with ranks of lieutenant-general and adjutant-general at his death (1846). The von Weymarns were an exceptionally ancient and illustrious Livonian family, ennobled in the seventeenth century. (One of Christel's sisters, Elisabeth Amalie, married Ferdinand von Weymarn, a major-general and also an adjutant-general.) Although Prosch, the devoted investigator of Barclay-von Weymarn family history, gives Christel's name as Christine Auguste (presumably baptismal order), she names herself as Auguste Christine von Weymarn in her memoirs. — Prosch letters to author, 1971–4; Auguste to BdT, Wieratz, 26 Dec. (O.S.) 1812, BdT Private Correspondence, 77; *Rigasche Biographien* (Riga 1881), I, 144.

35 Christel's memoirs, privately printed for her nine children in her eighty-fourth year (1886), are the principal source for what follows. Their bias against Auguste does not seem entirely justified, and Christel too patly assigns the 'bad mother' role to her aunt. Lina von Helffreich,

'motherless' as a result of her parents' divorce, gave (according to her daughter's memoirs) a far more kindly, maternal image of Auguste. There is no way of determining whether Christel's report of BdT's last words (below, in text) is fanciful. These are the memoirs of an old woman re-living the relationships of her childhood and early adolescence. — Auguste Christine von Weymarn, *Erinnerungen aus meinem Leben* (sl, sd [1886]); Sophie von Reutern, *Generalleutnant Christoph von Reutern und seine Familie* (Tübingen 1888).

6   A. C. v. Weymarn, *Erinnerungen* . . , 4.

7   Ibid., 10.

8   Ibid., 11.

9   Siegfried von Vegesack, *Vorfahren und Nachkommen: Aufzeichnungen aus einer altlivländischen Brieflade 1689–1887* (Heilbronn 1961), 276–7, quoting a letter from Ernestine von Campenhausen. The von Campenhausens were one of the grandest of the Baltic baronies. Leocadie von Campenhausen's father objected to her marrying BdT's son, a relative parvenu, and there was every temptation for the writer of this letter to present a nouveau-riche caricature of Auguste.

10 BdT to Auguste, St. Petersburg, 24 June (O.S.) 1811, BdT Private Correspondence, 6. BdT should have the last word on his marriage. This letter, for Auguste's forty-first birthday, concludes: 'May God let us live hand in hand many returns of this day and allow us to look back with bliss at the day when we were joined together.'

CHAPTER III

APPRENTICESHIP IN WAR

1   Cf. A. N. Kochetkov, *M. B. Barklai-de-Tolli* (pamphlet) (Moscow 1970), 6. The basic source for BdT material in this chapter is Mikhailovskii-Danilevskii and Viskovatov, *Imperator* . . , 2–3.

2   Cf. Louis-Philippe Comte de Ségur, *Mémoires, ou Souvenirs et anecdotes* (Paris 1824–6), III, containing some of the most memorable of the many entertaining descriptions which have been written about Catherine's voyage.

3   Charles Joseph Prince de Ligne, *Mémoires et mélanges historiques* (Paris 1827), I, 191–2 (letter to the Comte de Ségur while acting as Austrian observer at Potemkin's headquarters).

4   One of the principalities of Anhalt was Zerbst, birthplace of Empress Catherine II; another was Dessau, the capital, home of Count Friedrich Anhalt; still another was Bernburg-Schaumburg whence came Prince Anhalt-Bernburg. Prince Victor-Amadeus Anhalt-Bernburg (1744–90) was remotely related to the Empress (their common ancestor was Prince Joachim Ernst von Anhalt, 1536–85). This fact may have been one reason for his entering Russian service at the age of twenty-eight and perhaps explains his rapid promotion: three years after his arrival in Russia he was a major-general. He was a born soldier, however, and would have succeeded in any case.

5   V. A. Alekseev, 'Delo pod Ochakovym, 27 iuli'a 1788 goda', *Voenno-istoricheskii Sbornik* (St. Petersburg 1914), II, 77.

6   Cf. R. M. Tsebrikov, 'Vokrug Ochakova, 1788 god', *Russkaia Starina* (St. Petersburg), Sept. 1895, 147–212. Eyewitness Roman Maksimovich Tsebrikov was translator at Potemkin's field headquarters, handling the French correspondence.

7   Prince de Ligne to Emperor Joseph II, in Ligne, *Mémoires* . . , I, 127–9.

8   Mikhailovskii-Danilevskii and Viskovatov, *Imperator* . . , 2.

9   C. F. P. Masson, *Mémoires secrets sur la Russie pendant les règnes de Catherine II et de Paul Ier* (Paris 1859), 199 fn 1. Masson's scandal-mongerings, first published in 1800, are not entirely reliable.

10 In Russian, *Dezhurnyi Maior* (Duty Major). At this time the Russian army had two grades of major, junior and senior; BdT's promotion after Ochakov was to the junior grade. — *Russkii biograficheskii slovar'* (St. Petersburg 1900), II, 502.

11 L. P. de Ségur, *Mémoires* . . , III, 373.

12 A. G. Brikner, 'Voina Rossii s Shvetsiei v 1788–1799 godakh', *Zhurnal Ministerstva Narodnogo Prosveshcheniia* (St. Petersburg), March 1869, Part CXLII, 122.

13 Ernst Herrmann, *Geschichte des Russischen Staats* (Gotha 1866), Supplementary Volume, 643, quoting Helbig, a Saxon diplomat writing from St. Petersburg.

14 Foreign talent in the Russian navy was as prominent as in the army at this time. Of the foreign admirals serving Catherine in this war, the most able was the British Sir Samuel Greig, the most dashing and daring were Prince Charles de Nassau-Siegen, in charge of the oar-propelled galley fleet, and the American John Paul Jones who, whenever he took command of

a squadron, was faced by a revolt of British junior officers. — Brikner, 'Voina Rossii..', 130.

15 Mikhailovskii-Danilevskii and Viskovatov, *Imperator*.., 3.

16 *Russkii biografischeskii slovar'*, 1900, II, 502.

17 The St. Petersburg Grenadier Regiment had been founded in 1703 in the reign of Peter the Great. Potemkin ordered it to be re-formed and brought up to strength, insisting that only officers having outstanding records recognized by the highest military authorities be allowed to serve in it. The reputation that Barclay had acquired made him one of the first to be chosen.

18 Bartenev, 'Pamiati..', 137.

19 BdT to Auguste von Vermeulen, Grodno, 15 March (O.S.) 1796, BdT Private Correspondence, 1.

20 Mikhailovskii-Danilevskii and Viskovatov, *Imperator*.., 3, quoting Field-Marshal Prince Nicolas Repnin to his adjutant, the future Senator F. P. Liubanovskii: 'I shall no longer be in this world, but my words should be remembered: this general holds out much promise and he will go far.'

CHAPTER IV

CLASH OF EAGLES

1 Prince Adam Czartoryski, *Mémoires et correspondance avec l'Empereur Alexandre Ier* (Paris 1887), I, 370. Cf. Serge Tatistcheff, *Alexandre Ier et Napoléon* (Paris 1891), I, 1–39.

2 Napoleon to Vice-Admiral Villeneuve, Fontainebleau, 16 July (N.S.) 1805, in Napoléon, *Correspondance de Napoléon Ier* (Paris 1863), XI, 19 (item 8985).

3 J. Holland Rose, *William Pitt and the Great War* (London 1912), 529.

4 David G. Chandler, *The Campaigns of Napoleon* (London 1967), 384.

5 A plausible hypothesis has been advanced that the Austrians, in making their plans for the campaign of 1805, did not take into account the Julian calendar then in use in Russia, twelve days behind the Gregorian calendar, and thus miscalculated the date when the Russian troops would reach the Danube valley. — Cf. J. Holland Rose, *The Life of Napoleon* (London 1903), II, 20 fn; Chandler, *The Campaigns*.., 384.

6 General Levin August Gottlieb Count Bennigsen, 'Zapiski Grafa Bennigsena', ed. by L. L. Bennigsen, *Russkaia Starina* (St. Petersburg), Dec. 1896, 499.

7 Philip Longworth, *The Art of Victory: The Life and Achievements of Generalissimo Suvorov, 1729–1800* (London 1965), 285.

8 Aleksandr Shil'der, *Imperator Aleksandr Pervyi: ego zhizn' i tsarstvovanie* (St. Petersburg, 1904–5), II, 155.

9 Mikhail Bragin, *Kutuzov* (Moscow 1970), 87.

10 Czartoryski, *Mémoires*.., II, 122–5. Czartoryski not only showed more common sense than the Tsar but may have had a better historical memory: 105 years before Austerlitz, on the eve of the battle of Narwa, Peter the Great left the camp to avoid embarrassing his commander-in-chief. Five years after Austerlitz, however, Alexander's judgement had somewhat ripened: 'Let us forget that unfortunate battle where we, and I in the first place, did a lot of foolish things.' — Langeron, 'Zapiski grafa Lanzherona o russkom voiske (1796–1825 gg)', *Russkaia Mysl'* (Moscow 1896), XI, 1.

11 Cf. Chandler, *The Campaigns*.., 454–5; Oskar von Lettow-Vorbeck, *Der Krieg von 1806 und 1807* (Berlin 1893), I, 38.

12 Napoléon, *Correspondance*.., XIV, 127 (item 11530); cf. Graf Yorck von Wartenburg, *Napoleon als Feldherr* (Berlin 1904), 287.

13 Sir Robert Wilson, *Brief Remarks on the Character and Composition of the Russian Army and a Sketch of the Campaigns in Poland in the Years 1806 and 1807* (London 1810), 51.

14 The figures are given by Mikhailovskii-Danilevskii, *Opisanie vtoroi voiny Imperatora Aleksandra s Napoleonom v 1806, 1807 godakh* (St. Petersburg 1846), 72, and they accord with the figures cited by the equally authoritative German specialist von Hoepfner (cf. Chandler, *The Campaigns*.., 518). It is curious that Mathieu Dumas, who had no reason to deflate the Russian strength, arrives at a figure of only about 55,000, in *Précis de événements militaires ou essais historiques sur les campagnes de 1799 à 1824* (Paris 1826), XVII, 99. For Buxhoevden's army, Dumas lists a total of only 36,000. On arrival in the field, the Russian Field-Marshal Kamenskii wrote to the Tsar complaining that instead of the 55,000 effectives listed for Buxhoevden's army, he had found only 40,000 (Mikhailovskii-Danilevskii, *Opisanie vtoroi*.., 72).

15 Mikhailovskii-Danilevskii, *Opisanie vtoroi*.., 72 fn (letter in French).

6   Kamenskii to Alexander, 10 Dec. (O.S.) 1807, in Mikhailovskii-Danilevskii, *Opisanie vtoroi* . . , 76.
7   Chandler, *The Campaigns* . . , 525; cf. A. Thiers, *Histoire du Consulat et de l'Empire* (Paris 1847–56), VII, 268.
8   Barclay's report for the Tsar, 15 Dec. (O.S.) 1807, quoted by Mikhailovskii-Danilevskii, *Opisanie vtoroi* . . , 83.
9   The poet and partisan Denis Davydov met Barclay de Tolly in 1806: 'In those days,' he said, 'although his only decorations were the orders of St. George and St. Vladimir, both Fourth Class – for personal courage – and the medal for the storming of Ochakov, Barclay already had the reputation of a brave and accomplished general.' — Quoted by A. N. Kochetkov, *M.B. B-d-T* . . , 7.
10 Mikhailovskii-Danilevskii, *Opisanie vtoroi* . . , 95.
11 Eugen Prinz von Württemberg gives the following eyewitness account of Kamenskii's departure: 'Count Kamenskii left his cart, was helped on to a horse and, facing a grenadier regiment lined up before him, he shouted at the soldiers, "You have been betrayed and sold out. Everything is lost and you would do better to run home — I am running on ahead."' — Lettow-Vorbeck, *Der Krieg* . . , III, 129.
12 Mikhailovskii-Danilevskii, *Opisanie vtoroi* . . , 106.
13 Raymond A. P. J. Montesquiou, duc de Fezensac, *Souvenirs militaires de 1804 à 1814* (Paris 1863), V, 131.
14 Schubert, *Unter* . . , 94–5.
15 Bennigsen, 'Zapiski . .' (Jan. 1897), 107.
16 Mikhailovskii-Danilevskii, *Opisanie vtoroi* . . , 176.
17 Ibid., 178.
18 Ibid., 178–9; cf. Kochetkov, *M.B. B-d-T* . . , 7.
19 Petre, following General E. von Hoepfner, puts Russian losses at over 2,000, and French losses rather higher. — F. Loraine Petre, *Napoleon's Campaign in Poland 1806–7: A Military History of Napoleon's First War with Russia, Verified from Unpublished Official Documents*, new edition with introduction by David G. Chandler (London 1975), 159.
20 General Serge Andolenko, *Aigles de Napoléon contre drapeaux du Tsar* (Paris 1969), 118.
21 Wilson, *Brief Remarks* . . , 95–6.
22 Mikhailovskii-Danilevskii, *Opisanie vtoroi* . . , 182.
33 Report to his king by the Swedish ambassador to St. Petersburg, then Baron Kurt Ludwig von Stedingk: Feld-Maréchal Comte de Stedingk, *Mémoires Posthumes*, ed. by Général Comte de Björnstjerna (Paris 1844), II, 277.
34 Wilson, *Brief Remarks* . . , 93.
35 Ibid., 94.
36 *Russkii biograficheskii slovar'*, II, 502; cf. F. W. v. Weymarn, 'Barklai . .', 176.
37 Bennigsen, 'Zapiski . .' (July 1889), 209.
38 Jomini, quoted by Mikhailovskii-Danilevskii, *Opisanie vtoroi* . . , 205.
39 Mikhailovskii-Danilevskii, *Opisanie vtoroi* . . , 208.
40 Napoleon to Cambacérès, Eylau, 9 Feb. (N.S.) 1807, 1700 hours, in Napoléon, *Correspondance* . . , XIV, 293 (item 11791).
41 Not all Frenchmen agreed with Napoleon: 'The battle of Eylau, which remained indecisive, had thrown Paris into an incredible consternation; the Emperor's enemies could hardly hide the joy this public disaster caused them. Securities took a considerable tumble.' — L. P. E. Bignon, *Histoire de France depuis le 18 brumaire jusqu'à la Paix de Tilsit* (Paris 1830), VI, 147.
42 Dumas, *Précis* . . , XVIII, 39.
43 Napoléon, *Correspondance* . . , XIV, 363–4 (item 11917); cf. Albert Vandal, *Napoléon et Alexandre Ier: l'Alliance russe sous le premier Empire* (Paris 1891–6), I, 37.
44 Fezensac, *Souvenirs* . . , 148–9.
45 Wilson, *Brief Remarks* . . , 53.
46 Madame de Krudener, *Journal de 1806–1808*, quoted in Ley, *Madame de Krüdener* . . , 273–4.
47 Reutern, *Generalleutnant* . . , 24. The physician in question was either Sir James Wylie, a Scottish surgeon who was the Imperial Physician, or one of his three Scottish assistants. Cf. Steuart, *Scottish Influences* . . , 131–2; Alan Palmer, *Alexander I: Tsar of War and Peace* (London 1974), 388–9, fn.

CHAPTER V

MEMEL AND TILSIT: SHADOWS OF THE FUTURE

1   Mikhailovskii-Danilevskii and Viskovatov, *Imperator* . . , 9.

2 *Sbornik Imperatorskogo russkogo istoricheskogo obshchestva* (*SIRIO*), (St. Petersburg 1893), LXXXIX, 8, fn 1.

3 Leopold von Ranke, *Denkwürdigkeiten des Staatskanzlers Fürsten von Hardenberg* (Leipzig 1877), IV, 306.

4 Dumas, *Souvenirs du Lieutenant-Général Comte Mathieu Dumas de 1770 à 1836* (Paris 1839), III, 416–17.

5 Ranke, *Denkwürdigkeiten* . . , IV, 307.

6 *SIRIO*, LXXXIX, 9.

7 Ibid., LXXXIX, 16. This message was delivered by General Popov who was sent by the Tsar to make certain first that there was no other way out. Popov carried Bennigsen's dismissal in his pocket for later delivery and was empowered to name General Essen I as commander-in-chief; the Tsar had not yet received the news that Essen I had been wounded at Friedland.

8 Bennigsen, 'Zapiski . .' (March 1900), 757.

9 Ranke, *Denkwürdigkeiten* . . , III, 360.

10 Rose, *The Life of Napoleon* (London 1903), II, 124.

11 Wilson, *Diaries*, II, 18 June 1897, quoted in Herbert Butterfield, *The Peace Tactics of Napoleon 1806–1808* (Cambridge 1929), 239.

12 Bennigsen, 'Zapiski . .' (March 1900), 752.

13 Alexander to Prince Kurakin, Russian Ambassador to Austria and chief Tilsit negotiator, in *SIRIO*, LXXXIX, 24.

14 Second Report of General von Schladen to Hardenberg, 21 June 1807, in Ranke, *Denkwürdigkeiten* . . , V, 522.

15 Third Report of General von Schladen to Hardenberg, 23 June 1807, in Ranke, *Denkwürdigkeiten* . . , V, 524–5.

16 Butterfield, *Peace Tactics* . . , 239.

17 Bagration to Grand Duke Constantine, 19 June/1 July 1807, in *SIRIO*, LXXXIX, 40.

18 Vandal, 'Notes sur la cour de Russie et St. Petersbourg en 1807 et 1808 par le Général Savary', *Revue d'Histoire Diplomatique* (Paris 1890), III, 402–7; cf. Palmer, *Alexander I* . . , 151.

19 Butterfield, *Peace Tactics* . . , 248–9. Note also that French Marshal Soult warned British diplomat Lord Holland that Bennigsen was plotting to murder the Tsar; cf. Rose, . . *Napoleon*, II, 126, fn 1, quoting Lord Holland, *Foreign Reminiscences*, 185.

20 Shil'der, *Imperator* . . , II, 210. A French historian and diplomat during Napoleon's reign, Edouard Bignon, likewise wrote: 'In certain [English Party] salons the language used was quite unseemly. . . . Frightful prognostications led to fears for Emperor Alexander's very life.' — Bignon, *Histoire* . . , VI, 431.

21 Napoleon's lieutenants busied themselves in all kinds of 'black' operations, trying to counter anti-French feeling and manipulate the Tsar. General Savary supplied Alexander with stories of intercepted assassination threats and incendiary British propaganda supposedly circulating in St. Petersburg. In Paris, Minister of Police Fouché warned the high-ranking Russian prisoner of war there (General Meller-Zakomel'skii) to be on the lookout for anti-Napoleon talk among his fellow prisoners: 'In view of the great intimacy between the two Sovereigns, anyone holding such views must perforce be ill-intentioned towards his Sovereign.' — Ambassador Count Tolstoy to Foreign Minister Count Rumiantsev, Report No. 23, 7/19 Nov. 1807, in *SIRIO*, LXXXIX, 224.

22 Alexander to Catherine, Tilsit, 17 June (O.S.) 1807, in Nicolas Michaïlowitch, *Correspondance* . . , 18.

23 *Denkwürdigkeiten des Bayerischen Staatsministers Grafen von Montgelas* (Stuttgart 1887), quoted in Shil'der's introduction to *SIRIO*, LXXXIX, xxxviii.

24 Vandal, *Napoléon* . . , I, 66.

25 Shil'der's introduction to *SIRIO*, LXXXIX, xxxii.

26 Patricia Kennedy Grimsted, *The Foreign Ministers of Alexander I* (Berkeley, Calif. 1969), 167.

27 Alexander to Catherine, Weimar, 26 Sept. (O.S.) 1808, in Nicolas Michaïlowitch, *Correspondance* . . , 20.

CHAPTER VI

NORTHERN CONQUEST

1 *SIRIO*, LXXXIX, 61–2.

2 Tatistcheff, *Alexandre Ier* . . , 182.

3 Mikhailovskii-Danilevskii, *Opisanie Finliandskoi voiny na sukhom puti i na more v 1808 i 1809 godakh* (St. Petersburg 1841), 78.

4 Tatistcheff, *Alexandre Ier* . . , 382.

5 BdT's Corps consisted of one Jaeger and four line infantry regiments, two battalions of grenadiers, one battalion of Jaeger guards, one regiment of Uhlans, three squadrons of dragoons, 300 Cossacks, and one company of artillery guards. — Mikhailovskii-Danilevskii, *Opisanie Finliandskoi* . . , 113.

6 Ibid., 163.

7 Although no quarter was given in this war, certain civilities were practised. For instance, on departure from Kuopio, Sandels left some of his own soldiers behind to keep guard over the local prison, with a notice saying he was turning the inmates over to the Russians and expected the Russian commander to send back the Swedish guards. BdT promptly dispatched them to Sandels and put his own guards in their place. — F. Bulgarin, *Sochineniia* (St. Petersburg 1830), I, 197, quoted by M. Borodkin, *Istoriia Finliandii: vremia Imperatora Aleksandra I* (St. Petersburg 1909), 215.

8 Mikhailovskii-Danilevskii and Viskovatov, *Imperator* . . , 14.

9 Caulaincourt to Napoleon, Report No. 35, 29 May 1808, in Tatistcheff, *Alexandre Ier* . . , 411.

10 Borodkin, *Istoriia Finliandii* . . , 132, quotes a Finnish specialist who points out that these Finnish victories all happened when the Russians were outnumbered.

11 Borodkin, *Istoriia Finliandii* . . , 194. Borodkin gives no date for this consultation, but it must have taken place in early April 1808. He quotes BdT's reply as coming from his 'journal'. This journal, if it existed, has not been traced and this quotation from it seems to be unique.

12 Borodkin, *Istoriia Finliandii* . . , 194.

13 Ibid., 195.

14 Mikhailovskii-Danilevskii, *Opisanie Finliandskoi* . . , 358.

15 Borodkin, *Istoriia Finliandii* . . , 197–8. For the crossing of the Kvarken, besides Borodkin, see also Mikhailovskii-Danilevskii, *Opisanie Finliandskoi* . . , 396–408; Bulgarin, *Sochineniia*, I, 180–200; and General B. M. von Berg, 'Furst Barclay de Tollys tåg öfver Bottniska viken 1809', *Svensk Militär Tidskrift* (Stockholm 1914), 195–9: a Swedish translation of the posthumous memoirs of General von Berg, 1764–1838. F. Bulgarin, 1789–1859, was a twenty-year-old officer at the time of the crossing; his account appeared in 1830. Berg's and Bulgarin's accounts are almost identical, word-for-word, but without the original Berg (which I have been unable to obtain; an English translation of key passages of the Swedish was made for me) there is insufficient evidence for a sure judgement as to who is copying whom, though the background knowledge, for example of Arakcheev's message to BdT, suggests authorship by the older, higher-ranking Berg. In any case the descriptions are so vivid that the temptation to copy is fully understandable.

16 BdT to Auguste von Vermeulen, Vasa, 27 April (O.S.) 1809, BdT Private Correspondence, 2.

17 Berg, 'Furst Barclay de Tollys tåg . .', 196–7.

18 Ibid., 197.

19 Ibid., 198.

20 Mikhailovskii-Danilevskii, *Opisanie Finliandskoi* . . , 402.

21 Ibid., 405: BdT to General Knorring, Report No. 39, 11 March (O.S.) 1809.

22 Ibid.

23 Mikhailovskii-Danilevskii, *Opisanie Finliandskoi* . . , 407.

24 Ibid., 407: BdT to General Knorring, Report No. 41, 14 March (O.S.) 1809.

25 Ibid., 407: BdT to General Knorring, Report No. 43, 19 March (O.S.) 1809.

26 BdT to Auguste von Vermeulen, Vasa, 27 April (O.S.) 1809, BdT Private Correspondence, 2.

27 Bulgarin, *Sochineniia*, I, 200.

28 Viskovatov in Mikhailovskii-Danilevskii and Viskovatov, *Imperator* . . , 21.

29 Cf. Päiviö Tommila, *La Finlande dans la politique européenne en 1809–1815* (Helsinki 1962), 32.

30 Mikhailovskii-Danilevskii, *Opisanie Finliandskoi* . . , 424–5; Michael Jenkins, *Arakcheev: Grand Vizier of the Russian Empire* (London 1970), 123–4.

31 *Russkii biograficheskii slovar'*, II, 51; Robert Werlich, *Russian Orders, Decorations and Medals* (Washington 1968), 4–6.

32 Marc Raeff, *Michael Speransky: Statesman of Imperial Russia, 1772–1839* (The Hague 1969), 186.

33 Shil'der, *Imperator* . . , II, 239.

34 BdT to Alexander, 12 May (O.S.) 1809, quoted in F. V. v. Weymarn, 'Barklai-. . .', 178.

35 Ibid.

36 Mikhailovskii-Danilevskii and Viskovatov, *Imperator* . . , 21.

37 Ibid.

38 F. W. v. Weymarn, 'Barklai-. . .', 179, fn.

CHAPTER VII

FIRST IN FINLAND

1 Cf. Sprengporten to BdT, 14 June (O.S.) 1809, in State Archives of Finland (Helsinki), folder KKK-Da7.

2 Mikhailovskii-Danilevskii, *Opisanie Finliandskoi* . . , 439, citing BdT's order, No. 66, to Count Shuvalov, 22 May (O.S.) 1809.

3 Ibid., 446, citing BdT's report to the Tsar, No. 72, 27 May (O.S.) 1809.

4 Ibid., 458. Proving that, despite the ceasefire, St. Petersburg nevertheless brooked no signs of weakness in the field, the Tsar a few days later threatened General Alekseev with a court-martial if ever he let Umeå go without defending it to the last man. — Ibid., 454, citing Arkacheev's order to Alekseev, No. 139, 29 June (O.S.) 1809.

5 Ibid., 499, citing Captain E. P. Brenton, *The Naval History of Great Britain from the Year MDCCLXXXIII to MDCCCXXII* (London 1823–5).

6 Ibid., 485.

7 Ibid., 486.

8 The conference table had been set up at Frederikshamn and BdT was told to bar Stedingk's route at that point in order to prevent his going on to St. Petersburg where he would have found many sympathizers from his days at court.

9 Borodkin, *Istoriia Finliandii* . . , 279, citing Stedingk's dispatch, 16 Aug. (N.S.) 1809.

10 Ibid., 277, citing Skjöldebrand on Caulaincourt.

11 Prince S. G. Volkonskii, *Zapiski* (St. Petersburg 1902), 73.

12 Borodkin, *Istorii Finliandii* . . , 392, quoting from the papers of David Alopaeus.

13 Tatistcheff, *Alexandre Ier* . . , 381, citing Caulaincourt's 27th report to Napoleon, 4 April (N.S.) 1808, and letter of 5 April (N.S.) 1808.

14 Mikhailovskii-Danilevskii, *Opisanie Finliandskoi* . . , 25.

15 J. Rich. Danielson, *Finland's Union with the Russian Empire: with Reference to K. Ordin's Work 'Finland's Subjugation'* (Borgå 1891), 157.

16 The Order of St. Alexander Nevsky, of one class only, was Russia's third highest, after the Orders of St. Andrew and St. Catherine. The latter, for ladies only, was given to Auguste immediately after the Kvarken crossing. The Tsar's citation spoke of BdT's 'great contribution to the successful conclusion of the difficult campaign and for his having displayed sound judgement in the command of the armies entrusted to him'. — Mikhailovskii-Danilevskii and Viskovatov, *Imperator* . . , 25.

17 Borodkin, *Istorii Finliandii* . . , 267.

18 General von Weymarn, writing during the repressive reign of Nicolas II, found 'liberal principles' inconsistent with BdT's 'stoic character', and concluded that this suspect dedication implied no more than 'an esteem for human dignity and human rights' – as if such esteem in itself were not a rarity, especially in those wielding power. Weymarn conceded that his ancestor, BdT, favoured reforms when necessary 'to achieve a greater degree of perfection', and in this sense 'BdT was indeed a liberal, as he was to prove not only in his dealings with others but also in his approach to the administrative problems he faced'.— F. W. v. Weymarn, 'Barklai . .', 179.

19 Cf. Raeff, . . *Speransky*, 70–5.

20 K. Ordin, *Pokorenie Finliandii* (St. Petersburg 1889), II, Appendix 116, 131–2 (Archives of the Ministry of Foreign Affairs, *Affaires finlandaises, Camp. Suédoise 1809, ad. 28: Correspondance Speransky et Barclay de Tolly*), BdT memorandum to Speranskii, No. 134, Borgå, 28 June (O.S.) 1809.

21 Ibid., II, 132.

22 Ibid., II, 133.

23 Ibid., II, 130–4.

24 Ibid., II, 411.

25 Ibid., II, 131.

26 Ibid., II, Appendix 117, 134: BdT to Speranskii (no number), Åbo, 23 July (O.S.) 1809.

27 *SIRIO*, XXI (1877), 456.

28 State Archives of Finland, folder KKK Eb3: Speranskii to BdT, No. 176, St. Petersburg, 7 Aug. (O.S.) 1809.

29 Ibid.

30 Borodkin, *Istorii Finliandii* . . , 303.

31 Ibid.

32 Ibid., 304.

33 Ibid.

34 Senate Archives (Helsinki), Kejserliga Regerings Conseillens, Ekonomie Departements

Protocoller för år 1809, minutes of 29 Nov. (O.S.) 1809.

5 Tommila, *La Finlande* . . , 119–20.

6 Senate Archives (Helsinki), Kejserliga . . , minutes of 29 Nov. (O.S.) 1809.

7 Ibid., minutes of 1 Dec. (O.S.) 1809; State Archives of Finland, folder KKK Da7.

8 State Archives of Finland, folder KKK Eb3.

9 Ibid., Speranskii to BdT, No. 264, 19 Sept. (O.S.) 1809; Speranskii to BdT, No. 20, 12 Jan. (O.S.) 1810.

10 Reutern, *Generalleutnant* . . , 27.

CHAPTER VIII
MINISTER OF WAR

Archives du Ministère des Affaires étrangères (Paris), Correspondance Politique – Russie (1810), Vol. CL, item 226, report of 17 Jan. (N.S.) 1810.

The Ministry of Military Ground Forces (*Ministerstvo Voenno Sukhoputnykh Sil*) was so named in 1802 and was re-titled War Ministry (*Voennoe Ministerstvo*) only after the end of the Napoleonic wars. The title of War Minister, however, was introduced in June 1808 under Arakcheev; cf. Amburger, *Geschichte der Behördenorganisation Russlands von Peter dem Grossen bis 1917* (Leiden 1966), 295.

Cf. S. Mel'gunov, *Dela i liudi Alexandrovskogo vremeni* (Berlin 1923), 121.

Michael T. Florinsky, *Russia: A History and Interpretation* (New York 1953), II, 648.

Prince Peter Volkonskii, although not an especially able man, was a lifelong friend of the Tsar and had been concerned with Quartermaster duties throughout his military career. After Tilsit he spent two years in France at Napoleon's invitation, familiarizing himself with French army tactics and the functioning of the French General Staff.

P. A. Zhilin, *Gibel' Napoleonovskoi armii v Rossii* (2nd edn., Moscow 1974), 92.

Kochetkov, *M.B. B-d-T* . . , 13.

'Mémoire du Ministre de la guerre Barclay de Tolly, présenté à l'Empereur Alexandre Ier, au sujet de la protection des frontières occidentales de la Russie', *La Guerre Nationale de 1812: Publication du Comité scientifique du Grand État-Major russe* (French edition, Paris c. 1902), I, Pt 2, 15–21. Marginal notation: 'Read to His Majesty, 11 February 1810', and at the end: 'Read to His Majesty 2 March 1810'.

9 Zhilin, *Gibel'* . . , 95.

10 Secret report of 13 Nov. (O.S.) 1810, in *La Guerre Nationale* . . , I, Pt 2, 346.

11 BdT to Count Rumiantsev, 18 Aug. (O.S.) 1810, in *La Guerre Nationale* . . , I, Pt 1, 130.

12 Ibid., L, Pt 1, 129.

13 Grimsted, *Foreign Ministers* . . , 187.

14 *La Guerre Nationale* . . , I, Pt 1, 134.

15 Cf. Colonel D. P. Buturlin [Boutourlin], *Histoire militaire de la campagne de Russie en 1812* (St. Petersburg/Paris 1824), I, 57 ff.

16 Cf. Toll, *Denkwürdigkeiten* . . , I, 280–1.

17 Cf. L. O. Rakovskii, *Kutuzov* (Leningrad 1971), 230.

18 BdT to Alexander, Vilna, 9 April (O.S.) 1812, in F. W. v. Weymarn, 'Barklai- . .' (Aug. 1912), 203.

19 Wilson, *Brief Remarks* . . , 2, fn.

20 Richard Pipes, *Russia under the Old Regime* (London 1974), 122.

21 Foot soldiers were allotted to the following units: 6 imperial guard regiments, 14 grenadier regiments, 100 line infantry regiments, 50 Jaeger or light cavalry regiments, and 4 miscellaneous battalions.

22 Chandler, *The Campaigns* . . , 749.

23 Cavalrymen were allocated to 28 guard squadrons (6 regiments), 40 cuirassier squadrons (8 regiments), 180 dragoon squadrons (36 regiments), and 50 Uhlan squadrons (5 regiments).

24 Main sources for Russian armed forces figures are Buturlin, *Histoire militaire* . . , 55 ff.; F. W. v. Weymarn, 'Barklai- . .' (Aug. 1912), 189; Chandler, *The Campaigns* . . , 749; *Istoriia voennogo iskusstva* (Moscow 1966), I, 137. Figures are not always entirely reliable and sometimes represent paper rather than real effectives: not all units were brought up to strength. Figures for the Grande Armée are from Chandler's tables, *The Campaigns* . . , 1108 ff.

25 Edward A. Whitcomb, 'The Duties and Functions of Napoleon's External Agents', *History* (London), June 1972, 190.

26 *La Guerre Nationale* . . , I, Pt 2, 332, 339, 368–89, 414–22.

27 Ibid., I, Pt 1, 147−9, 154−5. See also *SIRIO*, XXI (1877), 258.

28 'Exposé du Procureur-général dans l'Affaire Michel', 21 April 1812, Archives Nationales (Paris), BB-3-145, Dossier A 4 2296.

29 *La Guerre Nationale* . . , I, Pt 1, 180.

30 Cf. Zhilin, *Gibel'* . . , 94, and Pipes, *Russia under* . . , 120.

31 *La Guerre Nationale* . . , I, Pt 2, 28. The Tsar's handwritten approval of these proposals read, 'Qu'il en soit ainsi' (So be it).

32 BdT to Lt.-Gen. Steinheil (BdT's successor in Finland), 9 June (O.S.) 1810, *La Guerre Nationale* . . , I, Pt 1, 93.

33 Ibid., 94.

34 Ibid.

35 BdT to the Marquis de Traversay, Admiral in command of the Baltic fleet and bases, 15 and 23 July (O.S.) 1810, *La Guerre Nationale* . . , I, Pt 1, 116, 123.

36 Mel'gunov, 'Barklai-de-Tolli i Bagration', *Otechestvennaia voina i russkoe obshchestvo* (St. Petersburg 1912), III, 91, quoting Mikhail Fonvizin.

37 Bignon, *Exposé Comparatif de l'État financier, militaire, politique et moral de la France et des principales puissances de l'Europe* (Paris 1814), 125.

38 Wilson, *Brief Remarks* . . , 22.

39 F. W. v. Weymarn, 'Barklai- . .' (Aug. 1912), 180−1.

40 Lt.-Col. Diebitsch to BdT, Dünaburg, 9 May (O.S.) 1810, *La Guerre Nationale* . . , I, Pt 2, 131.

41 Fonds Caulaincourt, Archives Nationales (Paris), 95 AP, No. 10, Dossier 18.

42 Mel'gunov, *Dela* . . , 121.

43 BdT to Auguste, St. Petersburg, 17 June (O.S.) 1811, BdT Private Correspondence, 3. Cf. above, Chapter II, 12−13.

44 Mikhail Magnitskii was a close friend and collaborator of Speranskii, whose ruin he unintentionally helped bring about by boastings and indiscretions. At the age of forty he turned fanatically obscurantist, and has gone down in Russian history as the 'wrecker' of Kazan University.

45 The Russian title: *Uchrezhdenie dlia upravleniia bol'shoi deistvuiushchei armii* (St. Petersburg 1812).

46 Schubert, *Unter* . . , 194−5.

47 'Uchrezhdenie dlia upravleniia bol'shoi deistvuiushchei armii', *Voenno-istoricheskii Zhurnal*, organ of the Ministry of Defence of the USSR (Moscow), Jan. 1962, 128.

48 Colonel (ret.) G. Os'kin, 'Vozniknovenie i razvitie sluzhby general'nogo shtaba v russkoi armii', *Voenno-istoricheskii Zhurnal* 3, March 1969, 96−7.

49 The seven departments were: Artillery, Engineers, Inspector General, Audits, Commissariat, Supplies, Medical. Special departments and services included the Quartermaster-General (forerunner of the General Staff) and the new Military Science Committee (*Voenno-Uchenyi Komitet*).

50 C. M. Woodhouse, *Capodistria: The Founder of Greek Independence* (London 1973), 74.

51 Rudolf Ibbeken, *Preussen 1807–1813* (Cologne 1970), 236.

52 Cf. ibid. The idea of a German Legion followed that of the *Tugendbund*, a league founded in 1808 by Prussian officers, functionaries, scholars, clergymen, etc. The *Tugendbund*, though (officially) short-lived, was the begetter of Prussian patriotism. Constantin de Grunwald's assertion that among the Russian officers who joined the league was BdT's son would seem to be erroneous: in 1810 when the league was dissolved by decree of the King, Magnus was twelve years old. It is not impossible, however, that BdT's nephew Andreas was a member. — Cf. Constantin de Grunwald, *Stein: L'Ennemi de Napoléon* (Paris 1936), 155, fn 2.

53 Cf. Kochetkov, *M.B. B-d-T-* . . , 14.

54 Even after Napoleon entered Moscow, the Tsar continued to promise Prussia and Austria that he would do everything in his power to see that they regained their independence. — Ibbeken, *Preussen* . . , 359.

55 Ludwig Freiherr von Wolzogen, *Memoiren des könig. preuss. Generals der Infanterie Ludwig Freiherrn von Wolzogen* (in *1807−14 in russischen Diensten*) (Leipzig 1851), Annexes 3−10.

56 Ibid.

57 V. V. Pugachev, 'K voprosu o pervonachal'-nom plane voiny 1812 goda', in *1812 god: k stoptiatidesiatiletiiu otechestvennoi voiny: sbornik stat'ei* (Moscow 1962), 34 and 43.

58 Wolzogen, *Memoiren* . . , Annex 1, v ff.

59 Friedrich von Smitt, *Aufklärung über den Krieg von 1812* (Leipzig 1861), 306; cf. 288 ff. for proposals.

60 Ranke, *Denkwürdigkeiten* . . , IV, 306; Général Armand de Caulaincourt, *Mémoires du Général*

de Caulaincourt, Duc de Vicence, Grand Ecuyer de l'Empereur, ed. Jean Hanoteau (Paris 1933), I, 291–3.

1 Caulaincourt, *Mémoires* . . , I, 293.

2 Ibid., 292.

3 BdT's wife acquired Beckhof in 1810 from her brother, Lt.-Col. Erich von Smitten, for the sum of 65,000 rubles, the price he had paid for it in 1805 to their elder brother, Heinrich von Smitten. Its value had been rising steadily – in 1763 it had been worth only 12,000 rubles, according to Stryk, *Beiträge* . . , 352–3 – though inflation accounted for some of the increase. (P. A. Viskovatyi, 'Fel'dmarshal Barklai-de-Tolli: k ego biografii', *Russkaia Starina*, Oct. 1888, 362–3, errs in stating that BdT's wife brought him Beckhof as her dowry.) Beckhof was on the Embach river in central Livonia, the part which is now southern Estonia.

A. C. v. Weymarn, *Erinnerungen* . . , 4.

Loewenstern, *Mémoires du Général-Major russe Baron de Löwenstern, 1776–1858*, 'published from the original manuscript and annotated by M. H. Weil' (Paris 1903), I, Pt 3, 167.

Otechestvennaia voina 1812 goda. Feb. 1812, archives published by the Scientific Committee of the Russian General Staff (St. Petersburg 1907, 1908) (= *La Guerre Nationale* . .), 410–17.

Ibid., March 1812, 91.

Barthold Georg Niebuhr to Dore Hensler, 21 April (N.S.) 1812 (the same day Niebuhr dined with Dumas), in *Die Briefe Barthold Georg Niebuhrs*, ed. D. Gerhard and W. Norwin (Berlin 1926), II, 264–5.

Dumas, *Souvenirs* . . , III, 416–17.

Niebuhr, *Die Briefe* . . , II, 264–5.

Dumas, *Souvenirs* . . , III, 416–17.

Schubert, *Unter* . . , 94.

L. G. Beskrovnyi, *Otechestvennaia voina 1812 goda* (Moscow 1962), 179.

CHAPTER IX

RETREAT

BdT to Alexander, 28 March (O.S.) 1812, cited by F. W. v. Weymarn, 'Barklai- . .', Sept. 1912, 309.

2 Ibid., 310.

3 Alexander to BdT (in his own hand), in *Russkii Arkhiv* (St. Petersburg 1892), I, 343, cited in Zhilin, *Gibel'* . . , 98.

4 Ibid.

5 Beskrovnyi, *Otechestvennaia* . . , 177.

6 Chandler, *The Campaigns* . . , 114.

7 Cf. Pugachev, 'K voprosu . .', 40.

8 Schubert, *Unter* . . , 216.

9 Cited in E. Tarlé, *La Campagne de Russie 1812* (Paris 1950), 18, trans. by Marc Slonim from the Russian edition, *Nashestvie Napoleona na Rossiiu – 1812 god* (Moscow 1936).

10 Pugachev, 'K voprosu . .', 41. He cites BdT to Wittgenstein, Tormassov, Bagration, and Platov, in TsG'VIA (Central State Military History Archives of the USSR).

11 Ibid., 41.

12 Beskrovnyi, *Otechestvennaia* . . , 179.

13 *Listovki otechestvennoi voiny 1812 goda: sbornik dokumentov* (Moscow 1962), 21.

14 Prince Clemens de Metternich, *Mémoires, documents et écrits divers laissés par le Prince de Metternich*, ed. by his son (Paris 1880), I, 122.

15 Napoleon, *Lettres inédites de Napoléon Ier à Marie-Louise: écrites de 1810 à 1814* (Paris 1935), 28: 30 May (N.S.) 1812.

16 Caulaincourt, *Mémoires* . . , I, 346.

17 Cf. Wolzogen, *Memoiren* . . , 99–100; cf. Loewenstern, 'Zapiski', Nov. 1900, 335–6.

18 Balashov's account of Napoleon's tirade, dated 29 Dec. (O.S.) 1836 and conserved in Scientific and Military Archives, Leningrad, is cited in Tarlé, *La Campagne* . . , 54. Balashov wrote his account almost a quarter of a century after the event and his reproduction of Napoleon's words cannot be taken as reliable, but no other testimony exists for his conversations with Napoleon.

19 Tarlé, *La Campagne* . . , 65, citing material from Archives of Headquarters (Vilna 1903), II, 46–7.

20 Pugachev, 'K voprosu . .', 44–5.

21 Paulucci, a native of Piedmont, was a protégé of Joseph de Maistre, the Sardinian ambassador at St. Petersburg, distinguished chiefly for his philosophical defence of political reaction.

22 In J. F. Baddeley, *The Russian Conquest of the Caucasus* (London 1908), 97, cited in Glynn Barratt, *The Rebel on the Bridge: A Life of the Decembrist Baron Andrey Rozen 1800–84* (London 1975), 171.

23 Alexander to BdT, Sventsiany, 16 June (O.S.) 1812, in V. I. Kharkevich, ed., 'Perepiska Imperatora Aleksandra i Barklaia-de-Tolli ot nachala voennykh deistvij do ot'ezda Gosudaria iz armii', *Voennyi Sbornik* (St. Petersburg), April 1906, 222.

24 Wilson, *Brief Remarks* . . , 47–8.

25 Alexander to BdT, Drissa, 26 June (O.S.) 1812, in Kharkevich, ed., 'Perepiska . .', June 1906, 231–2.

26 BdT to Auguste, Belmonte, 26 June (O.S.) 1812, BdT Private Correspondence, 16.

27 Carl von Clausewitz, *Der Feldzug von 1812 in Russland, der Feldzug von 1813 bis zum Waffenstillstand und der Feldzug von 1814 in Frankreich* (Berlin 1835), 29.

28 Tarlé, *Napoléon* (third French edition, Moscow, sd), 365.

29 W. G. F. Jackson, *Seven Roads to Moscow* (London 1957), 101.

30 Alexander to BdT, Sventsiany, 17 June (O.S.) 1812, in Kharkevich, ed., 'Perepiska . .', April 1906, 224.

31 BdT to Alexander, Bojarelli, 17 June (O.S.) 1812, in Kharkevich, ed., 'Perepiska . .', March 1906, 194.

32 BdT to Alexander, Belmonte, 25 June (O.S.) 1812, and Alexander to BdT, Drissa, 26 June (O.S.) 1812, ibid., June 1906, 230, 233.

33 BdT to Alexander, Belmonte, 25 June (O.S.) 1812, ibid., 230.

34 Ibid.

35 Clausewitz, *Der Feldzug* . . , 33.

36 Caulaincourt, *Mémoires* . . , I, 253.

37 Alexander to BdT, Drissa, 26 June (O.S.) 1812, in Kharkevich, ed., 'Perepiska . .', June 1906, 233–4.

38 Bagration to Arakcheev, 26 June (O.S.) 1812, cited in Tarlé, *La Campagne* . . , 77.

39 Bagration to Arakcheev (sl, sd [June 1812]) in General Petr Ivanovich Prince Bagration, *General Bagration: Sbornik dokumentov i materialov* (Leningrad 1945), 190.

40 Mikhailovskii-Danilevskii and Viskovatov, *Imperator* . . , 9.

41 BdT to wife, Drissa, 28 June (O.S.) 1812, BdT Personal Correspondence, 17.

42 Ibid.

43 Cf. *Listovki* . . , 5, based on TsGVIA (Central State Military History Archives), Fond VUA. The professors were Andrei S. Kaisarov (Russian Language and Literature) and Fedor E. Rambach (Political Economy).

44 Kochetkov, *M.B. B-d-T-* . . , 23.

45 Archives Nationales (Paris), 95 AP, Fonds Caulaincourt, No. 12, dossier 30.

46 Ibid.

47 Cf. Ibbeken, *Preussen* . . , 349–50. The Russo-German Legion began to gather momentum towards the end of the Russian campaign. In November 1812 it was 4,000-strong and stationed in Finland. It was finally absorbed by the Prussian army in April 1814.

48 Bagration to Alexander, 1 July (O.S.) 1812, in Bagration, . . *Sbornik dokumentov* . . , 187–8.

49 Bagration to Ermolov, 3 July (O.S.) 1812, in Tarlé, *La Campagne* . . , 78.

50 BdT's 'disdain for personal comfort was very great and any quarters would do as long as it kept him close to the army.' — Loewenstern, 'Zapiski', Nov. 1900, 351.

51 Catherine to Alexander, sl, sd [June (O.S.) 1812], in Nicolas Michaïlowitch, *Correspondance* . . , 76.

52 Kharkevich, *Barklai-de-Tolli v otechestvennuiu voinu: posle soedineniia armii pod Smolenskom*, with an Appendix of 20 letters exchanged between BdT and Alexander (St. Petersburg 1904), 6 and fn 2.

53 Bagration to Rostopchin, 14 Aug. (O.S.) 1812, in N. F. Dubrovin, *Otechestvennaia voina v pis'makh sovremennikov* (1812–1815 gg.), prilozhenie k XLIII tomu Zapisok imp. Akademii nauk, No. 1 (St. Petersburg 1882), 98.

54 Loewenstern, 'Zapiski', Nov. 1900, 351.

55 Alexander to BdT, St. Petersburg, 28 July (O.S.) 1812, in Kharkevich, *B-d-T* . . , Appendix No. 5, 12.

56 Bagration to Rostopchin, 'end of July' (O.S.) 1812, in Dubrovin, *Otechestvennaia* . . , 72.

57 BdT to Alexander, 12 July (O.S.) 1812, referred to in Kharkevich, *B-d-T* . . , 7.

58 Napoleon to Berthier, 6 and 15 July (N.S.) 1812, in Napoleon, *Correspondance*, XXIV, 23 and 63.

59 Général Antoine Henri Baron de Jomini, *Précis politique et militaire des campagnes de 1812 à 1814* (Lausanne 1886), I, 72. The Swiss Jomini fought the 1812 campaign as a brigadier-general in the French army. He changed sides and went over to the Russians only in August 1813.

60 Buturlin, *Histoire militaire* . . , I, 230.

BdT to Auguste, sl, 9 July (O.S.) 1812, BdT Private Correspondence, 18.

Clausewitz, *Der Feldzug* . . , 109.

Cf. Wolzogen, *Memoiren* . . , 109.

BdT to Bagration, 13 July (O.S.) 1812, in Toll, *Denkwürdigkeiten* . . , I, 358–9.

V. Glinka and A. Pomarnatsky, *Voiennaia galereia Zimnego Dvortsa* (Leningrad 1974), 137.

BdT, (I) 'Izobrazhenie voennykh deistvii pervoi armii v 1812 godu', *Chteniia v Imp. obshchestve istorii i drevnostei rossiiskiikh pri Moskovskom universete*, No. 4 (St. Petersburg 1859), 6.

Clausewitz, *Der Feldzug* . . , 109.

Cf. Wolzogen, *Memoiren* . . , 109–12.

Chandler, *The Campaigns* . . , 779.

Caulaincourt, *Mémoires* . . , I, 369.

Eugène Labaume, *The Campaign in Russia* (4th edn., London 1815), trans. by Edmund Boyce, 43. .

BdT to Alexander, Poreche, 18 July (O.S.) 1812, in Kharkevich, *B-d-T-* . . , Appendix No. 3, 6.

BdT, 'Opravdanie v deistviiakh ego vo vremia Otechestvennoi voiny s frantsuzami v 1812 godu', *Zhurnal Imperatorskogo Russkogo voenno-istoricheskogo obshchestva*, VI, Book 1 (St. Petersburg 1911).

BdT to Alexander, Krasnaia, 11 Sept. (O.S.) 1812, in Kharkevich, *B-d-T-* . . , Appendix No. 13, 30.

Caulaincourt, *Mémoires* . . , I, 293. 'Kamchatka' was a manner of speaking, as a Westerner might say 'Timbuktu'.

Napoleon, *Vie Politique et Militaire de Napoléon raconté par Lui-Même au Tribunal de César, d'Alexandre et de Frédéric* (Paris 1827), IV, 69.

Cf. Smitt, *Aufklärung* . . , 65–6. Smitt is the only author I have come across who confirms this interpretation.

CHAPTER X

'ALL BARK AND NO BITE'

1 Loewenstern, 'Zapiski', Nov. 1900, 358. Loewenstern takes credit for stage-managing the meeting with Bagration.

2 BdT to Bagration, Kholm, 19 July (O.S.) 1812, in his own hand in Russian, in BdT, (I) 'Izobrazhenie . . ', 53–5.

3 Bagration to Alexander, Smolensk, 23 July (O.S.) 1812, in Bagration, . . *Sbornik dokumentov* . . , 219.

4 BdT to Alexander, Smolensk, 22 July (O.S.) 1812, in Kharkevich, *B-d-T* . . , Appendix No. 4, 10.

5 Alexander to BdT, St. Petersburg, 28 July (O.S.) 1812, ibid., Appendix No. 5, 12.

6 *Otechestvennaia voina 1812 goda: sbornik dokumentov i materialov* (Leningrad/Moscow 1941), 42.

7 BdT to Alexander, Smolensk, 22 July (O.S.) 1812, in Kharkevich, *B-d-T* . . , Appendix No. 4, 10.

8 Cf. Wolzogen, *Memoiren* . . , 115–18; M. I. Bogdanovich, *Istoriia otechestvennoi voiny 1812 goda* (St. Petersburg 1859), I, 226–7; Kochetkov, *M.B. B-d-T-*, 35.

9 Général Georges Marquis de Chambray, *Oeuvres: Histoire de l'expédition de Russie* (Paris 1839), I, 294.

10 Loewenstern, *Denkwürdigkeiten eines Livländers: Aus den Jahren 1790–1815*, ed. Friedrich von Smitt (Leipzig 1858), I, 189.

11 BdT to Alexander, Smolensk, 22 July (O.S.) 1812, and Alexander to BdT, St. Petersburg, 28 July (O.S.) 1812, in Kharkevich, *B-d-T* . . , Appendix No. 4, 10, and Appendix No. 5, 13.

12 Bogdanovich, *Istoriia* . . , I, 233.

13 Clausewitz, *Der Feldzug* . . , 131.

14 Tarlé, *Nashestvie* . . , 473. Another German ridiculed Russia's continuing lavishness with medals: 'Although I have done nothing worthwhile I am nevertheless already a Knight of the Order of Vladimir.' — Clausewitz to wife, 30 Sept. (N.S.) 1812, in *Karl und Marie von Clausewitz: Ein Lebensbild in Briefen und Tagebuchblättern*, ed. Karl Linnebach (Berlin 1916), 297.

15 Cf. Wolzogen, *Memoiren* . . , 118–20.

16 BdT, (I) 'Izobrazhenie . .', 11.

17 Ibid., 12.

18 Cf. Loewenstern, 'Zapiski', Dec. 1900, 555.

19 Bagration to Arakcheev, 29 July (O.S.) 1812, in Bagration, . . *Sbornik dokumentov* . . , 226.

20 BdT to Bagration, 29 July (O.S.) 1812, in Bogdanovich, *Istoriia* . . , I, 237 and fn 19.

21 Cf. Tarlé, *Nashestvie* . . , 473. I am indebted to

Alan Palmer for the punning equivalent in English: *Napoleon in Russia* (London 1967), 57.

22   Cf. Clausewitz, *Der Feldzug* . . , 114–17.

23   BdT to Auguste (en route from Smolensk to Rudnia), 27 July (O.S.) 1812, BdT Private Correspondence, 20.

24   Bagration to BdT, Vydra, 30 July (O.S.) 1812, in Bagration, . . *Sbornik dokumentov* . . , 226–7.

25   Général Philippe-Paul Comte de Ségur, *Histoire de Napoléon et de la Grande Armée pendant l'année 1812* (Paris 1826), II, 254.

26   BdT, (I) 'Izobrazhenie . .', 16.

27   Yorck von Wartenburg, *Napoleon* . . , part II, 131.

28   Napoleon, *Napoléon, recueil . . . de ses lettres . . . , discours . . . formant une histoire de son règne*, ed. Jean Kermoysan (Paris 1857), II, 541: Treizième bulletin de la Grande Armée, Smolensk, 21 Aug. (N.S.) 1812.

29   Alexander to BdT, St. Petersburg, 28 July (O.S.) 1812, and BdT to Alexander, Korovina, 9 Aug. (O.S.) 1812, in Kharkevich, *B-d-T* . . , Appendix No. 5, 12, and Appendix No. 8, 17.

30   Cf. Wilson, *Narrative of Events during the Invasion of Russia by Napoleon Bonaparte, and the Retreat of the French Army, 1812*, ed. Rev. Herbert Randolph (London 1860), 105; Bogdanovich, *Istoriia* . . , I, 530.

31   Alexander to BdT, rescript, St. Petersburg, 30 July (O.S.) 1812, in Dubrovin, *Otechestvennaia* . . , 67.

32   Chandler, *The Campaigns* . . , 786. As usual, both sides maximized the other's losses and minimized their own. Napoleon claimed 4,500 Russian dead, 7,000 to 8,000 wounded, and 2,000 prisoners, as against 700 (sic) French dead and 3,100 or 3,200 wounded. The Russians estimated that the French had lost 8,000 to 10,000 men as against 4,000 of their own – though exaggeration-prone Bagration (who was not there) spoke of 20,000 French casualties and less than half of this for the Russians, figures which the Soviet military expert and historian Zhilin surprisingly makes his own.

33   Eugen Prinz von Württemberg, *Aus dem Leben des Kaiserlich Russischen Generals der Infanterie, Prinzen Eugen von Württemberg*, ed. Freiherr von Helldorf (Berlin 1861), part II, 19.

34   Cf. BdT, (I) 'Izobrazhenie . .', 17–19.

35   Chandler, *The Campaigns* . . , 789.

36   Bagration to BdT, from a coaching inn near Smolensk, 5 Aug. (O.S.) 1812, in Dubrovin, *Otechestvennaia* . . , 82.

37   Kharkevich, *B-d-T* . . , 13.

38   Wilson, *Narrative* . . , 105.

39   Wilson, *General Wilson's Journal, 1812–1814*, ed. Antony Brett-James (London 1964), 28, fn.

40   Cf. BdT, (I) 'Izobrazhenie . .', 19; Toll, *Denkwürdigkeiten* . . , I, 416–17; F. W. v. Weymarn, 'Barklai-..', Oct. 1912, 129; G. H. Pertz, *Das Leben des Ministers Freiherrn vom Stein* (Berlin 1848–55), III, 112.

41   Wilson, . . *Journal* . . , 32.

42   F. W. v. Weymarn, 'Barklai-..', Oct. 1912, 129, citing Zhirkevich in *Russkaia Starina*, 1874, 651.

43   Bagration to Arakcheev, 7 Aug. (O.S.) 1812, in *Otechestvennaia voina 1812 goda, sbornik dokumentov i materialov*, 54.

44   Bagration to Arakcheev, 8/20 Aug. 1812, in Brett-James, *1812: Eyewitness Accounts of Napoleon's Defeat in Russia* (London 1966), 96–7.

45   Bagration to Rostopchin, 14 Aug. (O.S.) 1812, in Dubrovin, *Otechestvennaia* . . , 96.

46   Dokhturov to wife, 9 Sept. (O.S.) 1812, in *Russkii Arkhiv* (Moscow 1873), 1099–1100.

47   Fiodor N. Glinka, *Pis'ma russkago ofitsera* (Moscow 1815), I, part IV, 43–5.

48   Cited in P. P. de Ségur, *Histoire* . . , I, 274.

49   Ibid., 108.

50   Ibid., 108–9.

51   S. F. Platonov, *Histoire de la Russie des origines à 1918*, trans. from the Russian (Paris 1929), 856.

52   P. P. de Ségur, *Histoire* . . , I, 109.

CHAPTER XI

CROSSFIRE

1   Wilson, *Narrative* . . , 109. Michael Glover (*A Very Slippery Fellow: The Life of Sir Robert Wilson 1777–1849* [Oxford 1977], 103) has suffered a slight slip of the pen in making Bagration the hero of this episode.

2   Clausewitz, *Der Feldzug* . . , 125.

Hilaire Belloc, *The Campaign of 1812 and the Retreat from Moscow* (London 1924), 74.

S. N. Golubov and Y. I. Kuznetsov, Introduction to Bagration, . . *Sbornik dokumentov* . . , 12.

Napoleon to BdT, Rouibiki, 28 Aug. (N.S.) 1812, in Baron A. J. F. Fain, *Manuscrit de Mil Huit Cent Douze* (Paris 1827), I, 433–4; Staël, *Dix Années* . . , 346.

Cf. René Laforgue, *Psychopathologie de l'échec* (Paris 1950), 167, 179.

Kochetkov, *M.B. B-d-T* . . , 50–1.

Clausewitz, *Der Feldzug* . . , 129; cf. BdT, (I) 'Izobrazhenie . .', 20.

Kharkevich, *B-d-T* . . , 20.

Ibid.

BdT to Rostopchin, cited in Kochetkov, *M.B. B-d-T-* . . , 52.

Catherine to Alexander, Jaroslavl', 5 Aug. (O.S.) 1812, in Nicolas Michaïlowitch, *Correspondance* . . , 81.

Count P. A. Shuvalov to Alexander, Moshinsk, 31 July (O.S.) 1812 (received 5 Aug. through Prince Volkonskii), in Dubrovin, *Otechestvennaia* . . , No. 65. 71–2.

Cf. V. I. Bakunina, 'Dvenatsatyi God', *Russkaia Starina*, Sept. 1885, 403.

Alexander to BdT, St. Petersburg, 24 Nov. (O.S.) 1812, in Kharkevich, *B-d-T* . . , Appendix No. 19, 48.

Alexander to Catherine, St. Petersburg, 18 Sept. (O.S.) 1812, in Nicolas Michaïlowitch, *Correspondance* . . , 87.

Clausewitz, *Der Feldzug* . . , 130.

Bogdanovich, *Istoriia* . . , II, 11. The Special Commission, presided over by Alexander's former tutor, the 76-year-old Field-Marshal Count Saltykov, consisted of Arakcheev, Balasheve, Privy Councillors Prince Lopukhin and Count Kochubei, and General Viazmitinov, Military Commandant of St. Petersburg.

Borodino – Dokumenty, pis'ma, vospominania, ed. L. G. Beskrovnyi and G. P. Meshcheriakov (Moscow 1962), 11–13 (the original text of the Commission's resolution is kept in TsGVIA, Fond VUA). Tormassov and Chichagov, as well as Bagration, had seniority in rank over Barclay.

Alexander to the Commanders-in-Chief, St. Petersburg, 8 Aug. (O.S.) 1812, in *Sbornik istoricheskikh materialov izvlechennykh iz arkhiva Sobstvennoj E. I. V. Kantselarii*, pt I (St. Petersburg 1876), letter No. 67, 52–3.

21 BdT to Alexander, Viaz'ma, 16 Aug. (O.S.) 1812, in Kharkevich, *B-d-T* . . , Appendix No. 11, 23–4.

22 Ibid., 24.

23 Ibid.

24 BdT to Auguste, sl [Viaz'ma], 16 Aug. (O.S.) 1812, BdT Private Correspondence, 21.

25 Alexander to BdT, St. Petersburg, 24 Aug. (O.S.) 1812, in *Sbornik istoricheskikh materialov* . . , pt I, letter No. 87, 68–9.

26 Alexander to Catherine, St. Petersburg, 18 Sept. (O.S.) 1812, in Nicolas Michaïlowitch, *Correspondance* . . , 87.

27 Cf. Bogdanovich, *Istoriia* . . , II, 119; in the 1820s the German military writer, Major J. L. Besson, inspected all conceivable positions between Viaz'ma and Moscow and judged Tsarevo to be by far the best defensive position in that area.

28 Cf. Zhilin, *Gibel'* . . , 139.

29 BdT to Auguste, sl [Tsarevo-Zaimishche], 18 Aug. (O.S.) 1812, BdT Private Correspondence, 22.

30 Toll, *Denkwürdigkeiten* . . , I, 409.

31 Kutuzov to Alexander, 19 Aug. (O.S.) 1812, in *Borodino – Dokumenty* . . , No. 11, 25–6.

32 Cf. Württemberg, *Erinnerungen aus dem Feldzuge des Jahres 1812 in Russland* (Breslau 1846), 64–5.

33 Kutuzov to wife, Gzhatsk, sd, in *Borodino – Dokumenty* . . , No. 27, 42.

34 BdT, (I) 'Izobrazhenie . .', 24.

35 Leo Tolstoy, *War and Peace*, trans. Louise and Aylmer Maude (London 1957), 835.

36 Tarlé, *La Campagne* . . . 141.

CHAPTER XII

BORODINO

1 Cf. E. R. Holmes, *Borodino, 1812* (London 1971), 32–6, for a detailed description of the area.

2 Beskrovnyi, *Borodinskoe srazhenie* (Moscow 1971), 33–4.

3   Cf. Christopher Duffy, *Borodino and the War of 1812* (London 1972), 82–3, diagrams.
4   P. P. de Ségur, *Histoire* . . , I, 367–8.
5   BdT, (I) 'Izobrazhenie . .', 18.
6   Ermolov, 'Zapiski', *Borodino – Dokumenty* . . , 350–1.
7   BdT to Alexander, Tatarina [Borodino], 24 Aug. (O.S.) 1812, in Kharkevich, *B-d-T* . . , Appendix No. 12, 27.
8   Ibid., 26–7.
9   Ermolov, *Zapiski* (Moscow 1863), 173.
10 BdT to Alexander, Tatarina [Borodino], 24 Aug. (O.S.) 1812, in Kharkevich, *B-d-T* . . , Appendix No. 12, 27.
11 Ibid.
12 Beskrovnyi, *Borodinskoe* . . , 43.
13 Napoleon, *Correspondance* . . , XXIV, 207, item 19182.
14 Beskrovnyi, *Borodinskoe* . . , 35.
15 *Borodino–Dokumenty* . . , 89–90 (trans. Duffy, *Borodino* . . , 87).
16 A. A. Zakrevskii, 'Bumagi Grafa Zakrevskago' (biographical note), *SIRIO*, LXXIII, v–vi.
17 For a complete study see Duffy's *Borodino* . . which is one of the most recent and reliable accounts; the account here is limited to Barclay's role.
18 Loewenstern, 'Zapiski', Dec. 1900, 573.
19 This bayonet charge, which made Colonel Vuich a major-general, has been used in a curious way. To enhance the sales value of a copy of BdT's (II) 'Izobrazhenie . .', the Russian word for Jaegers – *egery* – was tampered with some years ago to read *evreyi*, i.e. Jews, and it thus appeared that there was documentary evidence for a Jewish brigade in BdT's army. The late Constantin de Grunwald was misled by the falsification and, writing under the pseudonym of S. Nevskii, authenticated the fraud (S. Nevskii, 'Novoe ob otechestvennoi voine 1812 g.', *Russkie Novosti* (Paris, 16 Dec. 1955). A questionable source attesting to Jewish volunteer units under Potemkin helped induce Grunwald to accept this error. The altered copy of (II) 'Izobrazhenie . .' was sold to the library of one of the great universities of the West.
20 A. N. Murav'ev, 'Iz avtobiograficheskikh Zapisok', in *Borodino – Dokumenty*, 376.
21 Bogdanovich, *Istoriia* . . , II, 225.
22 Murav'ev, 'Iz avtobiograficheskikh . .', 376.
23 Loewenstern, 'Zapiski', Dec. 1900, 574.
24 Bogdanovich, *Istoriia* . . , II, 224.
25 Kharkevich, *B-d-T* . . , 25.
26 Württemberg, 'Aus den Papieren' in F. M. Kircheisen, ed., *Napoleons Untergang: Ausgewählte Memoirenstücke* (Stuttgart 1911, 1914), I, 167.
27 Württemberg, *Erinnerungen* . . , 81.
28 F. N. Glinka, *Ocherki Borodinskago strazheniia* (Moscow 1839), 50.
29 Loewenstern, *Denkwürdigkeiten* . . , I, 227–8.
30 Württemberg, 'Aus den Papieren', 167.
31 F. N. Glinka, *Ocherki* . . , 50; cf. Jean Baechler, *Les Suicides* (Paris 1975).
32 Tarlé, *La Campagne* . . , 159.
33 Loewenstern, 'Zapiski', Dec. 1900, 575.
34 Duffy, *Borodino* . . , 142.
35 Loewenstern, 'Zapiski', Dec. 1900, 577.
36 A. A. Shcherbinin, 'Zapiski', in *Borodino – Dokumenty* . . , 395.
37 BdT, (I) 'Izobrazhenie . .', 21.
38 Loewenstern, *Denkwürdigkeiten* . . , I, 226.
39 Schubert, *Unter* . . , 236.
40 BdT, (I) 'Izobrazhenie . .', 22.
41 Duffy, *Borodino* . . , 141.
42 BdT, (I) 'Izobrazhenie . .', 22.
43 Ibid., 23.
44 I. T. Rodozhitskii, 'Pokhodnyia zapiski artillerista s 1812 po 1816 god', in *Borodino – Dokumenty* . . , 388.
45 Wolzogen, *Memoiren* . . , 144.
46 Kharkevich, *B-d-T* . . , 28.
47 A. L. Wardenburg, quoted in Loewenstern, *Denkwürdigkeiten* . . , I, 227, fn 5.
48 G. P. Meshcheriakov, 'Vlianie boevogo opyta otechestvennoi voiny 1812 goda na razvitie taktiki v russkoi armii v pervoi polovine XIX veka', *1812 god: k stopiatidesiatiletiiu otechestvennoi voiny: sbornik statei* (Moscow 1962), 192; cf. Wardenburg in Loewenstern, *Denkwürdigkeiten* . . , I, 227, fn 5.
49 P. P. de Ségur, *Histoire* . . , I, 389.
50 Kircheisen, ed., *Napoleons* . . , 67, citing *Aus dem Leben des Generals Dr. Heinrich von Brandt* (Berlin 1869).
51 Wolzogen, *Memoiren* . . , 145. Citations below

Notes and Sources 245

are from Wolzogen, 145−7, unless otherwise indicated.

M. I. Kutuzov, *Sbornik dokumentov* (Moscow 1954), IV, 150.

Wolzogen, *Memoiren* . . , 147.

BdT, (I) 'Izobrazhenie . .', 24.

Duffy, *Borodino* . . , 141.

F. N. Glinka, *Ocherki* . . , 50.

Bogdanovich, *Istoriia* . . , II, 225; Zhilin, *Gibel'* . . , 162.

Toll, *Denkwürdigkeiten* . . , II, 114.

Chandler, *The Campaigns* . . , 807.

P. P. de Ségur, *Histoire* . . , I, 405.

L. F. J. Baron de Bausset, *Mémoires anecdotiques sur l'intérieur du Palais de Napoléon, sur celui de Marie-Louise, et sur quelques événements de l'Empire, de puis 1805 jusqu'en 1816* (Paris 1829), II, 110.

Kircheisen, ed., *Napoleons* . . , I, 178.

Borodino − Dokumenty . . , 101−2.

BdT, (I) 'Izobrazhenie . .', 24; Kharkevich, *B-d-T* . . , 29.

Kharkevich, *B-d-T* . . , 30.

Michaïlowsky-Danilewsky (Mikhailovskii-Danilevskii), *Die Geschichte des Vaterländischen Krieges im Jahre 1812* (Riga/Leipzig 1840), 221.

CHAPTER XIII
'HE OFFENDED FATHERLAND'

Beskrovnyi, *Otechestvennaia* . . , 409.

Chambray, *Histoire* . . , II, 87.

Clausewitz, *Der Feldzug* . . , 165.

BdT, (I) 'Izobrazhenie . .', 24−5.

Chambray, *Histoire* . . , II, 87.

BdT, (I) 'Izobrazhenie . .', 25.

Ibid., 25−6.

Ibid., 26.

Bogdanovich, *Istoriia* . . , II, 247.

Ermolov, *Zapiski*, 183.

Bogdanovich, *Istoriia* . . , II, 248. Major sources used for the Fili war council: Michaïlowsky-Danilewsky, *Die Geschichte* . . , 261−7; Toll, *Denkwürdigkeiten* . . , II, 143−8; Bennigsen, 'Extrait du contenu du Conseil de Guerre qui a eu lieu le 1er septembre' (report to Tsar written 19 Jan. 1813), *Voennyi Sbornik* (St. Petersburg), 1 Jan. 1903, 236−8; Ermolov, *Zapiski*, 184−7; Tarlé, *La Campagne* . . , 170−2; BdT, (I) 'Izobrazhenie . .', 26−8; Bogdanovich, *Istoriia* . . , II, 248−52.

12 Bogdanovich, *Istoriia* . . , II, 248; cf. I. P. Liprandi, *Materialy dlia otechestvennoi voiny 1812 goda* (St. Petersburg 1867), 96.

13 Bogdanovich, *Istoriia* . . , II, 248.

14 Kharkevich, *B-d-T* . . , 34.

15 Bennigsen, 'Extrait . .', 236−7.

16 Ermolov, *Zapiski*, 183.

17 Michaïlowsky-Danilewsky, *Die Geschichte* . . , 265.

18 BdT to Rostopchin, Fili, 1 Sept. (O.S.) 1812, in Dubrovin, *Otechestvennaia* . . , 118−19.

19 Wolzogen, *Memoiren* . . , 155.

20 Ibid.; cf. Daria Olivier, *L'Incendie de Moscou (15 Septembre 1812)*, (Paris 1964), 26.

21 BdT to Rostopchin, Fili, 30 Aug. (O.S.) 1812, in Dubrovin, *Otechestvennaia* . . , 116.

22 BdT, (I) 'Izobrazhenie . .', 28.

23 Ibid.

24 Prince N.B. Golitsyn, *Ofitserskiia zapiski ili vospominaniia o pokhodakh 1812, 1813 i 1814 godov* (Moscow 1838), 24.

25 Loewenstern, 'Zapiski', Jan. 1901, 106.

26 Michaïlowsky-Danilewsky, *Die Geschichte* . . , 271−2.

27 Olivier, *L'Incendie* . . , 46; Wolzogen, *Memoiren* . . , 156.

28 Wolzogen, *Memoiren* . . , 157.

29 Colonel Michaud, French-born, had been in Russia's service since 1805, when Napoleon had swallowed up the Kingdom of Sardinia.

30 Kutuzov to Tsar, report, 4 Sept. (O.S.) 1812, in Beskrovnyi, *Otechestvennaia* . . , 416; cf. Toll, *Denkwürdigkeiten*, II, 177−8.

31 Clausewitz, *Der Feldzug* . . , 116−18: these three pages are entirely devoted to demonstrating the indefensibility of Smolensk.

32 Loewenstern, 'Zapiski', Jan. 1901, 106.

33 Bennigsen to Arakcheev (in German), in Toll, *Denkwürdigkeiten* . . , II, 180.

34 Alexander to Kutuzov, rescript, St. Petersburg, 2 Oct. (O.S.) 1812, in Beskrovnyi, *Otechestvennaia* . . , 417.

35 Kutuzov, *Sbornik* . . , IV, 220 (item 250 dated Sept. 1812).

36 BdT, (I) 'Izobrazhenie . .', 28.

37 Ibid.

38 Cf. Kharkevich, *B-d-T* . . , 35; cf. A. N. Popov, 'Ot Moskvy do Krasnoi Pakhry', *Russkaia Starina*, June 1897, 530–1.

39 BdT to Alexander, Kaluga, 24 Sept. (O.S.) 1812, in Kharkevich, *B-d-T* . . , Appendix 15, 37.

40 Cf. Chandler, *The Campaigns* . . , 816–17.

41 BdT to Auguste, Krasnaia-Pakhra, 11 Sept. (O.S.) 1812, in Dubrovin, *Otechestvennaia* . . , 128–9 = BdT Private Correspondence 25.

42 Bennigsen to Marie, his wife, '32 versts from Moscow', 11 Sept. (O.S.) 1812, in Dubrovin, *Otechestvennaia* . . , 129.

43 Wolzogen, *Memoiren* . . , 160.

44 BdT to Alexander, Kaluga, 24 Sept. (O.S.) 1812, in Kharkevich, *B-d-T* . . , Appendix 15, 34–8.

45 Cf. Zhilin, *Kontrnastuplenie Kutuzova v 1812 g.* (Moscow 1950), 78; cf. Popov, 'Ot Moskvy . .', July 1892, 114.

46 Popov, 'Ot Moskvy . .', July 1892, 114.

47 BdT to Kutuzov, report, Tarutino, 18 Sept. (O.S.) 1812, in Popov, 'Ot Moskvy . .', July 1892, 115.

48 Kutuzov to Alexander, Tarutino, 19 Sept. (O.S.) 1812, in Kutuzov, *Sbornik* . . , 323–4.

49 Loewenstern, 'Zapiski', Jan. 1901, 112; cf. Loewenstern, *Denkwürdigkeiten* . . , I, 248–9.

50 Loewenstern, *Denkwürdigkeiten* . . , I, 246–7. The Russian and French versions of Loewenstern's memoirs do not mention the wagon metaphor; they vary in nuances but not in any significant way.

51 Ibid.

52 *Andreas* Otto Heinrich Barclay de Tolly, only surviving son of Barclay's eldest brother Erich and a von Smitten cousin *née* Margarete Sophie von Lilienfeld; adjutant to Barclay in 1812, rose to Tsar's chamberlain and state councillor, finishing his career as First Secretary of the Russian legation in Dresden; married the widow of General Ivan Bibikoff (d. 1812), *née* Alexandra von der Howen; died without issue in Mainz in 1847.

53 Clausewitz, *Der Feldzug* . . , 184–5.

54 Ibid., 9.

55 Loewenstern, 'Zapiski', Jan. 1901, 110.

56 Wilson, . . *Journal* . . , 52.

57 Wilson to Alexander, General Headquarters [Tarutino], 21 Sept. (O.S.) 1812, in Dubrovin, *Otechestvennaia* . . , 169.

58 Lieut.-Gen. Mikhail S. Vorontsov to Col. Arsenii A. Zakrevskii, 22 Sept. (O.S.) 1812, in Zakrevskii, 'Bumagi Grafa Zakrevskago', ed. N. F. Dubrovin, *SIRIO*, 1890, LXXIII, 477.

59 Ibid.

60 Ibid.

61 BdT to Alexander, Krasnaia-Pakhra, 11 Sept. (O.S.) 1812, in Kharkevich, *B-d-T* . . , Appendix 13, 31.

62 BdT to Alexander, Kaluga, 24 Sept. (O.S.) 1812, in Kharkevich, *B-d-T* . . , Appendix 15, 34–8.

63 Ibid., 35.

64 BdT to Auguste, Tula, 1 Oct. (O.S.) 1812, BdT Private Correspondence, 29.

65 Zakrevskii, 'Bumagi . .', vi. Several other versions of this incident have been published, erroneously locating it in Kaluga.

66 A. C. v. Weymarn, *Erinnerungen* . . , 7.

67 Cf. Iuri N. Tynianov, *Pushkin i ego sovremenniki* (Moscow 1968), 236–8.

68 Cf. Alexander Pushkin, 'Polkovodets', Appendix A, pp. 218–19.

69 BdT to Alexander, Vladimir, 25 Oct. (O.S.) 1812, in Kharkevich, *B-d-T* . . , Appendix 16, 43–4.

70 BdT to Auguste, Vladimir, 16 Oct. (O.S.) 1812, BdT Private Correspondence, 32.

71 BdT to Alexander, Vladimir, 25 Oct. (O.S.) 1812, in Kharkevich, *B-d-T* . . , Appendix 16, 43–4.

72 Ibid., 44.

73 The full title is 'Obiasneniia Generala ot Infanterii Barklaia-de-Tolli o deistviiakh pervoi i vtoroi zapadnykh armii v prodolzhenie kampanii sego 1812 goda' ('Explanations of Infantry General Barclay de Tolly Concerning Actions of the First and Second Western Armies in the Campaign of This Year 1812'). This first (October 1812) version Barclay revised in January or February 1813 for circulation in manuscript form – an early kind of samizdat in view of failure to obtain official publication. The revised version, 'Opravdanie

v deistviiakh ego vo vremia Otechestvennoi voiny s frantsuzami v 1812 godu', finally achieved publication in 1911, in *Zhurnal imperatorskogo russkogo voenno-istoricheskogo obshchestva*, No. 1 (St. Petersburg 1911), 1–8. Cf. N. Kazakov, 'O zapiskakh M. B. Barklaia-de-Tolli', *Voenno-istoricheskii Zhurnal* (Moscow 1974), 102–8.

BdT, 'Opravdanie . .', 7.

Ibid., 8.

Wolzogen, *Memoiren* . . , 161–2.

(I) 'Izobrazhenie voennykh deistvii pervoi armii v 1812 godu' ('Tableau of the Military Operations of the First Army in the Year 1812') was written by Barclay in German and corrected in his own handwriting. It was translated into Russian for sending to the Tsar. This translation was published in 1859 (not 1858 as Kazakov states) in the periodical of 'readings' put out by the Russian Historical Society: *Chteniia russkogo istoricheskogo obshchestva*, No. 4 (St. Petersburg 1859), 1–32. Both the German original and the Russian translation sent to the Tsar were kept in the nineteenth century in secret Government archives.

After Barclay's death in May 1818 several manuscript copies circulated among some of the participants in the 1812 campaign. At least one of these copies had General Zakrevskii as its source and was seen by Generals Ermolov and Denis Davydov. This version, which I have called (II) 'Izobrazhenie . .', is almost identical with (I) 'Izobrazhenie . .' except for certain copyist's errors, paragraphing, and four critical footnotes by Davydov. (II) 'Izobrazhenie voennykh deistvii 1812 goda' was published simultaneously in 1912 in *Trudy Imperatorskogo russkogo voenno-istoricheskogo obshchestva* (Works of the Imperial Russian Society for Military History) (St. Petersburg 1912), VI, book 2, 17–67, and as a pamphlet by a certain Nikolai Gastfreund. The latter inherited the manuscript from his father, a doctor, who must have received it from one of his patients or friends in the early 1860s. It was published together with various other documents relating to the 1812 campaign (printed by P. P. Soikin, Stremiannaia Street 12, St. Petersburg, 1912). In this biography only (I) 'Izobrazhenie . .' is used. Cf. Kazakov, 'O zapiskakh . .', 106–8.

BdT to Alexander, Novgorod, 9 Nov. (O.S.) 1812, in Kharkevich, *B-d-T* . . , Appendix 17, 44–5.

Ibid., 45.

Ibid.

BdT to Alexander von Maier, Beckhof, 16 Nov. (O.S.) 1812, in *Russkaia Starina* (Oct. 1888), 263–4 = BdT Private Correspondence, 33.

82 Ibid.

83 Cf. Kharkevich, ed., 'Perepiska . .', Jan. 1904, 280 fn.

84 A. C. v. Weymarn, *Erinnerungen* . . , 7.

85 Ibid.

86 BdT to Alexander, Fellin, 21 Nov. (O.S.) 1812, in Kharkevich, *B-d-T* . . , Appendix 18, 47.

87 Alexander to BdT, St. Petersburg, 24 Nov. (O.S.) 1812, in Kharkevich, *B-d-T* . . , Appendix 19, 48–50.

88 Ibid.

CHAPTER XIV

APPOINTMENTS IN GERMANY

1 Cf. Mikhailovskii-Danilevskii and Viskovatov, *Imperaor* . . , 75.

2 Wilson, *Private Diary of Travels, Personal Services, and Public Events* . . , ed. Rev. Herbert Randolph (London 1861), I, 278.

3 BdT to Alexander, Plock, 27 Jan. (O.S.) 1813, in Kharkevich, *B-d-T* . . , Appendix 20, 54.

4 Ibid., 55.

5 Kutuzov, *Sbornik* . . , V, 230.

6 Langeron, *Journal des campagnes faites au service de la Russie*, Archives du Ministère des Affaires étrangères (Paris), XXV, 26 Jan. to 5 Feb. 1813 (no page numbers).

7 Ibid.

8 Cf. Kutuzov, *Sbornik* . . , V, 543–5.

9 Tarlé, *La Campagne* . . , 323.

10 Cf. Petre, *Napoleon's Last Campaign in Germany, 1813*, introduction by David G. Chandler (London 1974, first published 1912), 66–90, for a detailed description. This battle is also referred to as the battle of Gross-Görschen.

11 Napoleon, *Correspondance* . . , XXV, 262.

12 Cf. Petre, *Napoleon's Last* . . , 112.

13 Cf. BdT, *Journal des opérations militaires des Armées Russes et Combinées depuis le 4/16*

décembre 1813, jusqu'au 19/31 Mars [1814]: Epoque de leur entrée à Paris (245-page manuscript produced under BdT's direct supervision by an anonymous adjutant) in Schroeder family archives, 12–14.

14 Cf. Toll, *Denkwürdigkeiten* . . , II, 475.

15 Ibid., II, 477.

16 Alexander to Catherine, Taner, 14 May (O.S.) 1813, in Nicolas Michaïlowitch, *Correspondance* . . , 150.

17 Mikhailovskii-Danilevskii and Viskovatov, *Imperator* . . , 79. According to Shil'der, *Imperator* . . , III, 152, the initiative came from Miloradovich, and Wittgenstein's generous statement applied to 'anyone the Tsar appoints in my place'.

18 Mikhailovskii-Danilevskii and Viskovatov, *Imperator* . . , 79.

19 Alexander to Catherine, Taner, 14 May (O.S.) 1813, in Nicolas Michaïlowitch, *Correspondance* . . , 150.

20 Ibid.

21 Ibid.

22 Rostopchin to Zakrevskii, Moscow, 19 June (O.S.) 1813, in 'Bumagi Grafa Zakrevskago', *SIRIO*, LXXIII, 462.

23 Toll, *Denkwürdigkeiten* . . , II, 483.

24 Ibid.

25 Cf. Napoleon, *Correspondance* . . , XXV, 346.

26 BdT, Order of the Day, 29 May (O.S.) 1813, in Mikhailovskii-Danilevskii and Viskovatov, *Imperator* . . , 80.

27 Stein to Count Münster, Hanoverian statesman, in Toll, *Denkwürdigkeiten* . . , II, 479.

28 Loewenstern, *Denkwürdigkeiten* . . , II, 72.

29 Friedrich Carl Ferdinand Freiherr von Müffling, *Aus meinem Leben* (Berlin 1851), 52.

30 Mikhailovskii-Danilevskii and Viskovatov, *Imperator* . . , 81.

31 A. Borisevich, 'Pamiati General-fel'dmarshala kniazia M. B. Barklaia-de-Tolli', *Voenno-istoricheskii Sbornik*, No. 3 (St. Petersburg 1912), 73.

32 Wilson, . . *Journal* . . , 180.

33 Vigel', *Zapiski*, II, 286.

34 Ioann Grafy Kapodistria, 'Zapiska Grafa Ioanna Kapodistria o ego sluzhebnoi deiatel'nosti', *SIRIO*, III, 174; cf. Woodhouse, *Capodistria* . . , 76.

35 Cf. Kapodistria, 'Zapiska . .', 175–6; and Woodhouse, *Capodistria* . . , 77–8.

36 Shil'der, *Imperator* . . , III, 154.

37 Brett-James, *Europe Against Napoleon: The Leipzig Campaign, 1813, from Eyewitness Accounts* (London 1970), 80.

38 Karl Fürst Schwarzenberg, *Feldmarschall Fürst Schwarzenberg: Der Sieger von Leipzig* (Vienna 1964), 223.

39 Friedrich von Kosen [F. v. K.], *Journal der Kriegsoperationen der Kaiserlich-Russischen und verbündeten Armeen von der Eroberung Thorns bis zur Einnahme von Paris* (Riga 1815), 38. Colonel von Kosen was a member of BdT's General Staff. This work is similar to the unpublished French-language *Journal des opérations* . . listed in note 13.

40 Cf. Petre, *Napoleon's Last* . . , 200–26, and Toll, *Denkwürdigkeiten* . . , III, 179–201, for descriptions of the battle.

41 Cf. Toll, *Denkwürdigkeiten* . . , III, 258.

42 Schwarzenberg to Francis II, report, Haus-, Hof-, und Staatsarchive, Vienna, 1813, Fz 490/229, in Schwarzenberg, *Feldmarschall* . . , 230–1.

43 Cf. Wilson, . . *Journal* . . , 179; and Toll, *Denkwürdigkeiten* . . , III, 348.

44 Karl Friedrich von Knesebeck, in Brett-James, *Europe Against* . . , 82.

45 Toll, *Denkwürdigkeiten* . . , III, 219.

46 Wilson to Lord Cathcart, Teplitz, 30 Aug. (N.S.) 1813, in Wilson, *Private Diary* . . , I, 484.

47 BdT to Auguste, Teplitz, 19 Aug. (O.S.) 1813, BdT Private Correspondence, 40.

48 Wolzogen, *Memoiren* . . , 204.

49 BdT to Auguste, sl, sd, BdT Private Correspondence, 43.

50 BdT to Auguste, Teplitz, 10/22 Sept. 1813, BdT Private Correspondence, 47.

51 BdT to Auguste, Teplitz, 29 Aug. (O.S.) 1813, BdT Private Correspondence, 44; BdT to Auguste, Teplitz, 5 Sept. (O.S.) 1813, BdT Private Correspondence, 46.

52 BdT to Auguste, Teplitz, 29 Aug. (O.S.) 1813, BdT Private Correspondence, 44.

53 BdT to Auguste, Teplitz, 14/26 Sept. 1813, BdT Private Correspondence, 49.

54 Cf. BdT, *Journal des opérations militaires* . . , 83–4.

55 Wolzogen, *Memoiren* . . , 214.

Notes and Sources

6 Napoleon to Murat, Dresden, 7 Oct. (N.S.) 1813, in Napoleon, *Correspondance* . . , XXVI, 304.

7 Otto von Odeleben, *Napoleons Feldzug in Sachsen im Jahr 1813* (Dresden 1816), 337.

8 Bulletin de la Grande Armée, Erfurt, 24 Oct. (N.S.) 1813, in Napoleon, *Correspondance* . . , XXVI, 347.

9 BdT, *Journal des opérations militaires* . . , 117.

10 Ibid. 121.

11 Cf. Petre, *Napoleon's Last* . . , 324–85, or Chandler, *The Campaigns* . . , 922–36, for detailed descriptions of the Battle of the Nations.

12 BdT to Auguste, sl [Leipzig], sd, BdT Private Correspondence, 55.

13 BdT to Auguste, Leipzig, sd [7 Oct. (O.S.) 1813], BdT Private Correspondence, 54.

CHAPTER XV
GLORY

1 Marmont, *Mémoires* . . , 2.

2 Cf. Toll, *Denkwürdigkeiten* . . , IV, pt 2, Appendix 1.

3 Thiers, *Histoire du Consulat* . . , XVI, 55.

4 BdT to Alexander von Maier, Langres, 15 Jan. (O.S.) 1814, BdT Private Correspondence, 60. At this time Alexander von Maier was employed as an assessor in the Ministry of Foreign Affairs in St. Petersburg; he finished his career as a *Geheimer Rat*. BdT was also on easy terms with Alexander's father, *Hofrat* Ludwig von Maier.

5 Ibid.

6 Henry Houssaye, *1814* (Paris 1888), 59.

7 Mikhailovskii-Danilevskii and Viskovatov, *Imperator* . . , 90.

8 Napoleon to Joseph, Epine-aux-Bois, 11 Feb. (N.S.) 1814, 8 p.m., in Joseph Bonaparte, *Mémoires et correspondance politique et militaire du Roi Joseph*, ed. A. du Casse (Paris 1854), X, 88.

9 Toll, *Denkwürdigkeiten* . . , IV, pt 1, 430.

10 Jomini, *Précis politique* . . , II, 238–9.

11 Schwarzenberg, *Feldmarschall* . . , 281–2.

12 Chandler, *The Campaigns* . . , 978; cf. Houssaye, *1814*, 70.

13 Napoleon to Joseph, Nangis, 18 Feb. (N.S.) 1814, in Joseph Bonaparte, *Mémoires* . . , X, 133.

14 Cf. Carl von Plotho, *Der Krieg in Deutschland und Frankreich, in den Jahren 1813 und 1814* (Berlin 1817), II, 257.

15 Milhailovskii-Danilevskii and Viskovatov, *Imperator* . . , 90.

16 Cf. Toll, *Denkwürdigkeiten* . . , IV, pt 2, 122–3.

17 BdT to Alexander, Smolensk, 22 July (O.S.) 1812, in Kharkevich, *B-d-T* . . , Appendix 4, 10.

18 Marmont, *Mémoires* . . , VI, 210.

19 Chandler, *The Campaigns* . . , 996.

20 Plotho, *Der Krieg* . . , II, 328.

21 Ibid.

22 Ibid., 342.

23 Cf. Toll, *Denkwürdigkeiten* . . , IV, pt 2, 313–14; cf. Houssaye, *1814*, 354–62.

24 Count Michael Orlov, narrative, Arch. topog. de Saint-Pétersbourg, 47 346, as cited in Houssaye, *1814*, 493.

25 Cf. ibid., 533.

26 'L'Ordre du Jour', *Le Journal des Débats*, No. IV (Paris), 3 April (N.S.) 1814; English translation in *The Times* (London), 8 April (N.S.) 1814.

27 Cf. Prince A.A. Lobanov-Rostovsky, Introduction, in M. Lyons, ed., *The Russian Imperial Army: A Bibliography of Regimental Histories and Related Works* (Stanford 1968), xiii.

28 Houssaye, *1814*, 552.

29 P. F. F. J. Giraud, *La Campagne de Paris, en 1814, précédée d'un coup-d'oeil sur celle de 1813* (Paris 1814), 96.

30 Sir Charles Stewart to Castlereagh, Paris, 1 April (N.S.) 1814, in Viscount Castlereagh, *Memoirs, Correspondence, Despatches* (London 1852), IX, 420.

31 Cf. *The World Population Situation in 1970*, United Nations Population Studies No. 49 (New York 1971), 9. Napoleon's campaigns in the end caused the death of five million soldiers in Europe – the third largest figure (for military personnel deaths in Europe) in European

32 Clausewitz, *Der Feldzug* . . , 468.
33 Stein to Hardenberg, Bruchsal, 12 July (N.S.) 1814, in G. H. Pertz, *Das Leben* . . , IV, 42.
34 Frederick William to BdT, rescript, in Mikhailovskii-Danilevskii and Viskovatov, *Imperator* . . , 92.
35 Maria Fedorovna to BdT, St. Petersburg, 28 April (O.S.) 1814, in Schroeder family archives.
36 Loewenstern, *Mémoires* . . , 424–5.
37 Cf. above, Chapter I, 1.
38 *The Times* (London), 9 June (N.S.) 1814.
39 Borisevich, 'Pamiati . .', 76–7.
40 Ibid., 77.
41 Ibid.
42 Alexander (in his own hand) to BdT, in Mikhailovskii-Danilevskii and Viskovatov, *Imperator* . . , 93.
43 BdT to Auguste, Saarbrücken, 20 June (O.S.) 1815, BdT Private Correspondence, 66.
44 BdT to Auguste Vermeulen, Châlons, 21 July (O.S.) 1815, BdT Private Correspondence, 68.
45 Mikhailovskii-Danilevskii and Viskovatov, *Imperator* . . , 93–4.
46 BdT to Auguste Vermeulen, Châlons, 21 July (O.S.) 1815, BdT Private Correspondence, 68.
47 Wellington to BdT, Paris, 12 Aug. (N.S.) 1815, Schroeder family archives.
48 Shil'der, *Imperator* . . , III, 358.
49 Ibid., 335.
50 C. A. Sainte-Beuve, *Portraits de Femmes* (Paris 1870), 403.
51 Mikhailovskii-Danilevskii, *Zapiski 1814 i 1815 godov* (St. Petersburg 1832), 270–1. For detailed description of the Vertus review, 261–78.
52 Ibid., 271.
53 H. L. Empaytaz [H.L.E.], *Notice sur Alexandre, empereur de Russie* (Geneva 1828), 36.
54 Cf. Schroeder family archives; *Goethe Handbuch: Goethe, seine Welt und Zeit, in Werk und Wirkung*, Gen. Ed., Alfred Zastrau (Stuttgart 1961), I, 754–5.
55 BdT to Auguste, St. Petersburg, 14 Dec. (O.S.) 1815, BdT Private Correspondence, 70.
56 Ibid.

CHAPTER XVI

THE LOST BATTLE AND THE LAST JOURNEY

1 Richard Pipes, 'The Russian Military Colonies, 1810–1831', *Journal of Modern History*, Chicago, Sept. 1950, 206.
2 Alexander to Catherine, Gruzino, 7 June (O.S.) 1810, in Nicolas Michaïlowitch, *Correspondance* . . , 33.
3 Cf. Kenneth R. Whiting, *Aleksei Andreevich Arakcheev*, unpublished dissertation, Harvard University Archives (Cambridge 1951), 141. This is the most complete and fully documented study of the military settlements available in English.
4 Pushkin, *Eugene Onegin*, trans. Vladimir Nabokov (New York 1964), II, 77; Pipes, '. . Military Colonies . .', 210.
5 BdT, 'Voenniya poseleniia v Rossii', *Voennyi Sbornik* (St. Petersburg 1861), XIX, 334–63.
6 Ibid., 334 fn.
7 Ibid., 337; cf. Jenkins, *Arakcheev* . . , 188.
8 BdT, 'Voenniya . .', 340; cf. Jenkins, *Arakcheev* . . , 189.
9 BdT, 'Voenniya . .', 345; cf. Jenkins, *Arakcheev* . . , 189.
10 BdT, 'Voenniya . .', 348.
11 Cf. Lieut.-Gen. Hans Diebitsch [Field-Marshal Ivan Ivanovich, Count Dibich-Zabalkanskii], 'Voennyia poseleniia v Rossii', *Voennyi Sbornik* (St. Petersburg 1861), XIX, 363–72.
12 Amburger, *Geschichte* . . , 325.
13 Shil'der, *Imperator* . . , IV, 26.
14 Pipes, '. . Military Colonies . .', 219.
15 Cf. A. C. v. Weymarn, *Erinnerungen* . . , 10.
16 Stryk, *Beiträge* . . , 183.
17 Cf. *Rigasche Stadtblätter*, 1818, No. 23, in *Baltische Monatsschrift* (Riga 1912), LXXIV, 264–5.
18 Alexander to Auguste, Moscow, 2 June (O.S.) 1818, in Schroeder family archives.
19 *The Mausoleum of Barclay de Tolly*, trilingual guidebook compiled by H. Uprus, published by the State Committee for Building and Architecture of the Council of Ministers of the Estonian SSR (Tallinn 1957), 27.
20 Ibid., 30.

Notes and Sources

1 Ibid., 25.
2 A. C. v. Weymarn, *Erinnerungen* . . , 14.
3 Ibid.
4 Vegesack, *Vorfahren* . . , 273.
5 Empress Elisabeth Alekseievna to Auguste (Feldmarschallin Fürstin Barclay de Tolly), in German, St. Petersburg, 16 Feb. (O.S.) 1824, in Archives of the University of Tartu, No. 1927: 1391, Ms. 577.
6 Vegesack, *Vorfahren* . . , 273.
7 Cf. Prosch, *Stammtafeln* . . , 39–42, and the typewritten revision of this work brought up to date in 1970 in Prosch family archives. Today there are collateral and female descendants living in Geneva, London, Jersey, and various places in Germany.

EPILOGUE

THE POET AND THE COMMANDER

1 Justine Kuechelbecker to Wilhelm Kuechelbecker, 24 Aug. (O.S.) 1812, in Tynianov, *Kiukhlia* (Moscow 1975), 444.
2 Alexander Pushkin to Pavel A. Katenin, 4 Dec. (O.S.) 1825, in A. S. Pushkin, *Polnoe sobranie sochinenii* (Moscow/Leningrad 1937–59), XIII, 247.
3 Pushkin, *Eugene Onegin*, trans. B. Deutsch (London 1964), 241.
4 *Moskovskii Telegraf*, No. 9, Sept. 1833, in V. A. Manuilov and L. B. Modzalevskii, '"Polkovodets" Pushkina', *Pushkinskii Vremennik* (Leningrad 1939), 139.
5 Manuilov and Modzalevskii, '"Polkovodets" Pushkina', 139.
6 N. N. Petrunina, '"Polkovodets"', *Stikhotvoreniia Pushkina, 1820–1830 godov* (Leningrad 1974), 287.
7 Georgii Koka, 'Pushkin o Polkovodtsakh dvenadtsatogo goda', *Prometei*, VII (Moscow 1969), 18.
8 Cf. ibid.
9 Manuilov and Modzalevskii, '"Polkovodets" Pushkina', 149.
10 Ibid., 150, citing *Pis'ma Gogolia*, I, 462.
11 Ibid., 150, citing *Zapiski N. I. Grecha* (St. Petersburg 1886), 275.
12 Pushkin, *Polnoe* . . , XVI, 164.
13 I. Trofimov, '"Polkovodets"', *Prometei*, X (Moscow 1974), 195.
14 D. S. Mirsky, *A History of Russian Literature* (London 1964), 93.
15 Elisaveta Mikhailovna Khitrovo to Pushkin, St. Petersburg, 4 Nov. (O.S.) 1836, in Pushkin, *Polnoe* . . , XVI, 180. For a detailed account of the controversy, cf. Manuilov and Modzalevskii, '"Polkovodets" Pushkina', 152–3.
16 Pushkin, 'Obiasnenie: O stikhotvorenii "Polkovodets"', *Sovremennik*, No. 4 (St. Petersburg 1836), in Pushkin, *Polnoe* . . , XII, 133–4.
17 Ibid.
18 Mikhailovskii-Danilevskii and Viskovatov, *Imperator* . . , 97.
19 BdT to Alexander, Plock, 27 Jan. (O.S.) 1813, in Kharkevich, *B-d-T* . . , Appendix 20, 55.
20 The Kutuzov–Barclay statues had been ordered by Alexander I in 1818 soon after Barclay's death and the unveiling of Moscow's monument to its early saviours, Minin and Pozharskii. Alexander's rescript made clear the parallel between 'immortal deeds in olden times' and 'in our own times'. In the monument competition which finally took place in 1828–9, only two sculptors took part, though they were Russia's best, S. I. Galberg and B. I. Orlovsky, the winner. The official intention was to commemorate Kutuzov as the supreme leader of the Russian armies in 1812, and Barclay de Tolly as 'The conqueror of Napoleon and liberator of Europe'. Accordingly, '1812' appears on Kutuzov's pedestal while '1813, 1814, 1815' are engraved on Barclay's. Cf. *Istoriia russkogo isskustva*, VIII (Moscow 1964), 413–20.
21 Cf. Koka, 'Pushkin o Polkovodtsakh . . ', 27–8.
22 In 1969 a series of nineteenth-century personal records held in the Central State Archives of the October Revolution (Leningrad) became accessible to scholars.
23 Cf. Trofimov, '"Polkovodets"', 192.
24 Ibid. Translation by W. W. Arndt.
25 Ibid.
26 Efim Etkind, 'Stikhotvorenie Pushkina "Polkovodets"; opyt interpretatsii', *Rossiia/Russia*, No. 2 (Turin 1975), 170.
27 Petrunina, '"Polkovodets"', 299.
28 Trofimov, '"Polkovodets"', 188.

29 V. A. Zhukovskii, *Stikhotvoreniia* (Moscow 1959), I, 149–67, 400–2.

30 Iraklii Andronikov, *Lermontov: issledovaniia i nakhodki* (Moscow 1964), 88–9.

31 Pushkin, *Polnoe* . . , XII, 133.

32 There is no memorial in Moscow, though there is a short street in the Kiev district of Moscow named Barclay de Tolly Street. Statues of Barclay and Bagration were finally to be erected on the monument-scattered field at Borodino, according to a government decree of 1962 to celebrate the 150th anniversary. Eight years later, however, they had not appeared and it is not known whether they are yet in sight. — Cf. Kochetkov, *M.B. B-d-T*, 76.

SELECT BIBLIOGRAPHY

This list serves only to bring together materials actually cited in the text or directly referred to in the Notes; it does not include background materials or many indirectly used Russian articles on Barclay de Tolly. (The editions quoted are for the most part those consulted by the author.) It is proper, however, that extant works written by Barclay de Tolly himself or produced under his direct supervision should be included even when they have not supplied direct quotations.

D. J.

ARCHIVES

FINLAND
Senaatin Talousosasto = Economic Department of the Senate Archives (Helsinki)
Suomen Valtionarkiste (SVA) = State Archives of Finland (Helsinki), KKK-Da 7, KKK-Eb 3

FRANCE
Archives du Ministère des Affaires étrangères (Paris): Vol. CL, Correspondance politique: Russie (1810); Vol. XXV, L. A. A. comte de Langeron, *Journal des campagnes faites au service de la Russie*
Archives nationales (Paris): Exposé du Procureur-général dans l'Affaire Michel (21 April 1812), BB-3-145; Fonds Caulaincourt 95 AP, 10, dossier 18; 95 AP, 12–13, dossier 30

CAMPENHAUSEN
Family archives of Baron Balthasar von Campenhausen (Meinerzhagen, Nordrhein-Westfalen)

PROSCH
Family archives of Georg R. von Prosch (Bad Homburg vor der Höhe)

SCHROEDER
Family archives of Johann Karl von Schroeder (Berlin): *Journal des opérations militaires des Armées Russes et Combinées depuis le 4/16 décembre 1813, jusqu'au 19/31 Mars [1814]: époque de leur rentrée à Paris; Journal militaire de la 3ème Armée de l'ouest depuis l'époque où le Général d'infanterie Barclay-de-Tolly en prit le commandement jusqu'à celle de l'Armistice*

PUBLISHED WORKS

Alekseev, V. A. 'Delo pod Ochakovym, 27 iul'ia 1788 goda', *Voenno-istoricheskii Sbornik* 2 (St. Petersburg 1914)
Amburger, Erik. *Geschichte der Behördenorganisation Russlands von Peter dem Grossen bis 1917* (Leiden 1966)
———'Wer war der Pflegevater Barclay de Tollys?', *Baltische Hefte* X, 4 (Hanover 1963)
Andolenko, General Serge. *Aigles de Napoléon contre drapeaux du Tsar* (Paris 1969)
———*Histoire de l'armée russe* (Paris 1967)

Andronikov, Iraklii. *Lermontov: issledovaniia i nakhodki* (Moscow 1964)
Bagration, General Petr Ivanovich, Prince. *General Bagration: Sbornik dokumentov i materialov*, introduction by S. N. Golubov and Y. I. Kuznetsov (Moscow 1945)
Bakunina, V. I. 'Dvenatsatyi god', *Russkaia Starina* (St. Petersburg, September 1885)
Barclay, The Rev. Charles W. *A History of the Barclay Family* (London 1924)
Barclay, Hubert F. *A History of the Barclay Family* (London 1933), being part II of the work begun by the Rev. Charles W. Barclay, and including 'The Barclays in Scotland' and 'The Russian Barclays de Tolly'
Barclay de Tolly, Field-Marshal Mikhail Bogdanovich, Prince. 'Doneseniia Barklaia Aleksandru I i pis'ma tsaria posle ostavleniia tsarem armii v 1812 godu', *Voennyi Sbornik* (St. Petersburg, November–December 1903, March–September 1904)
———— (I) 'Izobrazhenie voennykh deistvii pervoi armii v 1812 godu', *Chteniia v Imp. obshchestve istorii i drevnostei rossiiskiikh pri Moskovskom universitete* 4 (St. Petersburg 1859)
———— (II) 'Izobrazhenie voennykh deistvii 1812-go goda', *Trudy Imperatorskogo russkogo voenno-istoricheskogo obshchestva* (St. Petersburg 1912)
———— 'Opravdanie v deistviiakh ego vo vremia Otechestvennoi voiny s frantsuzami v 1812 godu', *Zhurnal Imperatorskogo russkogo voenno-istoricheskogo obshchestva*, VI, Book 1 (St. Petersburg 1911)
———— *Uchrezhdenie dlia upravleniia bol'shoi deistvuiushchei armii* (St. Petersburg 1812)
———— 'Voennyia poseleniia v Rossii', *Voennyi Sbornik* XIX (St. Petersburg 1861)
———— 'Zapiska', *Voennyi Zhurnal* (St. Petersburg 1859)
Barratt, Glynn. *The Rebel on the Bridge: A Life of the Decembrist Baron Andrey Rozen 1800–84* (London 1975)
Barrow, G. W. S. *The Kingdom of the Scots: Government, Church and Society from the eleventh to the fourteenth century* (London 1973)
Bartenev, A. *Biografii Generalissimusov i Generalfel'd-marshalov rossiskoi imperatorskoi armii* (St. Petersburg 1912)
———— 'Pamiati General-Fel'dmarshala kniazia M. B. Barklaia-de-Tolli, 1761–1818', *Voenno-istoricheskii Sbornik*, II, 1, 2 (St. Petersburg 1912)
Bausset, L. F. J., Baron de. *Mémoires anecdotiques sur l'intérieur du Palais de Napoléon, sur celui de Marie-Louise, et sur quelques événements de l'Empire, de puis 1805 jusqu'en 1816* (Paris 1829)
Belloc, Hilaire. *The Campaign of 1812 and the Retreat from Moscow* (London 1924)
Bennigsen, General Levin August Gottlieb, Count. 'Extrait du contenu du Conseil de Guerre qui a eu lieu le 1er septembre' [report to the Tsar written 19 January 1813], *Voennyi Sbornik* (St. Petersburg, 1903)
———— 'Zapiski Grafa Bennigsena', ed. by L. L. Bennigsen, *Russkaia Starina* (St. Petersburg, December 1896 to March 1900)
Berg, General B. M. 'Furst Barclay de Tollys Tåg Öfver Bottniska Viken 1809', *Svensk Militär Tidskrift* (Stockholm 1914)
Berlin, Isaiah. *The Hedgehog and the Fox* (London 1953, New York 1957)
Bernhardi, Theodore von. See Toll, *Denkwürdigkeiten* . .
Beskrovnyi, L. G. *Borodinskoe srazhenie* (Moscow 1971)
———— *Otechestvennaia voina 1812 goda* (Moscow 1962)
Bignon, L. P. E. *Exposé comparatif de l'état financier, militaire, politique et moral de la France et des principales puissances de l'Europe* (Paris 1814)
———— *Histoire de la France depuis le 18 brumaire jusqu'à la seconde abdication* (Paris 1830)

Select Bibliography

Boehtlingk, Arthur. *Frédéric-César Laharpe, 1754–1838* (Neuchâtel 1969)
Bogdanovich, M. I. *Istoriia Otechestvennoi voiny 1812 goda po dostovernym istochnikam* (St. Petersburg 1859–60)
Bonaparte, Joseph Napoléon. *Mémoires et correspondance politique et militaire du Roi Joseph*, ed. by A. du Casse (Paris 1854)
Borisevich, A. T. 'Pamiati General-fel'dmarshala kniazia M. B. Barklaia-de-Tolli', *Voenno-istoricheskii Sbornik* 3 (St. Petersburg 1912)
Borodino – dokumenty, pis'ma, vospominaniia, ed. by L. G. Beskrovnyi and G. P. Meshcheriakov (Moscow 1962)
Borodkin, M. M. *Istoriia Finliandii: Vremia Imperatora Aleksandra I* (St. Petersburg 1909)
Bragin, Mikhail. *Kutuzov* (Moscow 1970)
Brett-James, Antony. *1812: Eyewitness Accounts of Napoleon's Defeat in Russia* (London 1966)
────── *Europe Against Napoleon: The Leipzig Campaign, 1813, from Eyewitness Accounts* (London 1970)
Brikner, A. G. 'Voina Rossii s Shvedtsiei v 1788–1790 gg', *Zhurnal Ministerstva Narodnago Prosveshcheniia* CXLII (St. Petersburg, February, March, July 1869)
Brown, P. Hume. *History of Scotland*, 3 vols. (Cambridge 1899—1909
Bulgarin, F. V. *Sochineniia* (St. Petersburg 1830)
Butterfield, Herbert. *Napoleon* (London 1962)
────── *The Peace Tactics of Napoleon, 1806–1808* (Cambridge 1929)
Buturlin, Colonel D. P., Count [Boutourlin]. *Histoire militaire de la campagne de Russie en 1812* (St. Petersburg/Paris 1824)
Castlereagh, Robert, Viscount. *Memoirs, Correspondence, Despatches* (London 1848–52)
Capodistria, John. See Kapodistria
Caulaincourt, General Armand de, Duc de Vicence. *Mémoires du Général de Caulaincourt, Duc de Vicence, Grand Ecuyer de l'Empereur*, ed. by Jean Hanoteau (Paris 1933)
──────Fonds Caulaincourt, see under Archives, France
Chambray, Général Georges, Marquis de. *Histoire de l'expédition de Russie* (Paris 1839)
Chandler, David G. *The Campaigns of Napoleon* (London 1967)
Choiseul-Gouffier, Sophie de Ticsenhausen [Tyzenhaus], Comtesse de. *Mémoires historiques sur l'Empereur Alexandre et la Cour de Russie* (Paris 1829)
Clausewitz, General Carl von. *Der Feldzug von 1812 in Russland, der Feldzug von 1813 bis zum Waffenstillstand und der Feldzug von 1814 in Frankreich* (Berlin 1835)
────── and Marie. *Ein Lebensbild in Briefen und Tagebuchblättern*, ed. by Karl Linnebach (Berlin 1916)
Comité scientifique du Grand État-major russe. See *La Guerre nationale de 1812*
Czartoryski, Prince Adam. *Mémoires et Correspondance avec l'Empereur Alexandre Ier* (Paris 1887)
Danielson, J. Rich. *Finland's Union with the Russian Empire: with reference to K. Ordin's work 'Finland's Subjugation'*, translated from Swedish (Borgå 1891)
Diebitsch, Hans [Field-Marshal Ivan Ivanovich, Count Dibich-Zabalkanskii]. 'Voennyia poseleniia v Rossii', *Voennyi Sbornik* XIX (St. Petersburg 1861)
Dollinger, Philippe. *La Hanse (XIIIe–XVIIe siècles)* (Paris 1964)
Dubrovin, N. F. *Otechestvennaia voina v pis'mach sovremennikov (1812–1815 gg.)*, prilozhenie k XLIII tomu Zapisok imp. Akademii nauk, No. 1 (St. Petersburg 1882)
Duffy, Christopher. *Borodino and the War of 1812* (London 1972)
Dumas, General Mathieu, Comte. *Précis des événements militaires ou essais historiques sur les campagnes de 1799 à 1814* (Paris 1826)

―――――― *Souvenirs du Lieutenant-Général Comte Mathieu Dumas de 1770 à 1836* (Paris 1839)
Earle, Edward Meade, ed. *Makers of Modern Strategy* (Princeton 1943)
Empeytaz, H. L. [H. L. E.] *Notice sur Alexandre, empereur de Russie* (Geneva 1828)
Ermolov, General A. P. *Materialy dlia istorii voiny 1812 g* (Prilozheniia) (Moscow 1863)
―――――― *Zapiski* (Moscow 1863)
Etkind, Efim. 'Stikhotvorenie Pushkina "Polkovodets": opyt interpretatsii', *Rossia/Russia* 2 (Turin 1975)
Fain, A. J. F., Baron. *Manuscrit de Mil Huit Cent Douze* (Paris 1827)
Fezensac, General Raymond A. P. J., duc de. *Souvenirs militaires de 1804 à 1814* (Paris 1863)
Florinsky, Michael T. *Russia: A History and an Interpretation* (New York 1953)
Fon-Vizin, Mikhail A. *Zapiski Fon-Vizina, ochevidtsa smutnykh vremen tsarstvovanii Pavla I, Aleksandra I, Nikolaia I* (Leipzig 1859)
Genealogisches Handbuch der Baltischen Ritterschaften: Teil Estland (Görlitz 1929–31)
Giraud, P. F. F. J. *La Campagne de Paris, en 1814, précédée d'un coup-d'oeil sur celle de 1813* (Paris 1814)
Glinka, F. N. *Ocherki Borodinskago srazheniia* (Moscow 1839)
―――――― *Pis'ma russkago ofitsera* (Moscow 1815)
Glinka, V. M., and Pomarnatsky, A. V. *Voennaia galereia Zimnego Dvortsa* (Leningrad 1974)
Glover, Michael. *A Very Slippery Fellow: The Life of Sir Robert Wilson 1777–1849* (Oxford 1977)
Goethe Handbuch: Goethe, seine Welt und Zeit, in Werk und Wirkung, Gen. Ed. Alfred Zastrau (Stuttgart 1961)
Golenishchev-Kutuzov, M. I. See Kutuzov
Golitsyn, N. B., Prince. *Ofitserskiia zapiski ili vospominaniia o pokhodakh 1812, 1813 i 1814 godov* (Moscow 1838)
Grimsted, Patricia Kennedy. *The Foreign Ministers of Alexander I: Political Attitudes and the Conduct of Russian Diplomacy, 1801–25* (Berkeley, Calif. 1970)
Grunwald, Constantin de. *Alexandre Ier, le tsar mystique* (Paris 1957)
―――――― [Nevskii, S:, pseud.] 'Novoe ob otechestvennoi voine 1812 g.', *Russkie Novosti* (Paris, 16 December 1955)
―――――― *Stein: L'Ennemi de Napoléon* (Paris 1936)
La Guerre Nationale de 1812, Publication du Comité scientifique du Grand État-major russe (French edition, Paris c. 1902)
Harnack, Otto. 'Briefe de Feldmarschalls Fürsten Barclay de Tolly aus den Jahren 1812–1815', *Baltische Monatsschrift* XXXV, 6 (Reval 1888)
Haym, Rudolf. *Herder* (East Berlin 1958)
Herder, Johann Gottfried. *Journal meiner Reise im Jahre 1769*, ed. with an introduction by Johannes Nohl (Weimar 1949)
Herrmann, Ernst. *Geschichte des Russischen Staats* (Gotha 1866)
Holmes, E. R. *Borodino, 1812* (London 1971)
Houssaye, Henry. 1814 Paris 1888)
Ibbeken, Rudolf. *Preussen 1807–1813* (Cologne 1970)
Istoriia russkogo isskustva (Moscow 1964)
Istoriia voennogo isskustva (Moscow 1966)
Jackson, Lieut.-Col. W. G. F. *Seven Roads to Moscow* (London 1957)
Jenkins, Michael. *Arakcheev: Grand Vizier of the Russian Empire* (London 1970)
Jomini, General A. H., Baron de. *Précis politique et militaire des campagnes de 1812 à 1814*

extrait des souvenirs inédits du Général Jomini, avec une notice biographique (Lausanne 1886)

Kapodistria, Grafy Ioann. 'Zapiska Grafa Ioanna Kapodistria o ego sluzhebnoi deiatel'nosti', *Sbornik Imperatorskogo russkogo istoricheskogo obshchestva* III (St. Petersburg 1868)

Kazakov, N. 'O zapiskakh M. B. Barklaia-de-Tolli', *Voenno-istoricheskii Zhurnal* 4 (Moscow 1974)

Kharkevich, V. I. *Barklai-de-Tolli v otechestvennuiu voinu: posle soedineniia armii pod Smolenskom* (with an Appendix of 20 letters exchanged between BdT and Alexander), (St. Petersburg 1904)

──────, ed. 'Perepiska Imperatora Aleksandra i Barklaia-de-Tolli ot nachala voennykh deistvii do ot'ezda Gosoudaria iz armii', *Voennyi Sbornik* (St. Petersburg, November 1903–September 1906)

Kircheisen, F. M., ed. *Napoleons Untergang: ausgewählte Memoirenstücke* (Stuttgart 1911–14)

Kochetkov, A. N. *M. B. Barklai-de-Tolli* (pamphlet) (Moscow 1970)

Koka, Georgii. 'Pushkin o Polkovodtsakh dvenadtsatogo goda', *Prometei* VII (Moscow 1969)

Kosen, Friedrich von [F. v. K.]. *Journal der Kriegsoperationen der Kaiserlich-Russischen und der verbündeten Armeen, von der Eroberung Thorns bis zur Einnahme von Paris* (Riga 1815)

Kutuzov, Field-Marshal M. I., Prince Golenishchev-. *Sbornik dokumentov* (Moscow 1951–6)

Labaume, Eugène. *Relation circonstanciée de la campagne de Russie en 1812* (Paris 1816)

Laforgue, Dr René. *Psychopathologie de l'échec* (Geneva 1963)

Langeron, L. A. A., Comte de. *Mémoires de Langeron, Général d'infanterie dans l'armée russe: campagnes de 1812, 1813, 1814*, ed. by L. G. Fabry (Paris 1902)

────── 'Zapiski grafa Lanzherona o russkom voiske (1796–1824 gg)', *Russkaia Mysl'*, IX and XI (Moscow 1896)

Lermontov, M. I. *Stikhotvoreniia* (Leningrad 1940)

Lettow-Vorbeck, Oskar von. *Der Krieg von 1806 und 1807* (Berlin 1891–6)

Ley, Francis. *Madame de Krüdener et son temps, 1764–1824* (Paris 1961)

Ligne, Charles-Joseph, Prince de. *Mémoires et mélanges historiques et littéraires* (Paris 1827–9)

Liprandi, I. P. *Materialy dlia otechestvennoi voiny 1812 goda* (St. Petersburg 1867)

Listovki otechestvennoi voiny 1812 goda: sbornik dokumentov (Moscow 1962)

Loewenstern, General Waldemar Freiherr von.* *Denkwürdigkeiten eines Livländers: aus den Jahren 1790–1815*, ed. by Friedrich von Smitt (Leipzig/Heidelberg 1858)

──────* *Mémoires du Général-Major russe Baron von Löwenstern (1776–1858)*, publiés d'après le manuscrit original et annotés par M. H. Weil (Paris 1903)

──────* 'Zapiski', *Russkaia Starina* (St. Petersburg, November 1900, December 1900, January 1901)

*All three versions of Loewenstern, but especially the Russian, have been used here abundantly for source material. There are variations among all three: merely because a detail appears in only one of the three does not mean the detail is inauthentic. Loewenstern wrote his memoirs in French and the manuscript remained in the Department of Manuscripts of the Russian Imperial Public Library, appearing in print for the first time in the form of Russian-translation 'Zapiski' (Memoirs) in three consecutive numbers of *Russkaia Starina* in 1900–1. Before this, however, in 1859, immediately after Loewenstern's death, his friend Smitt edited *Denkwürdigkeiten* . . , using, according to *Russkaia Starina*, 'the words of Loewenstern in 1850 together with correspondence and various family documents which were put at his disposal'. Smitt himself said that his *Denkwürdigkeiten* should not be confused with Loewenstern's French-language manuscript memoirs kept in imperial

Longworth, Philip. *The Art of Victory: The Life and Achievements of Generalissimo Suvorov 1729–1800* (London 1965)
Lyons, M., ed. *The Russian Imperial Army: A Bibliography of Regimental History and Related Works* (Stanford 1968)
Manuilov, V. A., and Modzalevskii, L. B. '"Polkovodets" Pushkina', *Pushkinskii Vremennik* (Leningrad 1939)
Marmont, Maréchal, duc de Raguse. *Mémoires du Maréchal Marmont, Duc de Raguse, de 1792 à 1841* (Paris 1857)
Marx, Karl, and Engels, Friedrich. 'Barclay de Tolly', *New American Cyclopedia* II (New York 1858)
Masson, C. F. P. *Mémoires secrets sur la Russie pendant les règnes de Catherine II et de Paul Ier*, ed. by F. Barrière (Paris 1859)
The Mausoleum of Barclay de Tolly, trilingual guidebook compiled by H. Üprus, published by the State Committee for Building and Architecture of the Council of Ministers of the Estonian SSR (Tallinn 1957)
Mel'gunov, S. P. 'Barklai-de-Tolli i Bagration', *Otechestvennaia voina i russkoe obshchestvo* (St. Petersburg 1912)
——— *Dela i liudi Aleksandrovskogo vremeni* (Berlin 1923)
Meshcheriakov, G. P. 'Vlianie boevogo opyta otechestvennoi voiny 1812 goda na razvitie taktiki v russkoi armii v pervoi polovine XIX veka', *1812 god: k stopiatidesiatiletiiu otechestvennoi voiny: Sbornik statei* (Moscow 1962)
Metternich, Clemens, Prinz von. *Mémoires, Documents et écrits divers laissés par le Prince de Metternich*, ed. by his son (Paris 1880)
Mikhailovskii-Danilevskii, General A. I. [A. I. Michaïlowsky-Danilewsky], *Die Geschichte des vaterländischen Krieges im Jahre 1812*, trans. by Carl R. Goldhammer (Riga/Leipzig 1840)
——— *Opisanie Finliandskoi voiny na sukhom puti i na more v 1808 i 1809 godakh* (St. Petersburg 1841)
——— *Opisanie vtoroi voiny Imperatora Aleksandra s Napoleonom v 1806, 1807 godakh* (St. Petersburg 1846)
——— and Viskovatov, A. V. *Imperator Aleksandr I i ego spodvizhniki v 1812, 13, 14 i 1815 godakh: voennaia galeria Zimniago Dvortsa* (St. Petersburg 1848–9)
Mirsky, D. S. *A History of Russian Literature* (London 1964)
Monteith, General William, ed. *Narrative of the Conquest of Finland in the Years 1808–9*, from an unpublished work by a Russian officer of rank, written in 1827 (London 1854)
Montesquiou-Fezensac. See Fezensac
Müffling, General Friedrich Carl Ferdinand, Freiherr von. *Aus meinem Leben* (Berlin 1851)
Napoleon. *Correspondance de Napoléon Ier*, published by order of the Emperor Napoleon III (Paris 1858–69)
——— *Lettres inédites de Napoléon Ier à Marie Louise écrites de 1810 à 1814*, ed. by Louis Madelin (Paris 1935)
——— *Napoléon, recueil . . . de ses lettres . . ., discours . . . formant une histoire de son règne*, ed. by Jean Kermoysan (Paris 1857)
——— See also *Vie politique . . . de Napoléon*

archives. The French version published in Paris in 1903, 'after the original manuscript', contains two or three plausible details perhaps considered frivolous by the German and Russian editors. Loewenstern's name is also written as Woldemar Hermann Baron von Löwenstern and Vladimir Ivanovich Levenshtern.

Nevskii, S. See Grunwald, Constantin de
Nicolas Mikhaïlovich, Grand Duke [Grand-Duc Nicolas Michaïlowitch]. *Correspondance de l'Empereur Alexandre Ier avec sa sœur la Grande-Duchesse Catherine, 1805–1818* (St. Petersburg 1910)
Niebuhr, Barthold Georg. *Die Briefe Barthold Georg Niebuhrs*, ed. by Dietrich Gerhard and William Norvin (Berlin 1929)
Odeleben, Otto von. *Napoleons Feldzug in Sachsen im Jahr 1813* (Dresden 1816)
Olivier, Daria. *L'Incendie de Moscou (15 Septembre 1812)* (Paris (1964)
'Order of the Day', *The Times* (London, 8 April 1814)
Ordin, K. F. *Pokorenie Finliandii* (St. Petersburg 1889)
'L'Ordre du Jour', *Le Journal des Débats* (Paris, 3 April 1814)
Os'kin, G. 'Vozniknovenie i razvitie sluzhby general'nogo shtaba v russkoi armii', *Voenno-istoricheskii Zhurnal* 3 (Moscow, March 1969)
Otechestvennaia voina 1812 goda, archives published by the Scientific Committee of the Russian General Staff (St. Petersburg 1907, 1908) = *La Guerre Nationale*, q.v.
Otechestvennaia voina 1812 goda: sbornik dokumentov i materialov (Leningrad/Moscow 1941)
Palmer, Alan. *Alexander I: Tsar of War and Peace* (London 1974)
——— *Napoleon in Russia* (London 1967)
Pertz, G. H. *Das Leben des Ministers Freiherrn vom Stein* (Berlin 1849–55)
Petre, F. Loraine. *Napoleon's Campaign in Poland 1806–7: A Military History of Napoleon's First War with Russia, Verified from Unpublished Official Documents*, new edition with introduction by David G. Chandler (London 1975, first published 1901)
——— *Napoleon's Last Campaign in Germany, 1813*, introduction by David G. Chandler (London 1974, first published 1912)
Petrunina, N. N. 'Polkovodets', *Stikhotvoreniia Pushkina, 1820–1830 godov* (Leningrad 1974)
Pipes, Richard. 'The Russian Military Colonies, 1810–1831', *Journal of Modern History* (Chicago, September 1950)
——— *Russia under the Old Regime* (London 1974)
Platonov, S. F. *Histoire de la Russie des origines à 1918*, trans. from Russian (Paris 1929)
Plotho, Carl von. *Der Krieg in Frankreich und Deutschland* (Berlin 1813–18)
Popov, A. N. 'Ot Moskvy do Krasnoi Pakhry', *Russkaia Starina* (St. Petersburg, June and July 1897)
Prosch, Georg R. von. *Stammtafeln aus neuerer Zeit: Die Fürsten Barclay de Tolly* (Munich 1948)
Pugachev, V. V. 'K voprosu o pervonachal'nom plane voiny 1812 goda', in *1812 god: k stopiatidesiatiletiiu otechestvennoi voiny: sbornik stat'ei* (Moscow 1962)
Pushkin, Aleksandr S. *Eugene Onegin*, trans. by Babette Deutsch (London 1964)
——— *Eugene Onegin*, trans. by Vladimir Nabokov (New York, 1964)
——— 'The Field-Marshal', trans. by Eugene M. Kayden, *The Colorado Quarterly* XXII, 2 (Boulder, Autumn 1973)
——— *Polnoe sobranie sochinenii* (Moscow/Leningrad 1937–59)
Raeff, Marc. *Michael Speransky: Statesman of Imperial Russia, 1772–1839* (The Hague 1969)
Rakovskii, L. O. *Kutuzov* (Leningrad 1971)
Ranke, Leopold von. *Denkwürdigkeiten des Staatskanzlers Fürsten von Hardenberg* (Leipzig 1877)
Reutern, Sophie von. *Generalleutnant Christoph von Reutern und seine Familie*, private printing (Tübingen 1888)

Rigasche Biographien (Riga 1881)
Rose, J. Holland. *The Life of Napoleon* (London 1903)
―――― *William Pitt and the Great War* (London 1912)
Runeberg, Johan Ludwig. *The Songs of Ensign Stål*, trans. from Swedish by Clement Burbank Shaw (New York 1925)
Russkii biograficheskii slovar', ed. by A. A. Polovtsov (St. Petersburg 1896–1918)
Sainte-Beuve, C. A. *Portraits de Femmes* (Paris 1870)
Sbornik Imperatorskogo russkogo istoricheskogo obshchestva (*SIRIO*, I–CXXXXVIII), (St. Petersburg 1868–1916)
Sbornik istoricheskikh materialov izvlechennykh iz arkhiva Sobstvennoj E. I. V. Kantselarii (St. Petersburg 1876, 1889, 1890)
Sbornik voenno-istoricheskikh materialov (I–XVI), (St. Petersburg 1892–1904)
Schroeder, Johann Karl von. 'Michael Barclay de Tolly: zum 200. Geburtstag des Feldmarschalls', *Baltische Hefte*, IV, 2 (Hanover 1962–3)
Schubert, Friedrich von. *Unter dem Doppeladler: Erinnerungen eines Deutschen in russischem Offiziersdienst, 1789–1814*, ed. with an introduction by Erik Amburger (Stuttgart 1962)
Schwarzenberg, Prince Karl. *Feldmarschall Fürst Schwarzenberg: Der Sieger von Leipzig* (Vienna 1964)
Ségur, Louis-Phillipe, Comte de. *Mémoires, ou souvenirs et anecdotes* (Paris 1824–6)
Ségur, Général Paul-Philippe, Comte de. *Histoire de Napoléon et de la Grande Armée pendant l'année 1812* (Paris 1826)
Shil'der, Aleksandr N. K. *Imperator Aleksandr Pervyi', ego zhizn' i tsarstvovanie I-IV* (St. Petersburg 1904–5)
Smitt, Friedrich von. *Aufklärung über den Krieg von 1812* (Leipzig 1861)
――――, ed. See Loewenstern, *Denkwürdigkeiten*..
Smout, T. C. *A History of the Scottish People 1560–1830* (London 1969)
Staël, Germaine de. *Oeuvres complètes de Mme la Baronne de Staël*, XV, *Dix années d'exil* (Brussels 1821)
Stalin, I. V. 'Otvet tov. Stalina na pis'mo tov. Razina', *Bolshevik* 3 (Moscow 1947)
Stedingk, Maréchal Kurt Bogislaus Ludvig Christopher, Comte de. *Mémoires posthumes*, ed. by General Count de Björnstjerna (Paris 1844)
Stendhal [Marie Henri Beyle]. *Vie de Napoléon, fragments* (Paris 1876)
Steuart, A. Francis. *Scottish Influences in Russian History* (Glasgow 1913)
Stryk, L. von. *Beiträge zur Geschichte der Rittergüter Livlands* (Dorpat 1877)
Tarlé, E. *La Campagne de Russie 1812*, trans. from Russian by Marc Slonim (Paris 1950)
―――― *Napoléon*, trans. from Russian by J. Champenois (Moscow sd)
―――― *Nashestvie Napoleona na Rossiiu, 1812 god*. (original of *La Campagne de Russie 1812*) (Moscow 1936)
Tatistcheff, Serge. *Alexandre Ier et Napoléon*, from their unpublished correspondence 1801–1812 (Paris 1891)
Thiers, A. *Histoire du Consulat et de l'Empire* (Paris 1847–57)
Toll, Carl Friedrich, Graf von. *Denkwürdigkeiten aus dem Leben des Kaiserl. Russ. Generals von der Infanterie, Carl Friedrich Grafen von Toll*, ed. with introduction and notes by Theodor von Bernhardi (Leipzig 1865)
Tolstoy, Count Lev. *War and Peace*, trans. by Louise and Aylmer Maude (London 1959)
Tommila, Päviö. *La Finlande dans la politique européene en 1809–1815* (Helsinki 1962)
Trofimov, I. '"Polkovodets"', *Prometei* X (Moscow 1947)
Tsebrikov, R. M. 'Vokrug Ochakova, 1788 god', *Russkaia Starina* LXXXIV (St.

Petersburg, September 1895)

Tynianov, Iuri N. *Kiukhlia* (Moscow 1975)

—— *Pushkin i ego sovremenniki* (Moscow 1968)

'Uchrezhdenie dlia upravleniia bol'shoi deistvuiushchei armii', *Voenno-istoricheskii Zhurnal* (Moscow, January 1962)

Üprus, H., ed. See *The Mausoleum of Barclay de Tolly*

Vandal, Albert. *Napoléon et Alexandre Ier: l'alliance russe sous le premier Empire* (Paris 1891–6)

—— 'Notes sur la cour de Russie et St. Pétersbourg en 1807 et 1808 écrites en Décembre 1807 par le Général Savary', *Revue d'histoire diplomatique* III (Paris 1890)

Vegesack, Siegfried von. 'Die Briefe des Feldmarschalls Barclay de Tolly an seine Frau aus den Jahren 1812, 1813, 1815', *Baltische Hefte* (Hanover, January and March 1959)

—— *Vorfahren und Nachkommen: Aufzeichnungen aus einer altlivländischen Brieflade 1689–1887* (Heilbronn 1960)

Vie politique et militaire de Napoléon racontée par lui-même, au tribunal de César, d'Alexandre et de Frédéric (Paris 1827)

Vigel', F. F. *Zapiski*, ed. by S. Ya. Shtraikh (Moscow 1928, reprinted Cambridge 1974)

Viskovatyi, P. A. 'Fel'dmarshal Barklai-de-Tolli: k ego biografii', *Russkaia Starina* (St. Petersburg, October 1888)

Voenno-Entsiklopededicheskii Leksikon (St. Petersburg 1838, 1853)

Volkonskii, S. G., Prince. *Zapiski* (St. Petersburg 1902)

Watson, William J. *The History of the Celtic Place-Names of Scotland* (Edinburgh/London 1926)

Werlich, Robert. *Russian Orders, Decorations and Medals* (Washington 1968)

Weymarn, Auguste Christine von. *Erinnerungen aus meinem Leben*, private printing (sl,sd [1886])

Weymarn, F. W. von [V-n, V.]. 'Barklai-de-Tolli i otechestvennaia voina 1812 goda', *Russkaia Starina* (St. Petersburg, August, September, October, December 1912)

—— [von W-n, F. W.]. *Barklay de Tolly und der vaterländische Krieg* (Reval 1914)*

Whitcomb, Edward A. 'The Duties and Functions of Napoleon's External Agents', *History* LVII, No. 190 (London, June 1972)

Whiting, Kenneth R. *Aleksei Andreevich Arakcheev*, unpublished dissertation, Harvard University Archives (Cambridge 1951)

Wilson, General Sir Robert. *Brief Remarks on the Character and Composition of the Russian Army and a Sketch of the Campaigns in Poland in the Years 1806 and 1807* (London 1810)

—— *General Wilson's Journal, 1812–1814*, ed. by Antony Brett-James (London 1964)

—— *Narrative of events during the Invasion of Russia by Napoleon Bonaparte and the Retreat of the French Army, 1812*, ed. by the Rev. Herbert Randolph (London 1860)

—— *Private Diary of Travels, Personal Services, and Public Events, during Mission and Employment with the European Armies in the Campaigns of 1812, 1813, 1814, from the Invasion of Russia to the Capture of Paris*, ed. by the Rev. Herbert Randolph (London 1861)

Wittram, Reinhard. *Geschichte der Baltischen Deutschen: Grundzüge und Durchblicke* (Stuttgart 1939)

---

*Posthumous German book version, less authoritative than the Russian version serialized in *Russkaia Starina* 1912. This essay (173 pp.) is the only book heretofore devoted to BdT.

Wolzogen, Ludwig, Freiherr von. *Memoiren des königlich preussischen Generals der Infanterie Ludwig Freiherrn von Wolzogen* (Leipzig 1851)
Woodhouse, C. M. *Capodistria: The Founder of Greek Independence* (London 1973)
The World Population Situation in 1970, United Nations Population Studies No. 49 (New York 1971)
Württemberg, Eugen, Prinz von. *Aus dem Leben des Kaiserlich Russischen Generals der Infanterie, Prinzen Eugen von Württemberg*, ed. by Freiherr von Helldorf (Berlin 1861)
────── *Erinnerungen aus dem Feldzuge des Jahres 1812 in Russland* (Breslau 1846)
Yorck von Wartenburg, Feldmarschall Graf. *Napoleon als Feldherr* (Berlin 1904)
Zakrevskii, Arsenii Andr'evich, Count. 'Bumagi Grafa Zakrevskago', ed. by N. F. Dubrovin, *Sbornik Imperatorskogo russkogo istoricheskogo obshchestva* LXXIII (St. Petersburg 1890)
Zhilin, P. A. *Gibel' Napoleonovskoi armii v Rossii* (Moscow 1974)
────── *Kontrnastuplenie Kutuzova v 1812 g.* (Moscow 1950)
Zhukovskii, V. A. *Stikhotvoreniia* (Moscow 1959)

D. J.

GEOGRAPHICAL GLOSSARY

Åbo (Swedish) = Turku (Finnish)
Åland [Islands] (Swedish) = Ahvenanmaa (Finnish)
Alavo (Swedish) = Alavus (Finnish)
Austerlitz (then, German) = Slavkov u Brna (now, Czech)
Beckhof (then, German) = Jõgereste (now, Estonian)
Borgå (Swedish) = Porvoo (Finnish)
Courland (then, French) = Kurland (then, German) = part of the Lithuanian SSSR (now)
Danzig (German) = Gdańsk (Polish)
Dorpat (then, German) = Jurjev (Russian) = Tartu (now, Estonian)
Dünaburg (German) = Dvinsk (Russian) = Daugavpils (now, Latvian)
Elisavetgrad (then) = Kirovograd (now)
Embach (German) = Emajögi (Estonian)
Estland (then) = part of Estonia (now)
Fredrikshamn (Swedish) = Hamina (Finnish)
Friedland (German) = Pravdinsk (now, Russian)
Gaddarna (Swedish) = Gadan (Finnish)
Gamle-Karlebi (Swedish) = Gamlakarleby (Swedish variant) = Kokkola (Finnish)
Graudenz (German) = Grudziadz (Polish)
Helsingfors (Swedish) = Helsinki (Finnish)
Hogland (Swedish) = Suk-Sari (Finnish)
Karelia = Karelen (Swedish) = Karjala (Finnish) = south-west Finnish district and Finno-Karelian SSR (now)
Koenigsberg (then, German) = Kaliningrad (now, Russian)
Kovno (Russian) = Kowno (Polish, German) = Kobno (variant) = Kaunas (now, Lithuanian)
Krasnyi (Russian) = Krasnoye, Krasnoe, Krasnaia (Russian variants)
Kulm (German) = Chlumec (Russian) = Chełmno (Polish)
Kvarken (Finnish) = Quarken (variant)
Lappo (Swedish) = Lapua (Finnish)
Livonia (then) = region encompassing Latvia, part of Estonia, part of Lithuania (now)
Memel (then, German) = Klaipeda (now, Lithuanian) = Klaypeda (variant)
Neman' (Russian) = Niemen (Polish, English) = Memel (German) = Nemumas (Lithuanian)
Nesvizh (Russian) = Niesweirz (Polish)
Nizhni-Novgorod (then) = Gor'kiy (now)
Porech'e (Russian) = Porechie (Lithuanian) = Poredzie (Polish)
Preussisch-Eylau (then, German) = Bagration (now, Russian)
Reims (French) = Rheims (German, English)
Reval (then, German, Danish) = Revel' (Russian) = Tallinn (now, Estonian)
Revolaks (Russian) = Revolax (Swedish) = Revonlahti (Finnish)
Rhine (English) = Rhein (German) = Rhin (French)
Ruschuk (then, Russian) = Ruse (now, Bulgarian)
St. Petersburg (then) = Leningrad (now)

Saivar (Swedish) = Säfvar (Finnish)
Schaueln (then, German) = Shavli (Russian) = Siauliai (now, Lithuanian) = Shaulyai, Shaulyay (variants)
Sveaborg (Swedish) = Suomenlinna (Finnish)
Svenskound (Swedish) = Ruotsinsalmi (Finnish)
Sventsiany (Russian) = Święciany (Polish)
Tavastehus (Swedish) = Hämeenlinna (Finnish)
Tilsit (then) = Sovetsk (now)
Thorn (German) = Toruń (Polish)
Torneå (Swedish) = Tornio (Finnish)
Towie (Scots) = Tolly (Latin and Gaelic) = Tolli and Tollie (variants)
Uleaborg (Swedish) = Oulu (Finnish)
Vasa (Swedish) = Vaasa (Finnish)
Velizh (Russian) = Velish (Lithuanian)
Vilna (then, German, English) = Vil'na (Russian) = Wilna (then, French) = Wilno (Polish) = Vilnius (now, Lithuanian)
Vistula (then) = Weichsel (German) = Wisła (now, Polish)
Znaim (German) = Znojmo (Czech)

INDEX

Åbo, 47, 53, 59–60, 62, 65, 68–9, 72; Bishop of, 68
Adevile, Humphrey and Theobald de (BdT's ancestors), 2
Aix-la-Chapelle, Congress of (1818), 212
Akkerman, Battle of (1789), 19
Åland Islands, 47, 50, 53–4, 58, 60, 64–5
Alavo, Battle of (1808), 53
Albert, Bishop of Bremen, 3
Alekseev, General, 63
Alexander I (Tsar of Russia):
  education, 5
  1801 accession, 25
  1805–7 war of Third Coalition, 26–30, 33–4, 38–44
  1807 Bartenstein Convention, 40–1, 43–4
  1807 Treaty of Tilsit, 44–5, 65
  1808 war with Sweden in Finland, 46–50, 52–5, 58–61
  1809 Treaty of Frederikshamn, 65–6
  1812 Treaty of Bucharest, 77
  1812 retreat from Vilna, 94–6, 98
  1812 loss of Smolensk, 121
  1812 loss of Moscow, 149, 151, 153, 160
  1813–14 war of Fourth Coalition, 167–70, 172–80, 182–4, 186–94, 196–8
  1814 visit to England, 1
  1815 religiosity, 4, 201–3
  1816 military settlements, 205–7
  1818 BdT's death and burial, 208–9
  relationship with BdT, 13, 24, 27, 38–41, 45, 52–4, 60–1, 63–4, 66–7, 73–4, 83, 88, 90, 99–100, 114–17, 120, 129–32, 136–7, 139–40, 157, 159–69, 175, 179–80, 188–9, 192, 200, 203–4
  military/diplomatic strategies, 26–7, 42–6, 49, 52–4, 59–71, 74–5, 77, 80, 85–8, 90–5, 98, 104–6, 112, 128, 146, 149, 151, 161, 167, 170, 172, 174, 176–9, 186–8, 190, 193–4, 197–8
  command of Army, 91–3, 99–106, 125, 129–32, 157, 169–70, 172–3, 178
Alexander II (Tsar of Russia), 84, 210
Allonville, Count d', 87

Alopaeus, David, Count, 64
Andronikov, Iraklii, 216
Anhalt, Friedrich, Count, 17
Anhalt-Bernburg, Lieutenant-General Victor-Amadeus, Prince, 17–19, 21–3
Anstedt, Jean Protais, Baron d', 167, 198
Arakcheev, Alexei Andreevich, Count, 52, 54–5, 60, 71–5, 98, 102, 104, 106, 118, 124, 153—4, 205–7
Arcis-sur-Aube, Battle of (1814), 192–3
Armfelt, General Gustaf Mauritz, Count von, 100, 106
Army Regulations (1812), 83–5, 92, 105, 140, 156, 167, 169, 206, 213
Arundel, Roger, 2
Ascheraden, Karl Schultz von, Baron, 4
Auerstadt, Battle of (1806), 28, 37, 65
Augereau, Maréchal Pierre-François Charles, 31, 33, 38, 182, 191
Austerlitz, Battle of (1805), 26–8, 30, 37, 42, 45, 75, 90, 95, 130, 143, 170, 176, 197
Austria, 1, 16, 22, 26–7, 41, 43, 85, 92, 166–7, 170, 173–4, 176–7, 181, 195–6
Azerbaidjan, 76

Baggavut, General Karl Fedorovich, 32–4, 89, 96, 99, 140–1, 143, 145
Bagration, General Pyotr Ivanovich, Prince, 35, 43, 45–7, 55, 58, 60, 80, 87, 89, 91, 93–4, 96, 98–100, 102–11, 113–16, 118–20, 122, 124, 126–37, 139–42, 146, 158, 164, 173, 192, 203
Balashov, General Alexander Dmitrievich, 80, 95, 98, 100, 104, 106
Baltic Sea, 3–4, 66, 74
Barclay, Andrew (BdT's ancestor), 3
Barclay, David (BdT's ancestor), 2
Barclay, Johann Stephan (BdT's great-grandfather), 3–6
Barclay, John (BdT's ancestor), 2–3, 6
Barclay, Patrick (BdT's ancestor), 2
Barclay, Sir Patrick (BdT's ancester), 2, 6
Barclay, Peter (BdT's great-great-grandfather), 2–3, 6

Barclay, Colonel Sir Robert (Scottish relative of BdT), 1, 199
Barclay, William (BdT's ancestor), 2
Barclay de Tollie, Wilhelm (BdT's grandfather), 5–6
Barclay de Tolly, Andreas Otto Heinrich (BdT's nephew), 6, 88, 157
Barclay de Tolly, August Wilhelm, Baron von (BdT's cousin), 90
Barclay de Tolly, Christine Gertrude Anna (BdT's sister, married Magnus von Lueder), 6–9, 12, 88, 160, 163, 210
Barclay de Tolly, Erich Johann (BdT's elder brother), 6–7, 12, 22, 88, 209
Barclay de Tolly, Gotthard (BdT's father), 6–7, 9
Barclay de Tolly, Heinrich Johann (BdT's younger brother), 6–7, 27
Barclay de Tolly, Ernst Magnus August, Prince (Max; BdT's son), 13, 69, 88, 160, 200, 208–10
BARCLAY DE TOLLY, Field-Marshal Mikhail Bogdanovich, Prince:
  ancestors, 5–6
  childhood, 6–9
  character, 10–12, 17, 23, 25, 30, 32–3, 40, 51, 60, 66–7, 72, 74, 81, 139–40, 145
  1787 Turkish war, 16–19
  1790 Finnish war, 19, 21
  1792, 1794 Polish campaigns, 22
  1805–7 war of Third Coalition, 26–43
  1808–9 war with Sweden in Finland, 47, 50–61
  1809–10 Governor-General of Finland, 60–72
  1810–12 Minister of War, 72–91, 95, 102, 124, 129–31, 158, 173
  1812 Commander-in-Chief, First Army, 90–4, 96, 130–1, 156
  1812 retreat from Vilna, 96, 98–101, 103
  1812 retreat to Smolensk, 106–12
  1812 abandonment of Smolensk and growing unpopularity, 113–28
  1812 Borodino, 134–47
  1812 abandonment of Moscow, 151–4
  1812 departure from First Army, 157–8
  1813 Commander-in-Chief, Third Army, 167–8
  1813–14 war of Fourth Coalition, 167–98
  1813 Commander-in-Chief, Russian Main Army, 172–3, 188
  1813 named Count, 184
  1814 named Field-Marshal, 196
  1814 visit to England, 1, 199
  1814 Commander-in-Chief, First Army, 199
  1815 France, 200–3
  1815 named Prince, 203–4
  1816 military settlements, 205–7
  1818 death and burial, 208–9
  Pushkin's memorial: 'Polkovodets' ('The Commander'), 211–17, 218–219
  relationship with Tsar Alexander I, 13, 24, 27, 38–41, 45, 52–4, 60–1, 63–4, 66–7, 73–4, 83, 88, 90, 99–100, 114–17, 120, 129–32, 136–7, 139–40, 157, 159–69, 175, 179–80, 188–9, 192, 200, 203–4
  military career, 9, 17, 19, 23, 27, 41, 60, 72, 90, 129–31, 157, 167, 172, 196, 199
  marriage and family life, 12–15, 22–4, 27, 88–9, 163, 185, 198
  Fabian strategy, 20, 41–2, 45, 87, 89–90, 104–12, 114–15, 120, 122, 132–3, 135, 146, 148–51, 155
Barclay de Tolly Regiment, 209
Barclay de Tolly-Weymarn, Alexander Magnus, Prince (BdT's great-nephew), 15, 210
Barclay de Tolly-Weymarn, Ludwig Alexander, Prince (BdT's great-great-nephew), 210
Barclay de Tolly-Weymarn, Nicolas, Prince (BdT's great-great-great-nephew), 210
Bar-sur-Aube, Battle of (1814), 188, 190–1
Bartenstein, 40–1; Bartenstein Convention (1807), 41, 43–4
Batalin, Dr., 159–60, 163, 165–6
Bautzen, Battle of (1813), 169–70, 173–4, 177
Bavaria, 45, 181; Crown Prince of, 79
Beauharnais, Eugène, Prince de, 108, 116, 135, 141, 166, 191
Beckhof (BdT's home), 6, 12, 22, 88, 162–3, 165–6, 205, 208–10
Belinskii, Vissarion Grigorevich, 213

Benckendorff, General Aleksandr, Count von, 102
Bender, Battle of (1788), 19
Bennigsen, General Levin August Gottlieb, Count, 26, 28, 30–8, 41–4, 52, 87, 93–5, 100, 104, 106, 119, 123–4, 127, 130, 132–4, 136, 138, 146, 148–51, 153–6, 158–9, 167, 175–6, 181–3, 187, 199
Bennigsen, Baroness, 94, 156
Berchelei, Robert de (BdT's ancestor), 2
Berezina, river, 1, 75, 107
Berg, General Burchard Maximovich von 56
Berkeley, Agatha de (BdT's ancestor), 2
Berlin, 28, 31, 79, 89, 169, 177, 181, 186, 197, 208
Bernadotte, Maréchal Jean-Baptiste (Crown Prince of Sweden from 1810), 26, 31, 34, 37, 53, 76, 86–7, 93, 129, 169, 176, 182–3, 187, 191
Berthier, Maréchal Louis-Alexandre, 90, 112, 152
Bertrand, Général Henri-Gratien, Comte de, 170
Beskrovnyi, L. G., 90, 94
Bessarabia, 77
Bessières, Maréchal Jean-Baptiste, 31
Białystock, 89
Bignon, L. P. E. (Edouard), 79, 83
Bistrom, Colonel Karl Ivanovich, 138
Blücher, Marshal Gebhard von, 169–70, 172–4, 176–7, 181–3, 187–92, 194–5, 197–200
Bobruisk fortress, 75–6, 87, 107, 109
Bohemia, 13, 176–82, 207; Army of, 176–8, 181, 183, 187; see also Main Army
Bonaparte, Jérôme, King of Westphalia, 102, 106–7
Bonaparte, Joseph, King of Spain, 189–90, 195–7
Bonaparte, Letitia, 198
Bonaparte, Napoleon, see Napoleon I (Bonaparte)
Bondy, Château of, 194, 196–7
Borgå, 59, 63, 67, 71
Borodino, Battle of (1812), 11, 134–5, 138–9, 141–8, 150, 153–9, 161–3, 170, 192, 202, 214
Bothnia, Gulf of, 47, 49, 54–5, 62
Brandt, Captain Heinrich von, 143
Britain, 1–2, 16, 25–6, 36, 41–6, 60, 76, 86, 207
Bubna, General Ferdinand, Count von, 188
Bucharest, Treaty of (1812), 77, 85
Budberg, General Andrei, 45
Bulgarin, Faddei V., 215
Bülow, General Friedrich Wilhelm, Baron von, 191
Butterfield, Herbert, 44, 166
Buturlin, Colonel D. P., Count, 107
Buxhoevden, General Friedrich Wilhelm, Count von, 26, 30–4, 47, 49–54

Campenhausen, Christoph, Baron von, 209
Campenhausen, Leocadie von (first wife of Ernst Magnus Barclay de Tolly), 209–10
Capodistria, John, Count, 85, 175–6
Castlereagh, Robert Stewart, Viscount, 189, 197
Cathcart, Lord, 155
Catherine, Grand Duchess, 14, 44–5, 91, 104–5, 124, 129, 131, 153, 173, 204
Catherine II (the Great, Empress of Russia), 4, 16–23, 26, 30, 42, 66, 80, 203
Caulaincourt, Général Armand-Augustin Louis, Marquis de, 45, 49, 53, 55, 65, 73, 83, 87–8, 95, 110, 112, 189, 197
Caulaincourt, Général August J. G. de, 142
Chambray, Général Georges, Marquis de, 115, 147
Chandler, David G., 122, 190
Chaplits, General, 170, 172
Charles XII (King of Sweden), 65, 155
Châtillon, Congress of (1814), 189, 194
Chaumont, Treaty of (1814), 190
Chernyshev, Colonel, 79–80, 87, 89
Chichagov, Admiral Paul V., 85, 130, 154, 167, 175
Clarke, Général Henri-Jacques Guillaume, 195
Clausewitz, General Carl von, 100–2, 108, 118, 127–30, 134, 147, 153, 158, 167, 198
Colloredo (Colloredo-Mansfeld), General Hieronymus, Count von, 178, 180, 183
'Commander, The' ('Polkovodets' by Pushkin), 211–17, 218–19

Constantine, Grand Duke, 43, 96, 114–15, 117, 123, 177, 180, 184, 187–8, 197, 211–12
Constantinople, 65, 85
Continental System, The, 45–6, 65, 75–6, 92
Copenhagen, 46
Crimea, 16, 20
Crimean War, 207
Croanne, Battle of (1814), 191
Cronstedt, Admiral Carl Olaf, 57
Czartoryski, Adam, Prince, 25–7

Dalmatia, 85
Damas, Comte de, 18
Danube, river, 26, 77, 175, 179
Danubian Army, 82
Danzig, 28, 45
Darenthal, Anna Sophia von (BdT's great-grandmother, married Johann Stephan Barclay), 5
Daru, Général Pierre-Antoine Noël Bruno, Comte de, 112
Davout, Maréchal Louis-Nicolas, Duc d'Auerstadt, Prince d'Eckmühl, 31–3, 80, 89, 92, 94, 102–3, 106–7, 109–11, 121, 126, 135–6, 186–7
Davydov, Colonel Denis Vassil'evich, 45, 213
Dawe, George, 212, 218
Decembrists, 80, 124, 138, 194
Dejean, Général Jean-François, Comte de, 196
Delzon, Général A. J., Baron, 138, 144
Denmark, 21, 46, 65
Diebitsch, Hans [Field-Marshal Ivan Ivanovich, Count Dibich-Zabalkanskii], 167, 174–5, 177, 190–1, 193–4, 207–8
Dnepr, river, 75, 86, 109, 113, 116, 119–20, 126–7, 205
Dneprovskii Liman, 17–19
Dokhturov, General Dmitri Sergeevich, 33–4, 61, 80, 96, 99, 103, 107–8, 116, 120–4, 130, 137, 142, 144–6, 149–50, 200
Dorogobuzh, 122, 124, 126, 128
Dorokhov, General Ivan Semenovich, 155
Dorpat, 209; University, 103, 212
Dresden, Battle of (1813), 169, 177–8, 180–1

Drissa military camp, 86, 93–4, 96, 98–104, 106–7, 129, 149, 158
Dumas, General Mathieu, Comte, 89–90
Dünaburg, see Dvinsk
Dvina, river, 3, 75, 86, 107
Dvinsk, 75, 104

Ekaterinoslav Army, 16–19
Elba, 199
Elena Pavlovna, Grand Duchess, 215
Elizabeth Alekseevna (Empress of Russia, wife of Alexander I), 60, 165, 204, 209
Elizabeth Petrovna (Empress of Russia), 99–100
Enghien, Louis-Antoine de Bourbon Condé, Duc d', 25
England, see Britain
Erfurt, 203; Conference (1808), 53, 168
Ermolov, General Alexei Petrovich, 98, 104–5, 108, 111, 115, 117–18, 123–4, 136–7, 141, 148–50, 154, 156, 158, 169, 177, 179, 201, 213
Essen I, General Ivan Nikolaevich, 30, 41, 89–90
Essen II, General Pyotr Killillovich, Count, 61
Estonia, 3, 54, 83, 88, 208–9
Etkind, Efim, 216
Eylau, see Preussisch-Eylau

Fabian strategy 41, 89, 113, 122, 135; see also BARCLAY DE TOLLY
Fezensac, Raymond, Duc de, 33
Ficquelmont, Karl Ludwig, Count von, 214
Fili war council (1812), 148, 150, 153–4, 213
Filisov, Colonel, 56, 58
Finland, 19–22, 46–7, 49–55, 59–72, 76–7, 100, 140, 159, 169
Finland, Gulf of, 23, 47, 63
First (West) Army, 90–1, 93–6, 98–100, 102–4, 106–9, 111, 113–14, 119, 122, 126–7, 130, 132–3, 136–7, 140, 146, 156–7, 161–2, 175, 199–200, 211
Florinsky, Michael T., 74
Fontaine, Pierre-François, 202
France, 16, 25, 44, 46, 65, 73, 75–6, 85–6, 169, 186–9, 193, 195, 200–1, 207

Francis I (Emperor of Austria), 1, 178–80, 186, 190, 197, 200, 202, 212
Franco-Prussian Alliance (Feb. 1812), 86
Franco-Prussian Treaty (1807), 44
Frankfurt, 186, 188, 200
Frauendorf, Battle of (1807), 35–6, 39
Frederick the Great (King of Prussia), 7–8, 17, 28, 38, 74–5, 86, 167
Frederick William III (King of Prussia), 1, 26, 28, 34, 38, 40–1, 44, 85–7, 90, 167, 170, 172, 176, 178, 183, 186, 189, 191, 193–4, 196–8, 200, 202, 208, 212
Frederikshamn, Treaty of (1809), 65–6, 68–9, 71
Friedland, Battle of (1807), 27, 41–5, 90, 95, 170
Frimont, 192

Galberg, S. I., 215
German Legion, 85, 103
Germany, 3–5, 17, 25, 174, 186, 188, 201, 207
Giraud, P. F. F. J., 197
Glinka, Fiodor Nikolaevich, 124–5, 139, 145
Gneisenau, General August Wilhelm, Count von, 85, 169, 174, 187, 190
Goethe, Johann Wolfgang von, 203
Gogol, Nicolas Vassil'evich, 213
Golenishchev-Kutuzov, Login, 213–14
Golitsyn, General D. V., Prince, 33, 55, 61
Golitsyn, N. B., Prince, 118, 152
Golymin, Battle of (1806), 33
Gorchakov, General Andrei Ivanovich, Prince, 61, 90, 131, 177, 182
Gotland, Isle of, 47, 53
Grande Armée, 1, 26, 28, 31, 34, 78, 85, 95–6, 101, 103, 107–8, 110–11, 114–15, 127–8, 135, 143–5, 155, 162, 169–70, 192, 196–7
Graudenz garrison, 28, 168
Grech, Nicolas, 213
Greece, 175
Grodno, Battle of (1794), 22
Gros, Antoine-Jean, Baron, 38
Gruzino, 205
Gudin de la Sablonnière, Général C. E., Comte de, 126–7
Gustavus Adolphus (King of Sweden), 2
Gustavus III (King of Sweden), 20–2

Gustavus IV Adolphus (King of Sweden), 45–6, 49, 58
Gutstadt, 34
Gyulai, General Ignaz, Count, 195
Gzhatsk, 129, 131–4

Hamann, Johann Georg, 5
Hamburg, 186–7
Hanau, Battle of (1813), 186
Hanseatic League, 3
Hardenberg, Karl August von, 41–2, 169, 198
Helffreich, Caroline Elisabeth von (Lina; BdT's foster-daughter), 13–14, 38–9, 41, 69, 72
Helsingfors, 47, 59
Herder, Johann Gottfried von, 4–5
Hof, Battle of (1807), 35–6, 39, 140
Hogland, Battle of (1788), 21
Holland, 20, 187
Houssaye, Henry, 197
Hungarians, 79, 85

Igelström, General, 21–2
Illyria, 85
Innocent III, Pope, 3
Insterburg (BdT's death at), 208
Intelligence, Military, 78–80, 89–90, 117, 193
Italy, 25, 187, 200, 207

Jassy, Treaty of (1792), 19, 22
Jena, Battle of (1806), 28, 37, 65, 95, 170
Jomini, Général Antoine-Henri, Baron de, 106, 114, 177, 182, 187, 190
Junot, Général Andoche, Duc d'Abrantès, 121, 127, 135, 143

Kaisarov, Colonel Paisii Sergeevich, 133, 149, 152, 159, 192
Kalisch, Treaty of (1813), 167
Kallavesi, Lake, 47, 50
Kaluga, 154, 156, 158–9, 162
Kamenskii, General Nikolai Mikhailovich, 47, 50, 53, 61, 63–4, 68, 71, 159
Kamenskii, Field-Marshal Mikhail Fedorovich, Count, 30–2, 34, 41
Kant, Immanuel, 4–5
Karshany, Battle of (1789), 19

Katzbach, Battle of (1813), 181
Kernakoski, Battle of (1790), 21
Khitrovo, Daria, 214
Khitrovo, Elizabeth Mikhailovna, 214, 216
Kiev, 27, 66, 74–6, 86, 91
Kiselev, Lieutenant-Colonel, 55–6
Kleist, General Friedrich von, 170, 177–8, 180, 182–3, 196
Klenau [Klenau von Janowitz], General Johann, Count von, 182
Kliastitsy, Battle of (1812), 169
Klinger, Captain Alexander von, 139
Klingspor, Field-Marshal Wilhelm Mauritz, Count von, 47, 49–53
Knesebeck, General Karl Friedrich von, 87, 172, 175, 179, 187, 190
Knorring, General Bogdan Fedorovich von, 52, 54–5, 57–60, 62
Koenigsberg, 4–5, 28, 34–5, 37–8
Königswartha, Battle of (1813), 170, 173
Konovnitsyn, General Pyotr Petrovich, 108–9, 134, 149–50, 154
Korff, General Friedrich, Baron, 96, 126, 142
Kosciuszko, Thaddeus, 22–3
Kovno, 89, 92, 95, 100
Kramer, Alexandra von (second wife of Ernst Magnus Barclay de Tolly), 210
Krasnaia Pakhra, 154–5
Krasnyi, 116, 119
Kremenchug, 75
Kreutz, 142
Krüdener, Colonel, 118
Krüdener, Julie de, 4, 38, 201–3
Kudashev, Colonel Nikolai Danilovich, Prince, 133, 159
Kuechelbecker [Kiukhelbeker], Justine, 211, 213
Kuechelbecker [Kiukhelbeker], Wilhelm, 160, 211
Kulm, Battle of (1813), 180
Kul'nev, General Iakov Petrovich, 49, 60, 114
Kuopio garrison, 47, 49–53, 63
Kurakin, Alexander Borisovich, Prince, 44, 79
Kutaisov, General Aleksandr Ivanovich, Count, 122, 137, 141
Kutuzov, Field-Marshal Mikhail Illarionovich, Prince Golenishchev-, 11, 18, 26–7, 30, 65, 73, 77, 85, 129–38, 140, 142–62, 164–9, 175, 208, 211–17
Kvarken crossing (1809), 55–6, 58–63, 69, 140, 147, 200

Laharpe, Frédéric-César, 5, 187
Laizer, Marquis de, 89
Lamsdorff, 139
Langenau, General Friedrich Karl, Freiherr von, 182, 187
Langeron, Général Louis-Alexandre, Comte de, 12, 167–8, 170, 196, 202, 213
Langres, 187–8, 190–1
Lannes, Maréchal Jean, 32–3
Laon, Battle of (1814), 191–2
Lappo, Battle of (1808), 51, 53
La Rothière, Battle of (1814), 189
Lauriston, Général Alexandre Jacques Bernard Law, Marquis de, 170, 172–3, 182–4
Lavrov, General Nikolai Ivanovich, 98
Leipzig, Battle of (1813), 169, 176–7, 181–7, 193
Lermontov, Mikhail Iurevich, 205, 216
Lestocq, General Anton Wilhelm de, 28, 30–1, 36
Lieven, General Wilhelm, Count von, 87, 89
Ligne, Charles-Joseph, Prince de, 17–18
Likhachev, General Pyotr Gabrilovich, 141
Lilienfeld, Margarethe Sophie von (BdT's sister-in-law, married Erich Barclay de Tolly), 88
Lindenau, 181, 184
Lithuania, 3, 6, 26, 44, 92, 114, 121, 168
Livonia, 3–6, 8, 27, 72, 83, 88, 208, 210
Lobanov-Rostovskii, General Dmitri Ivanovich, Prince, 175
Loewenstern, General Waldemar, Freiherr von, 12, 105, 116, 118, 138–41, 152, 154, 157–8, 174, 198–9
London, 199, 203
Louis XVIII (King of France), 197
Louisa (Queen of Prussia), 40, 167
Lübeck, 28, 210
Lubino, Battle of (1812), 126–7
Lubomirski, Prince, 117
Lueder, Auguste Christine Anna von (Christel; BdT's foster-daughter,

married Wilhelm von Weymarn), 13–15, 88, 163, 207–10
Lueder, Major Magnus von (BdT's brother-in-law), 163
Lutheran Protestantism, 3–4, 8, 10, 22, 52, 59, 62, 69, 88, 208
Lützen, Battle of (1813), 169, 173
Lyons, 188, 191

Macdonald, Maréchal Jacques-Etienne Joseph Alexandre, 167, 181–2, 190
Mack, General Karl Freiherr von, 26
Magdeburg, surrender of (1806), 28
Magnitskii, Mikhail Leont'evich, 84
Maier, Alexander von, 163, 165, 188
Maier, Ludwig von, 249 n 4
Main Army (of Allies 1813–14), 187–8, 190–4
Malcolm IV (King of Scotland), 2
Malojaroslavets, Battle of (1812), 162
Marengo, Battle of (1800), 95, 143
Maria Fedorovna (Dowager Empress of Russia), 44, 60, 198, 203–4, 209
Marie-Louise (Empress of France), 95, 146, 189, 193, 196
Markov, General Evgenii Ivanovich, 34
Marmont, Maréchal August, Duc de Raguse, 179–80, 183, 186, 192, 194–6
Meller-Zakomel'skii, General, 83
Memel, 38, 40–1, 43, 45, 60, 69, 87, 89, 112, 208
Menshikov, General Aleksandr S., Prince, 109–11
Metternich, Klemens, Prince von, 1, 85, 167, 173, 178–9, 189
Michael, Grand Duke, 202, 215
Michaud, Colonel, 104, 153, 168
Mikhailovskii-Danilevskii, General A. I., 35, 189, 202–3
Mikhelson, General, 20
Military Intelligence, 78–80, 89–90, 117, 193
Miliutin, Dmitri Alexeevich, Count, 84, 90
Miloradovich, General Mikhail Andreevich, 105, 128, 133, 139, 141–2, 145, 147, 152, 154, 156, 169–70, 172, 177–8, 180
Mirsky, D. S., 213
Möckern, Battle of (1813), 183
Mogilev, 107, 109–10, 114, 205
Moldavia, 16, 19, 26, 76–7, 81, 118

Moldavian Army, 85, 154
Molevo-Boloto, Battle of (1812), 116–17
Moncey, Maréchal Bon-Adrien Jannot de, 195
Montgelas, Max Joseph, Count von, 45
Mordvinov, Admiral Nicolas Semenovich, Count, 87
Moreau, Général Jean-Victor, 177–8
Morillon, Général, 168
Mormant, Battle of (1814), 190
Mortier, Maréchal Edouard Adolphe Casimir Joseph, 182, 190, 195–6
Moscow, 5, 20, 44, 75, 80, 89, 93, 105–7, 112, 119–20, 122, 124, 126–9, 131–5, 137, 147–55, 160, 162–4, 166, 173, 186, 188, 197, 214
Moscow University, 80
Mozhaisk, 146–7, 152, 155, 162
Müffling, General Friedrich Karl Ferdinand, Freiherr von, 174–5
Mukhin, Quartermaster-General Sem'on Aleksandrovich, 98–9
Murat, Maréchal Joachim, 26, 31, 92, 96, 101, 107–8, 116–17, 119, 124, 126–8, 134–5, 152, 155, 162, 166, 179–80, 182, 191
Murav'ev, Aleksandr N., 138
Murav'ev-Apostol, Catherine (BdT's foster-daughter), 13–14
Musin-Pushkin, Ivan, Count, 20–1

Nangis, Battle of (1814), 190
Napoleon I (Bonaparte), 1, 25–8, 30–8, 40–7, 49, 53, 65, 74–80, 83, 85–90, 92–6, 98, 100–16, 119–28, 130–1, 133–7, 140, 142–6, 150–2, 154–5, 160–3, 166–70, 172–94, 196–202, 205, 212, 214
Napoleonic Wars:
  war of Third Coalition (1805–7), 25–45, 166
  Patriotic War (1812), 6, 94–162
  war of Fourth Coalition (1813–14), 168–98
Naryshkin, Maria, Countess, 88, 201
Nations, Battle of the (1813), *see* Leipzig, Battle of (1813)
Neman', river, 44, 74, 85–6, 92, 94–5, 98, 124, 163, 166, 168, 188
Nesselrode, Karl Robert, Count, 198
Neverovskii, General Dmitri Petrovich, 116, 119, 136

Ney, Maréchal Michel, 31, 34, 37–8, 89, 92, 119, 121, 126–7, 135, 170, 172, 181, 193
Nicolas Mikhailovich, Grand Duke, 202
Nicolas I (Tsar of Russia), 212–13, 215
Niebuhr, Barthold Georg, 41, 87, 89–90
Niebuhr, Karsten, 89
North, Army of the, 176, 181

Ochakov, Battle of (1788), 17–21, 35, 84, 140
Oder, river, 77, 86, 89, 93, 174
Oldenburg, George, Prince of, 143
opolchenie 133, 135–6, 144–5, 151, 162, 181
Oppermann, Major-General Karl Ivanovich, 75–6, 83, 88, 104, 168
Ordin, K. F., 67
Orlov, General Mikhail Fedorovich, Count, 194, 196
Orthodox faith, 3, 5, 10, 23, 181, 203, 208, 214
Ostermann-Tolstoy, General Aleksandr Ivanovich, Count, 32–4, 43, 61, 96, 99, 108–9, 137, 141, 149–51, 154, 177, 179–80
Ostrovno, Battle of (1812), 108
Ottoman Empire, 16, 19, 85, 130; *see also* Turkey
Oudinot, Maréchal Nicolas-Charles, 89, 92, 104, 107, 169, 172, 177, 182, 190–1, 193

Parr, Johann, Count von, 196
Pahlen, General Peter, Count von, 116, 129, 177, 182
Pardakoski, Battle of (1790), 21
Paris, 78–9, 87, 89, 187–91, 193–8, 200–3, 209, 212
Paskevich, Field-Marshal Ivan Fedorovich, Count, 142
Patkul, Major-General von, 17
Paul I (Tsar of Russia), 23, 25, 27, 30, 34, 44, 129
Paulucci, General Filippo, Marquis, 52, 98, 100
Pechersk fortress, 75
Peninsular War (1809–14), 87, 148
Persia, 76, 98
Peter I, the Great (Tsar of Russia), 3–4, 9, 20, 26, 65–6, 76–7, 80–1, 83, 98, 155, 203

Peter III (Tsar of Russia), 9
Peterswalde, Battle of (1813), 179–80
Petrunina, N. N., 216
Phull, Generl K. L. A. von, 75, 86–7, 90, 93–4, 96, 100–2, 104, 106, 112, 158
Pipes, Richard, 77, 207
Platonov, Sergei Feodorovich, 125
Platov, Ataman Matvei Ivanovich, Count, 96, 99–100, 103, 107, 109, 113, 116, 142, 156, 183, 192, 199
Pleiswitz, *see* Poischwitz
Plock, 28, 30–1, 166–7
Plotho, Karl von, 193
Poischwitz, Armistice of (1813), 174
Poland, 3, 20, 22–3, 26–7, 47, 77, 86–7, 92, 167–8, 174–5, 181, 201, 205
Poland, Army of, 176, 181
'Polkovodets', *see* 'Commander, The'
Poltava, Battle of (1709), 42, 65, 89, 104, 155
Pomerania, 169
Poniatowski, Maréchal Joseph-Antoine, Prince, 121, 135–6, 141, 143, 150, 182, 184
Porech'e, 116, 119, 121, 155
Portugal, 46, 86
Posen, 31
Potemkin, Field-Marshal Grigorii Aleksandrovich, Prince, 16–20, 89
Potsdam, 167
Praga (Warsaw), 22, 30–1
Prendel, Major, 79
Preussisch-Eylau, Battle of (1807), 36–42, 65, 140, 143, 146
Prince Regent of Britain (later George IV), 201
Prikaz-Vydra, 116, 119
Probstheida, Battle of (1813), 183
propaganda, 103
Protestantism, 3–4, 23; *see also* Lutheran Protestantism
Prussia, 1, 7, 10, 16, 22, 25–8, 30–1, 40–1, 43–5, 47, 52, 74, 85–7, 166–9, 174, 187, 198
Pskov, 75
Pugachev, V. V., 94, 98
Pultusk, Battle of (1806), 28, 30–2, 34, 39, 41–3
Pushkin, Alexander Sergeevich, 73, 160, 211–17

Radetzky, Field-Marshal Josef J. W., Count, 176

Raevskii, General Nikolai Nikolaievich, 49, 51–3, 109, 119–20, 122, 140–2, 149–51, 154, 170, 177, 180, 191, 195, 200, 213
Ranke, Leopold von, 42
Ratan, Battle of (1809), 64
Reims [Rheims], Battle of (1814), 192
Reitz, Major, 159
Repnin, Field-Marshal Nicolas, Prince, 23
Revolax, Battle of (1808), 49–51
Reynier, Général J. L. E., Comte, 184
Rhine, river, 26, 186–8, 192, 200
Rhine, Confederation of the, 186
Riazan', 151, 153–4, 156
Riga, 3–7, 34, 74–6, 90, 92, 158, 208
Roman Catholicism, 3, 23, 92
Rome, King of, 137, 196
Rostock, 2–3
Rostopchin, Feodor Vassileevich, Count, 105–6, 124, 128–9, 131–3, 135, 147, 151–3, 160, 173
Rudnia, 116–17, 119, 129, 155
Rumiantsev, Nikolai Petrovich, 64, 76, 95, 106
Rumiantsev, Field-Marshal Pyotr Aleksandrovich, Count, 16, 19
Runeberg, Johan Ludwig, 54
Ruschuk, Battle of (1812), 77
Russia, 3–5, 7, 9, 16, 20–5, 27, 40–6, 49, 52–4, 60, 64–8, 70–1, 73–80, 85–90, 92–3, 95, 98, 102–3, 105–9, 112, 114–15, 119–20, 125, 129, 132, 144, 149, 153–4, 158, 160, 162, 166–7, 169, 177, 179, 184, 188, 192, 198–9, 201, 205, 207, 209, 211–13, 215

Sabaneev, General Ivan Vasil'evich, 175
Sacken, General Fabian Gottlieb, Baron von der Osten-, 32, 61, 200
St. Cyr, Maréchal Gouvion de, 178–80
St. Helena, 201, 214
St. Petersburg, 5, 7–10, 12–14, 18, 20–2, 42–6, 49, 51, 53, 56, 60, 63–7, 70–3, 79–80, 85–6, 88–9, 92, 103, 106–7, 114, 123, 126, 128–30, 132, 146, 150, 153–5, 159–66, 169, 188, 197, 203, 207–8, 210, 214–15
Saint-Priest, Général Guillaume Emanuel, Comte de, 109, 115, 124, 130, 192
Saivar, Battle of (1809), 64
Salmi, Battle of (1808), 53
Saltanovka, Battle of (1812), 109
Saltykov, Nicolas I., Count, 21
Sandels, General Johann August, Freiherr von, 50–3, 63
Sanglen, Iakov Ivanovich de, 80, 101
Sardinia, 86
Savary, Général Anne-Jean Marie René, 43, 45
Savolax, 49–51
Saxe-Meiningen, Duchy of, 86
Saxony, 79, 168, 174, 176–7, 179; King of, 178, 183
Scharnhorst, General Gerhard Johann von, 85, 103, 169
Schaueln, 89
Schinkel, Karl Friedrich, 208
Schubert, Friedrich von, 33, 85, 93, 142
Schwarzenberg, Field-Marshal Karl Philipp, Prince, 167, 177–83, 186–94, 196–7
Scotland, 1–2
Sébastiani, Général Horace François de la Porta, Comte, 117, 182, 193
Second (West) Army, 86, 91, 96, 98, 102, 105, 107, 109, 111, 116, 119–20, 122, 132, 140, 142, 144–5, 156, 161, 199
Sedmoratskii, General, 30–1, 41
Ségur, Louis-Philippe, Comte de, 20
Ségur, Colonel Octave-Henri de, 96
Ségur, Général Paul-Philippe, Comte de, 96, 125, 146
Senff, Carl August, 212
Serasken, Baron Tuyll van, 87
Seslavin, Major-General, 139
Shevich, General Ivan Egorovich, 143
Shil'der, Alexander N. K., 176
Shishkov, Admiral Aleksandr Sem'onovich, 98, 100, 104, 106
Shuvalov, General Pavel Andreevich, Count, 55–6, 58–63, 96, 99–100, 129–30
Siikojaki, Battle of (1808), 49–51
Silesia, 169–70, 174–5
Silesia, Army of, 176, 181, 183, 189–91, 194–5, 198
Skjöldebrand, Colonel, 64
Slonim, 89
Smith, Admiral Sir Stanley, 203
Smitten, Auguste Wilhelmine von (BdT's foster-mother, married Georg Vermeulen), 7–8, 22–3, 59, 201

Smitten, Helene Auguste Eleonore von (Auguste; BdT's wife), 11–15, 22–3, 38–9, 56, 59–60, 69, 71–2, 83, 88, 94, 100, 103, 107, 119, 131–2, 155–6, 159–61, 163, 166, 180–1, 184–6, 198, 200, 203–4, 208–9
Smitten, Margarethe Elisabeth von (BdT's mother, married Gotthard Barclay de Tolly), 6–7
Smolensk, 3, 75, 92–3, 95, 106–7, 109–13, 115–22, 125–31, 134–7, 147, 150, 153, 155, 158–60, 162–4, 205
Soult, Maréchal Nicolas Jean de Dieu, 31, 33, 36
South, Army of the, 85; *see also* Moldavian Army
Spain, 53, 65, 169
Speranskii, Mikhail Mikhailovich, Count, 59, 66–9, 71–2, 80, 93, 98, 129, 213
Sprengporten, Göran Magnus, Baron, 20–1, 54, 59–60, 62
Stadion, Franz, Count von, 177
Staël, Anne-Louise Germaine de, 9
Stedingk, Field-Marshal Kurt Ludwig, Count von, 45, 64
Stein, Heinrich Friedrich Karl, Baron vom, 103, 117, 169, 174, 198
Steinheil, General Fadei Fedorovich, 64, 70
Stewart, Sir Charles, 197
Stockholm, 46, 49, 53–5, 57–8, 60, 64–5, 79
Stolben, 208–10
Storgrundset, Island of, 56–7
Suvorov, General Aleksandr Vassileevich, Count, 18–19, 22–3, 30, 43, 91, 130, 175, 211
Sveaborg, fortress of, 47, 49–50, 59, 63
Svenskund, Battle of (1790), 21
Sventsiany (Święciany), 96, 99
Sweden, 2–3, 5–6, 20–2, 42, 45–6, 49, 52–6, 58–60, 62–5, 68, 70–1, 75–6, 86, 210
Switzerland, 187

Talleyrand-Périgord, Charles-Maurice de, 44, 197
Tandefelt, Baron, 69
Tarlé, E. V., 133, 139

Tarutino, Battle of (1812), 155–6, 158, 162, 166
Tauroggen Convention (1812), 166
Tavastehus, 47, 53
Thiers, Adolphe, 93, 187
Third (West) Army, 94, 96, 105, 114, 154, 167–8, 170
Third Coalition (1805), 26–8
Thorn, Battle of (1806), 28, 30–1
Thorn, Battle of (1813), 168–9, 175
Tiesenhausen, Georg, Baron von, 210
Tilsit, Treaty of (1807), 44–6, 65, 85, 92, 167, 208
Toivala, 50–1, 53
Toll, Colonel Karl Friedrich, Baron von, 93, 99, 114–15, 117, 121, 123–4, 128, 130, 132–4, 136, 140–2, 144–6, 148–51, 154, 156, 169, 176–7, 179, 182, 193–4
Tolstoy, Leo Nikolaievich, Count, 133–4, 211, 216
Tolstoy, Pyotr Aleksandrovich, Count, 30, 61
Tomilovski, Cadet, 35
Torcy-le-Grand, Battle of (1814), 193
Tormassov, General Alexander P., Count, 94, 96, 114, 119, 130, 154, 169
Tornauw, Johanna Wilhelmina von (Jenny; BdT's foster-daughter, married Field-Marshal Diebitsch), 13–14, 207
Towie Castle, 1–2, 199
Trachenberg Operational Plan (1813), 176, 178
Transcaucasia, 76
Trofimov, I. T., 216
Troyes, Battle of (1814), 190–2
Tsarevo-Zaimishche, 129, 131–4, 156, 164
Tsarskoe Selo, 160, 211
Tsisianov, P. D., Prince, 22
Tuchkov IV, General Aleksandr Alekseevich, 34
Tuchkov I, General Nikolai Alekseevich, 47, 49–52, 61, 96, 107, 116, 120, 123, 126, 136, 140–1
Tuchkov III, General Pavel Alekseevich, 126–8
Tula, 154, 159–60
Turgenev, Alexander Ivanovich, 213
Turkey, 16–17, 21–2, 45, 53, 75–7, 85, 98; *see also* Ottoman Empire
Turskii, Colonel, 89

Tyzenhaus [Tiesenhausen], Sophie, Countess von, 94

Ukraine, 66, 74, 86, 109
Ukrainian Army, 16
Uleaborg, 62, 71
Ulm, Battle of (1805), 26, 37
Umeå, 55–8, 62, 64–5, 68
Utitsa, 134, 136, 141
Uvarov, General Fiodor Petrovich, 61, 96, 107, 147, 149–50, 154
Uvarov, Sergei Semenovich, Count, 214

Valutina Gora, Battle of (1812), see Lubino, Battle of
Vandal, Albert, 45
Vandamme, Maréchal Dominique-Joseph, 179–81, 197
Vasa, 51, 55–6, 58–9, 62, 69
Verelä, Treaty of (1790), 22, 47
Vermeulen, Brigadier Georg Wilhelm (BdT's foster-father), 7–9, 19, 88
Vertus Military Review (1814), 202
Viazemskii, Pyotr Andreevich, Prince, 213
Victor, Maréchal Claude-Perrin, 182–3, 190
Vienna, 79, 89, 173; Congress of (1814–15), 199
Vietinghoff, Otto Herman, Baron von, 4
Vilna, 22–3, 44, 75, 80, 89–92, 94–6, 98–103, 106, 120, 163, 165–6
Viskovatov, A. V., 59, 215
Vistula, river, 28, 30–1, 86, 95, 166, 168, 199
Vitebsk, 107–11, 114, 119, 128, 157
Vladimir, 149, 160–1
Volhynian Army (Second West Army), 80
Volkonskii, Pyotr Mikhailovich, Prince, 74, 83, 87, 98, 169, 193, 198
Volkonskii, Sergei Grigor'evich, Prince, 65
Vorontsov, General Michael S., Prince, 158–9, 196, 198
Vosges, 188
Vuich, Colonel Nikolai Vasil'evich, 138

Wachau, Battle of (1813), 182–4
Wagram, Battle of (1809), 95

Wagram, Prince of, see Berthier, Maréchal
Wallachia, 76–7
Warsaw, 22–3, 28, 30–1, 199
Warsaw, Grand Duchy of (1807–14), 74, 77, 79, 87, 92, 167, 175
Waterloo, Battle of (1815), 146, 200
Weimar, 203
Wellington, Duke of (Arthur Wellesley), 1, 87, 89, 177, 187, 191, 200–2, 212
Weymarn, Wilhelm Peter Jost von, 210
Weyrother, General Franz von, 27
William the Lion (King of Scotland), 2
Wilson, General Sir Robert, 42, 77, 83, 91, 120, 123, 127, 155, 158, 167, 175
Wintzingerode, General Ferdinand, Baron, 191, 194, 198
Wittgenstein, General Peter C., Graf zu Sayn-, 89, 96, 99, 103–4, 107, 114, 169–70, 172–5, 177–8, 181–2, 187–8, 191
Wolzogen, Ludwig, Freiherr von, 86–7, 108–10, 113–15, 117–18, 143–5, 151, 153, 156, 158, 161–3, 179–80, 182
Wrede, General Karl Philipp, Prince von, 191, 193
Württemberg, Alexander, Duke of, 106, 110
Württemberg, Army of, 103
Württemberg, General Eugen, Prince von, 121–3, 126, 133, 139, 141, 146, 148, 170, 177–80, 182–3, 191, 195
Württemberg, King of, 86
Württemberg, Princess of, 215

xenophobia, 34, 83, 99, 117–18, 130, 160, 198, 211, 214, 216

Yellow Book, see Army Regulations
Yorck von Wartenburg, General Hans David Ludwig, Count, 166–7, 169–70, 196

Zakret, 94, 96
Zakrevskii, Colonel Arsenii Andreevich, Count, 137, 159–64, 175–6, 213
Zheime (BdT's birthplace), 6
Zhitomir, 89
Zhukovskii, Vassilii Andreevich, 216
Ziethen, General, Graf von, 182